Major Acts of Congress

EDITORIAL BOARD

MAJOR ACTS
OF CONGRESS

VOLUME 2:
F-M

BRIAN K. LANDSBERG
Editor in Chief

**MACMILLAN
REFERENCE
USA™**

THOMSON
™
GALE

New York • Detroit • San Diego • San Francisco • Cleveland • New Haven, Conn. • Waterville, Maine • London • Munich

Major Acts of Congress

Brian K. Landsberg, Editor in Chief

Permissions Hotline:
248-699-8006 or 800-877-4253 ext. 8006
Fax: 248-699-8074 or 800-762-4058

Cover photographs: Capital dome (PhotoDisc, Inc.); Civil rights march (National Archives and Records Administration); IRS paperwork (PhotoDisc, Inc.); session of Congress (©AP/Wide World Photos. Reproduced by permission).

Since this page cannot legibly accommodate all copyright notices, the acknowledgements constitute an extension of the copyright notice.

LIBRARY OF CONGRESS CATALOGING-IN-PUBLICATION DATA

Major acts of Congress / Brian K. Landsberg, editor in chief.
  p. cm.
Includes bibliographical references and index.
  ISBN 0-02-865749-7 (set hardcover : alk. paper) — ISBN 0-02-865750-0
(v. 1 : alk. paper) — ISBN 0-02-865751-9 (v. 2 : alk. paper) — ISBN
0-02-865752-7 (v. 3 : alk. paper)
  1. Law—United States—Encyclopedias. I. Landsberg, Brian K.
  KF154.M35 2004
  348.73'22—dc22
                                                 2003018874

This title is also available as an e-book.
ISBN 0-02-865909-0 (set)
Contact your Gale sales representative for ordering information.

Printed in the United States of America
10 9 8 7 6 5

EDITORIAL AND PRODUCTION STAFF

Jeff Galas, *Project Editor*

Erin Bealmear, Joann Cerrito, Stephen Cusack, Mark Drouillard, Miranda Ferrara, Kristin Hart, Melissa Hill, Margaret Mazurkiewicz, Jennifer Wisinski, *Editorial Assistants*

Leitha Etheridge-Sims, Lezlie Light, Michael Logusz, Kelly Quin, *Imaging*

GGS Information Services (York, Pennsylvania), *Tables*

Taryn Benbow-Pfalzgraf, Laurie Di Mauro, Jessica Hornik Evans, Anne Janette Johnson, William L. Peper, *Copyeditors*

Deanna Raso, *Photo Researcher*

Douglas Funk, *Caption Writer*

Paula Kepos, *Sidebar Writer, unless otherwise specified*

Taryn Benbow-Pfalzgraf, Nicolet Elert, Elizabeth Henry, *Proofreaders*

Wendy Allex, *Indexer*

Pamela A. E. Galbreath, *Art Director*

Graphix Group (Fenton, Michigan), *Compositor*

Margaret A. Chamberlain, *Permissions*

Mary Beth Trimper, *Manager, Composition*

Evi Seoud, *Assistant Manager, Composition*

Rhonda Williams, *Manufacturing*

MACMILLAN REFERENCE USA

Jill Lectka, *Director, Publishing Operations*

Hélène Potter, *Director, New Product Development*

Frank Menchaca, *Vice President and Publisher*

CONTENTS

VOLUME 2

VOLUME 3

TOPIC OUTLINE

ECONOMIC DEVELOPMENT/TRADE

Bank of the United States (1791)
Community Development Banking and Financial Institutions Act of 1994
Community Reinvestment Act (1977)
Copyright Act of 1790
Copyright Act of 1976
Economic Cooperation Act of 1948 (Marshall Plan)
Economic Opportunity Act of 1964
Electronic Signatures in Global and National Commerce Act (2000)
Export-Import Bank Act of 1945
Federal Power Acts
Freedmen's Bureau Acts (1865, 1868)
Hill-Burton Act (1946)
Homestead Act (1862)
Housing and Urban Development Act of 1965
Internal Improvements Acts
Merchant Marine Act of 1920
National Industrial Recovery Act (1933)
North American Free Trade Agreement Implementation Act (1993)
Patent Acts
Tennessee Valley Authority Act (1933)
Trade Act of 1974
Trading with the Enemy Act (1917)

ECONOMIC AND FINANCIAL REGULATION

Agricultural Adjustment Act (1933)
Bank of the United States (1791)
Bankruptcy Act of 1841
Bankruptcy Act of 1978
Civil Service Acts
Clayton Act (1914)
Coinage Act of 1792
Coinage Acts
Commodity Exchange Act (1936)
Community Development Banking and Financial Institutions Act of 1994
Community Reinvestment Act (1977)
Consumer Credit Protection Act (1969)
Contract Disputes Act (1978)
Farm Credit Act of 1933

Farmers Home Administration Act (1946)
Federal Deposit Insurance Acts
Federal Employers' Liability Act (1908)
Federal Home Loan Bank Act (1932)
Federal National Mortgage Association Charter Act (1954)
Federal Reserve Act (1913)
Federal Trade Commission Act (1914)
Glass-Steagall Act (1933)
Gold Reserve Act of 1934
Gold Standard Act of 1900
Interstate Commerce Act of 1887
National Bank Act (1864)
Public Utility Holding Company Act of 1935
Pure Food and Drug Act (1906)
Securities Act of 1933
Securities Exchange Act of 1934
Sherman Antitrust Act (1890)
Small Business Act (1953)
Truth in Lending Act (1969)
Walsh-Healey Act (1936)

EDUCATION

Civil Rights Act of 1964
Elementary and Secondary Education Act of 1965
Higher Education Act of 1965
Individuals with Disabilities Education Act (1975)
Morrill Land Grant Act of 1862
No Child Left Behind (2001)
Richard B. Russell National School Lunch Act (1946)
Title IX, Education Amendments (1972)
Vocational Education Act of 1917

ENERGY

Atomic Energy Acts
Department of Energy Organization Act (1977)
Federal Power Acts
National Energy Conservation Policy Act (1978)
Natural Gas Act (1938)
Nuclear Waste Policy Act (1982)
Oil Pollution Acts
Rural Electrification Act (1936)

Tennessee Valley Authority Act (1933)

ENVIRONMENT

Clean Air Act (1963)
Comprehensive Environmental Response, Compensation, and Liability Act (1980)
Emergency Planning and Community Right-To-Know Act (1986)
Endangered Species Act (1973)
Federal Water Pollution Control Act (1948)
Fish and Wildlife Conservation Act of 1980
Food Quality Protection Act of 1996
Hazardous and Solid Waste Amendments of 1984
Highway Beautification Act (1965)
Homestead Act (1862)
Marine Mammal Protection Act (1972)
Migratory Bird Conservation Act of 1929
Mineral Leasing Act (1920)
National Emissions Standards Act (1965)
National Environmental Policy Act (1969)
National Historic Preservation Act (1966)
National Wildlife Refuge System Administration Act (1966)
Nuclear Waste Policy Act (1982)
Oil Pollution Acts
Outer Continental Shelf Lands Act (1953)
Plant Variety Protection Act (1970)
Safe Drinking Water Act (1974)
Solid Waste Disposal Act (1965)
Surface Mining Control and Reclamation Act (1977)
Toxic Substances Control Act (1976)

FOREIGN AFFAIRS/ INTERNATIONAL RELATIONS

Communist Control Act of 1954
Economic Cooperation Act of 1948 (Marshall Plan)
Espionage Act (1917) and Sedition Act (1918)

Export-Import Bank Act of 1945
Federal Civil Defense Act of 1950
Foreign Assistance Act (1961)
Foreign Service Act of 1946
Lend-Lease Act (1941)
North American Free Trade
  Agreement Implementation Act
  (1993)
Nonintercourse Act (1809)
Panama Canal Purchase Act (1902)
Trade Act of 1974
Trading with the Enemy Act (1917)
United Nations Participation Act
  (1945)
United States Information and
  Educational Exchange Act
  (1948)

GOVERNMENT STRUCTURE AND PROCESSES
Administrative Dispute Resolution
  Act (1990)
Administrative Procedure Act (1946)
Balanced Budget and Emergency
  Deficit Control Act (1985)
Civil Service Acts
Civil Service Reform Act (1978)
Congressional Budget and
  Impoundment Control Act
  (1974)
Contract Disputes Act (1978)
Ethics in Government Act (1978)
Federal Advisory Committee Act
  (1972)
Federal Election Campaign Act
  (1971)
Federal Tort Claims Act (1946)
Freedom of Information Act (1966)
Government in the Sunshine Act
  (1976)
Hatch Act (1939)
Judiciary Act of 1789
Judiciary Act of 1801
Legal Services Corporation Act
  (1974)
Lobbying Disclosure Act (1995)
Negotiated Rulemaking Act (1990)
Paperwork Reduction Act (1980)
Privacy Act of 1974
Public Debt Acts
Regulatory Flexibility Act (1980)

Walsh-Healey Act (1936)
Whistleblower Protection Laws
  (1978)

IMMIGRATION
Alien and Sedition Acts of 1798
Chinese Exclusion Acts
Immigration and Nationality Act
  (1952)
Immigration Reform and Control Act
  of 1986
Naturalization Act (1790)

LABOR
Americans With Disabilities Act
  (1990)
Civil Rights Act of 1964
Civil Service Acts
Employee Retirement Income
  Security Act of 1974
Employment Act of 1946
Equal Pay Act of 1963
Fair Labor Standards Act (1938)
Family and Medical Leave Act of
  1993
Federal Employers' Liability Act
  (1908)
Hatch Act (1939)
Keating-Owen Act of 1916
National Labor Relations Act (1935)
Norris-LaGuardia Act (1932)
Occupational Safety and Health Act
  of 1970
Pregnancy Discrimination Act (1978)
Taft-Hartley Act (1947)

NATIONAL SECURITY/WAR
Alien and Sedition Acts of 1798
Antiterrorism and Effective Death
  Penalty Act (1996)
Arms Control and Disarmament Act
  (1961) and Amendments
Atomic Energy Acts
Bonus Bill (1924)
Central Intelligence Agency Act
  (1949)
Civil War Pensions
Communist Control Act of 1954
Department of Homeland Security
  Act (2002)

Enrollment Act (1863)
Espionage Act (1917) and Sedition
  Act (1918)
Federal Civil Defense Act of 1950
First and Second Confiscation Acts
  (1861, 1862)
Foreign Intelligence Surveillance Act
  (1978)
Freedmen's Bureau Acts (1865,
  1868)
Militia Act (1862)
National Guard Acts
National Security Act of 1947
Neutrality Acts
Nonintercourse Act (1809)
Nuclear Non-Proliferation Act (1978)
Posse Comitatus Act (1878)
Reconstruction Acts
Selective Service Act of 1917
United States Housing Act of 1937
USA Patriot Act (2001)
Veteran's Preference Act of 1944
War Powers Resolution (1973)
Weapons of Mass Destruction
  Control Act (1992)

NATIVE AMERICANS
Alaska Native Claims Settlement Act
  (1971)
Indian Civil Rights Act (1968)
Indian Gaming Regulatory Act
  (1988)
Indian General Allotment Act (1887)
Indian Removal Act (1830)
Indian Reorganization Act of 1934

PUBLIC LANDS/PUBLIC WORKS
Agricultural Adjustment Act (1933)
Federal Land Policy and
  Management Act (1976)
Federal Power Acts
Freedmen's Bureau Acts (1865,
  1868)
Hill-Burton Act (1946)
Homestead Act (1862)
Internal Improvements Acts
National Forest Management Act
  (1976)
National Industrial Recovery Act
  (1933)
National Park Service Act (1916)

National Reclamation Act of 1902
National Wildlife Refuge System
    Administration Act (1966)
Northwest Ordinance (1787)
Soil Conservation and Domestic
    Allotment Act (1935)
Southwest Ordinance (1790)
Tennessee Valley Authority Act (1933)
Yellowstone National Park Act (1872)

SLAVERY

Compromise of 1850
Freedmen's Bureau Acts (1865,
    1868)
Fugitive Slave Acts (1793, 1850)
Kansas Nebraska Act of 1854
Missouri Compromise (1820)
Prohibition of the Slave Trade (1807)
Reconstruction Acts

**SOCIAL PROGRAMS/SOCIAL
WELFARE**

Agricultural Adjustment Act (1933)
Aid to Dependent Children (1935)
Alcoholic and Narcotic
    Rehabilitation Act (1968)
Antiquities Act of 1906
Bonus Bill (1924)
Born-Alive Infants Protection Act of
    2002
Civil War Pensions
Defense of Marriage Act (1996)

Domestic Volunteer Service Act of
    1973 (VISTA)
Drug Abuse Prevention, Treatment,
    and Rehabilitation Act (1980)
Family and Medical Leave Act of
    1993
Food Stamp Act of 1964
Freedom of Access to Clinic
    Entrances Act (1994)
Housing and Urban Development
    Act of 1965
McKinney-Vento Act (1988)
Medicaid Act (1965)
Medicare Act (1965)
National Housing Act (1955)
Occupational Safety and Health Act
    of 1970
Peace Corps Act (1961)
Personal Responsibility and Work
    Opportunity Reconciliation Act
    (1996)
Social Security Act of 1935
Truth in Lending Act (1969)
Violence Against Women Act of 1994

TAXES

Anti-Injunction Act (1793)
Bland-Allison Act (1878)
Corporate Income Tax Act of 1909
1894 Income Tax and the Wilson-
    Gorman Tariff Act
Employee Retirement Income
    Security Act of 1974

Estate and Gift Taxation
Federal Income Tax Act of 1913
Federal Unemployment Tax Act
    (1939)
Internal Revenue Act of 1954
Medicaid Act (1965)
Medicare Act (1965)
Smoot-Hawley Tariff Act (1930)
Social Security Act of 1935
Tariff Act of 1789
Tax Reform Act of 1986
Taxpayer Bill of Rights III (1998)

TRANSPORTATION

Civil Aeronautics Act (1938)
Federal Aviation Act (1958)
Hazardous Materials Transportation
    Act (1975)
Highway Act of 1956
Highway Beautification Act
    of 1965
Highway Safety Act of 1966
Motor Carrier Act (1935)
Mutual Security Act (1951)
National Aeronautics and Space Act
    (1958)
National Traffic and Motor Vehicle
    Safety Act of 1966
Rail Passenger Service Act (1970)
Shipping Acts
Staggers Rail Act of 1980
Urban Mass Transportation Acts

PREFACE

In the fall of 2001, Hélène Potter, director of development at Macmillan Reference, asked me to serve as editor in chief of an encyclopedia of major acts of Congress. I found the offer enormously exciting, because the world of reference books had seemingly neglected this area that is so central to American law, government, and history. Moreover, I helped to write, interpret, and enforce laws while at the U.S. Department of Justice Civil Rights Division, and I had taught and written about civil rights legislation. These experiences led me to appreciate how useful a clear and authoritative description of major American legislation could be. My duties as associate dean at the University of Pacific, McGeorge School of Law, initially precluded my undertaking this project. However, the publishing schedule for the encyclopedia changed, and in March of 2002 I enthusiastically signed up.

By the spring of 2002 an outstanding board of editors had agreed to join the project, and we were well underway. Each of the associate editors brings a rich understanding of legislation to the project, but each also contributes a different perspective. Professor Al Brophy of the University of Alabama School of Law is an accomplished and well-recognized legal historian. Professor Thomas Sargentich of American University's Washington College of Law has written extensively about the legal issues of the separation of powers; he serves as codirector of his law school's program on law and government. Professor Nancy Staudt of the Washington University School of Law (St. Louis) teaches and writes on tax law and social programs and has become known for her critical analyses of both tax and social policy.

Courses in American government typically teach students about the roles of the three branches established by the Constitution. Students learn that the Congress makes laws, the executive branch executes laws, and the courts apply laws. Often, however, that lesson may seem abstract. Students may fail to see the connection between these principles and their lives, the lives of their families and friends, or the history of the nation. *Major Acts of Congress* helps make concrete the law-making function of Congress and also casts light on the role of the other two branches in enforcing and applying law. It brings together for the first time, in one work, a selection from the product of the one hundred and seven Congresses which preceded this encyclopedia, as well as the current Congress.

In its first year, 1789, Congress enacted twenty-seven laws. The acts from its first ten years occupy 755 pages, in one volume of the *U.S Statutes At*

Large. By 2002, in the second and last year of the 107th Congress, we find 260 acts, occupying 3115 pages of volume 116 of the *U.S. Statutes.* The laws of the First Congress were mainly devoted to setting up the national government, which must have seemed quite distant to most Americans. By contrast, the 107th Congress enacted laws covering such subjects as agriculture (the names of fourteen laws begin with that word), education, the environment, foreign relations, intelligence, immigration, defense, crime, voter registration, radiation, securities, employment, social security, and so on. Today few aspects of our lives are untouched by federal law.

The acts described in this work demonstrate the range of congressional legislation, from the very first Congress's adoption of the Judiciary Act to the 108th Congress's enactment of legislation regulating so-called partial birth abortions. Described in more detail than one finds in most history books are landmarks of American history, such as the Fugitive Slave Act, the various civil rights acts, legislation from the New Deal and the Great Society, as well as acts that respond to such contemporary issues as terrorism and the rise of electronic technology.

Major Acts of Congress contains entries on 262 acts selected by the editorial board based on such criteria as historical significance, contemporary impact, and contribution to the understanding of American government. Hundreds of other laws are discussed in the entries and can be found through use of the comprehensive index. The entries vary in length from 2500 words down to 300 words. Entries describe the law, but they do much more than that. They typically explain the circumstances that led Congress to consider the law and the issues Congress discussed during its consideration of the law. They also provide information about the subsequent history of the law, including amendments or repeal, enforcement, and court cases.

As the list of contributors reflects, the 159 authors include legal scholars, historians, political scientists, economists, and lawyers from public and private practice. Some played a significant role in the adoption or enforcement of the act they wrote about. Others have literally written the book on the act or area of law.

The essays have been written to make accessible to students and lay persons the frequently complex, technical, arcane concepts and language of legislation. We have included brief excerpts from acts in those entries where a direct quotation would give a flavor of the law. Accessibility is enhanced by the use of sidebars to explain terms and historical allusions, as well as illustrations that help demonstrate the political and human dimension of these laws. Same-page definitions of terms and a glossary in the back matter further enhance access. Entries typically end with a short bibliography of books, articles, and Web sites, for those who wish to delve more deeply. To place the entries in perspective, *Major Acts* begins with an introduction that explains the role of the Congress and other branches. It also contains an in-depth time line in the back matter, showing who was president, the composition of each Congress, and what major events were taking place during the time when each law was enacted.

Major Acts has been a true team effort. The editorial board has worked closely with the publisher. Hélène Potter has skillfully guided the project. Jeff Galas, assistant editor at Macmillan Reference, has been invaluable in helping recruit authors and organize the work. And Kristin Hart has ably supervised the copyediting and the selection of illustrations.

Brian K. Landsberg
September, 2003
Sacramento, California

INTRODUCTION

In a democracy like the United States, congressional action reflects the will of the people. The impetus for acts comes from members of the House of Representatives who stand for election every two years and senators who—after 1916—have stood for election every six years. (Before 1916, they were selected by their state legislature.) The acts discussed in this encyclopedia illustrate the concerns of Americans, from the early national period, through the antebellum period, the Civil War, Reconstruction, the Gilded Age, the Progressive Era, the Great Depression, World War II, and the civil rights eras, right up to the administrations of Presidents Nixon, Ford, and Carter in the 1970s, and Presidents Reagan and Bush in the 1980s, and Presidents Clinton and Bush in the 1990s and 2000s.

At times, the nation is concerned with certain issues—like civil rights—and takes action. That happened in the wake of the Civil War, when Congress proposed and the states ratified three Constitutional amendments, including the Fifteenth Amendment to guarantee all adult males the right to vote, regardless of race. Congress also passed numerous acts to ensure the newly freed slaves had civil rights. Yet, after 1877 those acts lay largely dormant, until the civil rights era of the 1950s.

Examination of the Voting Rights Act of 1965 illustrates how the nation, awakened to the cause of civil rights, again turned to Congress to seek a national solution. Each law described in this encyclopedia went through the process that American students study in increasing detail as they advance through elementary and secondary school, college, and graduate school. The process is established by Article I of the U. S. Constitution. It is not easy to pass legislation, because many actors, representing a range of interests and ideologies, must reach agreement. Rather than simply providing another abstract description of the process in this introduction, we seek to bring the process to life by describing the course of one bill from initial concept to final adoption and enforcement and subsequent amendment. You will find an entry on this law, the Voting Rights Act of 1965, in volume three of this encyclopedia.

Although the Fifteenth Amendment had been added to the Constitution in 1870 in order to forbid official actions abridging the right to vote based on race, by the middle of the twentieth century most Southern states had placed a variety of obstacles in the way of African-American voter registration. The result was that by 1952 only about 20 percent of African Americans of voting age in the Deep South were registered to vote. Congress's first effort to address this problem came in the Civil Rights Act of 1957, the first modern federal civil rights law. It had been brilliantly steered through the United States Senate by Majority Leader Lyndon B. Johnson. It was, however, a bill with few teeth, principally the bare authorization for the Department of Justice to bring suits to remedy discrimination in official voting practices and race-based intimidation against potential voters. Johnson knew that it was not a strong bill, but regarded it as a start. "[I]t's only the first. We know we can do it now." As predicted, the 1957 act did not effectively end racial discrimination in voter registration. Congress tried again, in the Civil Rights Act of 1960, but again it was not politically possible to pass a strong bill. This time, Lyndon Johnson made the pragmatic argument that the legislation was "reasonable" and "the best that the able chairman of the House Judiciary Committee could get." After passage, Thurgood Marshall, the leading black lawyer in the country, said the 1960 act "isn't worth the paper it's written on." Congress made further very minor improvements in voting rights law in the Civil Rights Act of 1964, but that law primarily addressed other matters.

The weaknesses of the 1957 and 1960 acts stemmed largely from the political influence of Southern Democrats, who in those days regularly opposed all civil rights legislation. Though they were a minority in Congress, the availability of the filibuster in the Senate gave them added strength. To pass a bill over their objection required unusual consensus between Northern Democrats and the Republicans. You will see in the descriptions of many of the acts in this encyclopedia that compromises often are necessary in order to win passage and presidential approval of a bill.

Proponents of stronger legislation needed to find a way to convince Congress to abandon the approach of the prior acts. Civil rights groups believed that it would take very strong medicine indeed to effectively insure black voting rights. As you will see in Professor William Araiza's entry on the Voting Rights Act, the act interferes with state voter qualification laws, provides for federal officials to take over the registration process in some counties, and requires some changes in state law to be pre-approved by federal courts or officials before they may be implemented. Not since Reconstruction had such federal intervention into state law occurred.

Civil rights organizations mounted voter registration drives in Alabama, Mississippi, and Louisiana. The Department of Justice brought voter discrimination suits in federal court as Southern registrars turned away thousands of prospective voters. By early 1965, national newspapers and television networks began to report on events in such places as Selma, Alabama. In February 1965 during a civil rights demonstration in Marion, Alabama, Alabama State Troopers shot and killed an African American, Jimmie Lee Jackson, who had unsuccessfully tried in prior months to register to vote. To protest the killing and to dramatize the deprivations of the right to vote, civil rights organizations—the Student Nonviolent Coordinating Committee and Dr. Martin Luther King Jr.'s Southern Christian Leadership Conference—decided to march from Selma to the state capital, Montgomery. As the marchers left Selma and crossed the Edmund Pettus Bridge over the Alabama River, they were set upon by state troopers and sheriff's deputies, many of them mounted on horses. Many were beaten, all were tear-gassed, and they were pursued back to Selma by mounted men swinging billy clubs. The assault on the

Edmund Pettus Bridge in Selma occurred in broad daylight and was broadcast to an outraged nation. The following week President Lyndon Johnson gave a nationwide address in which he announced the outlines of the voting rights bill he was sending to Congress. In the flowery language of presidential addresses, he said that "the cries of pain and the hymns and protests of oppressed people have summoned into convocation all the majesty of this great Government—the Government of the greatest Nation on earth."

President Johnson's speech in the wake of the Bloody Sunday confrontation at the Edmund Pettus Bridge promised the country an effective voting rights act. The administration's interest in a new voting law predated Bloody Sunday by several months. The Department of Justice had begun drafting such a law in November of 1964, at the direction of President Johnson. The attorney general had sent the president a memorandum outlining three possible proposals by the end of December, and the president's State of the Union message on January 4, 1965, had already proposed that "we eliminate every remaining obstacle to the right and the opportunity to vote." However, Johnson had planned to delay the voting rights proposal until his Great Society social bills had passed. The events on Bloody Sunday changed all that.

In the above events we can see four important aspects of the legislative process. First, legislation normally responds to some felt need. It is necessary to mobilize public opinion and demonstrate that the nation faces a problem and that the problem requires legislation. Second, it is not enough to simply place a bill on a president's or a party's legislative agenda. The president and Congress face a myriad of problems that need solving, and they cannot solve them all. So they establish priorities. Unless a bill is given high priority, it is unlikely that Congress will enact it even if it has merit. Third, Congress is not the only player. The president plays an important role in setting the legislative agenda. Even the initial drafting of some laws may be done by executive agencies rather than Congress. Finally, Congress often addresses issues incrementally, with small starts, such as the 1957 and 1960 Civil Rights Acts, later leading to more ambitious legislation.

Within two days of President Johnson's speech, the administration proposal had been introduced in both the House and Senate. Each chamber referred the bill to its judiciary committee. The Committee on the Judiciary of the House of Representatives in turn referred the bill to a subcommittee chaired by Emanuel Celler of New York, with six other Democrats and four Republicans as members. The subcommittee began hearings the following day. It considered 122 bills dealing with voting rights, holding thirteen sessions, including four evening sessions. It then met in executive session for four days and substantially rewrote the administration bill and sent it to the full committee of twenty-four Democrats and eleven Republicans. The committee further rewrote the bill and then sent it to the House of Representatives, with a report and a recommendation that the House pass the bill in its amended form.

Meanwhile, the Senate faced a problem that flowed from the seniority system. The chair of the Senate Judiciary Committee was Senator James Eastland of Mississippi, a strong opponent of all civil rights legislation. And the committee's senior Democrats were also from the Deep South. The Senate responded by sending the bill to the committee with the mandate to report back to the Senate no later than April 9. The full Senate Judiciary Committee held hearings for nine days. It met the April 9 deadline and recommended that the Senate pass the bill, but instead of submitting a committee report submitted sets of "individual views" of the proponents and opponents.

The hearings before both the House and Senate committees began with testimony by Attorney General Nicholas Katzenbach, who presented voluminous exhibits, including the history of the fifty-one suits against voting discrimination and seventeen suits challenging intimidation against black voter registration that the Department of Justice had brought since adoption of the 1957 act. He argued that the litigation approach under these laws had not worked. He noted that the earlier laws "depended, as almost all our legislation does, on the fact that it is going to be accepted as the law of the land and is then going to be fairly administered in all of the areas to which it applies, by States officials who are just as bound as you and I by the Constitution of the United States and by Federal laws." The attorney general continued:

> I think, in some areas, it has become the theory that a voting registrar is not really required to do anything except what he has been doing until his records have been examined and he has been hauled into court and, at public expense, his case has been defended by the State, and all the delaying devices possible have been used, and then it has been taken on appeal, then appealed again with as much delay as possible. Then, when a decree is finally entered, that decree can be construed as narrowly as possible and he can do as little as he can get away with under that decree. Then that decree—what it means—can be questioned again in court, new evidence can be introduced, and meanwhile, election after election is going by.

After delivering his statement, Katzenbach was grilled for a day and half by the House committee and for three days by the Senate committee. Southern senators challenged him at every turn—on the need for legislation, the content of the legislation, and the constitutional basis of the legislation. Civil rights leaders, including the heads of the National Association for the Advancement of Colored People and the Congress for Racial Equality, testified in favor of the bill, as did religious leaders and other federal officials. Southern attorneys general and other public officials testified against the bill.

The hearings, in short, raised issues common to most legislation. First, does Congress have the authority under the Constitution to legislate on this issue? Here, the authority came from section 2 of the Fifteenth Amendment. In most cases Congress' authority is found in Article I, section 8, which contains a laundry list of areas on which Congress may pass laws. Second, why is legislation needed? For example, why isn't existing law sufficient to deal with the problem the bill addresses? Third, what should be the content of the new legislation? It is one thing to say that we need to solve a problem and quite another to agree on what are the appropriate means. For example, the act contains detailed criteria for determining which states will be subject to some of its provisions. One criterion is whether fewer than 50 percent of persons of voting age voted in the 1964 presidential general election. Why 50 percent, as opposed to 40 or 60 percent? Why the general election? These details must be worked out, usually at the committee level.

The Senate was the first chamber to debate the bill. The minority leader, Senator Everett Dirksen, Republican of Illinois, and the majority leader, Senator Mike Mansfield, Democrat of Montana, began the debate by describing the bill and supporting it. Each party had appointed other senators to lead the floor debate, Democrat Philip Hart of Michigan and Republican Jacob Javits of New

York. They spoke at length about the evidence of need. Southern opponents spoke at great length. In addition, Senator Edward Kennedy of Massachusetts proposed an amendment that would outlaw the poll tax, and Senators Robert F. Kennedy and Jacob Javits of New York proposed an amendment designed to protect the right of Puerto Ricans in New York to vote. The poll tax amendment was defeated; the Puerto Rico amendment passed. After over a month of debate, the Senate voted to impose cloture, thus preventing a full filibuster, and on May 26 the Senate adopted the bill with a vote of 79 to 18.

The House considered the bill for three days. It adopted an amendment outlawing the poll tax, and passed the bill on July 9, 328 to 74. Thus, at this point, overwhelming majorities in both chambers supported a voting rights bill, as did the president. However, the two chambers had passed different bills. Therefore the House and Senate appointed a conference committee, charged with the task of reconciling the two bills and agreeing on a final version. For example, what should be done about the poll tax? The conference committee decided that the bill would not outlaw the poll tax but would direct the attorney general to bring litigation challenging this barrier to voting. After almost a month of work, the conference committee reported on its work on August 2, 1965. As Representative Celler told the House of Representatives the next day, "The differences were many, wide, and deep. Mutual concession was essential otherwise there would have been ... no bill." The House adopted the conference bill on August 3, and the Senate did so on August 4. President Johnson signed it on August 6.

President Johnson had presented the legislation as having the highest urgency. Congress did act quickly, but the need for hearings and debates and conference committee meant that the legislative process occupied an enormous amount of the time of the members of Congress during the five months from introduction to passage. We see that, as is often the case, the House and Senate agreed on the general objective but not on the details of the bill. We also see the importance of bipartisan coalition building where, as here, a small group of senators opposes the general objective. And we see once again that compromise is often necessary in order to enact legislation.

This is the end of the story, right? Wrong! The story goes on. The attorney general had to enforce the law. The Southern states challenged its constitutionality, so the Supreme Court had to review the law's validity. Some provisions of the law were to expire after five years. Disputes arose as to the meaning of other provisions. For example, the law was silent as to whether private parties could bring suit to enforce the provision requiring preclearance of changes in voting practices. The Supreme Court therefore had to resolve that question, by trying to determine Congress's intent. Courts have interpreted and applied the act numerous times, while other provisions have been clarified by subsequent legislation, in which Congress has revisited and amended the law several times.

The history of the Voting Rights Act demonstrates that although Congress plays the primary role in enacting legislation, the president and the courts play important roles as well. The president may propose legislation and his signature is normally needed for a bill to become law. The courts may lay a legal and constitutional framework that guides the drafting of legislation, and they apply, interpret, and determine the validity of legislation once it has been enacted.

BIBLIOGRAPHY

"Article I." In *The Constitution and Its Amendments*, ed. Roger K. Newman. New York: Macmillan Reference USA, 1999.

Berman, Daniel M. *A Bill Becomes a Law: The Civil Rights Act of 1960*. New York: Macmillan, 1962.

Hawk, Barry E., and John J. Kirby. "Federal Protection of Negro Voting Rights." *Virginia Law Review* 51 (1965): 1051.

Marshall, Burke. "The Right to Vote." In *The Constitution and Its Amendments*, ed. Roger K. Newman. New York: Macmillan Reference USA, 1999.

Schwartz, Bernard, ed. *Civil Rights*. Statutory History of the United States. New York: Chelsea House, 1970.

Brian K. Landsberg

LIST OF CONTRIBUTORS

Melanie B. Abbott
Quinnipiac University School of Law
Civil Rights Act of 1964
McKinney-Vento Act (1988)

Norman Abrams
University of California, Los Angeles Law School
Violent Crime Control and Law Enforcement Act of 1994

Craig J. Albert
Reitler Brown LLC, New York
Highway Beautification Act (1965)

Ellen P. Aprill
Loyola Law School
Federal Unemployment Tax Act (1939)

William D. Araiza
Loyola Law School
North American Free Trade Agreement Implementation Act (1993)
Voting Rights Act of 1965

Carl Auerbach
University of San Diego School of Law and Northwest University School of Law
Communist Control Act of 1954

Reuven S. Avi-Yonah
University of Michigan Law School
Corporate Income Tax Act of 1909

Steven A. Bank
University of California, Los Angeles School of Law
Federal Income Tax of 1913
Internal Revenue Act of 1954

William Banks
Syracuse University College of Law
Foreign Intelligence Surveillance Act (1978)

Felice Batlan
New York University
Aid to Dependent Children (1935)

Jonathan S. Berck
University of Alabama, School of Law
Foreign Corrupt Practices Act (1977)

Richard K. Berg
Arlington, Virginia
Government in the Sunshine Act (1976)

Neil N. Bernstein
Washington University School of Law
Norris-LaGuardia Act (1932)

Christopher A. Bracey
Washington University School of Law
Civil Rights Act of 1866

Alfred L. Brophy
University of Alabama School of Law
National Historic Preservation Act (1966)

Darryl K. Brown
Washington and Lee University School of Law
Anti-Drug Abuse Act (1986)

Tomiko Brown-Nagin
Washington University School of Law
Elementary and Secondary Education Act of 1965

Alan Brownstein
Davis, California
Religious Freedom Restoration Act (1993)

Richard Buel, Jr.
Wesleyan University
Nonintercourse Act (1809)

Jennifer S. Byram
Orangevale, CA
Central Intelligence Agency Act of 1949
Electronic Communications Privacy Act of 1986
Immigration Reform and Control Act of 1986

Daniel P. Carpenter
Harvard University
Pure Food and Drug Act (1906)

Gilbert Paul Carrasco
Willamette University College of Law
Civil Rights Act of 1957

Federico Cheever
University of Denver College of Law
Endangered Species Act (1973)

Jim Chen
University of Minnesota Law School
Agricultural Adjustment Act (1933)

Gabriel J. Chin
University of Cincinnati
Chinese Exclusion Acts

Ruth Colker
Ohio State University, Michael E. Moritz College of Law
Americans with Disabilities Act (1990)
Individuals with Disabilities Education Act (1975)
Pregnancy Discrimination Act (1978)

Mikal Condon
Electronic Privacy Information Center, Washington, D.C.
Communications Decency Act (1996)

Bo Cooper
Paul, Hastings, Janofsky, and Walter, Washington, D.C.
Immigration and Nationality Act (1952)

Julie Davies
University of the Pacific, McGeorge School of Law
Ku Klux Klan Act (1871)
Title IX, Education Amendments (1972)

Derrek M. Davis
Austin Community College
Computer Security Act of 1987

Charles E. Daye
University of North Carolina School of Law
Housing and Urban Development Act of 1965
United States Housing Act of 1937

David G. Delaney
Brandeis University
Bonus Bill (1924)
Federal Civil Defense Act of 1950
Neutrality Acts

Corey Ditslear
University of North Texas
Public Broadcasting Act of 1967

Charles M. Dobbs
Iowa State University
Economic Cooperation Act of 1948 (Marshall Plan)

Keith Rollins Eakins
The University of Central Oklahoma
Brady Handgun Violence Prevention Act (1993)
Gun Control Act of 1968

Liann Y. Ebesugawa
University of Hawaii, Richardson School of Law
Civil Liberties Act (1988)

Gary J. Edles
American University, Washington College of Law and University of Hull Law School
Government in the Sunshine Act (1976)
Motor Carrier Act (1935)

Jonathan L. Entin
Case Western Reserve University
Balanced Budget and Emergency Deficit Control Act (1985)

Yonatan Eyal
Harvard University
Bank of the United States (1791)

Richard Finkmoore
California Western School of Law
National Wildlife Refuge System Administration Act (1966)

Lucinda Finley
State University of New York at Buffalo, School of Law
Freedom of Access to Clinic Entrances Act (1994)

Louis Fisher
Library of Congress
Congressional Budget and Impoundment Control Act (1974)

Employment Act of 1946
War Powers Resolution (1973)

Justin Florence
Harvard University
Alien and Sedition Acts of 1798

John P. Forren
Miami University, Ohio
Occupational Safety and Health Act of 1970

Julia Patterson Forrester
Southern Methodist University Dedman School of Law
Federal National Mortgage Association Charter Act (1954)

James W. Fox, Jr.
Stetson University College of Law
Naturalization Act (1790)

William Funk
Lewis and Clark Law School
Federal Advisory Committee Act (1972)

Fred Galves
University of the Pacific, McGeorge School of Law
Community Reinvestment Act (1977)

James P. George
Texas Wesleyan University School of Law
Anti-Injunction Act (1793)

Richard Gershon
Texas Wesleyan University School of Law
Estate and Gift Taxation
Taxpayer Bill of Rights III (1998)

Shubha Ghosh
State University of New York at Buffalo, School of Law
Copyright Act of 1790
Copyright Act of 1976
Patent Acts

Michele Estrin Gilman
University of Baltimore School of Law
Personal Responsibility and Work Opportunity Reconciliation Act (1996)

Mark Glaze
Campaign Legal Center, Washington, D.C.
Federal Election Campaign Act (1971)

Linda Gordon
New York University
Aid to Dependent Children (1935)

Brian E. Gray
University of California, Hastings College of the Law
Federal Power Acts
Mineral Leasing Act (1920)
National Park Service Act (1916)
Yellowstone National Park Act (1872)

Pamela L. Gray
Purdue University
Vocational Education Act of 1917

Stuart P. Green
Louisiana State University Law Center
Bribery Act (1962)
Federal Blackmail Statute (1994)

Steven J. Gunn
Yale University Law School
Alaska Native Claims Settlement Act (1971)
Fair Housing Act of 1968
Indian Gaming Regulatory Act (1988)
Indian General Allotment Act (1887)

Daniel W. Hamilton
New York University Law School
Enrollment Act (1863) (The Conscription Act)
First and Second Confiscation Acts (1861, 1862)
Militia Act (1862)
Morrill Land Grant Act of 1862
Reconstruction Acts

Douglas B. Harris
Loyola College in Maryland
Civil Aeronautics Act (1938)
Federal Aviation Act (1958)
National Aeronautics and Space Act (1958)

Philip J. Harter
Vermont Law School
Negotiated Rulemaking Act (1990)

Neil S. Helfand
Washington, D.C.
Department of Homeland Security Act (2002)
Mutual Security Act (1951)
National Security Act of 1947
USA Patriot Act (2001)

James E. Hickey, Jr.
Hofstra University School of Law
Public Utility Holding Company Act of 1935

Thomas M. Hilbink
University of Massachusetts

Omnibus Crime Control and Safe Streets Act of 1968

Arthur Holst
Philadelphia, Pennsylvania
Hazardous Materials Transportation Act (1975)
Oil Pollution Acts

Wythe W. Holt, Jr.
University of Alabama School of Law
Judiciary Act of 1789

Herbert Hovenkamp
University of Iowa
Clayton Act (1914)
Federal Trade Commission Act (1914)
Sherman Antitrust Act (1890)

James L. Huston
Oklahoma State University
Compromise of 1850
Homestead Act (1862)
Kansas Nebraska Act of 1854
Missouri Compromise (1820)

Mark D. Janis
University of Iowa College of Law
Plant Variety Protection Act (1970)

Barry L. Johnson
Oklahoma City University
Hobbs Anti-Racketeering Act (1946)
Mail Fraud and False Representation Statutes
Sentencing Reform Act (1984)

Warren F. Kimball
Rutgers University
Lend-Lease Act (1941)

Andrew R. Klein
Indiana University School of Law—Indianapolis
Rural Electrification Act (1936)

Stephen H. Klitzman
Bethesda, Maryland
Government in the Sunshine Act (1976)

Michael H. Koby
Washington University in St. Louis School of Law
Children's Online Privacy Protection Act (1998)

Thomas C. Kohler
Boston College Law School
National Labor Relations Act (1935)

David A. Koplow
Georgetown University Law Center

Arms Control and Disarmament Act (1961) and Amendments
Nuclear Non-Proliferation Act (1978)
Weapons of Mass Destruction Control Act (1992)

Andrew Koppelman
Northwestern University School of Law
Defense of Marriage Act (1996)

David E. Kyvig
Northern University Illinois
National Prohibition Act (1919)

Julia Lamber
Indiana University School of Law
Age Discrimination in Employment Act (1967)

David J. Langum
Samford University, Cumberland School of Law
Mann Act (1910)

Marc A. Le Forestier
Department of Justice, State of California
Migratory Bird Conservation Act of 1929

Arthur G. LeFrancois
Oklahoma City University School of Law
Fugitive Slave Acts (1793, 1850)
Organized Crime Control Act of 1970

Andreas Lehnert
Washington, D.C.
Federal Reserve Act (1913)

Jennifer Rebecca Levison
Independent Scholar
Narcotics Act (1914)

Alberto B. Lopez
Northern Kentucky University, Salmon P. Chase College of Law
Born-Alive Infants Protection Act of 2002

Kyle A. Loring
Boston College
National Reclamation Act of 1902
Safe Drinking Water Act (1974)
Soil Conservation and Domestic Allotment Act (1935)
Tennessee Valley Authority Act (1933)

Jeffrey S. Lubbers
American University, Washington College of Law

Administrative Procedure Act (1946)
Paperwork Reduction Act (1980)
Regulatory Flexibility Act (1980)

William V. Luneburg
University of Pittsburgh School of Law
Civil Service Acts (1883)
Federal Land Policy and
    Management Act (1976)
Federal Tort Claims Act (1946)
Hatch Act (1939)
National Environmental Policy Act
    (1969)
National Forest Management Act
    (1976)
Toxic Substances Control Act (1976)

Hether C. Macfarlane
University of the Pacific, McGeorge School of Law
Walsh-Healey Public Contracts Act
    of 1936

Shahla F. Maghzi
University of California, Berkeley Boalt Hall School of Law
Foreign Service Act of 1946
United States Information and
    Educational Exchange Act (1948)

Michael P. Malloy
University of the Pacific, McGeorge School of Law
Community Development Banking
    and Financial Institutions Act of
    1994
Glass-Steagall Act (1933)
International Emergency Economic
    Powers Act (1977)
National Banking Act (1864)
Tariff Act of 1789
Trading with the Enemy Act (1917)
United Nations Participation Act
    (1945)

Jerry W. Markham
University of North Carolina School of Law
Commodities Exchange Act (1936)
Gold Standard Act of 1900
Social Security Act of 1935

Edward J. McCaffery
University of Southern California Law School
Public Debt Acts

Michael D. McClintock
Mcafee & Taft, Oklahoma City
Merchant Marine Act of 1920

Travis McDade
Ohio State University, Michael E. Moritz College of Law
Administrative Dispute Resolution
    Act (1990)
Legal Services Corporation Act
    (1974)

W. Eric McElwain
University of the Pacific, McGeorge School of Law
Trade Act of 1974

Robert H. McLaughlin
University of Chicago
Antiquities Act of 1906

Eric J. Miller
Harvard University Law School
Juvenile Justice and Deliquency
    Prevention Act of 1974

Chandra Miller Manning
Pacific Lutheran University
Internal Improvements Acts

Kelly A. Moore
Washington University School of Law
Federal Cigarette Labeling and
    Advertising Act of 1965

William S. Morrow, Jr.
Washington Metropolitan Area Transit Commission
Urban Mass Transportation Acts

Mary-Beth Moylan
University of the Pacific, McGeorge School of Law
Highway Act of 1956

Roger K. Newman
Columbia University Graduate School of Journalism
Fair Labor Standards Act (1938)
Hill-Burton Act (1946)

Lawrence H. Officer
University of Illinois at Chicago
Bland-Allison Act (1878)
Coinage Act of 1792
Coinage Acts
Gold Reserve Act of 1934

Todd Olmstead
Yale University School of Public Health
Highway Safety Act of 1966
National Traffic and Motor Vehicle
    Safety Act of 1966

Craig Oren
Rutgers, The State University of New Jersey, School of Law, Camden
Clean Air Act (1963)

Kevin Outterson
West Virginia University College of Law
Medicare Act (1965)
Prohibition of the Slave Trade (1807)

Thomas Panebianco
Shepherd College; former General Counsel, Federal Maritime Commission
Shipping Acts

Sara M. Patterson
Claremont Graduate University
Indian Removal Act (1830)

Antonio F. Perez
The Catholic University of America School of Law
Foreign Assistance Act

Twila L. Perry
Rutgers, The State University of New Jersey, Center for Law and Justice
Family and Medical Leave Act of
    1993

Adam P. Plant
Montgomery, Alabama
Selective Service Act of 1917
Smoot-Hawley Tariff Act (1930)

Ellen S. Podgor
Georgia State University, College of Law
Counterfeit Access Device and
    Computer Fraud and Abuse Act
    of 1984

Steve Pollak
Shea and Gardner, Washington, D.C.
Economic Opportunity Act of 1964

James G. Pope
Rutgers University School of Law
National Industrial Recovery Act
    (1933)

Eric A. Posner
University of Chicago Law School
Bankruptcy Act of 1978

Trevor Potter
Campaign Legal Center, Washington, D.C.
Federal Election Campaign Act (1971)

L.A. Powe, Jr.
University of Texas School of Law
Judiciary Act of 1801

Ann Powers
Pace University School of Law
Federal Water Pollution Control Act
    (1948)

Steven Puro
St. Louis University
Electronic Signatures in Global and
    National Commerce Act (2000)
Food Stamp Act of 1964

Steven Ramirez
Washburn University School of Law
Federal Deposit Insurance Acts
Federal Home Loan Bank Act
    (1932)
Securities Act of 1933
Securities Exchange Act of 1934

Holly A. Reese
*Washington University School of
Law*
Taft-Hartley Act (1947)

Elizabeth Regosin
St. Lawrence University
Freedmen's Bureau Acts (1865,
    1868)

Sandra Rierson
Thomas Jefferson School of Law
Comstock Act (1873)

Eugene H. Robinson, Jr.
United States Marine Corps
Hazardous and Solid Waste
    Amendments of 1984
Solid Waste Disposal Act (1965)

Melissa Rogers
*Pew Forum on Religion and Public
Life, Washington, D.C.*
Religious Freedom Restoration Act
    (1993)

Stephen C. Rogers
Washington, D.C.
Rail Passenger Service Act (1970)

Sara Rosenbaum
George Washington University
Medicaid Act (1965)

Ross Rosenfeld
Brooklyn, New York
Atomic Energy Acts
Farm Credit Act of 1933
Farmers Home Administration Act
    (1946)
Force Act of 1871
Interstate Commerce Act of 1887
National Housing Act (1955)
Small Business Act (1953)

Seth Rosenfeld
Atomic Energy Acts
Small Business Act (1953)

William G. Ross
*Samford University, Cumberland
School of Law*
Keating-Owen Act of 1916

Theodore W. Ruger
*Washington University in St. Louis
School of Law*
Federal Food, Drug, and Cosmetic
    Act (1938)

Steve Russell
Indiana University
Indian Civil Rights Act (1968)

Lawrence Schlam
*Northern Illinois University College
of Law*
Domestic Volunteer Services Act of
    1973 (VISTA)
Equal Pay Act of 1963
Higher Education Act of 1965
Indian Reorganization Act of 1934
Peace Corps Act of 1961

Elizabeth M. Schneider
Brooklyn Law School
Violence Against Women Act of
    1994

Steven L. Schooner
*George Washington University Law
School*
Contract Disputes Act (1978)

John Cary Sims
*University of the Pacific, McGeorge
School of Law*
Emergency Planning and
    Community Right-To-Know Act
    (1986)
Privacy Act of 1974

David A. Skeel, Jr.
*University of Pennsylvania Law
School*
Bankruptcy Act of 1841

Richard Slottee
Lewis & Clark College Law School
Consumer Credit Protection Act
    (1969)
Truth in Lending Act (1969)

Charles Anthony Smith
University of California, San Diego
Outer Continental Shelf Lands Act
    (1953)

Donald F. Spak
Chicago-Kent College of Law
National Guard Acts
Posse Comitatus Act (1878)

Michael I. Spak
Chicago-Kent College of Law
National Guard Acts
Posse Comitatus Act (1878)

Andrew C. Spiropoulos
*Oklahoma City University School of
Law*
Flag Protection Act of 1989

Norman Stein
*University of Alabama School of
Law*
Civil War Pensions
1894 Income Tax and Wilson-
    Gorman Tariff Act

John P. Stimson
United States Marine Corps
Veterans' Preference Act of 1944

Robert N. Strassfeld
*Case Western University School of
Law*
Espionage Act (1917) and Sedition
    Act (1918)

Thomas Susman
Ropes & Gray, Washington, D.C.
Lobbying Disclosure Act (1995)

Matthew M. Taylor
Georgetown University
Panama Canal Purchase Act (1902)

Joseph P. Tomain
*University of Cincinnati College of
Law*
Department of Energy Organization
    Act (1977)
National Energy Conservation
    Policy Act (1978)
Natural Gas Act (1938)
Nuclear Waste Policy Act (1982)
Surface Mining Control and
    Reclamation Act (1977)

Mark Tushnet
Georgetown University Law Center
Antiterrorism and Effective Death
    Penalty Act (1996)
Civil Rights Act of 1875

James F. Van Orden
Duke University
Fish and Wildlife Conservation Act
    of 1980
National Emissions Standards Act
    (1965)

Robert W. Van Sickel
Indiana State University
Communications Act of 1934

Lynda D. Vargha
Skidmore College
Export-Import Bank Act of 1945

Robert G. Vaughn
American University, Washington College of Law
Civil Service Reform Act (1978)
Ethics in Government Act (1978)
Freedom of Information Act (1966)
Whistleblower Protection Laws (1989)

Wendy Wagner
University of Texas School of Law
Marine Mammal Protection Act (1972)

James Walker
Wright State University
Richard B. Russell National School Lunch Act (1946)

Valerie Watnick
Law Department, Baruch College, Zicklin School of Business
Food Quality Protection Act of 1996

Gregory S. Weber
University of the Pacific, McGeorge School of Law

Comprehensive Environmental Response, Compensation, and Liability Act (1980)

Richard Westin
University of Kentucky College of Law
Tax Reform Act of 1986

Daniel C. Wewers
Harvard University
Northwest Ordinance (1787)
Southwest Ordinance (1790)

Steven Harmon Wilson
Prairie View A&M University
Alcoholic and Narcotic Rehabilitation Act (1968)
Controlled Substances Act (1970)
Drug Abuse Prevention, Treatment, and Rehabilitation Act (1980)

John Fabian Witt
Columbia Law School
Federal Employers' Liability Act (1908)

Kelly A. Woestman
Pittsburg State University
No Child Left Behind (2001)

James A. Wooten
State University of New York at Buffalo, School of Law
Employee Retirement Income Security Act of 1974

Eric Yamamoto
University of Hawaii, Richardson School of Law
Civil Liberties Act (1988)

Diana H. Yoon
New York, New York
Chinese Exclusion Acts

Jeff Zavatsky
New York, New York
Farm Credit Act of 1933
National Housing Act (1955)

Christopher Zorn
Emory University
Staggers Rail Act of 1980

Lynne K. Zusman
Lynne Zusman & Associates, Washington, D.C.
Department of Homeland Security Act (2002)
Mutual Security Act (1951)
National Security Act of 1947
USA Patriot Act (2001)

F

FAIR HOUSING ACT OF 1968

Steven J. Gunn

Title VIII of the Civil Rights Act of 1968, commonly known as the Fair Housing Act (P.L. 90-284, 82 Stat. 81), prohibits discrimination in the sale and rental of residential housing. The act was designed to eradicate a wide range of discriminatory practices that, by the late 1960s, had resulted in the pervasive segregation of blacks and other minorities in ghettos in our nation's major cities.

The act was designed to eradicate a wide range of discriminatory practices that, by the late 1960s, had resulted in the pervasive segregation of blacks and other minorities in ghettos in our nation's major cities.

BACKGROUND

The Fair Housing Act was the final piece of civil rights legislation of the 1960s. It was enacted on April 11, 1968, just weeks after the National Advisory Commission on Civil Disorders released its report on racial discrimination and unrest in the United States. President Lyndon B. Johnson appointed the advisory commission in 1967 after a series of riots took place in the ghettos of many of America's largest cities, including Los Angeles, Chicago, Newark, and Detroit. The president asked the commission to investigate the triggers of the riots, the deeper causes of the racial unrest, and potential remedies.

The Commission's report, known as the Kerner Report after its chairman, Illinois governor Otto Kerner, found that the primary cause of racial unrest and violence was black rage against white racism, which the report stated was largely responsible for keeping blacks segregated in ghettos. The report concluded that America was "moving toward two societies, one black, one white—separate and unequal," noting that "white society is deeply implicated in the ghetto. White institutions created it, white institutions maintain it, and white society condones it." The report highlighted residential segregation as a primary cause of the urban riots of the middle to late 1960s. The Kerner Report recommended sweeping federal initiatives to eliminate housing discrimination and improve housing opportunities for urban blacks.

Congress responded by passing the Fair Housing Act. The act made many of the discriminatory practices that led to racial segregation in America's housing markets illegal. It was, in the words of the Supreme Court in

Jones v. Alfred H. Mayer Company (1968), a "comprehensive open housing law." The act made it U.S. policy to "provide, within constitutional limitations, for fair housing throughout the United States."

In broad terms, the act prohibited discrimination in the sale and rental of housing, in the provision of services or facilities in connection with the sale or rental of housing, and in **mortgage** brokerage services and other financing services in connection with the sale or rental of housing. The act also prohibited advertising with discriminatory preferences, and prohibited cities and counties from passing zoning laws to exclude or otherwise discriminate against minorities. In addition, the act empowered the U.S. Department of Housing and Urban Development (HUD) and the U.S. Attorney General to enforce its terms, to assist victims of discrimination, and authorized the federal courts to order the payment of damages to victims of discrimination.

mortgage: A loan to purchase real estate; the real estate purchased with the loan usually serves as collateral against default

When enacted in 1968, the act prohibited housing discrimination on the basis of race, color, national origin, and religion. It was expanded in 1974 to prohibit discrimination on the basis of sex, and again in 1988 to prohibit discrimination based on disability and familial status. ("Familial status" is a term that includes families with children, pregnant women, and individuals who are in the process of obtaining legal custody of a child.)

Congress responded by passing the Fair Housing Act. The act made many of the discriminatory practices that led to racial segregation in America's housing markets illegal.

SPECIFIC PROHIBITIONS

The Fair Housing Act contains several specific prohibitions against discrimination in the sale or rental of housing:

- *"It is unlawful for any person to refuse to rent or sell a dwelling, refuse to negotiate for the sale or rental of a dwelling, or otherwise make unavailable or deny a dwelling to any person because of race, color, national origin, religion, sex, familial status, or disability."* This prevents the classic forms of overt discrimination that were exceedingly common in the decades prior to the act's passage.
- *"It is unlawful for any person to represent to anyone because of race, color, national origin, religion, sex, familial status, or disability that a dwelling is not available for sale, rental, or inspection when the dwelling is in fact so available."* This prevents housing providers from giving minorities false information about the availability of housing or steering minorities to non-white neighborhoods.
- *"It is unlawful to discriminate against any person in the terms, conditions, or privileges of sale or rental of a dwelling because of race, color, national origin, religion, sex, familial status, or disability."* Among other things, this prevents housing providers from charging higher housing prices to minorities than whites.
- *"No one may discriminate against any person in the provision of services or facilities in connection with the sale or rental of a dwelling because of race, color, national origin, religion, sex, familial status, or disability."* For example, a landlord may not restrict minorities or families with children to a single portion of a housing complex or restrict their access to recreational facilities available to other tenants.

When enacted in 1968, the act prohibited housing discrimination on the basis of race, color, national origin, and religion. It was expanded in 1974 to prohibit discrimination on the basis of sex, and again in 1988 to prohibit discrimination based on disability and familial status.

Demonstrators picket outside the Sheraton-Blackstone Hotel in Chicago, where a Republican Party subcommittee meeting was taking place, July 21, 1960. Demands for an end to discrimination in the sale and rental of residential housing were met by the Fair Housing Act, enacted on April 11, 1968. (©BETTMANN/CORBIS)

- *"It is unlawful for any person to make any notice, statement, or advertisement, with respect to the sale or rental of a dwelling that indicates any preference, limitation, or discrimination based on race, color, national origin, religion, sex, familial status, or disability."* Advertisements may not refer to housing facilities as "white" or as reserved for any other race or color.

- *"It is unlawful, for profit, to persuade any person to sell or rent a dwelling by telling the person that people of a particular race, color, religion, sex, national origin, familial status, or disability are moving into the neighborhood."* This practice, known as "block-busting," was used to induce panic sales in which whites sold their properties and fled to suburban neighborhoods in order to avoid the prospect of living near minorities.

The Fair Housing Act also made it unlawful for mortgage lenders, brokers, and others involved in real estate related transactions to discriminate against minorities:

The Fair Housing Act also made it unlawful for mortgage lenders, brokers, and others involved in real estate related transactions to discriminate against minorities.

- *"It is unlawful to refuse to make a loan for the purchase, construction, improvement, repair, or maintenance of a dwelling to any person because of race, color, national origin, religion, sex, familial status, or disability."* Among other things, this provision was designed to prohibit "redlining," a practice in which banks refused to make loans to people who live in predominantly minority communities.
- *"It is unlawful to refuse to provide information regarding loans or other types of financial assistance to any person because of race, color, national origin, religion, sex, familial status, or disability. It is unlawful to discriminate against any person because of race, color, national origin, religion, sex, familial status, or disability in the terms and conditions of loans or other types of financial assistance."*

In addition, the act made it unlawful for local governments to pass housing laws that in any way discriminated against minorities. A city or township could not pass a law relegating low-income housing projects to predominantly minority neighborhoods, simply because the city expected the residents of the housing projects to be minorities. Similarly, under the act, a city could not pass a zoning ordinance that prohibited the use of private dwellings as places of religious worship.

SPECIAL PROTECTIONS FOR THE DISABLED

In the case of people with disabilities, the Fair Housing Act made it unlawful for any person to discriminate in the sale or rental of a dwelling because the potential buyer or renter had a disability, or because a disabled person intended to reside in the dwelling or happened to be associated with the buyer or renter of a property.

The act also required landlords of certain housing facilities to allow tenants with disabilities to make reasonable access-related modifications to their private living space, as well as to common use spaces, at the tenants' expense. Additionally, the act required landlords to make reasonable accommodations in their policies and operations to give people with disabilities equal opportunities to use and enjoy their housing. For example, a landlord with a "no pets" policy might have to allow an individual who is blind to keep a guide dog in the residence.

The act further required that new multifamily housing with four or more dwelling units must be built to allow access for persons with disabilities. This included accessible entrances and exits, common use areas, and doors, kitchens, and bathrooms built large enough for wheelchairs.

The Fair Housing Act applies to nearly all residential housing in the United States, including mobile home parks, homeless shelters, and summer homes. Certain housing, however, is not covered by the act, including single family houses sold or rented by the owner without a broker and without advertising, owner-occupied residences with no more than four units, dwellings within a private club, and dwellings operated by religious groups in which residency is limited to members of the group.

The Fair Housing Act applies to nearly all residential housing in the United States, including mobile home parks, homeless shelters, and summer homes.

CONSTITUTIONAL BASIS

The Fair Housing Act is authorized by the Commerce Clause of the U.S. Constitution, which grants Congress the power to regulate activities among the states, including inns and hotels catering to interstate guests. Insofar as the act prohibits racial discrimination, it is also authorized by the Thirteenth Amendment, which provides Congress with the power to abolish all badges and incidents of slavery in the United States. The Supreme Court ruled in *Jones v. Alfred H. Mayer Company* (1968) that, "when racial discrimination herds men into ghettos and makes their ability to buy property turn on the color of their skin, then it ... is a relic of slavery," and can be abolished by Congress. Finally, as applied to housing owned, operated, or subsidized by the federal or state governments, the Fair Housing Act is authorized by the Fifth and Fourteenth Amendments, in which Congress is given the power to pass laws ensuring that the federal and state governments do not deny any person the equal protection of the laws.

See also: CIVIL RIGHTS ACTS OF 1957, 1964; HOUSING AND URBAN DEVELOPMENT ACT OF 1965; NATIONAL HOUSING ACT.

BIBLIOGRAPHY

Metcalf, George R. *Fair Housing Comes of Age.* Westport, CT: Greenwood Press, 1988.

United States National Advisory Commission on Civil Disorders. *Report of the National Advisory Commission on Civil Disorders.* Washington, DC: U.S. Government Printing Office, 1968.

FAIR LABOR STANDARDS ACT (1938)

Roger K. Newman

The Fair Labor Standards Act regulates wages and hours in the workplace. Efforts to enact legislation limiting the number of hours a person could work in a week began early in the nineteenth century, but Congress was not able to adopt the Fair Labor Standards Act until 1938. Although many political and labor leaders were suspicious of federally-drawn labor standards, the minimum wage and hour laws are now widely believed to be an important piece of anti-poverty legislation.

> *Although many political and labor leaders were suspicious of federally–drawn labor standards, the minimum wage and hour laws are now widely believed to be an important piece of anti–poverty legislation.*

HUGO BLACK'S BILL

In December of, 1932, three months before Franklin D. Roosevelt's inauguration and at the **nadir** of the **Great Depression**, Senator Hugo L. Black of Alabama introduced a bill that would forbid interstate commerce of goods produced by persons working more than thirty hours a week or six hours a day. This early attempt to regulate the work week proved fruitless because of two Supreme Court cases that seemed to bar such laws. In the 1918 case *Hammer v. Dagenhart,* the Supreme Court held unconstitutional the federal child-labor law passed two years earlier. And in 1923, in *Adkins v. Children's Hospital,* the court voided a District of Columbia minimum wage law for women on the ground that such a law was "a naked, arbitrary exercise" of legislative power in violation of the due process clause of the Fifth Amendment.

nadir: the lowest point

Great Depression: The longest and most severe economic depression in American history (1929–1939); its effects were felt throughout the world.

Black tried to distinguish his proposal from the legislation rejected in *Hammer.* "Laws must be interpreted to meet conditions existing when the law is interpreted," he told the Senate which passed the bill in April of 1933. The bill never passed in the House. Congress passed the National Industrial Recovery Act (NRA) in May of 1933, one section of which addressed minimum wages and maximum hours.

THE SUPREME COURT AND THE NEW DEAL

The Supreme Court in 1935 unanimously struck down the NRA, holding that it exceeded the federal government's power under the Commerce Clause and that it was an unconstitutional delegation of legislative authority to the executive branch. One year later the Court ruled that a New York minimum wage law was unconstitutional. Based on these decisions it appeared that the court would not sanction a bill similar to the one that Hugo Black had proposed earlier on minimum wages and maximum hours. Nevertheless, after winning the 1936 presidential election in a landslide, Roosevelt asked labor secretary Frances Perkins, "What happened to that nice unconstitutional bill you had tucked away?" He had determined that the bill should be introduced in Congress. New Deal lawyers Benjamin V. Cohen and Thomas G. Corcoran, with help from Assistant Attorney General Robert H. Jackson started revising it extensively.

The proposal included a presidentially-appointed board with the authority to set minimum wage and maximum workweek standards.

In February of 1937 Roosevelt startled the nation by announcing his Reorganization of the Judiciary Proposal. The Supreme Court had invalidated six major New Deal laws over the previous two years, and Roosevelt wanted to **nominate** one justice, up to a total of six, for each one over the age of seventy who would not retire. This would make for a court of up to fifteen members. Roosevelt's "court-packing" proposal, as its opponents called it, produced a long and bitter political battle, but before it could come to fruition, the Supreme Court in *West Coast Hotel v. Parrish,* upheld a Washington state minimum wage law for women and minors similar to the New York statute it had overturned. *Adkins* was specifically overruled as the court emphasized the need for minimum wage regulation. "The Legislature," wrote Chief Justice Charles Evans Hughes, "was entitled to adopt measures to reduce the evils of the 'sweating system,' the exploiting of workers at wages so low as to be insufficient to meet the bare cost of living, thus making their very helplessness the occasion of a most injurious competition." And in April, in *N.L.R.B. v. Jones & Loughlin Steel Corporation,* the Court upheld the National Labor Relations Act. In short, Roosevelt no longer needed to "pack the court" with justices friendly to his labor legislation because the existing court ultimately found it compatible with the Constitution.

nominate: to propose one for appointment to office

CONGRESS CONSIDERS A BROADER BILL

The way was cleared for the introduction of a wages-hours bill. Cohen, its principal draftsman, based it on the newly reinvigorated Commerce Clause and hewed closely to the language and logic of the *West Coast Hotel* and *Jones & Loughlin* decisions. The proposal included a presidentially-appointed board with the authority to set minimum wage and maximum workweek standards. Black knew this discretion would draw strong opposition from Southern Democrats and most Republicans. The simpler the language, he

Boys working at an anthracite coal mine in a coal breaker, where coal was crushed, cleansed, and sorted (c. 1900–1910). (©CORBIS)

told Corcoran and Cohen in their frequent meetings, the easier it would be for him, a very persuasive advocate, to get the measure passed. Black introduced the bill in the Senate on May 27, 1937, and William P. Connery of Massachusetts brought it before the House. The bill provided for a forty cents per hour minimum wage, a forty-hour maximum workweek and a minimum working age of sixteen in interstate commerce except in certain industries outside of mining and manufacturing.

The bill's scope appalled conservatives, but the most strident opposition came from Southerners who wanted to maintain the "regional pay differential" that enabled Southern employers to pay lower wages than other areas of the country.

In late July of 1937 the Senate Labor and Education Committee unanimously, including the one Republican present, approved the bill. The powers of the proposed board were sharply curbed and different fields were exempted—agriculture, fishing and forestry, cannery workers, handlers of perishable foods, intrastate retail businesses, most transportation workers, and government employees. But there were no regional differentials on wages.

ENTANGLED IN THE HOUSE

The House Labor Committee passed the bill in early August, and it would have easily passed the House as a whole, but a coalition of Republicans and conservative Democrats stalled it in the Rules Committee. At one point not enough Democrats showed up to make a caucus official. Conservative groups teamed with Republicans and some labor leaders to try to bottle the measure—"bad medicine for us," a spokesman for the American Federation of Labor called it, even after work covered by collective bargaining was excluded.

Roosevelt called a special session of Congress in November of 1937 to force the House to consider it, and it reached the floor in December, only to see the House as a whole vote to send it back to the Rules Committee. Overall, members of Congress had proposed seventy-two amendments to weaken the bill. In April of 1938 the House Labor Committee passed a new version, but since it lacked a wage differential, Southerners again buried the bill in the Rules Committee. It seemed unlikely that it would ever become law.

PASSAGE

In early May of 1938 Florida's Senator Claude Pepper, basing his campaign on the wages-hours bill, decisively won the Democratic primary for re–nomination. This "put the fear of God in the hearts of some of the Democrats," one Republican congressman noted. Three days later, the rules committee sent the bill to the floor after a **discharge petition** gained the necessary 218 signatures in only two hours and twenty minutes as members of Congress jostled each other in a boisterous atmosphere on the floor. The House overwhelmingly passed the bill late that month, and on June 25, 1938, Roosevelt signed a compromise worked out with the Senate.

discharge petition: a method for moving a bill from a committee to the floor of the House when a committee refuses to do so itself. The bill must have been held by a committee for at least thirty legislative days, and half of the House membership must sign the petition for release that is filed

The Fair Labor Standards Act put the minimum wage at 25 cents an hour, below the rate then in effect in most union contracts, and the maximum workweek at forty-four hours for the first year of the act, forty-two for the second year, and forty hours thereafter, and it allowed seven years to reach the standards of a forty-cent minimum wage and forty-hour maximum work week. By 1943 all workers were covered by the forty-cent minimum. Advisory wage boards, under the authority of a newly established wage-hour division of the Labor Department, could consider but not be bound by "competitive conditions as affected by transportation, living, and production costs," and they have the authority to recommend higher levels. The act requires pay at the rate of time and one-half the regular rate for over forty hours worked in one week. And it forbids child labor, defined as the interstate shipment of goods made by firms that employed children under the age of sixteen, or children under eighteen in hazardous occupations. Initially, the law applied to industries whose employees combined represented about one-fifth of all workers.

The Fair Labor Standards Act put the minimum wage at 25 cents an hour, below the rate then in effect in most union contracts, and the maximum workweek at forty–four hours for the first year of the act, forty–two for the second year, and forty hours thereafter, and it allowed seven years to reach the standards of a forty-cent minimum and forty-hour maximum work week.

THE SUPREME COURT UPHOLDS

The Supreme Court upheld the law's constitutionality in *U.S. v. Darby* in 1941. "The power of interstate commerce," Justice Harlan F. Stone wrote for a unanimous court, "is 'complete in itself, may be exercised to its utmost extent, and acknowledges no limitations other than are prescribed in the Constitution.'" In 1942 in *A.B. Kirschbaum v. Walling,* the Supreme Court sustained the application of the act to employees who were not engaged in production for interstate commerce but operated a loft whose tenants produced garments for sale in interstate commerce. Subsequently, the court ruled that the law applied to a night watchman in a veneer plant, to window cleaners and to porters, elevator operators, and other employees of an office building, and in 1968 to nonprofessional employees of state-operated schools and hospitals.

EXPANDING COVERAGE

The original statute covered only workers "engaged in commerce or in the production of goods for commerce." Under this language, one of two employees hired by the same firm, performing essentially the same work, might be protected while the other would not be. These anomalies were ended in 1961 by extending coverage to all those "employed by an enterprise engaged in commerce or in the production of goods for commerce." Much litigation nevertheless continues to involve coverage issues, often focusing on the definition of "enterprise" or exemptions from coverage. Coverage of public employees has also been challenged before the Supreme Court. As of 2003, the statute protected employees of state governments, but whether they can enforce their rights depends upon whether the state has **waived sovereign immunity**. For private sector employees there can be enforcement by the federal Labor Department or by private rights of action. The law also regulates wages of employees who work for firms that provide goods and services to the federal government.

waive: to give up voluntarily

sovereign immunity: the doctrine that prevents bringing a lawsuit against the government, without the government's consent

Over the years the Fair Labor Standards Act has been amended repeatedly. Changes have included raising the minimum wage, expanding the classes of workers covered, redefining regular-time work and raising overtime payments so as to encourage the hiring of new workers, and equalizing pay scales for men and women. Amendments have also provided more effective enforcement. Amendments in 1966 extended the Act to workers in the retail and service industry, farm workers, government and transit employees, and restaurant, hotel, and domestic workers. Some job categories had a lower minimum wage, and it was not until 1978 that all employees covered by the act earned the same rate. In 1997 a sub-minimum wage of $4.25 was established for employees under the age of twenty for their first ninety days of employment. At the same time the minimum wage was raised to $5.15. States can set a wage higher than the federal minimum, and upwards of a dozen have.

"THE MOST VITAL LEGISLATION"

The Fair Labor Standards Act has been called "the most vital social legislation" in American history because it affects every worker in interstate commerce. Since its principal goal was to increase the purchasing power of the lowest-paid workers, it has also been called the original anti-poverty law. Another byproduct has been to help society maintain a healthy balance between work and the rest of life. The act's impact has eroded somewhat as more Americans have moved into professional

The Fair Labor Standards Act has been called "the most vital social legislation" in American history because it affects every worker in interstate commerce.

and other employment categories, such as executive and administrative, that are exempt from wage regulations. It does not cover approximately 50 million of the current 150 million workers. In 2003 strong union opposition in the House of Representatives doomed the passage of the Family Time Flexibility Act, which would have allowed employees the option of receiving overtime pay in the form of time off. This typifies continual attempts to change aspects of the law, but the Fair Labor Standards Act remains a major part of the American economic landscape.

See also: KEATING-OWEN ACT OF 1916; NATIONAL INDUSTRY RECOVERY ACT.

BIBLIOGRAPHY

Grossman, Jonathan, "Fair Labor Standards Act of 1938: Maximum Struggle for a Minimum Wage." *Monthly Labor Review* (June 1978).

Lash, Joseph P. *Dealers and Dreamers: A New Look at the New Deal.* New York: Doubleday, 1988.

Lasser, William. *Benjamin V. Cohen: Architect of the New Deal.* New Haven, CT: Yale University Press, 2002.

Newman, Roger K. *Hugo Black: A Biography.* New York: Pantheon, 1994.

Samuel, Howard D. "Troubled Passage: The Labor Movement and the Fair Labor Standards Act." *Monthly Labor Review* (December 2000).

FAMILY AND MEDICAL LEAVE ACT OF 1993

Twila L. Perry

Congress passed the Family and Medical Leave Act (P.L. 103-3, 107 Stat. 6) to help people who were stressed about trying to balance the competing demands of work and family. The law was signed by President William J. Clinton on February 5, 1993. Experts often refer to the legislation as the "FMLA."

Changes taking place in the American family over the past decades led to the need for the FMLA.

Changes taking place in the American family over the past decades led to the need for the FMLA. With an increasing number of single-parent families and two-parent families in which both parents work, the birth of a child or a serious family illness often placed workers in the position of having to choose between keeping their jobs or providing care to a family member.

Women were especially burdened because they have traditionally had the role of caregiver. Not only have parents sometimes lost time from work to attend to their families, but their own medical problems could lead to missed work days as well. These absences from work caused problems with employers who needed a reliable work force; too many absences due to illness, therefore, could get an employee fired. The FMLA allows employees to take unpaid leaves of absence from their jobs in these kinds of situations. It provides a minimum level of job security for people trying to balance the demands of their jobs with family obligations.

Section 2601 of the FMLA states the purpose of the law:

> ... to balance the demands of the workplace with the needs of families, to promote the stability and economic security of families, and to promote the national interests in preserving family integrity ... to entitle employees to take reasonable leave for medical reasons, for the birth or adoption of a child, and for the care of a child, spouse, or parent who has a serious health condition ... to promote the goal of equal employment opportunity for men and women.

Not everyone was in favor passing the FMLA; legislators extensively debated the proposed bill in Congress before it was passed. While many legislators thought the FMLA was needed to help families, some argued the FMLA would unnecessarily interfere with relationships between employers and employees and would hurt small businesses. Others argued that the leaves of absence taken by some workers would place unfair burdens of additional work on others who remained on the job.

The Supreme Court has noted that the power of Congress to pass the FMLA comes from two different sections of the U.S. Constitution: the Com-

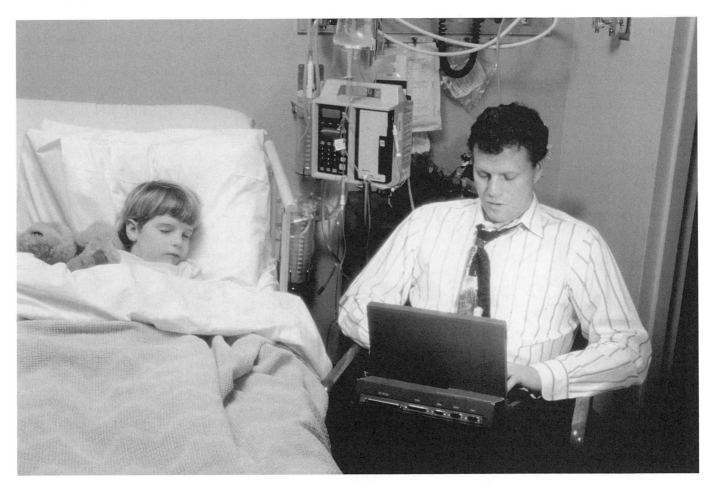

A father sits with his son while in the hospital, 1996. The Family and Medical Leave Act of 1993 allows an employee to take an unpaid leave of absence from his or her job, without a threat to job security, in the event of a family medical emergency. (©Tom Stewart/Corbis)

While many legislators thought the FMLA was needed to help families, some argued the FMLA would unnecessarily interfere with relationships between employers and employees and would hurt small businesses.

merce Clause and the Fourteenth Amendment. The Commerce Clause gives Congress the power to regulate businesses; the Fourteenth Amendment protects citizens from discrimination, including discrimination on the basis of gender. Section 5 of the Fourteenth Amendment gives Congress the power to adopt laws to enforce that Amendment.

DETAILS OF THE LAW

The FMLA allows employees to take up to twelve weeks of unpaid leave in any twelve-month period for the birth or adoption of a child, to care for a family member, or in the event of the employee's own serious health problems. The employee can take the leave in a continuous block or by working on a reduced schedule. In some circumstances the employee can take the leave on an intermittent, or off-and-on, basis. Finally, the employee can take leave under the FMLA in addition to other paid time off that might be available, such as vacation time.

An employee must, however, follow certain procedures in order to take FMLA leave. If the employee knows in advance that he or she will need a leave, he or she must give the employer thirty days notice. If the situation is an emergency, the employee must notify the employer as soon as it is practical; employers can also require that the employee submit written medical certification to verify any claimed health condition.

While an employee is on leave, the employer must maintain benefits for the individual such as group health care. If the employee was making payments for such benefits, the employee must continue those payments during the leave. At the end of the leave, the employee is entitled to return to the same job or to an equivalent job with the employer.

Not all employees are entitled to take leaves under the FMLA. The law only covers employees who have been working for their employers for at least twelve months and who have worked for at least 1,250 hours. State and local government employees are covered by the law, while private employers must offer the FMLA if they have fifty or more employees for each work day for at least twenty work weeks during the year.

LITIGATION AND CONTROVERSY

Workers have sued employers under the FMLA in a number of contexts. Examples of the kinds of issues courts have decided include whether an employer retaliated against an employee for taking a FMLA leave, if the job given to an employee upon return from leave was an equivalent job, whether an employee gave proper notice to an employer prior to a leave, and if an illness qualified as a "serious illness" under the FMLA.

The bipartisan Congressional Caucus for Women's Issues pushed for the enactment of FMLA.

The U.S. Supreme Court considered a case under the FMLA for the first time in 2002. In *Ragsdale v. Wolverine World Wide, Inc.*, the Department of Labor penalized an employer who failed to tell an employee the time she had taken off as unpaid leave counted as FMLA leave. The Supreme Court, however, ruled that the penalty was not valid. Even though the Department of Labor has the power to supervise the implementation of the FMLA, this case suggested it still was not completely clear in what it could and could not do in order to enforce this law.

In the 2003 case *Nevada Department of Human Resources v. Hibbs*, the Supreme Court upheld Congress's power to allow private suits against the states before the FMLA. The Court said that the FMLA protected against such discrimination in employment. Although the FMLA addresses some concerns employees have in trying to balance work with family, the benefits it gives are limited. The FMLA does not provide for paid leave; so the only workers who can take advantage of the law are those who can afford to take an unpaid leave. Some people take the position the FMLA should provide for paid leaves and that Congress should expand it to cover jobs where twenty or more workers are employed—rather than limiting it to employers with fifty or more employees. Experts also suggest that the FMLA should cover other family situations, such as doctor's appointments and parent-teacher conferences, situations that often require parents to take time off from work. It is likely that this debate over just how much the government should provide to families will continue well into the future.

> *Although the FMLA addresses some concerns employees have in trying to balance work with family, the benefits it gives are limited.*

See also: AID TO DEPENDENT CHILDREN; PREGNANCY DISCRIMINATION ACT.

BIBLIOGRAPHY

Dunston, Robert, and Frank Robins. *FMLA: A Practical Guide to Implementing the FMLA.* College and University Professional Association for Human Resources, 1994.

Dunston, Robert, and Frank Robins. *Practical Guide to Implementing the FMLA: 1996 Supplement.* College and University Professional Association for Human Resources, 1996.

Schwartz, Robert M. *The FMLA Handbook: A Union Guide to the FMLA.* Work Rights Project, 2001.

Wever, Kirsten S. "Changing Work in America: The Family and Medical Leave Act." <http://www.radcliffe.edu/pubpol/cwia_kw.html>.

Williams, Anne H. *FMLA Leave: A Guide Through the Legal Labyrinth.* M. Lee Smith Publishers and Printers, 2001.

INTERNET RESOURCES

U.S. Department of Justice. Family and Medical Leave Act (FMLA) Fact Sheet. <http://www.usdoj.gov/jmd/ps/fmla/htm>.

U.S. Department of Labor. Family and Medical Leave Act Fact Sheet. <http://www.dol.gov/dol/esa/faml.htm>.

FANNIE MAE

See FEDERAL NATIONAL MORTGAGE ASSOCIATION CHARTER ACT

Ross Rosenfeld and Jeff Zavatsky

Excerpt from the Farm Credit Act

The Governor of the Farm Credit Administration, herein after in this Act referred to as the "governor," is authorized and directed to organize and charter twelve corporations to be known as "Production Credit Corporations" and twelve banks to be known as "Banks for Cooperatives." One such corporation and one such bank shall be established in each city in which there is located a Federal land bank. The directors of the several Federal land banks shall be ex officio the directors of the respective Production Credit Corporations and Banks for Cooperatives.

Great Depression: the longest and most severe economic depression in American history (1929–1939); its effects were felt throughout the world

foreclosure: when a person defaults on (fails to pay) a mortgage debt, the owner's legal right to the property is terminated. The real estate may be sold at an auction by the creditor; the money raised is then put toward the mortgage debt

refinance: to pay off existing loans with funds secured from new loans

mortgage: a loan to purchase real estate; the real estate purchased with the loan usually serves as collateral against default

The Farm Credit Act of 1933 (48 Stat. 257) made it possible for many farmers to keep their farms and survive the **Great Depression**. It did so by offering short-term loans for agricultural production as well as extended low interest rates for farmers threatened by **foreclosure**. Small farmers were able to **refinance** their **mortgages** with the aid of twelve district banks, called Banks for Cooperatives. A thirteenth bank served larger farming operations. Local Production Credit Associations provided short and intermediate term loans for seasonal production, insuring that farmers would not lose out on essential crop yields.

The act was passed on June 16, 1933, the last day of President Franklin D. Roosevelt's "Hundred Days" initiative, an effort by his Administration to quickly put in place measures to fight the Depression. Its stated purpose was to "provide for organizations within the Farm Credit Administration to make loans for the production and marketing of agricultural products, to amend the Federal Farm Loan Act, to amend the Agricultural Marketing Act, to provide a market for obligations of the United States, and for other purposes."

CIRCUMSTANCES LEADING TO THE ACT

The Federal Farm Loan Act had been passed under President Woodrow Wilson's administration in 1916. It created twelve Federal Land Banks to provide long-term loans for farmers. The Agricultural Marketing Act provided loans to cooperatives, but it collapsed when prices fell in 1930. The Farm Credit Act built on these ideas by expanding the federal government's role and establishing short-term loan institutions. The Farm Credit Act coincided with the Emergency Farm Mortgage Act (passed on May 12, the same day as the Agricultural Adjustment Act), which provided $200 million in loans for farmers facing foreclosure. Under Executive Order No. 6340 (October 16, 1933), Roosevelt officially formed the Farm Credit Administration to oversee the day-to-day operations as set forth in the act.

The act was passed on June 16, 1933, the last day of President Franklin D. Roosevelt's "Hundred Days" initiative, an effort by his Administration to quickly put in place measures to fight the Depression.

From 1910 to 1930 the number of farms in the United States had decreased by 71,000, but nearly a quarter of the nation's 123 million people were still farmers. With 300,000 more people becoming tenant farmers, the day of the migrant worker or "day laborer" was quickly setting in. Technological advances made it possible for one person to do more work, and the average farm size grew from 139 to 157 acres. Unfortunately, the technology could not provide rain.

Since 1931 a period of severe drought had been destroying crops in the midwestern and southern plains. This region became known as the Dust Bowl. "Black blizzards" of dust settled over dry, overplowed land. The stock market crash and ensuing Great Depression exacerbated the problem by creating a lack of buying power. This resulted in production surpluses, causing farm and dairy prices to decline. Farmers found themselves without the necessary capital to support crop growth, and soon many of them were facing foreclosure.

During the campaign of 1932, Franklin Roosevelt had promised to reorganize the Department of Agriculture, lower taxes on farmers, raise tariffs, and provide federal credit for farm mortgages. Roosevelt may have been taking a cue from his famous uncle Theodore, who as president had proposed "an effective cooperation among farmers" back in 1908. The second Roosevelt, however, was more aggressive than the first on this subject. In addition to extending loan institutions, the administration advocated destroying crops and killing piglets to cut surpluses and prop up prices. Three months after the Farm Credit Act passed through Congress, six million piglets were put to death. Backlash from a deprived, often starving public, though, caused Roosevelt to reverse himself on this issue, and the administration instead offered subsidies for voluntary reduction.

Farmers found themselves without the necessary capital to support crop growth, and soon many of them were facing foreclosure.

RELATED ACTS

During the Great Depression, approximately three million people were forced to move off their farms. It is impossible to say exactly how many people the Farm Credit Act saved, but it is reasonable to estimate that without it the number forced off their farms would have been much larger. Other initiatives taken by Roosevelt and Congress to aid the farmer included the Frazier-Lemke Farm Bankruptcy Act, which limited the ability of banks to evict farmers during hard times, and the Emergency Relief Appropriation Act, which allocated $525 million for drought relief. The Farm Tenancy Act of 1937 helped tenant farmers buy their own land. Better farming methods also became a priority. The Soil Conservation Service taught farmers to preserve soil and prevent irreversible damage through techniques such as strip cropping and crop rotation.

In 1971 a new Farm Credit Act was drawn up, and it is the basis for the Farm Credit system today, which continues to help balance the risks of farming.

Like many **New Deal** laws, the Farm Credit Act was a tool of the times. But the idea took hold. Following the Depression, it went through many stages, being reworked in 1953, then repealed in 1966. In 1971 a new Farm Credit Act was drawn up, and it is the basis for the Farm Credit system today, which continues to help balance the risks of farming.

New Deal: the legislative and administrative program of President Franklin D. Roosevelt designed to promote economic recovery and social reform (1933–1939)

See also: AGRICULTURAL ADJUSTMENT ACT; FARMERS'S HOME ADMINISTRATION ACT; NATIONAL INDUSTRIAL RECOVERY ACT.

BIBLIOGRAPHY

Badger, Anthony J. *The New Deal: The Depression Years, 1933–1940.* New York: Noonday Press, 1989.

Burns, James MacGregor. *Roosevelt: 1882–1940: The Lion and the Fox.* San Diego: Harcourt Brace, 1956.

Watkins, T. H. *The Hungry Years: A Narrative History of the Great Depression in America*. New York: Holt, 1999.

INTERNET RESOURCE

PBS Online. "Timeline of Farming in the U.S." <http://www.pbs.org/wgbh/amex/trouble/timeline/>.

FARMERS HOME ADMINISTRATION ACT (1946)

Ross Rosenfeld

The Farmers Home Administration Act (FHAA) of 1946 grew out of the Dust Bowl of the 1930s, the Great Depression, and the Resettlement Act of 1935. Government was beginning to take a greater hand than it ever had in the life of the farmer. This involvement included price controls, surplus destruction, and farm loans. The Farmers' Home Administration (FHA) became part of what is known as the Farm Credit System.

The FHA was preceded by the Farm Security Administration (1937), which built cooperative structures where tenant farmers could work in a communal setting. The FHA differed from the former agency in that it concentrated on helping individual farmers acquire their own farms, just as the Federal Housing Authority helped people own their own homes. The main purpose of the act was "to simplify and improve credit services to farmers and promote farm ownership by ... authorizing government insurance of loans to farmers." The act consolidated various organizations so "eligible farmers" could "obtain their agricultural credit and services at one central point."

The FHA differed from the Farm Security Administration in that it concentrated on helping individual farmers acquire their own farms, just as the Federal Housing Authority helped people own their homes.

stipulate: to specify as a condition of an agreement

The FHA issued both direct and guaranteed loans to those who had trouble gaining credit lines through commercial banks. FHA assistance was directed toward young farmers just starting out, small farmers, poverty stricken farmers, veterans, and larger farming businesses struck by disaster. The FHA was to be their "last resort." Some states even took it upon themselves to **stipulate** that a loan applicant had to have been rejected for a commercial loan before applying to the FHA.

President Truman signed the bill into law on August 14, 1946, but had reservations. Section 9 of the act reads: "Any conveyance of real estate by the Government or any Government agency under this Act shall include all mineral rights." Truman, however, stated, "I do not concur with the objectives of this provision." He cited the Atomic Energy Act of 1946 and Executive Order 9701, both of which gave the government greater control over important natural resources such as gas and oil. The nuclear age was also just beginning, but private enterprise in this sector would have to wait for the Eisenhower Administration, which would prove to be more permissive.

The act went through various updates over the years, being reorganized to reflect the changing times. In general, the act's scope expanded to encompass all farmers in need. By 1977 this would come to include a growing amount of "emergency loans." These factors contributed to tremendous loan losses ($16.19 billion from 1986 to 1993 alone) and instigated a great deal of criticism. As a result of such losses, the agency made an effort to shift from predominantly direct loans to mostly insured loans. In 1980 "guaranteed loans" made up only 2.9 percent of farm owning and operating loans; by 1993 that number had risen to 70.5 percent.

In 1994 the Farmers' Home Administration was incorporated, along with the Agricultural Stabilization and Conservation Service, the Federal Crop Insurance Corporation, and others into the Farm Service Agency. This agency continues to oversee loans once controlled by the FHA.

See also: AGRICULTURAL ADJUSTMENT ACT; FAIR HOUSING ACT OF 1968; NATIONAL INDUSTRIAL RECOVERY ACT

BIBLIOGRAPHY

Rapp, David. *How the U.S. Got Into Agriculture and Why It Can't Get Out*. Washington, DC: Congressional Quarterly Inc., 1988.

Sumner, Daniel A., ed. *Agricultural Policy Reform in the United States*. Washington DC: American Enterprise Institute Press, 1995.

INTERNET RESOURCE

U.S. Farm Service Agency. <http://www.fsa.usda.gov>.

> *In 1994 the Farmers's Home Administration was incorporated into the Farm Service Agency, along with the Agricultural Stabilization and Conservation Service, the Federal Crop Insurance Corporation, among others.*

FEDERAL ADVISORY COMMITTEE ACT (1972)

William Funk

Both the president and federal agencies receive advice from committees that are at least partially made up of private persons. Congress passed the Federal Advisory Committee Act (P.L. 92-463, 86 Stat. 770) in 1972 to regulate the creation and operation of these committees. Congress was responding to two problems: (1) the large number of advisory committees, many of which were duplicative, wasteful, and of limited usefulness, and (2) the secretiveness of most advisory committees' operations and the undue influence certain private groups allegedly wielded in these committees.

THE ACT'S REQUIREMENTS

To address the issue of the number of federal advisory committees, the act requires both the president and the administrator of the General Services Administration (GSA), which is given general management responsibility for all federal advisory committees, to make an annual report on the activities and costs of advisory committees and to review whether committees should be retained or abolished. In addition, the act makes it more difficult to establish new advisory committees. Under section 9(a) of the act, no new advisory committee can be created unless

> *The Federal Advisory Committe Act is the legal foundation that defines how federal advisory committees must operate. The law places special emphasis on open meetings, chartering, public involvement, and reporting.*

the president or a statute has specifically authorized it, or the head of an agency formally determines after consultation with the administrator of GSA that the establishment of a new advisory committee is "in the public interest in connection with the performance of duties imposed on that agency by law." This prohibition is enforced by a separate requirement that no advisory committee shall meet or take any action until a charter for the committee has been filed with the administrator of GSA for presidential advisory committees, or with the head of the agency to which the advisory committee reports, and with the standing committees of the Senate and House having jurisdiction over such agency. Although an advisory committee cannot be established for longer than two years, the act allows the president or the head of an agency to renew committees created by them for additional and successive two-year periods.

To solve the problems of secretiveness and excessive influence of private groups, Congress required various procedures to open up advisory committee meetings:

- Each advisory committee meeting must be open to the public, and interested persons may attend, appear before, and file statements with the committee.
- Meetings or portions of meetings may be closed to the public only when the president or the head of an agency determines that closing is in accordance with the provisions of the Government in the Sunshine Act for closing meetings under that act.
- Agencies must provide effective public notice of committee meetings, including publication in the *Federal Register*.
- Detailed minutes must be kept of the meetings, and the minutes and other documents received by or generated by the committee must be made available to the public, subject only to the same limitations as records under the Freedom of Information Act.
- To limit the influence of any particular private group, the membership of advisory committees must be fairly balanced in terms of points of view represented and functions to be performed.
- Advisory committees cannot meet except with the approval of an officer or employee of the federal government who is designated to attend or chair their meetings and who also approves the agenda for the meeting.

Federal Register: a newspaper published daily by the National Archives and Records Administration to notify the public of federal agency regulations, proposed rules and notices, executive orders, and other executive branch documents

THE DEFINITION OF AN ADVISORY COMMITTEE

The definition of an advisory committee is a critical issue, because it determines whether the particular requirements governing the creation and operation of advisory committees are applicable. A fair amount of litigation has centered on this issue. Section 3(2) of the act defines "advisory committee" as: "any committee, board, commission, council, conference, panel, task force, or other similar group, or any subcommittee or other subgroup thereof ..., which is—(A) established by statute or reorganization plan, or; (B) established or utilized by the President, or; (C) established or utilized by one or more agencies, in the interest of obtaining advice or recommendations for the President or one or more agencies or officers of the Federal Government."

The definition of an advisory committee is a critical issue, because it determines whether the particular requirements governing the creation and operation of advisory committees are applicable.

However, the act exempts a number of groups from this definition that otherwise would be advisory committees.

These include any committee composed entirely of full-time or part-time employees of the federal government; any committee created by the National Academy of Sciences or the National Academy of Public Administration; any committee created or utilized by the Central Intelligence Agency or the Federal Reserve System; and, generally, local civic groups, state and local committees, and groups of state and local legislators. Statutes that create advisory committees sometimes also exempt those committees from the definition contained in the act.

INTERPRETING THE ACT

When do the president and the Department of Justice "utilize" a committee for the purpose of obtaining advice, thereby subjecting it to the act's requirements? In 1989 a Supreme Court case addressed this important question concerning interpretation of the act. The American Bar Association (ABA) maintained a standing committee to review candidates for judicial nominations. These names were forwarded to it by the Department of Justice, and the committee in return provided the president and the Department of Justice with the results of the committee's review. Thus, in a commonsense understanding of the term, the president and the department *utilized* the ABA committee for advice. Because the committee did not function in accordance with the requirements of the act, a public interest group sued to enforce the act in *Public Citizen v. U.S. Department of Justice*.

> *When do the president and the Department of Justice "utilize" a committee for the purpose of obtaining advice, thereby subjecting it to the act's requirements?*

In that case, the Supreme Court concluded that Congress could not have intended to impose the requirements of the act on any private group that the president or an agency happened to seek advice from. Rather, the Court said, the word "utilized" "appears to have been added simply to clarify that FACA applies to advisory committees established by the Federal Government in a generous sense of that term, encompassing groups formed indirectly by quasi-public organizations ... 'for' public agencies as well as 'by' such agencies themselves...." (491 U.S. at 462). The result of this very restrictive interpretation by the Court was largely to eliminate the requirements of the act for "utilized" advisory committees.

The other major interpretive issue, which has arisen on numerous occasions, is what constitutes the "establishment" of a group for the purpose of providing advice to an agency. Initially, it appears that the agency must establish the group so as to obtain the group's advice, as opposed to the individual advice of each of the members (*Association of American Physicians and Surgeons, Inc. v. Clinton* [1993]). The GSA, in its role of managing advisory committees generally, has taken the position that committees that are primarily operational and only incidentally provide advice are not subject to the act. In addition, the GSA advises that committees that only provide facts and information are not subject to the act. Court decisions have not definitively ruled on either of these interpretations. Nevertheless, the difficulty in policing the line between "operations" and "advice" and between "facts and information" and "advice" makes it risky for committees to use these two interpretations to avoid being covered by the act.

Finally, there is a question as to how formal the establishment of a group must be in order to trigger the act's requirements. An early case in a lower court found that biweekly, three-hour meetings between high executive offi-

private sector: the part of the economy that is not controlled by the government

cials and major business organizations and other groups in the **private sector** were not advisory committee meetings because the meetings involved different people from meeting to meeting and because the advice they provided was general advice as to whatever concerned these persons. On the other hand, other lower-court cases have found even a one-time meeting of agency officials with a group of outside experts on a particular policy initiative to be an advisory committee meeting.

JUDICIAL REVIEW

An agency's failure to comply with the act's procedural requirements applicable to meetings may be challenged under the federal Administrative Procedure Act. When the committee is engaged in a continuing enterprise, a court may order the committee to comply with the act. When, however, the committee has completed its work, it is less clear how the court should respond. One court prohibited an agency from using the advice and information provided to it by a committee, which resulted in the inability of the agency to list a species as endangered. Usually, however, courts merely order that the documents provided to or by the committee be made available to the public.

See also: ADMINISTRATIVE PROCEDURE ACT; FREEDOM OF INFORMATION ACT; GOVERNMENT IN THE SUNSHINE ACT.

BIBLIOGRAPHY

Croley, Steven P., and William F. Funk. "The Federal Advisory Committee Act and Good Government." 14 *Yale Journal on Regulation* 451 (1997).

Funk, William, Jeffrey S. Lubbers, and Charles Pou, Jr., eds. "Federal Advisory Committee Act." In *Federal Administrative Procedure Sourcebook*, 3d ed., Chicago: American Bar Association, 2000.

FEDERAL AVIATION ACT (1958)

Douglas B. Harris

Excerpt from the Federal Aviation Act

An Act: To continue the Civil Aeronautics Board as an agency of the United States, to create a Federal Aviation Agency, to provide for the regulation and promotion of civil aviation in such manner as to best foster its development and safety, and to provide for the safe and efficient use of the airspace by both civil and military aircraft, and for other purposes.

The Federal Aviation Act of 1958 (P.L. 85-726, 72 Stat. 731) created a Federal Aviation Agency (later called the Federal Aviation Administration; FAA) and empowered it to oversee and regulate safety in the airline industry and control civilian and military use of the airspace over the United States.

The authority to regulate air travel and the airline industry is based on Congress's power under Article I, section 8 of the Constitution to regulate interstate commerce. When the technological advance of air travel became commercially viable and a societal reality, Congress was empowered to regulate the airline industry. Although the Department of Commerce had regulated air travel since the 1920s, in 1938 Congress passed a law creating the Civil Aeronautics Board (CAB).

Building on the Civil Aeronautics Act of 1938, the Federal Aviation Act of 1958 reestablished the CAB, transferred its safety regulatory functions to the newly created FAA, and empowered the FAA to take control of all navigable airspace over the United States for both civilian and military purposes. The act provided for an influential Federal Aviation Administrator with broad latitude to implement airline safety regulations. In reconstituting the CAB, the act allowed for the CAB to continue regulating the commercial practices of the airline industry, fare regulations, and accident investigations. Finally, in holding that the Federal Aviation Administrator would have the authority to oversee military use of airspace, the act provided that the president of the United States would mediate jurisdictional conflicts between the Federal Aviation Administrator and military officials.

> *Building on the Civil Aeronautics Act of 1938, the Federal Aviation Act of 1958 reestablished the CAB, transferred its safety regulatory functions to the newly created FAA, and empowered the FAA to take control of all navigable airspace over the United States for both civilian and military purposes.*

TECHNOLOGICAL ADVANCES, AIR TRAGEDIES, AND THE CONSIDERATION OF THE ACT

In the 1950s, technological advances in aviation and a boom in the commercial airline industry crowded the national airspace, increased the speed of commercial airliners, and strained the government's capacity to regulate the safety of air travel. Deeming existing regulations inadequate to meet these demands, advocates for reform argued for the revamping of the federal government's role in regulating and promoting air travel. Although these reformers had been advocating such legislation since the early 1950s, it was not until several highly sensational and tragic aviation accidents occurred that the public and other policymakers perceived the need for new regulation. Most notably, a midair collision over the Grand Canyon provided the short-term rationale for immediate legislative action.

On June 30, 1956, two commercial airliners collided over the Grand Canyon resulting in 128 fatalities. As air travel was becoming increasingly common, this high-profile accident raised public concern, and top policymakers in Congress responded. In 1957 Congress passed the Airways Modernization Act that established the Airways Modernization Board (AMB) headed by General Elwood Quesada. Legislators were split on the sufficiency of the AMB to meet the long-term demands of aviation safety regulation. Some key legislators thought of the AMB as a temporary organization, whereas other legislators hoped to give the AMB time to work. The number of legislators in favor of delaying further legislative action diminished as another accident spurred lawmakers to quick action.

The collision of a military jet and a commercial airliner in Brunswick, Maryland, on May 20, 1958, not only led to a reconsideration of delaying legislative action, but also impressed upon legislative proponents the

The collision of a military jet and a commercial airliner in Brunswick, Maryland, on May 20, 1958, not only led to a reconsideration of delaying legislative action, but also impressed upon legislative proponents the need to unify control over both military and civilian use of airspace over the United States.

need to unify control over both military and civilian use of airspace over the United States. The primary proponent of the Federal Aviation Act was Senator Mike Monroney, a Democrat from Oklahoma. As chairman of the Aviation Subcommittee of the Senate Commerce Committee since its inception in 1955, Monroney had been a frequent critic of existing aviation policy in general and the CAB in particular. The day after the Brunswick collision, Monroney and House Interstate and Foreign Commerce Chairman Oren Harris, Democrat of Arkansas, introduced the Senate and House versions of the Federal Aviation Act.

By June 13, the White House had made its support of the legislation official when President Eisenhower sent a special message to Congress. Citing "recent midair collisions of aircraft occasioning tragic losses of human life," Eisenhower recommended the establishment of the FAA "in which would be consolidated among other things all the essential management functions necessary to support the common needs of our civil and military aviation." With the administration on board, committee consideration of the bill was fast, as the legislation cleared the Senate and House Interstate and Foreign Commerce Committees on July 9 and July 14, respectively.

The bill was considered on the Senate floor within a week of being reported out of committee. In floor debate Monroney summarized the need for the bill, arguing that advances in the technology of air travel demanded greater regulation. He said, "The combination of too many airplanes flying at supersonic speed and our entry into the jet air age have made necessary a more modern governmental agency to make use of the technological advances which are occurring in the aviation field." House proponents made many of the same arguments in floor debate in early August. That aviation technology had outstripped existing policy and the capacity of existing governing institutions was a problem many legislators expected to be exacerbated by technological progress in coming years. This point was underscored in legislative debate by Representative John J. Flynt, Jr., a Democrat from Georgia, who claimed to have been in favor of delaying legislative action until he became aware that "the first commercial jet transport may be in operation in the airspace between now and the convening of the 1st session of the 86th Congress.... We feel that it is necessary that this legislation be enacted into law and in operation prior to the time that the first commercial jet airliner takes off loaded with passengers."

That aviation technology had outstripped existing policy and the capacity of existing governing institutions was a problem many legislators expected to be exacerbated by technological progress in coming years.

Still, the existing regulatory structures and the CAB were not without their defenders, and the new FAA was not without its critics. Senator Edward Thye, Republican of Minnesota, was the chief critic of the Federal Aviation Act on the Senate floor. Thye's objections to the act were wide ranging. Expressing the view that the newly created FAA would be too powerful and unresponsive to the interests of airlines, Thye said, "I am most vitally concerned with the question of whether the bill will virtually set up a dictator over all aviation operations and all the companies which operate commercially." Arguing that the CAB was structured to have greater accountability mechanisms, Thye feared that the act was but a first step toward the elimination of the CAB altogether.

Despite these points of opposition, the Federal Aviation Act passed both the House and Senate by voice vote in the Senate on July 14 and in the House on August 4. To quell some of the concern over the power of the FAA and the loss of CAB authority, legislative proponents of the act in both the House and Senate debates made clear that legislative language encouraging "promotion" of civil aviation was not intended to connote economic promotion of the airline industry. This emphasis most likely was an effort to appease defenders of the CAB who feared that all of its essential functions might be transferred to the FAA. Relatively minor differences were reconciled in conference committee, and the Conference Report passed the House and Senate, again by voice vote, on August 13 and August 11, respectively. President Dwight D. Eisenhower signed the bill into law on August 23, 1958, appointed AMB Chairman Quesada the first FAA Administrator, and transferred, by executive order, AMB's authority to the FAA on November 1.

EXPERIENCE UNDER THE FEDERAL AVIATION ACT

Generally, the broader public is unaware of the political and policy questions that govern regulatory agencies like the CAB and the FAA. Although the

A Boeing 727 undergoes Federal Aviation Agency certification tests at Edwards Air Force Base in California, 1963. (©Hulton-Deutsch Collection/Corbis)

struggles within these narrow policy communities, known by political scientists as "subsystems," can be intense, they rarely draw outside attention. Although a small number of activists and congressional reformers had been pressing for increased regulation of the airline industry, the notable air tragedies over the Grand Canyon and in Brunswick, Maryland, fostered the political environment that led to passage of the Federal Aviation Act. As political scientist Emmette Redford wrote in *Democracy and the Administrative State,* "The passage of the Federal Aviation Act shows how a subsystem actor, in this instance, Senator Monroney, struggled within the subsystem for stronger rules and roles in safety protection and then was able, because of two accidents, to marshal support from outside the subsystem for amendment of the governing statute."

The FAA continues to function largely as it was designed by the 1958 act.

The FAA continues to function largely as it was designed to by the 1958 act. When the Department of Transportation (DOT) was created in 1967, the Federal Aviation Agency became the Federal Aviation Administration within the DOT. Still, it is notable that opponents' fears that this was a first step toward the elimination of the CAB seem to have materialized. The Transportation Act also transferred CAB's responsibilities to investigate airline accidents to the newly created National Transportation Safety Board. In 1978 the Airline Deregulation Act was enacted in an effort to decrease the amount of federal commercial regulation of the airline industry. As this was the primary function of the CAB after the 1958 Federal Aviation Act, airline deregulation eventually led to the demise of the CAB in 1985 under the Civil Aeronautics Board Sunset Act of 1984.

See also: CIVIL AERONAUTICS ACT.

BIBLIOGRAPHY

Redford, Emmette S. *Congress Passes the Federal Aviation Act of 1958.* Tuscaloosa: University of Alabama Press, 1961.

Redford, Emmette S. *Democracy in the Administrative State.* New York: Oxford University Press, 1969.

INTERNET RESOURCE

Federal Aviation Administration. <http://www1.faa.gov>.

FEDERAL BLACKMAIL STATUTE (1994)

Stuart P. Green

The federal blackmail statute (P.L. 103-322, 108 Stat. 2147), enacted in its current form as part of the Violent Crime Control and Law Enforcement Act of 1994, and based on earlier statutes dating from 1948 and 1909, makes it a crime to demand money or other items of value from a person in return for not informing on the person's violation of federal law. Along with the Hobbs Anti-Racketeering Act, which criminalizes extortion, the blackmail statute is one of a series of statutes that make it a crime to obtain money by means of threats. Extortion involves a threat to commit an act that is independently illegal, such as inflicting physical injury—give me money or I'll break your arm. Blackmail involves a threat to commit an act that is not independently illegal, such as revealing information about the commission of a crime—give me money or I'll tell the police what you did.

Along with the Hobbs Anti-Racketeering Act, which criminalizes extortion, the blackmail statute is one of a series of statutes that make it a crime to obtain money by means of threats.

The fact that blackmail entails the conjunction of two otherwise legal acts—namely, exercising one's right to make truthful statements about another person, and seeking payment in return for not exercising such a right—is thought by many commentators to constitute a kind of "paradox." Some legal scholars argue that the crime of blackmail makes a wrong out of two rights. For many years, scholars have sought to explain this puzzle. A minority have argued that blackmail ought not to be a crime at all because, they say, it violates no basic legal right of the victim. The vast majority of scholars believe that blackmail should be a crime, though they differ widely in their explanations as to why.

THEORIES ABOUT BLACKMAIL

One major theory about blackmail seeks to justify the criminalization of blackmail on the grounds that negative consequences would occur in a system that regularly tolerated it. For example, if blackmail were widely permitted, there would be a greater number of victims desperate to raise funds necessary to pay off their blackmailers, and many such victims would likely resort to criminal acts such as theft and fraud. Allowing blackmail to go unpunished would also tend to encourage people to engage in greater deception in their social dealings. In addition, it would create new incentives for people to invade people's privacy, much as the tabloid media now invade the privacy of celebrities, because such private information would have increased economic value.

The second major theory views blackmail as wrong in and of itself. One variant of this approach views blackmail as involving a triangular relationship among blackmailer, party blackmailed, and a third party with an interest in the information that has been suppressed. For example, imagine that a blackmailer threatens to tell Smith's wife that Smith is having an affair. According to this view, it is Smith's wife who has the strongest interest in having such information. By depriving her of that information, the blackmailer is wrongly attempting to use leverage that properly belongs to her. Another related theory suggests that blackmail resembles theft or robbery, because the blackmailer intends to take money from one who does not wish to part with it.

Despite the ongoing controversy among scholars as to the underlying rationale for making blackmail a crime, there is little disagreement that it should be a crime. The federal blackmail statute remains an important complement to the Hobbs Anti-Racketeering Act and a significant, if only occasionally used, tool in the federal prosecutor's arsenal.

See also: BRIBERY ACT; HOBBS ANTI-RACKETEERING ACT; SENTENCING REFORM ACT.

Despite the ongoing controversy among scholars as to the underlying rationale for making blackmail a crime, there is little disagreement that it should be a crime.

BIBLIOGRAPHY

Berman, Mitchell N. "The Evidentiary Theory of Blackmail: Taking Motives Seriously." *University of Chicago Law Review* 65 (1998): 795–878.

"Blackmail." Symposium. *University of Pennsylvania Law Review* 141 (1993): 1565–2168.

Feinberg, Joel. *Harmless Wrongdoing*. Oxford, U.K.: Oxford University Press, 1988.

Katz, Leo. *Ill-Gotten Gains: Evasion, Blackmail, Fraud, and Kindred Puzzles of the Law*. Chicago: University of Chicago Press, 1996.

Lindgren, James. "Unraveling the Paradox of Blackmail." *Columbia Law Review* 84 (1984): 670–717.

FEDERAL CIGARETTE LABELING AND ADVERTISING ACT OF 1965

Kelly A. Moore

Americans expect cigarette packaging and advertisements to include a warning such as "Smoking causes lung cancer, heart disease, emphysema, and may complicate pregnancy." These warnings, however, are a relatively recent development and came about after Congress adopted legislation in the 1960s requiring tobacco companies to inform consumers of the health risks associated with the use of their products. Congress required tobacco companies to place warnings on cigarette packaging beginning in 1965 when it enacted the Federal Cigarette Labeling and Advertising Act (known as the "Original Act,") (P.L. 89–92, 79 Stat. 282), and in print advertising 1969 when it adopted the Public Health Cigarette Smoking Act.

Health warnings are a relatively recent development and came about after Congress adopted legislation in the 1960s requiring tobacco companies to inform consumers of the health risks associated with the use of their products.

Researchers and statisticians began to suspect a link between smoking and lung cancer as early as 1900. The first medical studies linking smoking to this and other illnesses began to appear in the 1920s. Between 1920 and 1960 over 7,000 studies established a link between smoking and health problems. In 1962, with this ever expanding body of medical research as a backdrop, Dr. Luther L. Terry, the Surgeon General of the U.S. Public Heath Service, convened an advisory committee to examine the issue of the link between smoking and illness.

On January 11, 1964, the advisory committee released its conclusion that "cigarette smoking is a health hazard of sufficient importance in the United States to warrant appropriate remedial action." After requesting that the Federal Trade Commission (FTC) postpone acting on regulations it had developed to address the advisory committee's conclusion, Congress enacted the Original Act in 1965. Whereas the FTC had proposed requiring warnings on containers and print advertisements, the Original Act only required such warnings on packaging. The 1969 act, however, went further and required warnings be placed within any and all print advertising of cigarettes. The 1969 act also banned cigarette advertising in any medium of electronic communication subject to the jurisdiction of the Federal Communications Commission.

Congress amended the act again when it adopted the Comprehensive Smoking Education Act of 1984. This law required tobacco companies to

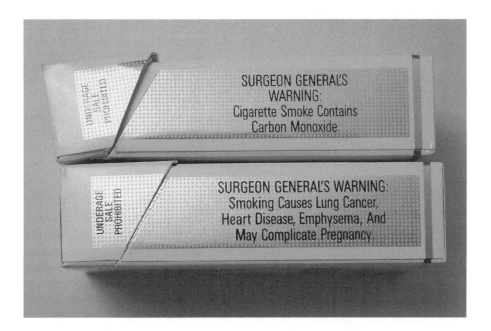

Since the passage of the Federal Cigarette Labeling and Advertising Act of 1965, it has been illegal to sell or distribute cigarettes in packaging without labels like the above. (©2003 KELLY A. QUIN)

place one of the following warnings on cigarette packaging and in print advertisements:

(1) "SURGEON GENERAL'S WARNING: Smoking Causes Lung Cancer, Heart Disease, Emphysema, and May Complicate Pregnancy"
(2) "SURGEON GENERAL'S WARNING: Quitting Smoking Now Greatly Reduces Serious Risks to Your Health"
(3) "SURGEON GENERAL'S WARNING: Smoking by Pregnant Women May Result in Fetal Injury, Premature Birth, and Low Birth Weight"
(4) "SURGEON GENERAL'S WARNING: Cigarette Smoke Contains Carbon Monoxide"

Congress had two purposes for adopting these statutes—to adequately inform the public of the health hazards of smoking, and to protect the national economy from the potential impact on the cigarette manufacturing industry if each of the fifty states enacted its own packaging and advertisement regulations. The acts achieved the first purpose by making it unlawful to sell or distribute any cigarette unless its packaging displays the appropriate label; the second goal was achieved through the language of Section 1334, which provided that "no requirement or prohibition based on smoking and health shall be imposed under state law with respect to the advertising or promotion of any cigarettes the packages of which are labeled in accordance with the provisions of this Act."

The second goal was furthered by the Supremacy Clause of the U.S. Constitution, contained in Article 6, clause 2, which provided that "any Thing in the Constitution or Laws of any state to the Contrary notwithstanding," the laws of the United States shall

Congress had two purposes for adopting these statutes—to adequately inform the public of the health hazards of smoking, and to protect the national economy from the potential impact on the cigarette manufacturing industry if each of the fifty states enacted its own packaging and advertisement regulations.

be the supreme law of the land. In *McCulloch v. Maryland* (1819), the Supreme Court determined state laws that conflict with federal law are without effect under the Supremacy Clause. Subsequent cases, however, have held that there is a presumption against **preemption** of state police power regulations and that the scope of any such preemption must be narrowly defined.

preemption: when a conflict of authority arises between the federal and state governments, the federal government prevails

In the decades since the adoption of the acts, the preemption issue has led to several court cases. In *Cipollone v. Liggett Group, Inc.* (1992), the Supreme Court addressed the extent to which state law was preempted by the federal acts. In *Cipollone,* the plaintiff, a woman who ultimately died of lung cancer after years of smoking, sued cigarette manufactures under various state laws. The cigarette manufacturer argued that federal law barred her claims and the Supreme Court agreed with the argument to the extent that state law imposes a "requirement or prohibition based on smoking and health ... with respect to ... advertising or promotion." The Court based its decision on the fact that this was a narrow area of the law Congress had intended the acts to regulate and that the states could not interfere. Federal law, however, did not bar the plaintiff's claims that did not relate to the use of tobacco products.

BIBLIOGRAPHY

U.S. Department of Health and Human Services, report of the Surgeon General. *Reducing the Health Consequences of Smoking: 25 Years of Progress.* Washington, DC: 1989.

U.S. Department of Health, Education and Welfare, U.S. Surgeon General's Advisory Committee. *Smoking and Health* 33 (1964).

FEDERAL CIVIL DEFENSE ACT OF 1950

David G. Delaney

A lthough the United States government sponsored a civil defense program during World War I, modern American civil defense did not begin until May 1941, when President Franklin D. Roosevelt created the Office of Civilian Defense (OCD). Military technological developments since World War I, especially in airplanes and submarines, had made attacks on American soil real possibilities and challenged the government to defend the United States and protect civilians without overly militarizing American society.

"The new technique of war has created the necessity of developing a new technique of civil defense. It is not just {...} sweater knitting, and basket weaving that is needed." —Fiorello H. La Guardia to Franklin D. Roosevelt, 1942

The OCD created defense-related programs like air-raid procedures and black-out drills to minimize damage from aerial bombardment, and it relied on community volunteers to carry them out. The OCD also sponsored programs like day-care and family health services to strengthen communities' social ties. Although the OCD closed in June 1945, policymakers facing the beginning of the **Cold War** reestablished a small civil defense program in March 1949 under the National Security Resources Board (NSRB), an agency created by the National Security Act of 1947. Within two years, however, international events

Cold War: a conflict over ideological differences carried on by methods short of military action and usually without breaking off diplomatic relations usually refers to the ideological conflict between the U.S. and the former U.S.S.R.

would spur Congress to significantly expand this program and tailor America's civil defense programs to the age of nuclear warfare under the Federal Civil Defense Act of 1950 (64 Stat. 1245).

THE THREAT OF NUCLEAR WAR

When the NSRB was established, only the United States possessed nuclear weapons. The Soviet Union's successful nuclear bomb test in August 1949 surprised American defense planners and forced them to reconsider America's military and civilian preparedness and capabilities. Then, in October of that year, Mao Zedong, the head of the Chinese Communist Party who became leader of the nation, declared China a Communist state. By November 1950 China was supporting North Korean attacks against South Korea and a United Nations force led by, and consisting mostly of, members of the United States armed forces. These events forced government leaders to reconsider whether they could prevent nuclear war with the Soviet Union or an allied Communist government—or at least whether government planning could help the United States survive one.

The task of averting nuclear war fell largely within the realms of military and foreign policy. Surviving a war became the central mission of civil defense planners. Congress and policymakers recognized the impossibility of providing **absolute** protection from nuclear weapons. Although they considered comprehensive, community-level bunker systems, these were rejected as too costly or too difficult for most of America's 150 million people to reach during an attack. Instead, they decided on a program that encouraged Americans to learn how to protect themselves until the government could respond. Returning to the volunteerism that characterized civil defense during the world wars, this concept of "self-help" appealed to Republicans and Democrats, conservatives and liberals alike. Many wanted to reduce federal spending in the aftermath of the **New Deal** or were skeptical of greater military responsibility for civilian, peacetime programs. Others simply found it unnecessary or unwise to implement elaborate shelter systems, evacuation plans, or health care and social programs based on the mere possibility of a nuclear attack. Educating Americans to protect themselves from nuclear weapons became the centerpiece of civil defense policy.

absolute: complete, pure, free from restriction or limitation

New Deal: the legislative and administrative program of President Franklin D. Roosevelt designed to promote economic recovery and social reform (1933–1939)

GOALS AND ACHIEVEMENTS OF THE ACT

On December 1, 1950, President Harry S. Truman issued an executive order creating a new agency, the Federal Civil Defense Administration (FCDA), and transferring civil defense responsibilities to it from the NSRB. With the Federal Civil Defense Act of 1950, Congress charged the FCDA with creating shelter, evacuation, and training programs that state and local governments would implement. Local governments could request federal funds for these programs and for post-attack health care and reconstruction. However, the Federal Civil Defense Act did not fund any of these programs, and subsequent legislation throughout the administrations of Truman and Dwight D. Eisenhower provided only minimal resources to carry out these goals. Both Congress and the executive branch preferred instead to invest in military and diplomatic programs that might prevent nuclear war and eliminate the need for expensive, long-term reconstruction programs.

Educating Americans to protect themselves from nuclear weapons became the centerpiece of civil defense policy.

Bomb Shelters

During the late 1950s, as Cold War fears became part of everyday life, one survey showed that 40 percent of American families were considering building a shelter in which to wait out the effects of a nuclear attack. With bomb shelters selling from $100 for the basics to as much as $5,000 for a deluxe model, Wall Street analysts predicted that the shelter industry could become a $20 billion business. The magazine *Popular Mechanics* published a blueprint for those who preferred to build their own, and civil defense films provided instructions for those who intended to seek protection in their basements. Shelters were stocked with survival kits that included fallout protection suits, first-aid supplies, canned goods, flashlights, and water. Nuclear war was a recurring theme in movies and on television, and air-raid drills in elementary schools taught "duck-and-cover" techniques. Fears peaked in 1962 with the Cuban missile crisis; afterward, as the imminence of the nuclear threat began to fade, and there was some realization that backyard fallout shelters would provide little protection anyway, most people abandoned their shelters. An enlightened few converted them to wine cellars.

An employee of the Civil Defense Commission of New York State displays the official "CD" logo, November 1950—just over a year after the Soviet Union tested its first atomic bomb. (©Bettmann/Corbis)

With its limited funding the FCDA produced films, pamphlets, and other materials teaching Americans how to build family shelters and stock them with food and supplies. In conjunction with leading universities, the FCDA also studied the psychological effects of the threat and occurrence of nuclear war to better prepare their education and assistance plans. And through extensive public relations programs with print and television media outlets, the FCDA reinforced the idea that, aside from effective defense and foreign policy, individual preparedness was the next best response to nuclear threats.

CIVIL DEFENSE AFTER 1958

The FCDA lasted only until 1958, but federally supervised and funded civil defense programs continued throughout, and even beyond, the Cold War. The Federal Civil Defense Act adapted the World War II model that had combined defense and social programs, but it scaled back the latter considerably. To allay concerns about militarizing a democratic society, the act made the FCDA a civilian-led agency. But civil defense remained a secondary issue behind broader defense and diplomatic programs. Theories of containment—preventing the spread of Communism—and military strategies shaped policymakers' budgetary priorities. Nevertheless, programs under the Federal Civil Defense Act spurred large numbers of Americans to become more deeply engaged in the political processes shaping foreign policy, defense spending, and nuclear policies. Even today, the legacy of the Civil Defense Act is apparent in the civilian-led Department of Homeland Security, whose programs are organized around a different national security threat—international terrorism.

Programs under the Federal Civil Defense Act spurred large numbers of Americans to become more deeply engaged in the political processes shaping foreign policy, defense spending, and nuclear policies.

See also: DEPARTMENT OF HOMELAND SECURITY ACT; NATIONAL SECURITY ACT OF 1947.

BIBLIOGRAPHY

Gaddis, John Lewis. *Strategies of Containment: A Critical Appraisal of Postwar American National Security Policy.* New York: Oxford University Press, 1982.

McEnaney, Laura. *Civil Defense Begins at Home: Militarization Meets Everyday Life in the Fifties.* Princeton, NJ: Princeton University Press, 2000.

PBS Online, The American Experience. "Race for the Superbomb." <http://www.pbs.org/wgbh/amex/bomb/index.html>.

FEDERAL DEPOSIT INSURANCE ACTS

Steven Ramirez

When President Franklin D. Roosevelt took office in 1933 the banking industry was on the verge of collapse. Governors of thirty-four states ordered banks to close their doors to stem the tide of the massive withdrawals, causing millions of panic-stricken Americans to withdraw their funds from the national banking system. This led five thousand banks to fail between 1929 and 1933.

In 1933 Congress acted to restore depositor confidence in the banking system by adopting a law that would insure bank deposits even in the face of a failing bank system. Legislators hoped deposit insurance would encourage the flow of money back into the nation's banking system. At the time, Congress understood that when a bank failed, depositors lost the value of their deposits, causing panic and destabilizing the economy. Accordingly, Congress adopted the Banking Act of 1933 and created the Federal Deposit Insurance Corporation (FDIC) to administer a deposit insurance program. The law required the banking industry to fund deposit insurance which in turn assured depositors they would get their money back even if their bank failed.

As an independent federal agency, the FDIC is governed by a three member board that includes the Comptroller of the Currency. The FDIC has a number of responsibilities, including regulating banks to assure they do not expose the insurance fund to undue risks, and administering failed banks. The FDIC acts as a bankruptcy court for insured depository institutions and in this capacity it frequently brings civil suits against those whose misconduct caused the bank to fail.

In 1933 Congress acted to restore depositor confidence in the banking system by adopting a law that would insure bank deposits even in the face of a failing bank system.

The act has successfully achieved two economic benefits. Because the full faith and credit of the United States backs deposit insurance, banks enjoy a lower cost of capital than they would otherwise pay. This cost-cutting enables the bank to lend out funds at a lower cost to borrowers and entrepreneurs. The act has also successfully warded off bank failures.

Many economists have widely regarded deposit insurance as a brilliant solution to a significant and exceedingly difficult problem. Economist John Kenneth Galbraith may have put it best by stating that deposit insurance remedied a "grievous defect" in laissez-faire economics (the belief that free markets alone can best secure economic prosperity) and that "rarely has so much been accomplished by a single law."

The act, however, was not without critics. One of the most vehement opponents of deposit insurance was the American Bankers Association. Yet in the decade following the adoption of the law, total bank failures decreased dramatically and so the major opponents of the legislation also seemed to be its primary beneficiaries. Nevertheless, market enthusiasts continue to believe depositors themselves can exert discipline over banks that take too many risks—and that deposit insurance is not needed to prevent bank failures. Under this approach, depositors will punish weak banks and create market disincentives for poor management. These laissez faire enthusiasts fail to explain why market discipline did not prevent the onslaught of bank failures in the 1930s, nor do these commentators fully admit that the line between market discipline and a bank panic is thin indeed. By the time depositors realize a bank is in precarious condition, the bank is just as likely to fail as reform its management practices.

CIRCUMSTANCES LEADING TO THE ADOPTION OF THE ACT

The Banking Act of 1933 was a key component of President Franklin D. Roosevelt's New Deal, the first major attempt to regulate the economy and to resolve the Great Depression. The Depression was an unprecedented economic calamity that ultimately gave rise to an unemployment rate of 25 percent and to a 33 percent contraction of the nation's economy. In the election of 1932, Franklin D. Roosevelt promised to deliver economic reform, and the New Deal was an effort to adhere to that promise. Banking regulation was a natural starting point for the New Deal, and the Banking Act of 1933 was enacted as part of the historic first Hundred Days of the Roosevelt administration. The Banking Act of 1933 included many measures designed to stem the devastation in the banking industry, and deposit insurance was one of the keys to resolving the banking crisis.

The U.S. Supreme Court has interpreted the 1933 Banking Act on a number of occasions. For example, in *FDIC v. Philadelphia Gear Corporation Act* (1986), the Supreme Court held that the term "deposit" under the act included a standby letter of credit backed by a promissory note (a promise to pay a debt). This case suggested that deposit insurance extended to much more than a traditional savings or checking account, with the Court giving the act surprising depth when deciding this case. A decade later, however, the Court decided a case that limited the scope of the act. In *Atherton v. FDIC* (1997), the Supreme Court held that there

Many economists have widely regarded deposit insurance as a brilliant solution to a significant and exceedingly difficult problem.

was not sufficient federal interest warranting the creation of any common law duty of care (the obligation of directors to pay for the costs of their negligence) for directors of insured banks. This meant that states are generally free to insulate directors from liability for negligent bank management and are basically able to impose the costs of sloppy banking on the U.S. taxpayers instead.

SUBSEQUENT LEGISLATION

The federal deposit insurance program has evolved over the decades. In 1934, under the National Housing Act, Congress created the Federal Savings and Loan Insurance Corporation to insure the deposits held in the nation's savings and loans. Under the Federal Deposit Insurance Act of 1950, Congress extended deposit insurance to state banks, created under state laws. In the 1970s Congress extended deposit insurance to credit unions in the Federal Credit Union Act, and during the 1980s the regulation of banking, in accordance with the deregulatory **dogma** of the time, was dramatically loosened, leading to a new set of bank failures. Congress responded with the Financial Institutions Reform Recovery and Enforcement Act. This act served to broadly

The federal deposit insurance program has evolved over the decades.

dogma: an established opinion expressed as an authoritative statement

Thanks to the Banking Act of 1933, which created the Federal Deposit Insurance Corporation, the customers of D'Auria Bank and Trust Co. in Newark, New Jersey, did not lose their deposits when the bank went under (1936). (©BETTMANN/CORBIS)

Depositors are now secure enough that even if a bank becomes financially insolvent, they know the U.S. government stands behind virtually every bank in the land.

strengthen the hand of bank regulators and to recapitalize the depleted insurance funds. Since this act, the FDIC has administered both the Bank Insurance Fund for banks and the Savings Association Insurance Fund for savings and loans. In 1991 the Federal Deposit Insurance Corporation Improvement Act instituted a regime of risk-based assessments upon insured banks, requiring weaker banks to pay more for deposit insurance than financially strong banks.

Prior to deposit insurance, bank runs were embedded in our culture. For example, in the classic film *It's a Wonderful Life,* a central scene is a run on the Bailey Brothers Building and Loan, operated by George Bailey (played by James Stewart). To today's audience the concept of running down to the bank to get your cash back before they run out is an altogether foreign idea. Bank runs no longer exist; even when banks are known to be in adverse financial straits, depositors no longer rush to the bank to withdraw deposits. Depositors are now secure enough that even if a bank becomes financially insolvent, they know the U.S. government stands behind virtually every bank in the land. But in the 1930s fear could grip a community at the slightest whiff of financial trouble—having a very real and corrosive effect on the economy. For this reason, the Banking Act of 1933 was signed into law:

> The purpose of this legislation is to protect the people of the United States in the right to have banks in which their deposits will be safe. They have a right to expect of Congress the establishment and maintenance of a system of banks in the United States where citizens may place their hard earnings with reasonable expectation of being able to get them out again upon demand... [T]he purpose of the bill is to ensure that the community is saved from the shock of a bank failure, and every citizen [is] given an opportunity to withdraw his deposits.

See also: GLASS-STEAGALL ACT; NATIONAL HOUSING ACT

BIBLIOGRAPHY

Davis, Kenneth S. *FDR: The New Deal Years.* New York: Random House, 1986.

Ramirez, Steven. "The Law and Macroeconomics of the New Deal at 70." In *Maryland Law Review* 62, no. 3 (2003).

Schlesinger, Arthur M., Jr. *The Coming of the New Deal.* Boston: Houghton Mifflin, 1958.

FEDERAL ELECTION CAMPAIGN ACT (1971)

Mark Glaze and Trevor Potter

With the Federal Election Campaign Act (FECA) of 1971, (P.L. 92-225), Congress attempted to establish comprehensive regulations on the way American political campaigns for Congress and the presidency raise money and disclose the amount and sources of contributions. This act, and its subsequent amendments, governs nearly all aspects of federal campaign finance activity, including the four dominant issues: the size of contributions to political campaigns, the source of such contributions, public disclosure of campaign financial information, and public financing of presidential campaigns.

HISTORY OF FECA

Prior to FECA, legislators made many attempts to regulate campaign finance practices, all with the aim of upholding the national principle of "one person, one vote." These attempts sought to guarantee that election results and government policies reflected the public will and national interest rather than the demands of a relatively small group of major campaign contributors. The constitutional basis for campaign finance laws is article I, section 4 of the U.S. Constitution, which allows the federal government to regulate the "time, place and manner" of federal elections.

Public concern over the influence of money on politics stretches back at least to the Civil War era. Congress began to pass major campaign finance regulations, however, only in the late nineteenth century. By that time political contributions by major corporate interests and business leaders dominated campaign fundraising, and this development sparked the first major movement for national reform. Progressive reformers and investigative journalists, called **"muckrakers,"** charged that these business interests were attempting to gain special access and favors, thereby corrupting the democratic process. This reform movement, combined with allegations of financial impropriety in the 1904 presidential election, resulted in a number of important reforms:

- The 1907 Tillman Act prohibited corporations from using their general treasury funds (as opposed to their political action committees) to contribute to federal campaigns.

- The Federal Corrupt Practices Acts of 1910 and 1925 required political parties and federal candidates to publicly report their receipts and expenditures.
- The Taft-Hartley Act of 1947 prohibited labor unions, which had become a major source of campaign money, from using their general treasury funds to make contributions for federal office.

Despite these reforms, the lack of an effective administrative body and enforcement mechanisms, along with serious gaps in the laws, rendered the statutes largely unenforceable. As a result, they were often evaded. Meanwhile, broadcast advertising became a primary means of political campaigning in the mid-twentieth century. The costs of campaigns began to skyrocket, with the accompanying need for even greater fundraising.

Concern over the escalating amount of corporate and labor union money in elections, combined with the campaign finance abuses of the **Watergate** scandal, set the stage for the Federal Election Campaign Act of 1971 and its 1974 amendments.

FEATURES OF THE 1971 ACT AND THE 1974 AMENDMENTS

In FECA, Congress put the pieces of federal campaign finance legislation together into a single, coherent statute. It also added significant new reforms designed to offset the skyrocketing costs and perceived corruption of American political campaigns in the late twentieth century.

Among the act's major features are the creation of the Federal Election Commission and rules concerning disclosure, public financing, and contribution limits:

This act, and its subsequent amendments, governs nearly all aspects of federal campaign finance activity, including the four dominant issues: the size of contributions to political campaigns, the source of such contributions, public disclosure of campaign financial information, and public financing of presidential campaigns.

muckraker: one who tries to find and expose real or alleged evidence of corruption

Watergate: the scandal following the break-in at the Democratic National Committee headquarters located in the Watergate apartment and office complex in Washington, D.C., in 1972

- *Federal Election Commission (FEC).* The act created an agency solely responsible for administering federal election law. Among its duties, the six-member, full-time commission serves as the repository of all disclosure reports; establishes regulations to implement federal election law; and investigates all complaints of campaign violations, including through the use of its power to subpoena witnesses and information and to seek civil injunctions to ensure compliance.
- *Disclosure.* FECA requires every candidate or committee active in a federal campaign to establish a central committee through which all contributions and expenditures must be reported. Among other requirements, such committees must file with the FEC a quarterly report of receipts and expenditures, which must list any contribution or expenditure of $100 or more and must include extensive information about donors. The FEC makes this information available for public inspection.
- *Public financing.* The act created a voluntary program of full public financing for presidential general election campaigns, and a voluntary system of public matching subsidies for presidential primary campaigns. Under the program, presidential candidates from the major parties who agree to abide by a voluntary spending limit can receive an equivalent amount from the federal government as long as they agree not to raise additional private money. Minor party or independent candidates may also qualify for a proportional share of the subsidy.
- *Contribution limits.* The act continued the preexisting bans on contributions by corporations and labor unions. It also added contribution limits on all other sources of funding, sharply limiting the amount any individual, committee, or group could contribute to candidates or political committees in any election.

The act imposed several other regulations that were soon struck down by the U. S. Supreme Court.

COURT CHALLENGE

The Supreme Court has ruled repeatedly that campaign spending constitutes an essential form of "political speech" that is closely protected by the First Amendment. In order to regulate political spending, therefore, the government's action must be justified by a particularly compelling reason and be narrowly crafted to achieve the law's purpose. The only government interest the Court has found sufficient to justify campaign finance regulations is the prevention of either actual or apparent corruption in the political process.

The Supreme Court applied that analysis in *Buckley v. Valeo,* a 1976 case that challenged virtually every aspect of FECA. In its ruling, the Court struck down several provisions of the 1974 amendments. Congress had established a number of spending limits on candidates and political groups, including limits on the personal funds candidates could expend on their own elections. The Court held that these were unconstitutional restrictions on political speech. The Court reasoned that such spending limits were acceptable only as voluntary limits agreed to as a condition of public campaign financing.

Similarly, though the Court found disclosure requirements and contribution limits to be constitutional, including the prohibition on corporate and union contributions, the justices narrowed the ban substantially. They held that only

Soft Money

By law, individuals are limited to contributing no more than $1,000 to any given candidate for a federal election, and no more than $20,000 per year to a political party. Corporations and labor unions are prohibited from contributing to campaign funds at all. These regulations are intended to prevent individuals and organizations from buying influence by making huge contributions to a candidate, then calling in favors when the candidate is in office. "Soft money" is the term used to describe donations made to circumvent these rules. It is donated to political parties for the ostensible purpose of "party building," which describes activities not directly related to electing candidates. Soft money contributions in the presidential election of 2000 were estimated at approximately $500 million. In 2002 soft money contributions were banned with the passage of the Bipartisan Campaign Reform Act (known as McCain-Feingold); however, the ban was ruled unconstitutional in federal court. The Supreme Court was expected to hear the appeal in September 2003.

participation by those groups amounting to "express advocacy," or expressly calling for the election or defeat of a federal candidate could be forbidden.

The *Buckley* decision therefore gave Congress authority to craft disclosure requirements and contribution limits, and left prohibitions on corporate and union electioneering spending to elect or defeat a particular candidate in place. However, over the next generation these prohibitions on sources of funding would be radically undermined, leading to the next major cycle of public outrage and legislative reform.

SUBSEQUENT CHANGES IN THE LAW

Congress has substantially revised FECA three times since 1974. In 1976 the law was rewritten to comply with the terms of *Buckley*. In 1979 Congress acted primarily to ease the administrative burdens that resulted from the law's disclosure requirements. In addition, the 1979 amendments gave state and local political parties an important, limited exemption from the rules that normally limit the amount party organizations can spend on (technically, contribute to) campaigns. This exemption allowed state and local political parties

Public Citizen, a nonprofit public interest organization founded by Ralph Nader in 1971, unveils a "for sale" sign on Capitol Hill, June 4, 1996. The activist group supported a 1996 bill that would limit the amount spent on campaigns for elections to Congress. The bill did not make it into law. (© AP/WIDE WORLD PHOTOS)

grassroots: originating or operating at the basic level of society

to fund certain **grassroots** and "party-building" activities, such as voter registration and get-out-the-vote drives, without having those funds count against the parties' normal limits on contributions to individual candidates. The exemption was designed to counter a perceived weakening of influence at the state and local party level.

After the *Buckley* decision, this 1979 exemption and a number of other factors combined to substantially undermine the ban on corporate and union electioneering. Under *Buckley,* only corporate and union campaign activity "expressly advocating" the election or defeat of a candidate could constitutionally be prohibited. This part of the *Buckley* ruling was intended to clarify the specific restrictions of FECA on speech that is on corporate and union groups' ability to participate in a "discussion about political and policy issues." According to a longstanding Supreme Court precedent, such discussion may not be restricted without violating the First Amendment, unless there is some overwhelming justification for that restriction.

Since Buckley, *the Court has been more tolerant of limitations on contributions than those on campaign expenditures.*

Over time, the Court's interpretation of the First Amendment right to discussion of political issues led to outright evasion of the prohibition on corporate and union electioneering. The political parties ultimately determined that they could both solicit and spend campaign funds for grassroots, "party-building" activities. The parties argued that these functions did not constitute "express advocacy" of any particular candidate's election or defeat, and were therefore not subject to the FECA prohibitions.

As a result, unprecedented amounts of so-called soft money began pouring into party accounts. The parties used these funds disproportionately to fund negative attack advertisements on television and radio. This phenomenon

Watergate

On June 17, 1972, five members of President Richard Nixon's Committee to Re-Elect the President were arrested after they broke into the headquarters of the Democratic National Committee (DNC) in the Watergate residential and office complex in Washington, D.C. The break-in—an attempt to tap the DNC phones—did little damage to Nixon's re-election campaign, and he won in November with an overwhelming majority. However, two *Washington Post* reporters, Robert Woodward and Carl Bernstein, pursued the story until they had uncovered a wide-reaching scandal. Nixon and his associates—driven by Nixon's obsession with discrediting his "enemies"— tapped phones, stole medical records, and paid off potential witnesses to buy their silence. In 1973, as their illegal activities and attempted cover-up came to light, three key administration officials and Attorney General Richard Kleindienst resigned. The new Attorney General, Elliot Richardson, appointed a special prosecutor, Archibald Cox, to investigate.

At the same time, the Senate's Committee on Presidential Campaign Activities began a series of televised hearings which revealed that the president had secretly tape-recorded conversations in the Oval Office. Cox subpoenaed the tapes, but Nixon refused to hand them over and fired Cox. Richardson and his deputy resigned in protest. The Supreme Court ruled that Nixon was obligated to release the tapes, and the House of Representatives voted to begin impeachment proceedings. Nixon surrendered three tapes that clearly implicated him in the cover-up. He had little support, as the public was outraged over what was seen as the administration's attack on democracy, which included committing crimes to subvert the democratic process, suppressing civil liberties, using espionage and sabotage against political enemies, and intimidating members of the news media. In August 1974 Nixon resigned rather than face impeachment. He was pardoned by his successor, Gerald Ford.

reached epidemic proportions in the 1990s. To avoid the ban on using these corporate and union funds to electioneer, the ads carefully avoided use of words such as "vote for" or "support." Still, it was often clear that their purpose was to help elect or defeat particular candidates. The prevalence of these funds grew exponentially through the last part of the twentieth century. More than a half-billion dollars in soft money was spent in the 2000 federal elections.

Once again, public outrage over this evasion of basic campaign finance principles became powerful enough to prompt legislative action. Republican Senator John McCain of Arizona, who campaigned for the Republican presidential nomination in 2000 with campaign finance reform at the center of his platform, helped contribute to the public appetite for reform legislation.

In March 2002 Congress passed the Bipartisan Campaign Reform Act, popularly know as "McCain-Feingold" after its two main sponsors, Senator John McCain and Democratic Senator Russell Feingold of Wisconsin. The act's primary effect was to reinstate the pre-Watergate ban on corporate and union contributions by banning the solicitation or spending of soft money by the national political parties. The bill also supplied a new definition of "express advocacy" designed to allow corporations and unions to engage in legitimate discussion of issues while keeping them out of campaign-related advertising. Under the act's terms, corporate or union funds could not be used to pay for broadcast ads against a clearly identified national candidate, targeted at that candidate's electorate, within thirty days of a primary or sixty days of a general election.

These new provisions banning soft money faced immediate constitutional challenge, and **partisans** on both sides awaited the U.S. Supreme Court's decision in *McConnell v. FEC* as of late 2003.

partisan: someone loyal to a particular party, cause, or person

BIBLIOGRAPHY

Corrado, Anthony, Thomas Mann, Daniel Ortiz, Trevor Potter, and Frank Sorauf, eds. *Campaign Finance Reform: A Sourcebook*. Washington, DC: Brookings Institution Press, 1997.

INTERNET RESOURCE

The Campaign Legal Center. <http://www.campaignlegalcenter.org>.
The Brookings Institution. <http://www.brookings.org/gs/cf/hp.htm>.

FEDERAL EMPLOYERS' LIABILITY ACT (1908)

John Fabian Witt

Congress adopted the Federal Employers' Liability Act (FELA) (35 Stat. 65) in 1908. FELA governs the circumstances under which an injured employee of any interstate railroad (as well as any railroad in the District of Columbia or a United States Territory) may recover damages in a lawsuit against the railroad. During America's great economic expansion, FELA has served as an important component of the law addressing workplace injuries. At the same time, the Act has been a subject of considerable controversy.

Over time, the Court's interpretation of the First Amendment right to discussion of political issues led to outright evasion of the prohibition on corporate and union electioneering.

LEGAL AND WORKPLACE HISTORY LEADING TO FELA

In the United States, legal rules for the governance of workplace injuries first developed in state courts in the 1830s and 1840s. Employees injured on the nation's early railroads brought the first lawsuits to recover damages from their employers for injuries arising out of the course of their employment. In court decisions such as the leading case of *Farwell v. Boston & Worcester Railway* (1842), a Massachusetts Supreme Judicial Court decision, nineteenth-century state courts held that in order to recover damages from an employer in an injury case, an injured employee had to establish that the employer's negligence caused the injury. Moreover, although the doctrine of vicarious liability generally deemed an employer liable for damages caused by its employee's negligence, nineteenth-century courts ruled that an injured employee could not recover from the employer when co-workers' negligence caused the injury. Instead, courts held that employees assumed the ordinary risks of employment (including injury at the hands of a negligent fellow servant) as part of their employment contract. Finally, courts held that even where an injured employee could establish to a jury that the employer's own negligence had been a cause of the injury, the employee nonetheless could not recover any damages if the employee had also been negligent and that negligence had also contributed to the injury. Together these three rules—the fellow servant rule, the doctrine of assumption of risk, and the doctrine of contributory negligence—comprised the "unholy trinity" of rules that made it exceedingly difficult for injured employees to recover damages from their employers.

During the second half of the nineteenth century, the early trickle of injured employee lawsuits became a steady stream as the number of work accidents increased dramatically during these years. By the turn of the twentieth century, work-related accidents killed one in three hundred railroad employees each year, and one in fifty was injured in an accident. In 1908 alone, 281,645 employees were injured at work, and some 12,000 killed.

Against the background of an industrial accident crisis, state governments began enacting statutes limiting one or another of the rules that made it difficult for employees to sue their employers for work injuries. By 1911, twenty-five states had enacted laws that abolished the fellow servant rule (making employers liable for injuries to one employee caused by the negligence of another), abolished the rule of assumption of risk, or amended the doctrine of contributory negligence.

Pressure to enact such a statute also arose at the federal level in Congress, where increasingly powerful railway labor unions as well as President Theodore Roosevelt, argued that the law should make it easier for injured railroad employees to recover damages from their employer. In 1906, notwithstanding bitter opposition from the nation's railroad corporations, Congress responded to the unions and President Roosevelt by enacting a sweeping employers' liability reform statute pursuant to its authority to regulate interstate commerce in Article I, Section 8 of the Constitution. Known as the First Federal Employers' Liability Act, the 1906 statute sought to amend the law of employers' liability for work injuries for all employees of railroads and other "common carriers" engaged in interstate commerce. The act would have abolished the fellow servant rule and would have provided that where the contributory negligence of an injured employee was slight and the negligence of the employer was gross in comparison, the employee would not be precluded by that contributory negligence from recovery. Rather, in such cases, the damages recoverable from the employer would be reduced in proportion to the total negligence attributable to the employee.

The 1906 act would have constituted a massive expansion of federal authority into a realm that had theretofore been governed by state law. In the *First Employers' Liability Act Cases,* decided in 1908, however, the United States Supreme Court struck down the act as beyond Congress's power under the Commerce Clause. The Court reasoned that the Commerce Clause might allow Congress to enact legislation governing the liability of interstate railroads to injured employees who were themselves injured in interstate commerce, but that the clause did not allow Congress to enact legislation governing the liability of a railroad (interstate or otherwise) to an employee who was injured in the course of purely local, non-interstate business.

A NEW FEDERAL LAW: FELA

At President Roosevelt's urging, Congress quickly took up the matter of interstate railroad injuries following the Supreme Court's decision, and in 1908 enacted the Second Federal Employers' Liability Act, now generally known simply as the FELA. This act applied only to employees of interstate railroads who were themselves employed in interstate commerce, or to employees of railroads who were themselves employed in the District of Columbia or in a United States Territory. Under the Act, a railroad covered by the act

> shall be liable in damages to any person suffering injury while he is employed by such carrier in such commerce, or, in case of the death of such employee, to his or her personal representative, ... for such injury or death resulting in whole or in part from the negligence of any of the officers, agents, or employees of such carrier, or by reason of any defect or insufficiency, due to its negligence, in its cars, engines, appliances, machinery, track, roadbed, works, boats, wharves, or other equipment.

The Transcontinental Railroad

Considered one of the greatest technological achievements of the nineteenth century, the transcontinental railroad linked the eastern states to California, reducing the time it took to cross the continent from four months to one week and providing the critical key to rapid westward expansion. The project was first proposed in 1845, but arguments between the North and South over the route to be taken and whether slavery would be allowed in the western territories delayed a decision until the Civil War. In 1862 the Union eliminated Southern concerns from consideration, and President Abraham Lincoln formally launched the project by signing the Pacific Railroad Act. The railroad was to be built by two companies, each receiving government loans, land grants for every mile completed, and permission to use building materials from the public domain. The two companies raced to cover as much territory as possi-

ble in order to secure the maximum possible land and financing. The Central Pacific Railroad, building east from Sacramento, employed seven thousand Chinese immigrants to carve a route through the Sierra Nevada mountains. Progress was slowed by winter snowstorms and by the danger of the work: using explosives to tunnel through rock, many workers were killed. The Union Pacific Railroad, building west from Omaha, was working on flat terrain, but its progress was slowed by conflicts with Native Americans who saw the railroad as a violation of their treaties with the U.S. government and a threat to their way of life. In May 1869 the companies met at Promontory Point, Utah, where a golden spike was driven to join the two rail lines. The nation celebrated when both coasts received the telegraph announcing the project's completion, which read simply, "Done."

FELA amended the contributory negligence doctrine by providing that "the fact that the employee may have been guilty of contributory negligence shall not bar a recovery, but the damages shall be diminished by the jury in proportion to the amount of negligence attributable to such employee." Amendments Congress enacted in 1939 further provided that injured employees "shall not be held" to have assumed the risks of their employment, thereby abolishing the doctrine of assumption of risk for workplace accidents.

The history of the FELA indicates the early difficulties lawmakers faced in expanding the authority of the federal government. The federal legislation encroached boldly on the areas ostensibly allocated to the control of the states, leading the Supreme Court to strike down the law. Since the late 1930s, however, the courts have afforded Congress much wider authority in exercising its Commerce Clause power. After a 1939 amendment to the FELA that extended its reach to any injured railroad employee whose work furthered or affected interstate commerce, the FELA once again reaches virtually all employees of interstate railroads.

More broadly, for the first century of its existence, the FELA has been the leading representative of the country's two main approaches to the problem of providing compensation to injured employees. Under the FELA, injured railroad employees sue their employers in a federal or a state court and seek to prove to a jury that the negligence of the employer or other employees caused the plaintiff's injury. When the jury finds that the employee has satisfied these requirements, it then awards damages based on its determination of such factors as the lost wages, medical care costs, and pain and suffering of the employee. Not all cases result in damages to injured employees, however. One estimate in 1990 found that as many as 26 percent of FELA lawsuits resulted in victories for the employer.

THE INTERACTION BETWEEN FELA AND STATE LAW

The other leading approach is represented by state workers compensation laws, which were enacted in every state beginning in 1910. Under the workers' compensation approach, injured employees file claims with state administrative boards, and all claims for injuries arising out of or in the course of employment result in awards of compensation. Compensation amounts, however, are limited to a statutory schedule, often amounting to medical care costs, plus one-half to two-thirds of weekly wages during the period of disability, subject to a maximum of one-half to two-thirds the state average weekly wage. Compensation awards under state workmen's compensation systems are thus virtually automatic, regardless of whether the injured employee is able to establish the negligence of the employer, but are generally much lower than damages awards under the FELA.

Controversy abounds among railroad employers and railroad labor unions as to which approach—employers' liability under the FELA or workers' compensation—is better policy. In 1912 railroad employers resisted the adoption of a workers' compensation system for railroad employee injuries—a system that many railroad labor unions supported. Today the positions are reversed. Employers argue strongly in favor of replacing the FELA with workers' compensation, reducing exposure to monetary judgments to employees at relatively low maximum limits. They argue that the FELA results in unjustified awards for damages in dubious cases, and that employees' lawyers in

FELA cases take large portions of damages awards for their fees—money that thus does not go to injured railroad employees and their families. Railroad labor unions, by contrast, favor maintaining the FELA. They contend that the relatively unfettered jury discretion in damages awards under the FELA provides more significant compensation to injured railroad employees and their families than limited workers' compensation awards do. Moreover, they argue that the threat of damages awards in FELA cases creates powerful incentives for railroad employers to maintain safe work facilities.

Perhaps most significantly, since at least the 1990s, the FELA has become a national pacesetter for the developing **tort** law in state and federal courts around the nation. Many of the most significant issues in American tort law—questions such as when emotional distress damages are available and how to allocate damages among joint wrongdoers—are being decided in FELA cases by the U.S. Supreme Court. Though these decisions are not binding on state and federal court torts decisions outside of the FELA context, they have become enormously influential in shaping the trajectory of state and federal tort decisions. In a sense, the FELA at the beginning of the twenty-first century has brought the American law of torts full circle. In 1908, the FELA borrowed from the developing state tort law; a century later, state tort law has begun to model itself after the FELA.

tort: any wrongdoing other than a breach of contract for which a civil lawsuit can be brought. Examples include physical injury, damage to property, and damage to one's reputation

BIBLIOGRAPHY

Dobbs, Dan B., et al. *Prosser and Keeton on Torts,* 5th ed. St. Paul, MN: West Publishing Co., 1984.

Dodd, Walter F. *Administration of Workmen's Compensation.* New York: Commonwealth Fund, 1936.

Friedman, Lawrence M. *A History of American Law,* 2nd ed. New York: Basic Books, 1985.

Friedman, Lawrence M., and Jack Ladinsky, "Social Change and the Law of Industrial Accidents." *Columbia Law Review* 67 (1967): 50–82.

Levey, Leonard W. *The Law of the Commonwealth and Chief Justice Shaw.* Cambridge, MA: Harvard University Press, 1957.

Thomas, William G. *Lawyering for the Railroad: Business, Law, and Power in the New South.* Baton Rouge: Louisiana State University Press, 1999.

Witt, John Fabian. *The Accidental Republic: Crippled Workingmen, Destitute Widows, and the Remaking of American Law.* Cambridge, MA: Harvard University Press, 2003.

FEDERAL FOOD, DRUG, AND COSMETIC ACT (1938)

Theodore W. Ruger

Americans are avid consumers, and the Federal Food, Drug, and Cosmetic Act (FDCA) (52 stat. 1040) covers products that represent nearly a quarter out of every dollar spent. The FDCA and the agency that administers it, the Food and Drug Administration (FDA), govern the safety and accurate labeling of a trillion dollars worth of products annually, including prescription and over-the-counter drugs, cosmetics, medical devices, blood and tissue products, and the nation's entire food supply except for meat and poultry.

The FDCA and the agency that administers it, the Food and Drug Administration (FDA), govern the safety and accurate labeling of a trillion dollars worth of products annually, including prescription and over-the-counter drugs, cosmetics, medical devices, blood and tissue products, and the nation's entire food supply except for meat and poultry.

Despite frequent amendments since the statute's inception in 1938, two longstanding and complementary regulatory goals remain at the core of the FDCA. The first is to protect the public's safety—the FDCA mandates the safety, purity, and in some cases the "effectiveness" of the products within its scope. For most food products, the FDA ensures safety through inspections of products already on the market, controls the manufacturing practices of companies, and possesses recall and seizure authority. For new drugs, medical devices, and food additives, the FDA has even more robust authority. Unlike most goods sold in the United States, new drugs, medical devices, and food additives must obtain the FDA's stamp of approval as "safe" before being marketed to the public, and drugs and devices must satisfy the added standard of "effectiveness." In a process that often takes years, FDA scientists review extensive empirical research submitted by manufacturers to assess the safety and effectiveness of each new drug or device. Once a product is on the market, the FDCA directs the FDA to monitor emerging information and authorizes it to withdraw approval of products in light of new safety concerns.

The FDCA's second major goal is to disclose information—the statute requires truthfulness and completeness in product labeling and other marketing communications. The act and related FDA regulations contain both prohibitions and affirmative requirements in this area. The act forbids "misbranding," and provides a range of civil and criminal enforcement mechanisms against inaccurate product labeling. It also grants FDA authority to require certain information on product labels, such as the standardized nutritional content box that appears on almost every food label and listing possible side effects and drug interactions on pharmaceutical labels.

Systematic federal regulation of the nation's food and drug supply dates back almost a century, and various public health crises have been instrumental in congressional decisions to implement or strengthen the federal regulatory regime. Upton Sinclair's widely-read book, *The Jungle* portrayed extremely unsanitary conditions in the meat packing industry and created wide public support for the precursor to the FDCA, the Pure Food and Drug Act of 1906. Numerous deaths from a popular consumer medicine (elixir of sulfanilamide) in the 1930s led Congress to enact the FDCA in 1938. The FDCA significantly expanded federal regulatory authority, most notably by requiring premarket safety approval for new drugs, adding cosmetics to the statutory scheme, and providing express authority for factory inspections.

The act also grants FDA authority to require certain information on product labels, such as the standardized nutritional content box that appears on almost every food label and listing possible side effects and drug interactions on pharmaceutical labels.

Congress further strengthened the FDCA in 1958 with the Food Additives Amendment (also called the "Delaney Clause" after its House sponsor), precluding FDA approval of any food additive found to cause cancer in humans or animals; and in 1962 Congress required that drug manufacturers produce scientific evidence not just that their products were "safe" before marketing them, but also that they were "effective" in their intended use. In 1976 the FDCA's scope was expanded to cover all medical devices used in the United States.

Throughout its long history the FDCA has been relatively secure from serious constitutional challenge, primarily

Experiments like the one above where poultry is sprayed with good bacteria to fight off bad bacteria fall under the jurisdiction of the FDA for approval, which has authority to restrict antibiotic use in food-producing animals. (© AP/WIDE WORLD PHOTOS)

because the statute regulates only products that are "in interstate commerce" and thus comfortably within Congress's Commerce Clause authority. Courts have also upheld the FDCA against a different sort of constitutional challenge brought by terminally ill patients claiming a fundamental privacy right to use whatever substances they and their doctors think will relieve their suffering despite the FDA's failure to approve its "safety" or "effectiveness," as in *Rutherford v. United States* (1980) (which holds that "[t]he premarketing requirement of the [FDCA] is a [valid] exercise of Congressional authority to limit the patient's choice of medication."

More significant than any serious constitutional questions are some important limitations on the scope of the FDCA's coverage. The act does not regulate the "practice of medicine" by individual physicians, meaning that once a drug is on the market, doctors can prescribe it in doses, in combinations with other

The act does not regulate the "practice of medicine" by individual physicians, meaning that once a drug is on the market, doctors can prescribe it in doses, in combinations with other drugs, or in patient populations (such as children or pregnant women) that differ significantly from the terms upon which the drug was tested and approved, and physicians are free to use a drug approved for one disease to treat a different medical condition.

drugs, or in patient populations (such as children or pregnant women) that differ significantly from the terms upon which the drug was tested and approved, and physicians are free to use a drug approved for one disease to treat a different medical condition. Such medical use of approved drugs for unapproved uses (termed "off-label" use) is widespread in certain specialties such as cancer, AIDS treatment, and pediatric medicine. A U.S. Supreme Court decision in *FDA v. Brown and Williamson Tobacco Corp.* (2000) upheld another key limitation on the FDCA's coverage by placing cigarettes and other tobacco products outside of the statute's scope. Despite these limitations at the margins, the FDCA remains one of the nation's most important consumer protection statutes.

See also: FOOD QUALITY PROTECTION ACT OF 1996; PURE FOOD AND DRUG ACT.

BIBLIOGRAPHY

Dunn, James Harvey. *Federal Food, Drug, and Cosmetic Act* Chicago: Clearinghouse Press, 1938.

Hutt, Peter Barton and Richard A. Merrill. *Food and Drug Law: Cases and Materials* 2d ed. New York: Foundation Press, 1991.

Young, James Harvey. *Pure Food: Securing the Federal Food and Drugs Act of 1906* Princeton, NJ: Princeton University Press, 1989.

INTERNET RESOURCE

FDA Home Page. <http://www.fda.gov>

FEDERAL HOME LOAN BANK ACT (1932)

Steven A. Ramirez

The Great Depression was an unprecedented economic calamity that ultimately gave rise to an unemployment rate of 25 percent and to a 33-percent contraction of the nation's economy. A quarter of a million families lost their homes in mortgage foreclosure proceedings. President Herbert Hoover initially responded to the downturn in accordance with mainstream economic doctrine of the day and conventional political conceptions of the role of the federal government. Unfortunately, the downturn proved to be very unconventional. President Hoover is to be credited with pursuing a far more interventionist concept of the federal government's role as the downturn intensified. By 1932 the conditions in the housing sector and the closely related savings and loan industry were so dire government intervention was necessary. President Hoover responded with the first federal regulation of the housing and savings and loan industry—the Federal Home Loan Bank Act (FHLB)(P.L. 72-304, 47 Stat. 785).

One major purpose of the Federal Home Loan Bank Act was to create a credit reserve intended to increase the supply of credit available to the housing market, thereby allowing people to buy and maintain homes. Much to President Hoover's great disappointment, however, the credit program was a complete failure. While 41,000 homeowners applied for FHLB loans in the first two years after its enactment, the government agency administering the program approved just three applications.

SUBSEQUENT LEGISLATION

The lack of initial success, however, did not prevent the act from laying the foundation for federal regulation of the housing market in general, and the savings and loan industry (also known as the thrift industry) in particular. On the contrary, the FHLB system was central to the success and regulation of the thrift industry—consisting of twelve regional FHLB banks and the Federal Home Loan Bank Board (FHLBB) in Washington, D.C.

The system, patterned after the Federal Reserve Bank, acted as a lender of last resort when thrifts faced financial strain. Having the FHLB system in place enabled Congress to adopt additional legislation to help fund home ownership. For example, in 1933 Congress adopted the Home Owners' Loan Act, which awarded $770 million to the thrift industry to help deal with borrowers who could not repay their loans. Again, in 1934, Congress acted by adopting the National Housing Act, which extended deposit insurance to the thrifts industry.

At the peak of its power, the FHLBB chartered federal thrifts and regulated the activities of federal savings and loans and savings and loan holding companies. None of these regulatory tasks had been part of the federal government's responsibilities prior to the Federal Home Loan Bank Act. Congress promulgated the act under its authority to regulate interstate commerce, pursuant to Article II, Section 8 of the U.S. Constitution.

As of 1981 some 44 percent of the savings and loan industry was federally chartered and 93 percent of the nation's savings and loans were members of the FHLB bank system. By the early 1980s the federal regulatory framework founded by the Federal Home Loan Bank Act had successfully strengthened the savings and loan industry and facilitated home ownership—which soared in the U.S. from 40 percent to 66 percent from the pre-Depression era to the 1970s. The FHLB Act was a key part of this success.

In the 1980s, however, problems arose as interest rates soared in the face of an increasingly restrictive monetary policy, and savings and loans were faced a high percentage of their assets committed to low interest, long-term mortgages. In an effort to alleviate this problem Congress deregulated the industry and permitted savings and loans to pursue more risky activities. Predictably, thrift failures soared; by 1989 thrift failures had become such an enormous problem Congress was forced to act. The Financial Institutions Reform Recovery and Enforcement Act of 1989 (FIRREA) radically changed the regulatory geography for thrifts. The FHLBB was abolished and replaced with the Office of Thrift Supervision, which has remained the primary regulator of federal thrifts.

Certainly the thrift crisis was notable; nevertheless, equally notable was that there were no runs on the thrift industry in

During the Great Depression a quarter of a million families lost their homes in mortgage foreclosure proceedings.

Having the FHLB system in place enabled Congress to adopt additional legislation to help fund home ownership.

In an effort to alleviate this problem Congress deregulated the industry and permitted savings and loans to pursue more risky activities.

light of its financial difficulties, and there were no macroeconomically significant thrift failures. The housing industry did not collapse, as it had in the Great Depression. The thrift industry has managed to prosper and continues to fulfill its original role to support the nation's housing industry and make housing available to more Americans.

SUPREME COURT RULINGS

The courts have given the act surprising breadth. In the *Fidelity Federal Savings and Loan Association v. De la Cuesta* (1982) case, the Supreme Court held that federally created savings and loan associations, chartered by the FHLBB, were immune from state laws prohibiting "due-on-sale clauses." These clauses were helpful to federal savings and loans because they limited the risk of raising interest rates by requiring all of a mortgage to be paid off, rather than assumed by the purchaser. The FHLBB had issued regulations permitting such clauses but state laws prohibited them. The Supreme Court upheld the FHLBB regulations because it found that Congress had vested the FHLBB with broad powers over federally chartered savings and loans and that federal law governed a broad array of activities of federally chartered thrifts, "from its cradle to corporate grave." Still, this broad power had its limits, as shown in 1997 when the Supreme Court held in *Atherton v. FDIC* that there was insufficient federal interest in federally chartered and federally insured thrifts to warrant a federal common law standard of care for thrift directors.

The courts have given the act surprising breadth.

In *United States v. Westar,* the Supreme Court summarized the history and extent of the Federal Home Loan Bank Act as follows:

> The modern savings and loan industry traces its origins to the Great Depression, which brought default on 40 percent of the Nation's $20 billion in home mortgages and the failure of some 1,700 of the Nation's approximately 12,000 savings institutions. In the course of the debacle, Congress passed three statutes meant to stabilize the thrift industry. The Federal Home Loan Bank Act created the Federal Home Loan Bank Board (Bank Board), which was authorized to channel funds to thrifts for loans on houses and for preventing foreclosures on them. Next, the Home Owners' Loan Act of 1933 authorized the Bank Board to charter and regulate federal savings and loan associations. Finally, the National Housing Act created the Federal Savings and Loan Insurance Corporation (FSLIC), under the Bank Board's authority, with responsibility to insure thrift deposits and regulate all federally insured thrifts. The resulting regulatory regime worked reasonably well until the combination of high interest rates and inflation in the late 1970s and early 1980s brought about a second crisis in the thrift industry. Many thrifts found themselves holding long-term, fixed-rate mortgages created when interest rates were low; when market rates rose, those institutions had to raise the rates they paid to depositors in order to attract funds. When the costs of short-term deposits overtook the revenues from long-term mortgages, some 435 thrifts failed between 1981 and 1983.

See also: Federal National Mortgage Association Charter Act; National Housing Act.

BIBLIOGRAPHY
Davis, Kenneth S. *FDR: The New Deal Years*. New York: Random House, 1986.

Kennedy, David M. *Freedom from Fear.* New York: Oxford University Press, 1999.

Lovett, William A. *Banking and Financial Institutions Law.* St. Paul, MN: West, 2001.

Ramirez, Steven. "The Law and Macroeconomics of the New Deal at 70." In *Maryland Law Review* 62, no. 3 (2003).

Schlesinger, Arthur M., Jr. *The Coming of the New Deal.* Boston: Houghton Mifflin, 1958.

FEDERAL INCOME TAX OF 1913

Steven A. Bank

Although the modern income tax emerged in 1913, it pales in comparison to the Internal Revenue Code in effect at the beginning of the twenty-first century. Because of a generous $3,000 exemption, plus an additional $1,000 exemption for married couples, the tax applied to fewer than four percent of the population. Even for those it affected, the impact was relatively mild. The act levied a tax of one percent on all incomes above the exemption with additional surtax rates imposed for progressively higher incomes. Those surtax rates started at one percent for those making $20,000 or more and topped out at a mere six percent on incomes in excess of $500,000. Given such a limited taxpayer base and low rates, it is not surprising that the income tax had only a minor role in the federal revenue system during its infancy. In its first year in operation, it was responsible for raising less than 10 percent of federal revenues. By contrast, the income tax accounted for 45 percent of federal revenues in 1950 and nearly 73 percent in 1985. The 1913 version of the income tax did not even merit its own act; rather, it was adopted as part of the Underwood/Simmons Tariff Act of 1913. Despite the income tax's relatively minor role, even contemporary observers recognized its larger significance. It marked the beginning of a transformation from taxation based upon the need to consume to taxation based upon the ability to pay. It also provided the vehicle for a rapid expansion of the federal government over the next thirty years.

> *The income tax applied to some 4 percent of the population, so it is not surprising that, early on, it played only a minor role in the federal revenue system.*

EARLY HISTORY OF THE INCOME TAX

In the nineteenth and early twentieth centuries, the United States relied primarily on taxes levied on products manufactured in the United States (**excise taxes**) or imported into the country from elsewhere (**tariffs**) for the bulk of federal revenues. Two notable problems resulted from this heavy reliance on what are called consumption taxes. First, the revenue from tariffs was easily disrupted when trade fell. Second, both types of taxes were typically passed on to consumers in the form of higher prices, and this disproportionately impacted the poor. Both of these problems with the consumption-based tax system led to consideration of an income tax during the nineteenth century.

When the War of 1812 began, the federal government doubled the customs duties it had been using to raise the majority of its revenues. As a drop in trade caused these sums to dwindle and the national debt to increase, Alexander Dallas, Thomas Jefferson's Secretary of the Treasury, sought alter-

excise tax: a tax levied on the manufacture or sale of specific—usually non-essential—commodities such as tobacco or liquor

tariff: a tax imposed on goods when imported into a country

During the Civil War (1861–65), Congress could no longer avoid the income tax.

protectionism: the use of tariffs to protect domestic industries from foreign competition

The Tax Protest Movement

Tax protesters differ from run-of-the-mill tax evaders in that protesters feel that they have a moral, ethical, or legal right to avoid paying taxes. The first organized tax protest movements began to emerge during the 1950s and 1960s. Protesters on the Left refused to pay taxes that would support the war in Vietnam and other aspects of American foreign policy they considered unjust or immoral. Protesters on the right felt that income taxes were unfair because of their progressive nature, resented being coerced into giving up income, and found the withholding process intrusive. In 1957 Congressman Elmer Hoffman of Illinois proposed an amendment calling for the abolition of income taxes; since then, the so-called Liberty Amendment has been reintroduced repeatedly, but with no success. During the 1970s the tax protest movement grew more radical, with protesters on the far Right taking the lead, and the movement came to be associated with anti-government organizations that have harassed and even killed government and law enforcement officials and burned or bombed government facilities.

native sources of revenue. Dallas turned first to internal revenues from excise and property taxes before deciding to push forward with proposals for income and inheritance taxes. Although these latter proposals were raised too late to secure passage, the war had exposed the vulnerability of a tariff-based system.

During the Civil War (1861–65), Congress could no longer avoid the income tax. Imports were on the decline in part because of a drop in demand after the Panic of 1857, a severe recession that began with the discovery of a Wall Street embezzlement scheme and an ensuing run on the banks. Moreover, Abraham Lincoln assumed the presidency in March of 1861 with a pre-war debt of almost $75 million. The onset of war, with its accompanying naval blockades and other economic dislocation, only exacerbated this situation. Thus, in 1862 Congress adopted an income tax. Not only was it the country's first income tax, but it was the first use of graduated rates, or rates that increased progressively with the rise in a taxpayer's income. Some contend that the progressive rates were intended merely to raise more revenue, rather than to redistribute wealth, but it is enough to say that they helped shift some of the revenue-raising burden from the poor to the rich. After the war ended, the economy began to improve, prices fell, and budget surpluses replaced deficits. In the face of growing opposition to what the *New York Tribune* called "the most odious, vexatious, inquisitorial, and unequal of all of our taxes," the income tax was repealed in 1872.

A CONSTITUTIONAL CHALLENGE TO THE INCOME TAX

The income tax issue continued to simmer during the 1870s and 1880s, but a number of influences converged to make it a reality in 1894. Great fortunes were amassed during the high prosperity and **protectionism** of the 1880s. This focused attention back to the inequities of the tariff system during the election of Democrat Grover Cleveland in 1892. Coupled with the popular and economic unrest resulting from the Panic of 1893—a depression in which the stock market collapsed—thousands of businesses went bankrupt, million of people were left jobless, and the national income dropped ten percent. Congress once again adopted an income tax as part of the Tariff Act of 1894. Although the rates were flat rather than graduated as in the Civil War version, the goal was more clearly to redress inequity than in the early experiment with an income tax.

The 1894 income tax was never actually implemented because of a judicial challenge. Although the Supreme Court had upheld the Civil War version in *Springer v. United States* (1880), two shareholder suits were soon filed to prevent their respective corporations from paying the 1894 act's income tax. In the case that followed, *Pollock v. Farmers' Loan and Trust Co.* (1895), the Supreme Court struck down the income tax as unconstitutional. According to the Court, the income tax was a direct tax under Article I, Section 9 of the Constitution, and therefore must be levied "in proportion to the Census or Enumeration." Since the income tax would be collected at a uniform national rate on the basis of income rather than population, the Court found it to be an unapportioned direct tax.

THE SIXTEENTH AMENDMENT

With the Court's decision to strike down the income tax as unconstitutional, Congress once again turned to the tariff. Republicans had blamed the Panic of 1893 on Cleveland's tariff reform efforts. They regained control of both houses of Congress during the midterm elections of 1894 and the presidency in 1896 with the election of William McKinley on a platform of protectionism. Armed with this mandate, Republicans passed the highly protective Dingley Tariff Act in 1897.

The Republicans' push for high tariff rates came back to haunt them when prices rose over the next decade. While there is only mixed evidence that the tariff was responsible for this inflation, Democrats took advantage of the public's perception of a link between tariffs and high prices in order to bolster their anti-tariff, pro-income tax stance. The Panic of 1907, with its ensuing economic instability, furthered this cause. By the 1908 elections, both parties pledged their support for tariff reform. Presidential candidates William Jennings Bryan and William Howard Taft each expressed their support for an income tax; Taft, the eventual winner, declared in his acceptance speech that it was both constitutionally permissible and potentially desirable to have an income tax under circumstances of dire need.

On March 4, 1909, Taft formally called a special session of Congress to discuss the issue of tariff reform. This contentious session illustrated the political breakdown that had developed over the subject. While Republicans ostensibly dominated both houses of Congress, a rift was growing in their ranks. Regular Republicans adhered to the traditional party **dogma** of protectionism. A small but significant group of Republicans, however, were straying from this stance. Known as "**Insurgents**," this group of primarily western representatives and senators were opposed to favoritism toward big business. They sought a scientifically drawn tariff, which would provide protection for certain deserving industries, supplemented by an income tax designed to add a measure of tax equity. Given this changing political landscape, Republicans had to take seriously calls for an income tax during the 1909 special session.

In an attempt to forestall income tax proposals supported by a coalition of Democrats and Insurgents, regular Republicans, led by Senator Nelson Aldrich and Representative Sereno Payne, both of New York, managed to secure a compromise. They agreed to submit a constitutional amendment to the states that would allow Congress to levy a tax upon incomes. At the same time, they enacted an excise tax on corporate income in part to offset revenue lost through tariff revision. The resulting Payne-Aldrich Tariff Act, enacted on August 5, 1909, delayed the income tax, but fell far short of the fundamental reform of the tariff system that had led to the special session.

This failure of tariff reform helped fuel efforts toward ratification of the constitutional amendment for an income tax. Prior to 1910, two-thirds of the states had not even considered the proposed amendment. During the 1910 elections, however, Democrats and Insurgents rode a wave of anti-tariff sentiment to victories at both the state and federal levels. The following year, income tax supporters secured passage of the constitutional amendment in all but eight of the states necessary for ratification. Although there was a subsequent delay because most state legislatures only met every other year, ratification was achieved when Delaware voted to accept the amendment on February 3, 1913. Under what became the Sixteenth Amendment to the U.S. Constitution, "[T]he Congress shall have the

On March 4, 1909, Taft formally called a special session of Congress to discuss the issue of tariff reform.

dogma: an established opinion expressed as an authoritative statement

insurgent: one who revolts against authority; especially a member of a political party who rebels against its leadership

The failure of tariff reform helped fuel efforts toward ratification of the constitutional amendment for an income tax.

power to lay and collect taxes on income, from whatever source derived, without apportionment among the several states, and without regard to any Census or Enumeration."

INCOME TAX OF 1913

In his inaugural address in March 1913, newly elected Democratic President Woodrow Wilson quickly took advantage of the new amendment by calling for tariff reduction and the adoption of an income tax. Within a month, during an emergency session of Congress, House Ways and Means Chair Oscar Underwood, a Democrat from Alabama, introduced a tariff reform bill that provided for an income tax with progressive rates. Underwood and the income tax section's principal drafter, Representative Cordell Hull of Tennessee, had originally sought to introduce a flat rate income tax to ensure judicial approval, but pressure from other Democrats, including future Vice-President John Nance Garner of Texas, led them to opt for the graduated rates.

The ensuing debates over the income tax primarily centered on the rate and exemption amount for an income tax, rather than the propriety of the income tax itself.

The ensuing debates over the income tax primarily centered on the rate and exemption amount for an income tax, rather than the propriety of the income tax itself. Regular Republicans pushed for flatter rates and lower exemptions. Since they did not concede that the tariff was itself a tax, they viewed any exemption to the income tax to be class legislation and, in the words of Michigan Senator Charles E. Townsend, a "danger to the Republic." When combined with progressive rates, Senator Henry Cabot Lodge of Massachusetts argued, the exemption would "set a class apart and say they are to be pillaged, their property is to be confiscated."

Insurgents and members of the newer Progressive party saw the income tax very differently from regular Republicans. They advocated steeply progressive rates as a method of redistributing wealth. In the most extreme example, Representative Ira Copley proposed an income tax with a top marginal rate of 68 percent on incomes exceeding one million dollars. Others, such as Senator Robert La Follette of Wisconsin, proposed rates as high as 11 percent to reach what he called the "menace" of "great accumulation of wealth."

Standing between these two extremes were the Democrats, who proposed a more mild progression of rates to offset the burden of tariff taxes on the poor. Senator John Sharp Williams from Mississippi, one of the Democratic caucus's spokesmen in the Senate, rebuked the Insurgent and Progressive position by stating "[n]o honest man can make war upon great fortunes per se.... I am not going to make this tariff bill a great panacea for all the inequalities of fortune existing in this country." Nevertheless, he recognized that a modicum of progressivity, accompanied by a high exemption, was necessary as long as tariff taxes remained in place. According to Williams, the regular Republicans' plea for flat rates and low exemptions should be left for "when the good day comes—the golden day—when there will be no taxes upon consumption at all."

The Democrats' position carried the day. The Underwood/Simmons Tariff Act, which went into effect on October 3, 1913, levied an income tax that imposed mildly progressive rates and was accompanied by a healthy exemption. The graduated rate feature was later challenged, but the Supreme Court

Prior to the 1913 income tax, the majority of the government's tax income came from consumption taxes, which were a greater burden on the working class than on the rich (the taxes consumed proportionally more of the working class's income). This 1913 cartoon reflects the notion that the rich would begin to share more equally in the burden of taxation with the passage of a progressive income tax. (LIBRARY OF CONGRESS, PRINTS AND PHOTOGRAPHS DIVISION)

upheld it in *Brushaber v. Union Pacific R.R. Co.* (1916) on the ground that it did not "transcend the conception of all taxation" so as "to be a mere arbitrary abuse of power."

Although the income tax act of 1913 instituted only mild progressivity and raised a relatively small amount, it was still a monumental development. It began the process of converting the tax system from a regressive consumption-based system to a system that levied taxes based on the ability to pay. Moreover, it offered the vehicle for a rapid expansion of the tax system during World War I (1914–1918) when consumption taxes proved inadequate. It was not until World War II (1939–45), however, when Congress permitted payroll deduction and a significant cut in the exemption, that the income tax truly

Although the income tax act of 1913 instituted only mild progressivity and raised a relatively small amount, it was still a monumental development.

became a tax for all people. Nevertheless, it was in the income tax act of 1913 that the seeds were planted for this development.

See also: CORPORATE INCOME TAX ACT OF 1909; ESTATE AND GIFT TAXATION; TAX REFORM ACT OF 1986; TAXPAYER BILL OF RIGHTS III.

BIBLIOGRAPHY

Brownlee, W. Elliot. *Federal Taxation in America: A Short History.* New York: Woodrow Wilson Center Press and University of Cambridge Press, 1996.

Buenker, John D. *The Income Tax and the Progressive Era.* New York: Garland, 1985.

Ratner, Sidney. *Taxation and Democracy in America.* New York: W.W. Norton, 1967.

Roberts, Paul C., and Lawrence M. Stratton, "The Roots of the Income Tax." *National Review* (April 17, 1995): 42.

Stanley, Robert. *Dimensions of Law in the Service of Order: Origins of the Federal Income Tax 1861-1913.* New York: Oxford University Press, 1993.

Waltman, Jerold L. *Political Origins of the U.S. Income Tax.* Jackson: University Press of Mississippi, 1985.

Weisman, Steven R. *The Great Tax Wars.* New York: Simon & Schuster, 2002.

FEDERAL LAND POLICY AND MANAGEMENT ACT (1976)

William V. Luneburg

Excerpt from the Federal Land Policy and Management Act

The Congress declares that it is the policy of the United States that ... the national interest will be best realized if the public lands and their resources are periodically and systematically inventoried and their present and future use is projected through a land use planning process coordinated with other Federal and State planning efforts.

The land west of the Mississippi River was acquired by the United States by conquest, treaty, and purchase during the first seven decades of the nineteenth century. Even today hundreds of millions of acres located within the lower forty-eight states and Alaska remain the property of the federal government, subject to the plenary, or absolute, constitutional authority of Congress to provide for its disposition, regulation, and protection. Various federal agencies have been assigned the statutory authority to manage this land. One of those agencies is the Bureau of Land Management (BLM), formed by a merger in 1946 of the Grazing Service and the General Land Office and located in the Department of the Interior. The BLM is now in charge of 261 million acres of the public domain. Of that, 176 million acres located in western states (excluding Alaska) are rangelands for 90 percent of which livestock grazing is approved.

Even today hundreds of millions of acres located within the lower forty-eight states and Alaska remain the property of the federal government subject to the plenary, or absolute, constitutional authority of Congress to provide for its disposition, regulation, and protection.

The Grand Staircase-Escalante National Monument near Boulder, Utah, is under the care of the Bureau of Land Management (BLM). Due to population growth in the West, BLM lands are increasingly used for recreational activities, such as hiking. (© AP/WIDE WORLD PHOTOS)

Between the federal acquisition of the land in the West and 1938, ranchers freely grazed livestock, both cattle and sheep, on the public domain. As the herds grew, forage scarcities developed and were aggravated by droughts, blizzards, and homesteading. Overgrazing became a continual problem, one that provoked a variety of reactions including violence on the range and calls

Dust Bowl: a semiarid region in the south-central United States where the topsoil was lost by wind erosion in the mid-1930s

for congressional regulation. While bills were routinely introduced in Congress even prior to 1900 to deal with the issues created by livestock grazing on federal land, it was not until the development of the **Dust Bowl** of the 1930s that Congress mustered the will to overcome political opposition to enact the Taylor Grazing Act of 1938. That statute aimed to "stop injury" to the public land from overgrazing and soil deterioration and to improve the range—goals that have ever since been the consistent theme of public land legislation, although they have yet to be fully realized in practice. The Secretary of the Interior was given the authority to create grazing districts, to determine the amount of land in each that could be subject to grazing, to issue permits to graze livestock on the land, and to charge fees for those permits.

With few statutory standards in the Taylor Grazing Act to limit its discretion, the BLM generally accommodated ranchers' desires without focusing on improvement of range condition. As a result, rangeland productivity continued to suffer. Yet for several more decades, BLM "management" was not a matter of intense public debate. That all changed, however, during the 1960s and 1970s as aggressive environmental and conservation organizations came into existence and called for drastic changes in the BLM's approach. During this period,

> *With few statutory standards in the Taylor Grazing Act to limit its discretion, the BLM generally accommodated ranchers' desires without focusing on improvement of range condition.*

litigation in the federal courts was a potent force for change in the way federal agencies dealt with natural resource and environmental issues, and the regulation of public rangeland was no different in that regard. The seminal case was decided in 1974, *Natural Resources Defense Council v. Morton*, where the court ordered the BLM to prepare environmental impact statements (a type of cost/benefit analysis) for livestock grazing on over 140 million acres of public land pursuant to the National Environmental Policy Act of 1969. While Congress had long ignored the BLM's stewardship of public land, the result in this case made it difficult for the legislature to duck the issues presented regarding the adequacy of federal land management. Moreover, the BLM itself had been pressing Congress to give it a comprehensive "organic" statute; the agency had labored since its inception under hundreds of unrelated and often conflicting laws. The result of these pressures was the Federal Land Policy and Management Act of 1976 (FLPMA) (P.L. 94-579, 90 Stat. 2743), which does not repeal but rather operates in tandem with the Taylor Grazing Act.

PROVISIONS OF THE FLMPA

At the outset of the FLPMA, Congress sets forth thirteen ambitious (and not always consistent) policies, including that the public lands should remain in federal ownership unless the national interest requires disposition, that those lands should be inventoried and managed through a planning process, that management of the lands should be on the basis of the principles of multiple use and sustained yield and "in a manner that will protect the quality of scientific, scenic, historical, ecological, environmental, air and atmospheric, water resource, and archeological values," and that the United States should receive fair market value in exchange for the use of the public lands and their resources by private persons.

The specific provisions of the FLPMA that follow the initial declaration of congressional policies encompass numerous and diverse subject matters, including:

(1) the organization of the BLM and the creation of authority to implement the statute through the issuance of rules and the commencement of civil actions in the courts to enforce those regulations;

(2) the development of land use plans;

(3) restrictions on sales and acquisitions of public land, exchanges of federal land for private land, and withdrawals of federal lands to limit their use;

(4) range management (e.g., grazing permits and fees); and

(5) the grant and renewal of rights-of-way across federal land (e.g., to build an oil pipeline).

Of particular importance are the statutory mandates directed to the BLM first to inventory the public lands under its control for the resources and "values" (e.g., for grazing, for recreation, etc.) they potentially offer and then to divide those lands into various areas for each of which a plan must be devised determining the use or uses to which the area will be put for a period of time. The FLPMA rejects grazing as necessarily the dominant use for rangeland, opting instead to require that the BLM plan and manage on the basis of "multiple use and sustained yield" (MUSY) principles that have, since at least 1960, governed the management of the National Forest System by the Forest Service located in the Department of Agriculture. MUSY does not offer a fixed formula for determining the use of land. Rather, it requires the agency to survey all the feasible uses of an area (e.g., grazing, wildlife, recreation, timber), giving each use equal weight, and to choose the one or ones that maximize the land's present value (not necessarily monetary) without impairing the land's ability to provide benefits of various kinds in the future. Once the BLM has approved a land use plan for a particular area, then any management actions later taken by the agency with regard to that land, including issuance of grazing permits, must be consistent with the plan.

Of particular importance are the statutory mandates directed to the BLM first to inventory the public lands under its control for the resources and "values" (e.g. for grazing, for recreation, etc.) they potentially offer and then to divide those lands into various areas for each of which a plan must be devised determining the use or uses to which the area will be put for a period of time.

Once the BLM has approved a land use plan for a particular area, then any management actions later taken by the agency with regard to that land, including issuance of grazing permits, must be consistent with the plan.

The Dust Bowl

Beginning in the 1890s, farmers began to plow areas on the Great Plains that were previously considered too arid for anything but grazing livestock. The practice accelerated after World War I as the demand for wheat increased and tractors and combines became common. Before they were plowed, these lands were covered in buffalo grass, whose roots trapped water and held the soil in place. With the grass removed the soil was easily picked up by the wind, setting the stage for ecological disaster. In the mid-1930s, in a 300,000-square mile area that became known as the Dust Bowl, "black blizzards" drew the topsoil into swirling clouds of dense brown fog. Crops were buried or torn out at the roots, and cattle were choked. The dirt clogged engines and infiltrated homes, despite wet blankets hung over windows. Hospitals reported "dust pneumonia," and some farmers caught by unexpected storms suffocated in their fields. One storm covered an area nine hundred miles wide and fifteen hundred miles long and dropped an estimated 12 million tons of soil on Chicago. In April and May of 1934 alone, 650 million tons of soil were blown off the plains. During the 1930s, more than 350,000 people were driven from their homes in the the afflicted areas, which included Kansas, Texas, Oklahoma, Colorado, and New Mexico. Many of the refugees settled in California.

CHALLENGES AND ADDITIONS TO LAND MANAGEMENT POLICY

Subsequent to the enactment of the FLPMA, Congress attempted to further specify the required approach to range management. One pertinent statute is the Public Rangelands Improvement Act of 1978, which establishes range condition improvement as the first priority.

As the BLM has accumulated authority to manage federal land under multiple use principles and range improvement mandates, its actions have been challenged by ranchers fearful of the effect on their grazing privileges. However, so far the Supreme Court has rejected those legal arguments on a variety of bases, including that the agency has substantial discretion to limit grazing privileges consistent with governing land use plans (*Public Lands Council v. Babbitt* [2000]).

See also: NATIONAL FOREST MANAGEMENT ACT.

BIBLIOGRAPHY

Foss, Phillip O. *Politics and Grass: The Administration of Grazing on the Public Domain.* Seattle: University of Washington Press, 1960.

Nelson, Robert H. *Public Lands and Private Rights: The Failure of Scientific Management.* Lanham, MD: Rowman & Littlefield, 1995.

Wilkinson, Charles F. "The Rancher's Code." In *Crossing the Next Meridian: Land, Water, and the Future of the West.* Washington, DC: Island Press, 1992.

INTERNET RESOURCE

Bureau of Land Management. <http://www.blm.gov/nhp/index.htm>.

FEDERAL NATIONAL MORTGAGE ASSOCIATION CHARTER ACT (1954)

Julia Patterson Forrester

Excerpt from the Federal National Mortgage Association Charter Act

The purposes of this subchapter are to establish secondary market facilities for residential mortgages, to provide that the operations thereof shall be financed by private capital to the maximum extent feasible, and to authorize such facilities to—

(1) provide stability in the secondary market for residential mortgages;

(2) respond appropriately to the private capital market;

(3) provide ongoing assistance to the secondary market for residential mortgages (including activities relating to mortgages on housing for low- and moderate-income families involving a reasonable economic return that may be ⟵ the return earned on other activities) ... ;

(4) promote access to mortgage credit throughout the Nation (including central cities, rural areas, and underserved areas) ... ; and

(5) manage and liquidate federally owned mortgage portfolios....

The Federal National Mortgage Association Charter Act (Charter Act) (68 Stat. 612) reorganized and reestablished the Federal National Mortgage Association (now called Fannie Mae), originally created in 1938, in order to encourage a **secondary market** for residential **mortage loan**, and in 1968 created the Government National Mortgage Association (Ginnie Mae) to take on some of the functions of Fannie Mae. In the secondary market, mortgage companies and other parties that originate mortgage loans sell the loans or interests in groups of loans to investors such as banks, insurance companies, pension funds, and individuals, as well as to Fannie Mae. These investors purchase loans or interests in loans as an alternative to other investments like stock, bonds, or real estate. The mortgage companies and other originators make money by charging fees for origination and in some cases by charging fees to collect loan payments from borrowers for the investors (called servicing the loans). Because the loans are sold after they are made, the originators do not need to have a lot of money in order to make a lot of loans.

By encouraging investment in home mortgages through the secondary market, the Charter Act is intended to make mortgage funds more readily

secondary market: the market in which mortgage loans are bought and sold by investors

mortgage loan: a loan to purchase real estate; the real estate purchased with the loan usually serves as collateral against default

A home for sale in a suburb of Detroit, Michigan. The mortgage that was used to buy this home was likely sold on the secondary market. (©2003 KELLY A. QUIN)

By encouraging investment in home mortgages through the secondary market, the Charter Act is intended to make mortgage funds more readily available throughout the nation, especially in areas that have traditionally been underserved and to low- and moderate-income households.

available throughout the nation, especially in areas that have traditionally been underserved and to low- and moderate-income households. Before the growth of the secondary market, most home mortgages were made by local savings and loan institutions using funds from savings accounts of depositors. The number of loans that could be made by a savings and loan depended on the amount of deposits it held. The secondary market makes mortgage funds more available because so many types of companies can invest in the loans and because investors in one part of the country may buy loans made to homeowners in other areas. In addition, if more funds are available for making mortgage loans, then more borrowers, including low income borrowers, can get loans.

Great Depression: the longest and most severe economic depression in American history (1929–1939); its effects were felt throughout the world

refinance: to pay off existing loans with funds secured from new loans

foreclosure: when a person defaults on (fails to pay) a mortgage debt, the owner's legal right to the property is terminated. The real estate may be sold at an auction by the creditor; the money raised is then put toward the mortgage debt

interest rate: the fee for borrowing money, expressed as a percentage of the amount borrowed

HISTORICAL BACKGROUND

Fannie Mae had its origins during the **Great Depression** under the leadership of President Franklin D. Roosevelt. In the early 1930s the typical loan made for the purchase of a home had only a three- to five-year term. Homeowners were required to **refinance** their homes frequently, and when refinancing was not available, many Americans lost their homes to **foreclosure**. In addition, **interest rates** and the availability of home mortgage financing varied widely throughout the country. In response to these problems, President Roosevelt's National Emergency Council recommended the establishment of a program for long-term, federally insured mortages and the creation of national mortgage associations to purchase these mortgages. The National Housing Act of 1934 implemented these proposals. In 1938 the National Mortgage Association of Washington was created and later that year was renamed the Federal National Mortgage Association (now Fannie Mae). Fannie Mae was originally a government corporation that borrowed money by issuing government bonds to raise funds for the purchase of mortgages insured by the Federal Housing Administration (FHA) and, beginning in 1944, those guaranteed by the Veteran's Administration (VA) as well. In 1950 Fannie Mae became part of the Housing and Home Finance Agency that later became the Department of Housing and Urban Development (HUD)

LEGISLATIVE HISTORY AND FEATURES OF THE ACT

In the early 1950s traditional lenders complained to Congress that Fannie Mae competed unfairly with private companies because Fannie Mae, as part of a government agency, could borrow money to buy mortgages at lower interest rates than private lenders. Traditional lenders encouraged Congress to abolish Fannie Mae altogether or to make it a private company. As a compromise between the interests of traditional lenders and those parties who recommended keeping Fannie Mae and even expanding its operations, Congress passed the Charter Act as a part of the National Housing Act of 1954. The Charter Act reestablished and reorganized Fannie Mae. It made Fannie Mae a partially private entity, meaning it would be owned in part by shareholders. The Charter Act also gave Fannie Mae three functions:

(1) secondary market operations—purchasing of FHA-insured and VA-guaranteed mortgages to make mortgage funds more available throughout the country;

(2) special assistance—providing assistance for mortgages originated under housing programs for those unable to obtain adequate housing or for mortgages in general if necessary to stop a decline in home building;

(3) management and liquidation—managing and eventually selling the mortgages owned by the old Fannie Mae.

During the period after the Charter Act, Fannie Mae became the most important institution in residential mortgage finance by purchasing significant numbers of mortgages each year: 11 percent of all residential mortgages originated in 1957, 9 percent in 1960, and 18 percent in 1966.

As a compromise between the interests of traditional lenders and those parties who recommended keeping Fannie Mae and even expanding its operations, Congress passed the Charter Act as a part of the National Housing Act of 1954. The Charter Act reestablished and reorganized Fannie Mae.

RELATED ACTS

In 1968 Congress enacted the Housing and Urban Development Act, which divided the functions of Fannie Mae between two entities. Fannie Mae became a government-sponsored private corporation and was allocated the secondary market operations of the former entity. Ginnie Mae remained a division of HUD and was given the special assistance and the management and liquidation functions of the former Fannie Mae. In 1970 the Emergency Home Finance Act authorized Fannie Mae to purchase **conventional mortgages** and created the Federal Home Loan Mortgage Corporation (Freddie Mac) which is now almost identical in its charter and functions to Fannie Mae. Finally, the Housing and Community Development Act of 1992 established the Office of Federal Housing Enterprise Oversight (OFHEO) as an office of HUD to monitor both Fannie Mae and Freddie Mac. The 1992 act also increased the role of both Fannie Mae and Freddie Mac in making mortgages available to borrowers with very low, low, and moderate incomes by requiring them to make money available for the purchase of these mortgages.

conventional mortgage: a home mortgage loan that is not federally insured

Fannie Mae is a government-sponsored entity.

HOW FANNIE MAE WORKS

Fannie Mae is a government-sponsored entity. It is a private corporation owned by shareholders, but it operates under a federal charter that imposes restrictions on its activities while granting certain benefits that other private corporations do not enjoy. These benefits include exemption from state taxes, except for real property taxes, and exemption from **federal securities laws**. Under the Charter Act, the president appoints five of Fannie Mae's eighteen **directors**, while the rest are elected by shareholders.

Fannie Mae still purchases residential mortgages on the secondary market, including conventional mortgages as well as FHA-insured and VA-guaranteed mortgages. Fannie Mae purchases some residential mortgage loans to retain in its portfolio of investments; however, most of the loans that Fannie Mae purchases today are securitized. This means that Fannie Mae collects a group of similar home mortgage loans (called a pool of loans), then issues securities (called mortgage-backed securities) that represent an ownership interest in the pool of loans. Investors who purchase the securities are thus purchasing an interest, not in an individual loan, but in the pool of mortgage loans. Most of the securities are pass-through securities, which means that Fannie Mae collects principal and interest payments from the mortgages in the pools and

federal securities laws: federal securities laws include the Securities Act of 1933, the Securities Exchange Act of 1934, and various rules and regulations under these acts. These acts regulate the offer and sale of securities as well as secondary markets for securities. They require numerous disclosures and prohibit deceptive practices

directors: those who establish the policies of the corporation

Through its purchases and securitization of residential mortgage loans, Fannie Mae is the largest source of home mortgage financing in the nation.

originate: a loan is originated when the loan is first made by the lender to a borrower. The origination function includes taking the borrower's loan application, checking the borrower's credit history and employment, obtaining an appraisal or valuation of the home, and funding the loan

default: the failure by the borrower to comply with the terms of the loan, usually the failure to make payments

passes them on to the investors who own the securities. Fannie Mae guarantees these payments to the investors. Because Fannie Mae is not a government agency, its guarantee is not backed by the full faith and credit of the federal government, but there is an assumption that the federal government would honor Fannie Mae's obligations in the event that Fannie Mae experiences financial trouble because of too many defaults on the loans it owns or with respect to which it guarantees payments. Securitization of mortgages by Fannie Mae makes more money available for mortgage loans by reducing the risk of investment in mortgage loans. An investor who purchases a mortgage loan risks the loss of that investment because the borrower may default on payment of the loan and foreclosure often does not leave the lender whole. By investing in mortgage-backed securities, an investor gets an interest in a portion of a large group of loans rather than in one loan, and the risk of loss is reduced since it is less likely that a large number of borrowers will default. Fannie Mae's guarantee of loan payments also reduces the risk of the investment.

Through its purchases and securitization of residential mortgage loans, Fannie Mae is the largest source of home mortgage financing in the nation. Fannie Mae and Freddie Mac together purchased 40 percent of all conventional mortgages **originated** in 2001. Also, because of Fannie Mae's successful involvement in securitizing mortgage loans, private companies have begun to securitize mortgage loans as well. Fannie Mae purchased $568 billion of residential mortgage loans and issued $515 billion of mortgage-backed securities in 2001. Fannie Mae thus facilitates the flow of money into the residential mortgage market in accordance with the purposes set out in its charter.

Fannie Mae facilitates a secondary market in other ways as well. In cooperation with Freddie Mac, Fannie Mae has developed standardized forms for use by lenders who make conventional mortgage loans. These forms are almost universally used by conventional lenders to facilitate the sale of their loans on the secondary market. Fannie Mae and Freddie Mac also maintain lists of approved private mortgage insurance companies. These companies make conventional mortgages more marketable by insuring investors in the mortgages against some of the risks of borrower **default**.

HOW GINNIE MAE WORKS

Ginnie Mae's primary activity today is to operate a program for guaranteeing mortgage-backed securities. Ginnie Mae does not issue securities but rather guarantees securities issued by mortgage lenders. The securities are backed by pools of loans guaranteed by the FHA, VA, and Rural Housing Service. These are mostly loans to low- and moderate-income homeowners and first-time home buyers. Thus, Ginnie Mae's program serves primarily these borrowers. Because the Ginnie Mae guarantee of the securities is backed by the full faith and credit of the federal government, the securities are desirable to investors. Thus Ginnie Mae also channels money into the residential mortgage market, particularly for low- and moderate-income homeowners. According to Ginnie Mae's web site, in 2002 Ginnie Mae reached the $2 trillion mark in its total guarantees of mortgaged-backed securities since it was formed in 1968.

The Charter Act has been successful in creating a secondary market for home mortgage loans and in making mortgage funds available throughout the nation, but there are critics. Some critics say that Fannie Mae and Freddie Mac compete unfairly against entirely private companies that purchase and securitize loans because of the advantages they receive from the federal government. Critics also say Fannie Mae and Freddie Mac should be more heavily regulated by the federal government because the failure of either would cause such a great disruption in the operation of the secondary market. Finally, critics say that Fannie Mae and Freddie Mac have not been sufficiently involved in purchasing and securitizing loans to low income households. Ginnie Mae's program of guaranteeing mortgage-backed securities does serve low-and moderate-income borrowers, and Fannie Mae and Freddie Mac have increased their involvement in this area in recent years. Because of the strength of the secondary market and because of securitization, the home mortgage loan market today operated in an entirely different manner from its operation prior to the 1970s, and the availability of mortgage funds no longer depends on local savings and loans.

See also: HOUSING AND URBAN DEVELOPMENT ACT OF 1965; NATIONAL HOUSING ACT.

BIBLIOGRAPHY

Nelson, Grant, and Dale Whitman. *Real Estate Finance Law.* St. Paul, MN: West, 1994.

INTERNET RESOURCES

Federal National Mortgage Association. <http://www.fanniemae.com>.

Government National Mortgage Association. <http://www.ginniemae.gov>.

FEDERAL POWER ACTS

Brian E. Gray

Article I, Section 8 of the United States Constitution grants Congress authority to "regulate Commerce with foreign Nations, and among the several States, and with the Indian Tribes." Historically, the **commerce clause** has been the greatest source of Congress's constitutional power to enact laws that govern economic and social activity within the United States.

Many Supreme Court decisions of the early nineteenth century that sanctioned the expansion of federal regulatory power involved protection of navigation. In the famous case *Gibbons v. Ogden* (1824), for example, Chief Justice John Marshall declared that the "power over commerce, including navigation, was one of the primary objects for which the people of America adopted their government." In subsequent cases, the Court recognized that the United States has paramount authority to protect and to regulate all navigable waters to ensure that they remain free and unobstructed avenues of commerce.

During the late nineteenth and early twentieth centuries, Congress passed a series of statutes to govern the use of the nation's navigable waterways. The Rivers and Harbors Act of 1890, for example, prohibited "the creation of any obstruction

commerce clause: the provision of the U.S. Constitution (Article I, section 8, clause 3) which gives Congress exclusive powers over interstate commerce—the buying, selling or exchanging of goods or products between states

Many Supreme Court decisions of the early nineteenth century that sanctioned the expansion of federal regulatory power involved protection of navigation.

not affirmatively authorized by Congress, to the navigable capacity of any of the waters of the United States." In the Federal Water Power Act of 1920 (41 Stat. 1063), Congress enacted the first general law to regulate the use of navigable rivers for the generation of hydroelectric power.

FEDERAL WATER POWER ACT OF 1920

As the Supreme Court has explained (*Federal Power Commission v. Union Electric Co.* [1965]), the "central purpose of the Federal Water Power Act was to provide for the comprehensive control over those uses of the Nation's water resources in which the Federal Government had a legitimate interest; these uses included navigation, irrigation, flood control, and, very prominently, hydroelectric power—uses which, while unregulated, might well be contradictory rather than harmonious." Congress believed that the earlier Rivers and Harbors Acts were inadequate because they focused exclusively on protection of the federal interest in navigability. In contrast, the Federal Water Power Act "was the outgrowth of a widely supported effort of the conservationists to secure enactment of a complete scheme of national regulation which would promote the comprehensive development of the water resources of the Nation, in so far as it was within the reach of the federal power to do so" (*First Iowa Hydro-Electric Coop v. FPC* [1946]).

> *Congress believed that the earlier Rivers and Harbors Acts were inadequate because they focused exclusively on protection of the federal interest in navigability.*

The act created a Federal Power Commission, now called the Federal Energy Regulatory Commission, and granted it exclusive authority to license the construction and operation of hydroelectric projects on the navigable waterways of the United States. The statute authorizes the Commission:

> To issue licenses to citizens of the United States, or to any association of such citizens, or to any corporation organized under the laws of the United States or any State thereof, or to any State or municipality for the purpose of constructing, operating, and maintaining dams, water conduits, reservoirs, power houses, transmission lines, or other project works necessary or convenient for the development and improvement of navigation and for the development, transmission, and utilization of power across, along, from, or in any of the streams or other bodies of water over which Congress has jurisdiction under its authority to regulate commerce with foreign nations and among the several States, or upon any part of the public lands and reservations of the United States (including the Territories), or for the purpose of utilizing the surplus water or water power from any Government dam.

If any part of a proposed hydroelectric project would be located within the boundaries of a federal reservation (such as a national forest or Native American reservation), the commission must ensure that the project "will not interfere or be inconsistent with the purpose for which such reservation was created or acquired." In addition, if the project might affect the "navigable capacity" of the waters of the United States, the act prohibits the commission from granting a license until the plans for the project have been approved by the Army Corps of Engineers (the federal agency with principal jurisdiction over protection of navigability). The terms of new and renewed licenses are thirty to fifty years.

As the number of America's rivers being used as sources of hydroelectric power has increased, and as public values have changed over time, Congress has amended the Federal Water Power Act to broaden its original utilitarian purpose of promoting the development of hydroelectric power. The two most important amendments occurred in 1935 and 1986.

FEDERAL POWER ACT OF 1935

In the Federal Power Act of 1935 (49 Stat. 803), Congress changed the Federal Power Commission from an interdepartmental body (composed of the secretaries of the Agriculture, Interior, and War Departments) to an independent regulatory agency with five members appointed by the president and confirmed by the Senate. Congress also granted the new Federal Power Commission authority over both the interstate transmission of electricity and the sale of hydroelectric power at the wholesale level. The act requires the commission to ensure that electricity rates are "reasonable, nondiscriminatory and just to the consumer."

The Federal Power Act of 1935 also amended the criteria that the commission must apply in deciding whether to license the construction and operation of new hydroelectric facilities. In addition to evaluating the need for additional power and the capabilities of the applicant, the commission also must determine that the project "will be best adapted to a comprehensive plan for improving or developing a waterway or waterways for the use or benefit of interstate or foreign commerce, for the improvement and utilization of water-power development, and for other beneficial public uses, including recreational purposes."

ELECTRIC CONSUMERS PROTECTION ACT OF 1986

Although the Supreme Court has held that this directive to consider "other beneficial public uses" included protection of native fish populations, Congress enacted the Electric Consumers Protection Act of 1986 (ECPA) (100 Stat. 1243) to make this protection explicit. The statute also broadened the commission's authority to protect the recreational uses of the nation's rivers, fish and wildlife, and other environmental values. As amended by ECPA, the Federal Power Act now provides that, "in addition to the power and development purposes for which licenses are issued," the Federal Energy Regulatory Commission "shall give equal consideration to the purposes of energy conservation, protection, mitigation of damages to, and enhancement of, fish and wildlife (including related spawning grounds and habitat), the protection of recreational opportunities, and the preservation of other aspects of environmental quality."

FEDERAL POWER ACT TODAY

Today, there are approximately 250,000 hydroelectric projects that operate with licenses issued under the Federal Power Act. Although these facilities account for only about 10 percent of the United States' power-generating capacity, they produce more than 95 percent of the nation's renewable energy, such as solar power, wind assisted power, and power generated by flowing water. As the original fifty-year licenses for the early hydroelectric projects have expired over the past two decades, the mandate that the Federal Energy Regulatory Commission give "equal consideration" to power production and environ-

Pros and Cons of Hydroelectric Power

The United States has come to rely heavily on hydroelectric power because it is a safe, clean, reliable method of generating large amounts of energy. Water-generated power does not burn fossil fuels; in addition, reservoirs created for use by hydroelectric plans can provide recreational opportunities and serve as a steady source of water for agriculture. However, critics point out that hydropower can cause extensive environmental damage. Dams alter the natural flow of rivers, degrade water quality, and prohibit the migration of fish. Ecosystems can be damaged by flooding, and reservoirs can alter the pressure on the Earth's crust and trigger earthquakes.

As the original fifty-year licenses for the early hydroelectric projects have expired over the past two decades, the mandate that the Federal Energy Regulatory Commission give "equal consideration" to power production and environmental interests has had two important consequences.

mental interests has had two important consequences: most of the new licenses include conditions to protect fish, wildlife, water quality, and recreational uses that may be adversely affected by project operations; and a number of old projects have been decommissioned and removed because they could no longer operate profitably under the new regulatory regime. The number of decommissioned dams is close to 500.

See also: FISH AND WILDLIFE CONSERVATION ACT OF 1980; TENNESSEE VALLEY AUTHORITY ACT.

BIBLIOGRAPHY

American Rivers. *Dam Removal Success Stories.* Washington, DC: American Rivers, 1999.

Coggins, George Cameron, Charles F. Wilkinson, and John D. Leshy. *Federal Public Land and Resources Law,* 4th ed. New York: Foundation Press, 2001.

Echeverria, John, Pope Barrow, and Richard Roos-Collins. *Rivers at Risk.* Covelo, CA: Island Press, 1990.

Federal Energy Regulatory Commission. *Hydropower: The Use and Regulation of a Renewable Resource.* <http://www.ferc.gov/hydro/hydro2.htm>.

FEDERAL RESERVE ACT (1913)

Andreas Lehnert

The question of how to regulate financial affairs was one of the earliest and most enduring problems facing the American republic. Congress formally resolved the issue only in 1913 with the passage of the Federal Reserve Act (38 Stat. 251), which created, for the first time, a permanent national central bank. The product of this act, the Federal Reserve System, was in some ways an awkward compromise among all sides of the national debate, but by the end of the twentieth century, it had become one of the most respected American public institutions. The European Union would use the Federal Reserve System as a model for its own European Central Bank.

HISTORICAL DEVELOPMENT

From the founding of the republic to the Civil War, no national consensus existed on banking or monetary policy. **Agrarian** and **populist** interests were deeply suspicious of the concentration of wealth in Eastern financial institutions and sought regulations to constrain their power. At the same time, business and manufacturing interests sought regulations to ease commerce and expand trade.

After the Civil War, the political debate centered on the **gold standard**, which the United States had left in 1861. Agrarian, populist, and labor interests opposed the **deflation** required to resume the standard. Because of the massive expansion in incomes following the war, the gold standard was

agrarian: having to do with farming or farming communities and their interests

populist: someone who identifies with and believes in the rights and virtues of the common people (often as the foundation of a political philosophy)

gold standard: a monetary standard under which the basic unit of currency is equal in value to and can be exchanged for a specified amount of gold

deflation: a general decline in the prices of goods and services

resumed with relatively little pain in 1879. Nonetheless, opposition to the gold standard continued under the free silver movement, championed by William Jennings Bryan. Indeed, the novel *The Wizard of Oz* by L. Frank Baum is an extended allegory favoring free silver. In the novel, as opposed to the film, the magic slippers Dorothy uses to save herself are silver, not ruby.

The period after the Civil War was also marked by successive financial panics and crises. Banks at that time were required to hold only a fraction of their deposits in reserve, that is, in the form of **specie**, vault cash or government securities, and could lend the remaining portion of the deposits to businesses and individuals. These loans were often **illiquid**, in the sense that although they were fundamentally sound investments in the long run, in the short run they could only be converted into cash for a fraction of their value. Such a system is prone to bank runs, in which a bank's depositors literally race each other to the bank to withdraw their deposits. Following the Panic of 1907, all political parties agreed that a mechanism had to be found to supply banks with short–term liquidity (known as an "elastic currency" at the time).

specie: money in the form of coins, usually in a metal with intrinsic value, such as gold or silver

illiquid: incapable of being readily converted to cash

CONGRESSIONAL PASSAGE AND EARLY IMPLEMENTATION

Congress passed the Aldrich-Vreeland Act in 1908 in reaction to the Panic of 1907. The act provided for a system of temporary liquidity for banks (slated to expire in 1914), and it also created a National Monetary Commission chaired by Senator Nelson Aldrich to find a permanent solution to the problem of bank runs. The Aldrich Commission's report was submitted to Congress in 1912. Although Woodrow Wilson, a Democrat, won the 1912 election, the Republican Aldrich's plan shaped the extensive debate that followed. A Democrat, Carter Glass of Virginia, shepherded the Federal Reserve Act through the Congress, and on Dec. 23, 1913, Congress adopted the Federal Reserve Act, also known as the Owens-Carter Act. Although Glass went to some lengths to distinguish the Federal Reserve Act from the Aldrich Commission's plan, the two acts had quite a bit in common.

The product of this act, the Federal Reserve System, was in some ways an awkward compromise among all sides of the national debate, but by the end of the twentieth century, it had become one of the most respected American public institutions.

The Federal Reserve Act provided for the creation of between eight and twelve Reserve Banks in cities throughout the United States. These institutions were to be capitalized by the member banks within each Reserve District; the member banks would control the board of directors of each Reserve Bank and appoint its president and chairman. The entire system was to be overseen by an appointed Federal Reserve Board, based in Washington, D.C. By 1914 a full complement of twelve Federal Reserve Banks had been established in Boston, New York, Philadelphia, Cleveland, Richmond, Atlanta, Chicago, St. Louis, Minneapolis, Kansas City, Dallas, and San Francisco.

In keeping with the act's central requirement that the Federal Reserve System provide an "elastic" currency (that is, one whose quantity could grow or shrink as required by economic policy), the system required its member banks to keep a certain fraction of their assets on deposit with the Reserve Banks as Federal Funds. In addition, the system issued Federal Reserve notes, the immediate ancestors of the familiar paper banknotes used today. The founders of the system hoped to prevent further banking panics by providing their member banks with ready and

The Federal Reserve Act provided for the creation of between eight and twelve Reserve Banks in cities throughout the United States.

discount window: a lending facility available to member banks of the Federal Reserve System

ex officio: (Latin) from office, by virtue of office; powers may be exercised by an officer which are not specifically conferred upon him, but are necessarily implied in his office

The Federal Reserve System officially opened for business in November, 1914, shortly after the start of World War I.

Great Depression: the longest and most severe economic depression in American history (1929–1939); its effects were felt throughout the world

collateral: property put up by a borrower to secure a loan that could be seized if the borrower fails to pay back the debt

Because the U.S. economy had become more complex and dependent on the smooth functioning of capital markets, the damage wrought by the bank runs of the early 1930s was much greater than in previous episodes.

immediate access to liquidity via the **discount window** at which member banks could borrow at a published discount rate. Finally, as the United States was still on the gold standard in 1914, all Federal Reserve notes and deposits were backed by gold.

The Federal Reserve System's initial design, however, assured a continuing struggle between the twelve Reserve Banks and the Washington-based Federal Reserve Board. The Federal Reserve Bank of New York, in particular, had a relatively sophisticated understanding of financial markets and often advocated policies different from those pursued by the Federal Reserve Board. The tension between the Reserve Banks and the Federal Reserve Board was heightened by the fact that the Secretary of the Treasury and the Comptroller of the Currency were *ex officio* members of the Board.

The Federal Reserve System officially opened for business in November of 1914, shortly after the start of World War I. Conceived in peacetime to prevent banking panics, the system's first duty would be to manage the monetary dislocations of the period of American neutrality, and then to assist the Treasury in financing the war expenditures.

After the war, the United States was one of the first nations to resume the gold standard. Other nations attributed the relatively easy resumption of the gold standard in America to, in part, the newly–established Federal Reserve System. In the 1920s the system was held in high regard domestically and abroad. Indeed, the period is sometimes known as "the high tide of the Federal Reserve"

In October of 1929 the U.S. stock market crashed, losing a considerable fraction of its value. This probably would not have been enough to cause the **Great Depression**; however, beginning in October of 1930 a series of small Midwestern banks failed and a full-scale nationwide banking panic began. This panic was the first of three banking crises that would culminate with the long "banking holiday" of March of 1933, when the entire U.S. banking system was closed by presidential directive. The system, along with all mainstream academic and government economists, firmly believed in the "real bills doctrine," which held that providing liquidity against purely financial claims (including U.S. government bonds) was bad policy. In short, when banks came to the discount window, they were required to present as **collateral** claims against viable business interests, which they did not have. The Great Depression began, in essence, as a classic banking panic of the late 1800s. Because the U.S. economy had become more complex and dependent on the smooth functioning of capital markets, the damage wrought by the bank runs of the early 1930s was much greater than in previous episodes.

REFORMS OF THE NEW DEAL AND BEYOND

The Roosevelt legislative program contained several measures designed to address the problem of bank runs and general financial instability. Many of the key New Deal laws affected the functioning of the Federal Reserve System.

Among the first laws passed under the Roosevelt administration was the Banking Act of 1933, also known as the Glass-Steagall Act. This act provided the first nationally-guaranteed system of insuring bank deposits by creating the Federal Deposit Insurance Company (FDIC). Deposit insurance ended forever the problem of bank runs and banking panics (although it would open the door to the thrift crisis of the late 1980s). The Glass-Steagall Act contained several other provisions that have since been modified or **superannuated**, but which in their time were extremely important. These included prohibiting banks from paying interest on short-term deposits (known as "**Regulation Q**"); prohibiting banks from **underwriting** securities ("investment banking"); and prohibiting banks from engaging in many other forms of non-bank activities such as underwriting insurance.

The Banking Act of 1935 renewed and extended many of the 1933 provisions to banks outside the Federal Reserve System. However, this act is of particular note because it finally clarified several of the institutional tensions designed into the Federal Reserve System. Under the act, the Federal Reserve Board became the supreme institution; it was renamed the Board of Governors of the Federal Reserve System, and members of the Board were given the title of "Governor," the traditional title for central bankers. In addition, the act ended the *ex officio* membership of the Secretary of the Treasury and Comptroller of the Currency on the Board. Finally, the act formally recognized the Federal Open Market Committee (FOMC) as a separate legal entity.

The Employment Act of 1946 directed the Federal Reserve System to implement policies designed to balance the two goals of full employment and low inflation. Achieving these goals has been the guiding principle of the system, and indeed almost all modern central banks, since.

The final step in the modernization of the Federal Reserve System was the Treasury Accord of 1951. Before the accord, the system acted as a buyer of last resort for Treasury debt. If investors demanded interest rates on government bonds above a ceiling (set to 2.5 percent at the time of the accord) the system would step in to buy the residual debt. With government spending hitting new records during the Korean War, this support rule demanded an inflationary monetary policy. Under the terms of the accord, the Federal Reserve System was relieved of the responsibility of keeping interest rates low.

superannuated: retired or discharged because of age; obsolete; out of date

Regulation Q: a banking regulation that prohibits paying interest on short-term deposits; the scope of this regulation has narrowed over time, so that most non-commercial deposits are unaffected

underwrite: to assume financial responsibility and risk for something

The formal laws governing the conduct of monetary policy have remained largely unchanged since the 1950s.

THE MODERN FEDERAL RESERVE SYSTEM

The formal laws governing the conduct of monetary policy have remained largely unchanged since the 1950s. Monetary policy decisions are largely made by the Federal Open Market Committee (FOMC). The FOMC is a separately-recognized legal entity made up of the seven Governors in Washington, D.C., the president of the Federal Reserve Bank of New York, and the presidents of four of the remaining eleven Reserve Banks (chosen on a rotating basis). It typically meets eight times a year. The FOMC dictates the conduct of **open market operations**, the technical means by which the Federal Reserve System affects short term interest rates.

The Full Employment and Balanced Growth Act of 1978, also known as the Humphrey-Hawkins Act, amended the Federal Reserve Act to require that the Board of Governors submit reports on the state of the U.S. economy and the conduct of monetary policy twice a year (typically in February and July). In addition, the chairman typically testifies before the relevant House and Senate Committees as part of the report. This appearance, referred to as the Humphrey-Hawkins testimony, has become a closely-watched event.

open market operations: purchases and sales of government securities by the Federal Reserve Bank, designed to control the money supply and short-term interest rates

Several of the financial regulatory reforms of the 1980s and 1990s involved the Federal Reserve System to some extent, either in its role as a bank regulator or by amending the Federal Reserve Act directly. The most important of these include the Depository Institutions Deregulation and Monetary Control Act of 1980, the Financial Institutions Reform, Recovery, and Enforcement Act of 1989, and the Gramm-Leach-Bliley Act.

Finally, several consumer protection and anti-discrimination laws also involve the Federal Reserve System. Among of the most important of these are the Home Mortgage Disclosure Act of 1975 and the Community Reinvestment Act of 1977.

See also: BANK THE OF UNITED STATES, BLAND-ALLISON ACT; COINAGE ACT OF 1792; COINAGE ACTS; GLASS-STEAGALL ACT; GOLD RESERVEE ACT OF 1934; GOLD STANDARD ACT OF 1900.

An employee of the Federal Reserve Bank in New York inspects gold bricks in the bank's vault in January 1965. (© AP/WIDE WORLD PHOTOS)

BIBLIOGRAPHY

Board of Governors of the Federal Reserve System. *Federal Reserve Act and Other Statutory Provisions Affecting the Federal Reserve System (As Amended Through October 1998)*. Washington, DC, 1998.

Federal Reserve Bank of Kansas City. *Fed 101*. <http://www.kc.frb.org/fed101/>.

Federal Reserve Bank of Richmond. *The Fiftieth Anniversary of the Treasury–Federal Reserve Accord*. 2001. <http://www.rich.frb.org/research/specialtopics/treasury/>.

Friedman, M. and A. J. Schwartz. *A Monetary History of the United States, 1867-1960*. Princeton, NJ: Princeton University Press, 1963.

Friedman, M. and A. J. Schwartz. *Monetary Trends in the United States and the United Kingdom*. Chicago: University of Chicago Press, 1982.

Hamilton, J. D. "The daily market for Federal Funds." 1 *Journal of Political Economy* 104 (1996): 26–56.

Rockoff, H. "'The Wizard of Oz' as a Monetary Allegory." 4 *Journal of Political Economy* 98 (1990): 739–760.

FEDERAL TORT CLAIMS ACT (1946)

William V. Luneburg

Excerpt from the Federal Tort Claims Act

The United States shall be liable, respecting the provisions of this title relating to tort claims, in the same manner and to the same extent as a private individual under like circumstances, but shall not be liable for interest prior to judgment or for punitive damages.

For centuries, the law has provided for compensation to individuals injured physically or otherwise by the actions of other private persons, including artificial "persons" such as corporations whose employees cause the harm. Significant parts of this liability fall within what is known as the law of torts. However, when the personal injuries are inflicted by the government through the actions of its employees, the ordinary rules of compensation do not apply unless the government takes special action to allow itself to be held liable. With regard to the federal government in particular, it is, as a general matter, immune from all liability under the law unless Congress consents to suit. This is the doctrine of sovereign immunity. As to the United States, the doctrine is not created by the Constitution itself but, rather, recognized by the federal courts in cases decided during the nineteenth century whose rationales have been criticized by various legal commentators. One of the conceptual underpinnings of the doctrine is that there can be no legal right against the authority that makes the law on which the right depends (*Kawananakoa v. Polyblack* [1907]).

> *When personal injuries are inflicted by the government through the actions of its employees, the ordinary rules of compensation do not apply unless the government takes special action to allow itself to be held liable.*

The significance of allowing the United States government to be immune from suit can be fully appreciated only when it is realized that it employs millions of people to do its work, and that work is, more often than not, very similar, if not identical, to that which gives rise to tort liability of private persons. For example, federal employees routinely drive government-owned vehicles as part of their daily routine and, not surprisingly, are involved in automobile accidents. The federal government runs hundreds of hospitals and medical clinics that serve veterans and others; mistakes in treatment are no less common there than in private medical practices against which medical malpractice suits are common. And this is just the tip of the proverbial "iceberg." Of course, the potential magnitude of the government's legal liability can be—and has been—seen as a reason to urge for restricting the government's ability to be sued for compensation.

Given sovereign immunity, the traditional means for affording compensation to persons injured by the federal government was not a suit in court but rather, a so-called private bill enacted by both houses of Congress and signed by the president (as in the case of other legislation). Indeed, the first private bill providing redress for a tort claim was enacted as long ago as 1792. However, the mounting volume of these bills during the nineteenth century, the burdens on Congress in considering them, the perceived capriciousness of the process for their introduction and enactment, and the unfairness of leaving persons without any compensation for serious injuries provoked Presidents Fillmore and Lincoln, among others, to suggest that some type of **adjudicatory** process outside Congress was required to deal adequately with the claims presented.

> *The first private bill providing redress for a tort claim was enacted as long ago as 1792.*

adjudicatory: having to do with the process of settling something judicially

In 1855, and then in 1887, with the enactment of the Tucker Act, Congress waived the sovereign immunity of the United States with regard to monetary claims other than tort claims (e.g., claims based on contracts with the government). As time went on, Congress enacted various limited **waivers of immunity** with regard to tort liability, as in connection with the federal operation of railroads during World War I and the operation of government maritime vessels. Those limited provisions for liability were part of a thirty-year debate on the need for a more comprehensive waiver of immunity from suit with regard to the torts committed by federal employees.

waivers of immunity: legal statement that gives up the government's right to sovereign immunity (the doctrine that the government cannot be sued without its consent)

With the number of private bills being introduced each year in Congress growing into the thousands, and the majority of tort claimants being left without any remedy, resistance to change in the law weakened significantly. After an army bomber flew into the Empire State Building on a misty Saturday morning in July 1945, killing or injuring a number of people who found, to their dismay, that the most obvious party to sue (the United States) was immune from liability, whatever was left of the argument in favor of general United States immunity from suit for the **tortuous** acts of its employees rapidly dissipated. One year later, the Federal Tort Claims Act (FTCA) (P.L. 79-601, 60 Stat. 842) became law, and the victims of the Empire State Building crash were among the first to bring suit under the new statute.

tortuous: legal unlawful conduct that subjects a person to tort liability

PROVISIONS OF THE FEDERAL TORT CLAIMS ACT

The FTCA grants exclusive jurisdiction to the federal courts to dispose of claims by individuals and corporations against the United States where the lawsuits seek compensation ("money damages") "for injury or loss of property, or personal injury or death caused by the negligent or wrongful act or omission of any employee" of the United States where that employee acted in performance of his or her governmental duties *if* the same action resulting in injury would impose liability on a private individual under state law in similar circumstances.

There is a deceptive simplicity with regard to this statement of a general waiver of immunity from suit for tort claims, as is demonstrated by the numerous decisions issued by the Supreme Court and other federal courts attempting to interpret and apply the FTCA over the past sixty years. For example, can the United States be liable without a showing of "fault" (e.g., negligence)? (No.) When can it be said that a governmental employee inflicted injury in the course of the employee's duties (e.g., the car accident occurred on the way from the employee's lunch to his or her duty station)? Do there exist unique governmental functions (e.g., running a lighthouse where the light goes out causing a shipwreck) as to which Congress intended to preserve immunity? (Perhaps, but the Supreme Court has not yet identified them.) And, finally, if the wrongful act takes place in one state and the injury in another and the laws of each state are different, what law applies? (The FTCA is itself clear only in requiring that "state law" must apply.)

One issue that the FTCA, as originally enacted, did not address was the liability of the federal employee to the injured person.

One issue that the FTCA, as originally enacted, did not address was the liability of the federal employee to the injured person. Both before and after 1946, the law was clear that federal employees could themselves be liable to the injured person under state law in some circumstances. However, one of the potential costs of such liability is that federal employees become unduly timid in doing their jobs to avoid lawsuits and, as a result, the public interest suffers. Congress dealt squarely with this problem in the Federal Employees Liability Reform and Tort Compensation Act of 1988, commonly known as the Westfall Act after the Supreme Court case that it overruled. Today, when a federal employee is sued to collect money damages for an action performed within the scope of his or her employment, the United States is substituted as the defendant and the employee is excused from the case without the potential for any personal liability. This substitution is not available, however, if the employee's action violated the United States Constitution in circumstances where the courts allow a damage remedy against the employee for that violation.

EXCEPTIONS TO FEDERAL TORT CLAIM LIABILITY

If all of this is not complicated enough, Congress has enacted numerous exceptions to FTCA liability, and the Supreme Court itself has created an important one. The same rationale cannot be offered to support each and every exception. A few of these exceptions should be noted here.

Many torts involving the intentional conduct of federal employees (like assault and battery) cannot be the basis for United States liability under the FTCA. In such cases, it might be argued that it is unfair to penalize the government where the employee is more directly at fault. Nevertheless, there is a category of intentional torts for which the United States can be held liable, including those attributable to the actions of a federal investigative or law enforcement officer.

Not surprisingly, claims arising out of combatant activities in time of war (e.g., one serviceman shoots another by mistake during battle) are excluded.

Claims arising out of combatant activities in time of war (e.g., one serviceman shoots another by mistake during battle) are excluded.

Although the FTCA has not removed all of the inequities imposed by the doctrine of sovereign immunity, as a general matter, it goes a long way toward ensuring that the government itself is not above the law.

Another exception of immense importance encompasses actions of federal employees that are considered to involve a "discretionary function." The Supreme Court has struggled, with mixed success since 1953 (*Dalehite v. United States*) in trying to impose limits on this exception to prevent it from almost entirely swallowing tort liability (since almost every action of a government official involves some discretion, i.e. choice) while, at the same time, protecting governmental functions that Congress probably did not want to affect by the imposition of tort liability (e.g., making important policy decisions).

Finally, the Supreme Court itself has created an exception to FTCA liability: U.S. service personnel injured "incident to service" cannot sue the United States in tort (*Feres v. United States* [1950]). While the rationales offered for this exception have varied over the years, the one most prominently invoked today is an alleged concern for the effect of liability on military discipline.

In order to encourage the administrative resolution of tort claims arising under the FTCA and to avoid costs imposed by litigation, the injured person must first present his or her claim to the federal agency whose employee allegedly caused the injury. Only after waiting a designated period or obtaining a denial of the claim from the agency (whichever first occurs) can the claimant resort to federal court in a suit against the United States under the FTCA.

Although the FTCA obviously has not removed all of the inequities imposed by the doctrine of sovereign immunity, as a general matter, it goes a long way toward ensuring that the government itself is not above the law.

See also: ADMINISTRATIVE PROCEDURE ACT; FEDERAL EMPLOYERS' LIABILITY ACT.

BIBLIOGRAPHY

"Developments in the Law—Remedies against the United States and Its Officials." *Harvard Law Review* 70 (1957): 827–938.

Jaffe, Louis. "Suits against Governments and Officers: Sovereign Immunity." *Harvard Law Review* 77 (1963): 1–39.

Jayson, Lester S. *Handling Federal Tort Claims: Administrative and Judicial Remedies.* Albany, NY: Matthew Bender, 1964.

Lester, Urban A., and Michael F. Noone, eds., "The Federal Tort Claims Act." *Litigation with the Federal Government,* 3d ed. Philadelphia, PA: American Law Institute–American Bar Association, 1994.

Wright, William B. *The Federal Tort Claims Act Analyzed and Annotated.* New York: Central Book Co., 1957.

INTERNET RESOURCE

U.S. Department of Justice Home Page. <http://www.usdoj.gov/>.

FEDERAL TRADE COMMISSION ACT (1914)

Herbert Hovenkamp

The Federal Trade Commission Act (38 Stat. 717) was originally passed in 1914 with President Woodrow Wilson's enthusiastic support. In its current form, the act states that "unfair methods of competition ... and unfair or deceptive acts or practices in or affecting commerce, are hereby declared unlawful." The statute created a new government agency, the Federal Trade Commission (FTC), a five-member board with broad authority to regulate unfair and deceptive business practices. No more than three of the FTC members can be from the same political party, and they are appointed for overlapping seven-year terms. This was intended to limit the amount of control that any particular president and his political party have over the FTC.

> *The statute created a new government agency, the Federal Trade Commission (FTC), a five-member board with broad authority to regulate unfair and deceptive business practices.*

SUPPORT FOR THE FTC AND OTHER COMMISSIONS

Many political groups supported the creation of the commission. First, Progressive Party members believed that the courts were too conservative about condemning anticompetitive practices and tended to side with big business. Further, court processes were cumbersome and took a long time. Often, many years went by from the filing of a complaint until a final decision. By contrast, an administrative agency was not obligated to follow strict rules of evidence and did not have to use juries. The commissioners themselves could listen to evidence and then issue "cease and desist" orders telling firms that certain practices must be stopped. Even businesses largely supported the FTC because of cumbersome court procedures and the inconsistent results of jury trials in many different courts. Many businesses believed that a single commission could clarify and give them advance notice of the kinds of practices that were unfair.

The Federal Trade Commission Act was part of a broad-based movement in the late nineteenth and early twentieth centuries to use commissions rather than courts to regulate various forms of business conduct. Commissions were regarded both as more streamlined in their decision-making process and also as more specialized. However, early in its history the FTC was hampered by a conservative Supreme Court that was highly suspicious of regulatory agencies and limited their power.

> *The Federal Trade Commission Act was part of a broad-based movement in the late nineteenth and early twentieth centuries to use commissions rather than courts to regulate various forms of business conduct.*

Several commissions were set up as part of this movement:

- The Interstate Commerce Commission supervised railroads and other public transportation and cargo carriers.
- The Securities Exchange Commission regulated corporate stocks and bonds.
- The Civil Aeronautics Board regulated interstate air traffic.
- The Federal Power Commission (now called the Federal Energy Regulatory Commission) regulated the provision of electric power.
- The Food and Drug Administration regulated medicines, pharmaceuticals, foods, and a few related products such as cosmetics.

The FTC eventually was divided into two bureaus, or branches. The Competition Bureau was intended to enforce that part of the law dealing with "unfair methods of competition." The Consumer Protection Bureau was intended to enforce that part of the law condemning "unfair or deceptive acts or practices." Each bureau has broad power to define the business practices that violate the statute. However, the power is not unlimited. If the commission decides to condemn a certain practice, it ordinarily issues a "cease and desist" order, telling the company that it must stop that practice. The company can either agree or appeal the FTC's order to a court. If the court agrees with the FTC, it will "enforce" the order. If it disagrees it will "vacate" the order and either let the company off entirely or else send the case back to the FTC so that the FTC can consider other issues it may have overlooked.

COMPETITION

When the FTC's Bureau of Competition is enforcing the law against "unfair methods of competition," its power overlaps extensively with the power of the Department of Justice to enforce the **antitrust** laws. The FTC has the power to enforce the Clayton Act directly, but its power over offenses covered by the Sherman Act is even broader. The Supreme Court held in *FTC v. Brown Shoe Co.* (1966) that the phrase "unfair methods of competition" includes everything that the Sherman Act includes plus some additional practices that might not violate the Sherman Act.

One example of this broader power is part of the law of price fixing. The Sherman Act, which prohibits contracts, combinations, and conspiracies "in restraint of trade," condemns price fixing by cartels (groups of businesses that try to limit competition). But under the terms of the Sherman Act, this price fixing must be done by *agreement* for the practice to be considered illegal. Economists know, however, that there are some markets called "oligopolies" in which firms can achieve cartel-like results without ever agreeing with each other. For example, if there are four gasoline stations on a busy intersection, each one of them can see what the other ones are charging for gas. If one station puts up its price in the morning, each of the others can match the price, acting entirely on its own. The four stations may effectively *fix* the price at a higher level without ever formally agreeing with each other to do anything. Although this would not be a Sherman Act violation, the FTC has taken the position since the 1940s that it could be an "unfair method of competition" under the Federal Trade Commission Act (*Triangle Conduit and Cable Co. v. FTC* [1948]). Since the early 1980s, however, the courts have cut back the FTC's power to condemn oligopoly pricing unless there is a fairly explicit agreement among the parties.

The FTC also enforces the Clayton Act provision against anticompetitive mergers. In general, when the FTC enforces the merger laws the standards are the same as when the Justice Department enforces the Clayton Act. As a result, we have one set of merger standards for most firms. In general, the merger laws come into play when a merger either creates a monopoly or makes it more likely that the firms will engage in price-fixing or oligopoly behavior. If a market contains several dozen firms of roughly the same size, then price fixing is unlikely. The concern for possible price fixing gets stronger as the number of firms in the market falls below seven or eight. This is because price-

antitrust: laws protecting commerce and trade from monopolistic restraints on competition

In general, the merger laws come into play when a merger either creates a monopoly or makes it more likely that the firms will engage in price-fixing or oligopoly behavior.

fixing agreements tend to work better when the number of participants in the agreement is fairly small.

CONSUMER PROTECTION

The Bureau of Consumer Protection in the FTC is concerned with deceptive practices. One division of this Bureau is concerned with false and misleading advertising. Another is concerned with misleading credit practices by lenders. The FTC has also established rules regarding how car dealers must report features such as the miles that a used car has been driven or its gasoline mileage. Increasingly the FTC has become involved in enforcement against fraudulent practices by telemarketers as well as practices by sellers over the Internet, including complaints about spam, or unsolicited e-mails.

In this 1934 cartoon, monopolies block the "highway of competition," creating a barrier to small business. The Federal Trade Commission has fallen by the wayside—it is criticized here as "an idle threat." (© MICHAEL J. SANDERS/USAF/GETTY IMAGES)

Do Not Call

In 2003 the Federal Trade Commission (FTC) instituted a National Do Not Call Registry that allowed citizens to register their phone numbers in order to cut down on the number of telemarketing calls they received. Political organizations, charities, and telephone surveyors were still allowed to call. Organizations with whom the citizen had an established business relationship were allowed to call for up to eighteen months after the most recent transaction. The FTC was scheduled to begin enforcing the Do Not Call Registry on October 1, 2003.

The FTC also has always paid very close attention to health claims, particularly for products that are said to be "miracle" drugs or to cause dramatic weight loss.

EFFECTIVENESS

The FTC has made many hundreds of rules governing many aspects of business behavior. Some of the rules are very complicated, but others are quite simple. Here are two examples, the first concerning advertising and the second concerning product warranties:

> Advertising must tell the truth and not mislead consumers. A claim can be misleading if relevant information is left out or if the claim implies something that's not true. For example, a lease advertisement for an automobile that promotes "$0 Down" may be misleading if significant and undisclosed charges are due at lease signing.

> If your ad uses phrases like "satisfaction guaranteed" or "money-back guarantee," you must be willing to give full refunds for any reason. You also must tell the consumer the terms of the offer.

These rules, simple and straightforward, have protected the average consumer from unfair business practices for decades. Although the FTC is a large government agency, it encourages consumers to file complaints when they believe they have been the victim of a false or misleading claim. The FTC actively maintains a web site for this purpose.

See also: Clayton Act; Sherman Antitrust Act.

BIBLIOGRAPHY

Chamberlain, John. *The Enterprising Americans: A Business History of the United States*. New York: Harper and Row, 1974.

Faulkner, Harold U. *American Economic History*. New York: Harper, 1960.

Hovenkamp, Herbert. *Federal Antitrust Policy: The Law of Competition and Its Practice,* 2d ed. St. Paul, MN: West Group, 1999.

Sklar, Martin J. *The Corporate Reconstruction of American Capitalism, 1890–1916*. Cambridge, U.K.: Cambridge University Press, 1988.

INTERNET RESOURCE

Federal Trade Commission. <http://www.ftc.gov>.

FEDERAL UNEMPLOYMENT TAX ACT (1939)

Ellen P. Aprill

Great Depression: the longest and most severe economic depression in American history (1929–1939); its effects were felt throughout the world

The Federal Unemployment Tax Act (FUTA) (P.L. 76-379) emerged from the country's experience during the **Great Depression**. By 1932, 25 percent of the workers in the United States were unemployed. In his presidential message of June 8, 1934, President Franklin D. Roosevelt declared that the American people wanted "some safeguard against misfortunes which cannot be wholly eliminated in this man-made world of ours." In the summer of 1934, President Roosevelt created the Committee on Economic Security to draft legislation that would help alleviate the pain of the Great Depression and prepare for future economic downturns.

Members of the committee gave the highest priority to the establishment of some form of unemployment insurance. They believed that involuntarily unemployed workers had earned the right to a temporary and partial wage replacement. A wage replacement program would not only prevent the need for welfare relief but also maintain workers' purchasing power and thus stabilize and stimulate the economy during recessions. Sections of the Social Security Act of 1935 created such a program, and the Federal Unemployment Tax Act of 1939 established the framework for a joint state and federal scheme of unemployment insurance as set out in the 1935 act.

In the summer of 1934, President Roosevelt created the Committee on Economic Security to draft legislation that would help alleviate the pain of the Great Depression and prepare for future economic downturns.

FEATURES OF THE ACT

FUTA applies a uniform nationwide tax to "employers" on certain "wages" paid to individuals with respect to "employment." Since the time of enactment, the definition of these terms has excluded large numbers of agricultural and domestic workers from coverage. As originally enacted, FUTA applied only to employers of eight or more. It now applies to employers that pay at least $1,500 in wages in any calendar quarter or who have at least one employee on any given day in each of twenty different calendar weeks.

Both as originally enacted and under current law, FUTA provides that, if a state has a state unemployment law that satisfies certain requirements, an employer can claim a 90 percent credit against the federal tax otherwise due for contributions to the state fund. The federal government also makes grants to the state for the administrative costs of any qualifying program. For employers to be eligible for the credit and for states to qualify for federal money to cover administrative costs, federal law requires that (1) the money from any state funds go to a central fund controlled by the federal government, (2) money from the fund be spent only on unemployment compensation, (3) a state account for how it spends the money, and (4) the state provide certain due process procedures in administration of the fund. All fifty states, the District of Columbia, Puerto Rico, and the Virgin Islands have unemployment programs satisfying these requirements.

THE FEDERAL-STATE SYSTEM

Subject to the relatively minimal federal requirements, states have had wide discretion in their unemployment compensation laws. Each state determines its own rate of compensation, waiting periods before compensation is made available to the unemployed worker, and the maximum duration of the benefits. States vary widely in the benefits they provide. Typically, state programs provide up to twenty-six weeks of benefits and replace on average 38 percent of a worker's immediate previous wages. State eligibility generally depends on amounts of earnings from recent

Subject to the relatively minimal federal requirements, states have had wide discretion in their unemployment compensation laws.

employment as well as the worker's demonstrated ability and willingness to seek and accept suitable employment.

At the time FUTA was enacted, proponents of unemployment insurance believed that a nationwide system was necessary. Without a nationwide system, they argued, no state would enact an unemployment scheme because each state feared competition with states that did not impose such a burden on employers. Although some proponents argued that the federal government should set the level and duration of unemployment benefits, the program as enacted involved both state and federal control. This joint control was designed to enable the plan both to pass Congress and to withstand constitutional scrutiny. In two 1937 cases involving five-to-four votes, *Steward Machine Co. v. Davis* and *Carmichael v. Southern Coal & Coke Co.*, the Supreme Court upheld the joint federal-state unemployment system. The Court rejected the argument that federal inducement for state participation through the 90 percent credit coerced states in violation of the constitutional guarantee of state autonomy.

CHANGES TO THE ACT

Congress has made various changes to the unemployment system since its enactment. In addition to the basic federal-state benefit, the current system of unemployment compensation includes an extended benefits program, funded half by the federal government and half by state governments. The extended benefit program, which was first enacted in 1970 and revised substantially in 1981, provides additional weeks of benefits to jobless workers in particular states where unemployment has worsened dramatically. Moreover, in times of national recession, the federal government has historically provided funding for additional weeks of benefits in every state. For example, the federal government did so in March 2002 under a program called Temporary Emergency Unemployment Compensation. Such additional weeks of benefits are financed entirely by funds from the federal unemployment tax, without contribution from state funds. Federal funds are also available to make loans to insolvent state unemployment funds. Under the Reed Act of 1954, transfers are made to state unemployment funds when the federal unemployment fund balance reaches a certain high level. Since 1986 unemployment benefits have been subject in full to federal income tax.

In addition to the basic federal-state benefit, the current system of unemployment compensation includes an extended benefits program, funded half by the federal government and half by state governments.

Congress has from time to time adjusted both the tax rate and amount of wages subject to FUTA taxes. The taxable wage base was set at $3,000 in 1939, raised to $4,200 in 1972, $6000 in 1978, and $7,000 in 1983. The effective tax rate (after credit for state unemployment taxes) began at 0.3 percent in 1939 and was raised to 0.8 percent in 1983. This 0.8 percent rate includes a surtax of 0.2 percent enacted by Congress in 1976. The surtax, extended several times, was extended through 2007 by the Taxpayer Relief Act of 1997. Further changes can be expected.

See also: SOCIAL SECURITY ACT OF 1935.

BIBLIOGRAPHY

Jannsson, B. *The Recluctant Welfare State: American Social Welfare Policies: Past, Present, and Future,* 4th Ed. Cambria, CA: Wadsworth Thomson Learning, 2000.

INTERNET RESOURCES

Cornell University Law School. <http://www.law.cornell.edu/topics/unemployment
compensation.html>.

U.S. Department of Labor, Employment and Training Administration. <http://workforce
security.doleta.gov/uitaxtopic.asp>.

University of Texas at Dallas. <http://www.utdallas.edu/~jargo/green2000/Section_
4.pdf>.

FEDERAL WATER POLLUTION CONTROL ACT (1948)

Ann Powers

Excerpt from the Federal Water Pollution Control Act

[I]n consequence of the benefits resulting to the public health and welfare by the abatement of stream pollution, it is ... the policy of Congress to recognize, preserve, and protect the primary responsibilities and rights of the States in controlling water pollution, to support and aid technical research to devise and perfect methods of treatment of industrial wastes which are not susceptible to known effective methods of treatment, and to provide Federal technical services to State and interstate agencies and to industries, and financial aid to State and interstate agencies and to municipalities, in the formulation and execution of their stream pollution abatement programs.

The Federal Water Pollution Control Act (FWPCA) (P.L. 80-845, 62 Stat. 1155) of 1948 was the first major law enacted by Congress to address the problems of water pollution in the United States. Legislators had made numerous attempts, totaling over 100 bills, to pass legislation over the previous half century, but without success. By 1948 industrial and urban growth fueled by World War II had led to obvious, and often notorious, pollution of the country's rivers, streams, and lakes, impelling Congress finally to confront the issue. Unfortunately, the act was not well designed and achieved little. It did not generally prohibit pollution, gave only limited authority to the federal government, and provided an extremely cumbersome enforcement mechanism. In 1972 Congress totally rewrote the act to provide adequate protection for the nation's waters.

WATER POLLUTION CONTROL PRIOR TO THE ACT

Before 1948 various minor laws dealt with aspects of water pollution. The only notable one was the Refuse Act, actually a section of the Rivers and Harbors Appropriations Act of 1899. The Refuse Act was not aimed at preventing water pollution but rather at preventing the dumping of materials that might impede navigation. In the five decades following the Refuse Act, waterways continued to be used as a convenient place to dispose of waste. Indeed, waste disposal was seen as a legitimate use of these waters. As a result, sub-

A fish killed by water pollution, photograph taken by the Environmental Protection Agency, 1972. (US NATIONAL ARCHIVES AND RECORDS ADMINISTRATION)

stantially more pollutants were being discharged into the nation's waters at a greater rate than the waters could absorb. In the years just prior to World War II, states and municipalities took some steps to deal with water pollution, but the pressure of war production essentially put those efforts on hold.

In the postwar period, attention again turned to the country's polluted waters. It was reported in 1945 that over 3,500 communities pumped 2.5 billion tons of raw sewage into streams, lakes, and coastal waters every day. The Surgeon General warned that, as a consequence, over half of the U.S. population relied on drinking water supplies of doubtful purity. In a report that eventually accompanied the 1948 legislation, the Senate Committee on

Public Works declared that "pollution of our water resources by domestic and industrial wastes has become an increasingly serious problem due to the rapid growth of our cities and industries.... Polluted waters menace the public health (through contamination of water and food supplies), destroy fish and game life, and rob us of other benefits of our natural resources" (House Report no. 1829, to accompany Senate Bill 418, 80th Congress, 2d session, April 28, 1948).

It was reported in 1945 that over 3,500 communities pumped 2.5 billion tons of raw sewage into streams, lakes, and coastal waters every day.

Nevertheless, it was difficult to gain political support for a water pollution proposal. Legislators generally considered the control of water bodies a responsibility of the states and viewed federal regulation with suspicion. Still, some conservationists and public officials recognized the need for action at the federal level. After years of failed bills, the 80th Congress in 1948 achieved a legislative compromise with the support of President Harry S. Truman.

LEGISLATIVE DEBATE

Although there was general consensus on the need to clean up polluted water, there was strong disagreement on the extent of waters to be covered, the rights of the states, and the role of the federal government. Some legislators envisioned extending protection not only to interstate waters (waters that came in contact with more than one state), but also to intrastate waters (rivers and tributaries within individual states) that might contribute pollution to interstate waters. They urged that both intra- and interstate waters be protected by a strong federal program with substantial enforcement authorities.

Although there was general consensus on the need to clean up polluted water, there was strong disagreement on the extent of waters to be covered, the rights of the states, and the role of the federal government.

However, the final bill that reached the House floor at the end of the legislative session, under a gag rule permitting no amendments, was far weaker. The legislation applied only to interstate waters, eliminating from protection under the act heavily polluted waters that were wholly contained within one state, and it restricted the role of the federal government. These weaknesses led

The Cuyahoga River Fire

On June 22, 1969, an oil slick on the Cuyahoga River, just southeast of downtown Cleveland, caught fire. By the time the fire was extinguished, twenty minutes later, severe damage had been done to two railroad trestles. The cause of the fire was not determined, but an investigation noted that the "highly volatile petroleum derivatives" on the water could have been ignited by sparks from a passing train. The Cuyahoga had seen other fires, including one in 1936 and a fire in 1952 that caused thirty times as much damage as the 1969 fire—in fact, the police chief, William E. Barry, said of the 1969 blaze, "It was strictly a run-of-the-mill-fire." But the 1969 fire caught the attention of the national press, lead by *Time* magazine, which reported: "Some river! Chocolate- brown, oily, bubbling with subsurface gases, it oozes rather than flows. 'Anyone who falls into the Cuyahoga does not drown,' Cleveland's citizens joke grimly. 'He decays'." The resulting publicity was a significant factor in the passage of important environmental legislation, including the Clean Water Act, and the creation of state and national Environmental Protection Agencies. Today, the Cuyahoga has gone from a complete lack of life forms (not even slugs or leeches could be found in it), to boasting twenty-seven species of fish, including bass and bluegill. The Cleveland riverfront has also been revitalized with bars, restaurants, and riverboats. Still, the Cuyahoga is considered a "recovering system," and officials warn swimmers to stay away. Cleanup continues.

Water pollution. Discharge and refuse from the pictured ship floats near a Navy pier.
(US National Archives and Records Administration)

members of Congress who had worked long and hard on a water protection bill to speak and vote against the legislation. Nevertheless, many proponents of broader legislation felt that a weak bill was better than no bill at all. The bill passed the House of Representatives by a vote of 138 to 14.

PROVISIONS OF THE ACT

Congress declared that the act's purpose was "to provide a comprehensive program for preventing, **abating**, and controlling water pollution," and that it

abate: to reduce in amount; put an end to; make void or annul

was congressional policy "to recognize, preserve, and protect the primary responsibilities and rights of the States in controlling water pollution." The act gave individual states most of the responsibility for abating water pollution and encouraged interstate agreements. In addition to preserving states' control of their waterways, the act limited federal authority for the most part to preparing pollution abatement plans and providing support to the states. It established federal technical services and grants to state and interstate government bodies. The law did not specifically prohibit polluting activities, set standards, or limit new sources of pollution.

Although the act did declare pollution of interstate waters a public nuisance subject to abatement, this applied only when water pollution endangered "the health or welfare of persons in a State other than that in which the discharge originates." When this situation occurred, the Surgeon General of the United States was authorized to bring an abatement action, but only after a cumbersome process and with the permission of the state where the pollution originated. This provision gave the states virtually unlimited power to override a federal action to prevent water pollution. Not surprisingly, in the following twenty years there were essentially no enforcement actions filed under the act.

WATER POLLUTION CONTROL AFTER THE ACT

The Federal Water Pollution Control Act was not effective in preventing and abating water pollution. Because of the federal government's inability to require any direct reduction in discharges, pollution continued to increase and the quality of the nation's waters did not significantly improve. However, the act demonstrated both popular and political support for pollution control efforts. It also established the basic framework for water pollution control, which Congress subsequently amended. Congress changed the act six times before completely rewriting it in the 1972 Federal Water Pollution Control Act Amendments. Today the statute is commonly known as the Clean Water Act and bears little resemblance to its 1948 ancestor.

Because of the federal government's inability to require any direct reduction in discharges, pollution continued to increase and the quality of the nation's waters did not significantly improve.

See also: FISH AND WILDLIFE CONSERVATION ACT OF 1980; NATIONAL ENVIRONMENTAL POLICY ACT; SAFE DRINKING WATER ACT.

BIBLIOGRAPHY

Barry, Frank J. "The Evolution of the Enforcement Provisions of the Federal Water Pollution Control Act: A Study of the Difficulty in Developing Effective Legislation." 68 *Michigan Law Review* 1103 (1969–70).

Clean Water Deskbook. Washington, DC: Environmental Law Institute, 1988.

Rodgers, William H., Jr. *Environmental Law.* St. Paul, MN: West Publishing, 1992.

FIRST AND SECOND CONFISCATION ACTS
(1861, 1862)

Daniel W. Hamilton

In the first summer of the Civil War, Abraham Lincoln called the thirty-seventh Congress into special session on July 4, 1861. On August 6, the last day of this short first session, Congress passed and Lincoln signed the First Confiscation Act. This law authorized the federal government to seize the property of all those participating directly in rebellion. Enacted in the wake of the first battle of Bull Run, this hurriedly passed law did not break much new ground. It was essentially a restatement of internationally recognized laws of war and authorized the seizure of any property, including slave property, used by the Confederacy to directly aid the war effort.

This First Confiscation Act authorized the federal government to seize the property of all those participating directly in rebellion.

When the second session of the Thirty-seventh Congress convened in December 1861, public pressure was mounting in the North for another, more vigorous confiscation bill. Senator Lyman Trumbull, a Republican from Illinois and the chairman of the Judiciary Committee, quickly emerged as the most important figure on confiscation. On December 2, 1861, Trumbull took the floor to introduce a new confiscation bill. This bill envisioned the seizure of all rebel property, whether used directly to support the war, or owned by a rebel a thousand miles away from any battlefield.

After several months of debate, Congress came to a stalemate over the confiscation of rebel property. This paralysis was not the result of incompetence, or because confiscation was considered relatively unimportant; it was instead an issue of ideological differences debated by a country in the midst of war. The debate, to the surprise and ultimate frustration of the legislators themselves, reflected deep-seated, nearly intractable divisions over the social role of property and the extent of sovereign power over property in American law and the Constitution.

Within a few weeks of the introduction of Trumbull's bill, different ideological coalitions emerged. Trumbull took the lead of a group of radicals sponsoring a vigorous confiscation bill, joined by Charles Sumner of Massachusetts and Benjamin Wade of Ohio in the Senate and George Julian of Indiana in the House. To their amazement these confiscation radicals soon faced bitter opposition both from outside and from within their own Republican Party. A group of conservatives soon began to condemn the radical bill as a violation of the Fifth Amendment and the Constitution's prohibition of bills of attainder. Republican senator Orville Browning of Illinois, a powerful friend of President Lincoln, led these conservatives in condemning the radical confiscation plan. As winter turned to spring and spring to summer, Congress argued endlessly over confiscation. Was property confiscation a legitimate power of the national legislature? Was confiscation in violation of the Constitution? Were slaves a type of property subject to confiscation? These basic questions drew intense scrutiny and the congressional debates were remarkable for their sustained

Congressional debate, to the surprise and ultimate frustration of the legislators themselves, reflected deep-seated, nearly intractable divisions over the social role of property and the extent of sovereign power over property in American law and the Constitution.

consideration, in the midst of war, of the power of government and the rights of property.

Between these two warring camps, a group of confiscation moderates brokered a compromise bill that, unfortunately, proved mostly unworkable. These moderates were led by John Sherman of Ohio, Daniel Clark of New Hampshire, and Henry Wilson of Massachusetts in the Senate, and Republican Thomas Eliot of Massachusetts in the House. The moderates sent Trumbull's bill to a select committee, where they reworked it into a much less radical bill providing a much greater role for the judiciary than the radicals wanted. On July 17, President Lincoln signed the Second Confiscation Act into law, after first insisting that Congress pass an "explanatory resolution" to the act. This resolution reflected President Lincoln's concern that permanent property confiscation was a "corruption of blood" prohibited by the Constitution and provided that property seized from individual offenders under the act could not be seized beyond the lifetime of the offender. President Lincoln had fully intended to veto the bill if Congress did not pass his resolution, and in an effort to ensure his objections were an official part of the congressional record, after signing the bill he also sent the veto message he had prepared to Congress.

On paper, the Second Confiscation Act permitted the Union government to seize all the real and personal property of anyone taking up arms against the government, anyone aiding the rebellion directly, or anyone offering aid or comfort to the rebellion. In practice though, the act did not really work. From the summer of 1862 to the end of the war, only a small amount of rebel property was ever confiscated. President Lincoln's ambivalence about confiscation soon led to reluctant enforcement of the Second Confiscation Act by the attorney general. Even more importantly, the Confiscation Act provided little by way of instructions on its enforcement. The act simply asserted, "it shall be the duty of the President of the United States to cause the seizure of all the estate and property, money, stocks, credits and effects."

On the slavery question, the act was also confusing. The last part of the act, section 9, was mostly radical and provided for the immediate liberation of all slaves who escaped to Union lines. This section pleased radicals, however, even as it avoided resolution of the debate over the legitimacy of slave property. In particular, the act made no attempt to explicitly remove slaves from provisions dealing with the seizure of property. As a result, both sides of the slavery question claimed victory, radicals asserting that the bill freed slaves who came in contact with the Union Army, and conservatives asserting that judges could treat slaves as property.

The Lincoln administration's lackluster enforcement of confiscation drew considerable criticism from Congress and from the Northern public. Perhaps most famously, on August 19, Horace Greeley, editor of the *New York Tribune,* published an open letter to the president, "The Prayer of Twenty Millions." The *Tribune* was the most widely read Republican newspaper in the country and was sure to grab President Lincoln's attention. Greeley seized upon the sections of the law freeing slaves that came within Union lines and demanded the President enforce them: "We think you are strangely and disas-

> *On paper, the Second Confiscation Act permitted the Union government to seize all the real and personal property of anyone taking up arms against the government, anyone aiding the rebellion directly, or anyone offering aid or comfort to the rebellion.*

A list of General Robert E. Lee's personal property at Arlington House, Virginia. A "libel of information," to which this list was attached, was brought by U.S. Attorney Lucius Henry Chandler against Lee in 1864. It was claimed that Lee's property should be forfeited to the United States under the Second Confiscation Act. (US NATIONAL ARCHIVES AND RECORDS ADMINISTRATION)

trously remiss in the discharge of your official and imperative duty with regard to the emancipating provisions of the new Confiscation Act."

Lincoln received pressure not just from the press but also from his own cabinet. In his 1863 Report to Congress, Treasury Secretary Salmon P. Chase urged Lincoln to move quickly against property located in the North and owned by those aiding the rebellion. "Property of great value in loyal states is held by proprietors who are actually or virtually engaged in that guilty attempt to break up the Union," he wrote. Such property "should be subjected by sure and speedy processes to confiscation."

This is not to suggest Lincoln blocked any and all property confiscation. After the passage of the first act in August 1861, U.S. attorneys were given wide discretion to instigate proceedings and began to seize Confederate property located in the North. For proponents of confiscation the prospects for enforcement were made considerably worse when Andrew Johnson became president in April 1865. The Johnson administration began to radically restrict the enforcement of the Confiscation Acts, as part of his administration's drive to placate white Southerners and restore the Union. In the summer and fall of 1865 Johnson began to issue special pardons that restored the property rights of former rebels.

Johnson's attorney general, James Speed, took a narrow view of confiscation and by June of 1866 he ordered a halt to any more seizures. President Johnson ordered that land seized by the federal government under the Confiscation Acts, land to which the United States had title, should be returned to its owners, unless it had already been sold to a third party. All told, total proceeds from confiscation by 1867 amounted to roughly $300,000.

Congress failed to pass an effective confiscation law not because property confiscation was not important, but because property confiscation was too important. The confiscation debates were significant for the amount of ideological agonizing and self-reflection they produced. They show the Thirty-seventh Congress torn between competing ideas of property. The Congress in Civil War confiscation legislation, attempted—ultimately unsuccessfully—to occupy an ideological middle ground recognizing both the power of legislature and the expanding conceptions of individual property rights.

See also: FREEDMAN'S BUREAU ACTS; MILITIA ACT.

> *Congress failed to pass an effective confiscation law not because property confiscation was not important, but because property confiscation was too important.*

FISH AND WILDLIFE CONSERVATION ACT OF 1980

James F. Van Orden

Excerpt from the Fish and Wildlife Conservation Act of 1980

(a) *Findings*—The Congress finds and declares the following:

(1) Fish and wildlife are of ecological, educational, esthetic, cultural, recreational, economic, and scientific value to the nation.

(2) The improved conservation and management of fish and wildlife, particularly nongame fish and wildlife, will assist in restoring and maintaining fish and wildlife and in assuring a productive and more esthetically pleasing environment for all citizens.

The Fish and Wildlife Conservation Act of 1980 (FWCA) (P.L. 96-366, 94 Stat. 1322), or "Nongame Act," was designed to support state efforts to protect the 83 percent of fish and wildlife species that were neglected under prior American law. EPA Administrator Russell Train had complained that "97 percent of federal money for wildlife management 'goes to less than three percent of the species—the ones used for hunting, fishing and trapping'" (*Washington Post,* October 7, 1976). In addition, the Endangered Species Act (ESA) protected only those species near extinction. The FWCA attempted to fill the gap left by these laws and provide measures to protect nongame species that were diminishing due to habitat loss from development and other environmental ills such as pollution. Congress recognized that people place many different values on wildlife resources, including ecological, cultural, scientific, and recreational values. Therefore, the FWCA took steps to protect species *before* they became imperiled and merited ESA protection.

commerce clause: the provision of the U.S. Constitution (Article I, section 8, clause 3) which gives Congress exclusive powers over interstate commerce—the buying, selling or exchanging of goods or products between states

The constitutional foundation for this law is the **commerce clause**, which allows Congress to regulate commerce among the several states (Article I, section 8). Congress called upon state wildlife agencies to inventory their wildlife resources and assess the status of their species, and ultimately to develop statewide conservation plans. Plans would be submitted to the Secretary of the Interior for approval. Next, states were to take the necessary actions set forth in their conservation plans. They could apply for federal reimbursement of much of the cost associated with developing, revising, or implementing plans that were ultimately approved. Generally, the law provided for federal and state partnerships, whereby the federal government would provide technical and financial support to the states.

The FWCA took steps to protect species before *they became imperiled and merited Endangered Species Act protection.*

The FWCA reflected the notion that fish and wildlife resources are best managed at the state level due to the understanding within states of their unique resources. It also recognized that the problem of species loss crosses state and even national boundaries, creating a need for coordination among states, as well as federal financial support of protection of wildlife resources that benefit all Americans. Finally, it encouraged federal agencies and departments to use their statutory and administrative authority to the maximum extent possible in order to conserve and protect nongame species and their habitats.

excise tax: a tax levied on the manufacture or sale of specific—usually non-essential—commodities such as tobacco or liquor

The source of federal funding for state conservation plans was widely debated. Other game-focused wildlife laws had successfully raised funds through **excise taxes** on hunting and fishing equipment. Advocates for the FWCA hoped to find a similar stream of money for nongame efforts, and called for an 11 percent tax on birdseed and birdfeeders. This provision ultimately was dropped from the text of the act because it would not have raised much and it would disproportionately harm the small birdseed and bird feeder industry. Instead, the act called for the use of the general tax revenues of the federal government while the Fish and Wildlife Service (FWS) studied other funding options. Also, it provided funds only for vertebrates because including the daunting number of invertebrates would spread federal resources too thin.

Although the FWS studied funding options, it failed to recommend any in the years following. A reliance on general federal revenues has since proven to be inadequate. In 1988, when Congress revisited the act, it had yet to be funded at all. Ronald Lambertson of the FWS testified that forty-nine states used portions of their budgets for nongame activities, and twenty-three states had actually undertaken comprehensive planning. Consensus arose among state agencies, biologists, and environmentalists that federal funding would foster many other important nongame conservation activities that were then neglected at the state level for lack of funds.

It was not until 2001 that Congress actually appropriated money to the states through the State and Tribal Wildlife Grants program. It was funded at $80 million per year beginning in **fiscal year** 2002 to fund state and tribal conservation efforts. Federal aid has since gone to aid the fish and wildlife agencies in all fifty states. In fiscal year 2002 the Fish and Wildlife Service dispersed a total of $77.6 million dollars through this program to states and territories. The Fish and Wildlife Conservation Act has authorized a large amount of nongame research and planning at the federal level, and over two decades after its enactment, the key state conservation plan funding mechanism is in place.

See also: ENDANGERED SPECIES ACT; MARINE MAMMAL PROTECTION ACT.

It was not until 2001 that Congress actually appropriated money to the states through the State and Tribal Wildlife Grants program.

fiscal year: the term used for a business's accounting year; the period is usually twelve months which can begin during any month of the calendar year

BIBLIOGRAPHY

Bean, Michael J. *The Evolution of National Wildlife Law*. New York: Praeger Publishers, 1983.

"Policy on Wildlife." *Washington Post* (October 7, 1976).

Musgrave, Ruth S., and Judy Flynn-O'Brien, et al. *Federal Wildlife Laws Handbook with Related Laws*. Rockville, MD: Government Institutes, 1998.

"State Wildlife Grants Apportionment for FY 2002." U.S. Fish and Wildlife Service. <http://www.fws.gov/>.

Subcommittee on Environmental Protection, One Hundredth Congress. *Reauthorization of the Fish and Wildlife Conservation Act of 1980* (1988): 3–4.

FLAG PROTECTION ACT OF 1989

Andrew C. Spiropoulos

In 1989 the U.S. Supreme Court, in *Texas v. Johnson*, considered the constitutionality of a Texas statute making it a crime to "deface, damage, or otherwise physically mistreat an American flag in a way that the [person] knows will seriously offend one or more persons likely to observe or discover his action." The Court ruled that the First Amendment to the Constitution prevented the use of the statute to prosecute Gregory Lee Johnson, who had burned a flag to protest President Ronald Reagan's renomination as a presi-

Five senators meet with reporters on Capitol Hill on June 14, 1990, to show their support for a Constitutional Amendment that would give Congress the power to make a law against the desecration of the U.S. flag. United States v. Eichman, *in which the Supreme Court declared the Flag Protection Act unconstitutional, was decided only three days prior. Pictured in the photo (from left to right) are Alfonse D'Amato (R-N.Y.), James McClure (R-Idaho), Bob Dole (R-Ind.), John McCain (R-Ariz.), and Bennett Johnson (D-La.).* (© AP/WIDE WORLD PHOTOS)

free expression: the right to state opinions without interference or censorship

dential candidate. Justice William Brennan, writing for a 5–4 majority, found that the state's declared interest in "preserving the flag as a symbol of nationhood and national unity" was "related 'to the suppression of **free expression**.'"

The state's concern, the Court reasoned, was triggered "only when a person's treatment of the flag communicates some message," meaning that the state prosecuted only those who mistreated the flag so as to express a particular message that others found offensive. The Court concluded: "If there is a bedrock principle underlying the First Amendment, it is that the Government may not prohibit the expression of an idea simply because society finds the idea itself offensive or disagreeable."

Many Americans expressed disappointment, and even outrage, at the Court's decision in *Johnson,* including President George H. W. Bush and overwhelming majorities in both houses of Congress. By July 1, 1989, less than a month after the decision, members of Congress had introduced thirty-nine separate resolutions calling for a constitutional amendment authorizing laws forbidding desecration of the flag. The leaders of both houses of Congress opposed a constitutional amendment but agreed that Congress needed to do something to reverse the effect of the *Johnson* decision. On October 28, 1989, the Flag Protection Act of 1989 (P.L.101-131, 103 Stat. 777), despite President Bush's refusal to sign the bill, became law. The act states that "whoever knowingly mutilates, defaces, physically defiles, burns, maintains on the floor or ground, or tramples upon any flag of the United States shall be fined under this title or imprisoned for not more than one year, or both." The act "does not prohibit any conduct consisting of the disposal of a flag when it has become worn or soiled."

The supporters of the act believed that the Court would hold it constitutional because the statute was carefully written to make clear that Congress intended to protect the flag from defacement or other forms of ill treatment no matter the motive or intended message of the accused. In other words, the law punished flag desecration without regard to whether, as with the Texas law in *Johnson,* anyone found the actions in question offensive. However, in 1990 the Court, in *United States v. Eichman,* found that the prosecution of an individual for burning a flag in violation of the act was inconsistent with the First Amendment. The Court held that, despite the absence of the explicit restriction of particular messages found in *Johnson,* the government's declared interest in protecting the "physical integrity" of the flag "rests upon a perceived need to preserve the flag's status as a symbol of our Nation and certain national ideals." This defense of the nation's symbol and the ideas it represents would be necessary only when a person's treatment of the flag communicates a message at odds with those ideals. In other words, the government's legal protection of the flag is by definition, whether stated explicitly or not, aimed at the suppression of particular messages.

The remaining option for those who wish to provide legal protection against flag desecration is the path abandoned in 1989—an amendment to the Constitution. Amendment proposals, however, were defeated by the Senate in 1989, 1995, and 2000, and by both houses in 1990.

> *The supporters of the act believed that the Court would hold it constitutional because the statute was carefully written to make clear that Congress intended to protect the flag from defacement or other forms of ill treatment no matter the motive or intended message of the accused.*

BIBLIOGRAPHY

Dorsen, Norman. "Flag Desecration in Courts, Congress, and Country." *Thomas M. Cooley Law Review* 17 (2000): 417–442.

Goldstein, Robert Justin. "The Great 1989–1990 Flag Flap: An Historical, Political, and Legal Analysis." *University of Miami Law Review* 45 (1990): 19–106.

Police arrest Scott Tyler, 24, on the steps of the Capitol for setting fire to an American flag on October 31, 1989. The Flag Protection Act became law on October 28, 1989, and was declared unconstitutional by the Supreme Court on June 11, 1990. (© AP/WIDE WORLD PHOTOS)

Tiefer, Charles. "The Flag-Burning Controversy of 1989–1990: Congress' Valid Role in Constitutional Dialogue." *Harvard Journal on Legislation* 29 (1992): 357 398.

FOOD QUALITY PROTECTION ACT OF 1996

Valerie Watnick

At the time of its passage, the Food Quality Protection Act of 1996 (FQPA) (P.L. 104-170, 110 Stat. 1489) was called "one of the most significant environmental and public health bills passed in 20 years, [which] indeed may distinguish itself in time as the most significant." In response to major scientific findings by the National Research Council (NRC) and others in the area of children's susceptibilities to pesticides, Congress intended the FQPA to strengthen protections for children by requiring the Environmental Protection Agency (EPA) to consider these special susceptibilities in assessing the risk of a pesticide.

Environmentalists and consumer groups used the Delaney clause, passed in 1958 as part of the Federal, Food, Drug and Cosmetic Act, as a bargaining chip in the effort to gain regulatory protection for children from pesticides. The Delaney clause provided that food additives had to be safe; and that if a substance was found to cause cancer, it could not be designated as safe and thus could not be added to processed foods. This standard was known as a "zero tolerance" standard. Raw agricultural commodities were generally considered unsafe for use unless a legal limit was in place for pesticide residue found on that food.

Given scientists' current ability to detect certain chemicals in extremely minute amounts, scientists and politicians urged that the Delaney clause's zero tolerance standard for **carcinogenic** food additives needed revision. In September 1993 the Clinton administration proposed a reform package that attempted to please the chemical industry and the environmentalists. The proposal included abolishing the Delaney zero-tolerance standard and setting limits on pesticide residues that would be safe for children.

carcinogenic: cancer-causing

After the Clinton administration made its proposal, the House and Senate Agriculture Committees held a series of hearings on pesticide regulation. The debates focused on assessing dietary risks to different groups of consumers, the method of assessing consumer exposure, and whether and when to consider a pesticide's benefits when setting legal limits on pesticide residues.

The presidential election in November 1996 and public opinion that food safety laws needed revision played roles in developing a consensus. In July of that year the House approved a bill that included provisions proposed by the Clinton administration that were designed to ensure that pesticide limits would protect infants and children. On July 24, 1996, the child protective bill was passed by the Senate, and President Clinton signed the FQPA into law on August 3, 1996.

The act resulted in three major changes in the regulation of pesticides and their use on food products. First, the FQPA contains provisions specifically designed to protect the health of infants and children. The most significant aspect of these protections for children originated with the report by the National Research Council on the dangers of pesticides to children. It generally requires the EPA to assess the risks of a given pesticide residue and to use an additional ten-fold margin of safety when setting legal limits for certain pesticide residues on food. The FQPA also requires the EPA to take into account the special susceptibilities and consumption habits of infants and children in establishing pesticide limits.

Moreover, the act requires the EPA to consider all of the different exposures to pesticides that adults and children face when setting limits for pesticide residues on food. This provision requires the EPA to consider all of a consumer's exposures to pesticide residues, including exposure through the air and water.

Finally, the FQPA eliminated Delaney's zero-tolerance standard for cancer-causing substances in processed foods and replaced it with a negligible risk standard for all foods. This standard of negligible risk is generally assumed to mean that there exists a one-in-one-million chance that a harmful effect will occur.

If implemented as intended, the Food Quality Protection Act has great potential. The act could help to make the food supply safer for this generation of children and adults by limiting the amount of pesticide residue on all food sold in the United States.

See also: FEDERAL FOOD, DRUG, AND COSMETIC ACT; PURE FOOD AND DRUG ACT.

BIBLIOGRAPHY

National Research Council. Committee on Pesticides in the Diets of Infants and Children. *Pesticides in the Diets of Infants and Children.* Washington, DC: National Academy of Sciences, 1993.

Watnick, Valerie J. "Risk Assessment: Obfuscation of Policy Decisions in Pesticide Regulation and the EPA's Dismantling of the Food Quality Protection Act's Safeguards for Children." *Arizona State Law Journal* 31 (Winter 1999): 1315. Source from which portions of this essay have been adapted.

Watnick, Valerie J. "Who's Minding the Schools: Toward Least Toxic Methods of Pest Control in Our Nation's Schools." *Fordham Environmental Law Journal* 8 (Fall 1996): 73.

FOOD STAMP ACT OF 1964

Steven Puro

The Food Stamp Act (P.L. 88-525) was part of President Lyndon Johnson's Great Society Program. The Great Society Programs substantially expanded social welfare programs within the national government. Designed to "safeguard the health and well-being of the Nation's population and raise levels of nutrition among low-income households," the Food Stamp Act received strong support from legislators—including Lenore Sullivan (D-MO), Hubert Humphrey (D-MN), Stuart Symington (D-MO), and George Aiken (R-VT)—as well as the U.S. Department of Agriculture, the National Farmers Union, and poverty groups, particularly those groups located in the Appalachian Mountains, a poverty-stricken area of the country.

The goal of the Food Stamp Act of 1964 was to prevent hunger, improve the social conditions of citizens with low-incomes, and provide a foundation for U.S. agriculture. In particular, Congress designed the act "To strengthen the agricultural economy; to help achieve a fuller and more effective use of food abundances; to provide for improved levels of nutrition among low-income households through a cooperative Federal-State program of food assistance to be operated through normal channels of trade." This nutritional program, it was hoped, would reduce the incidents of health problems in poverty-stricken areas, in particular, problems associated with low birth weight, anemia, and osteoporosis.

To accomplish its goals, Congress adopted a new mechanism to distribute agricultural surpluses to poor individuals—food stamps—stamps that people could exchange for food at grocery stores. The U.S. Department of Agriculture provided these stamps through state welfare offices, and this, in turn, created a key linkage between federal and state governments on agricultural matters. The Food Stamp Act required the federal government pay for the benefits, but the state agencies determined individual eligibility, distributed the stamps, and conducted audits and monitored vendors' food stamp inventories. The federal and state governments, however, shared the administrative costs of the program. The food stamp program is best described as an "in-kind" benefit that ensures recipients use the government support on groceries and nutrition. Not only did the program feed poor individuals, but it also provided an economic boost to grocery stores because the food stamps worked as a cash-equivalent, enabling customers to buy more goods and items not subsidized by the program. The Food Stamp Act, however, was not free of controversy. At the time of its adoption and for many years after, legislators have debated funding, eligibility standards, accessibility, and accountability.

AMENDMENTS AND ALTERATIONS

Shortly after the initiation of the program, there were major additions to the existing law. In 1967 Congress amended the act to allow for greater distribution of food and food stamps to both children and retirees over sixty-five. A range of groups supported these amendments, including the National Grange and National Milk Producers Federation, and poverty rights advocates, represented by the Poverty Rights Action Center of the National Welfare Rights Organization.

To some supporters, the Food Stamp Act of 1964 and its amendments played an important role in a network of programs that served to promote individuals' health and prevent hunger. Ellen Haas, Undersecretary of the Department of Agriculture, testified on June 8, 1995, before the U.S. House Committee on Agriculture Department Operations, Nutrition and Foreign Agriculture, Food Stamp and Commodity Program that: "[T]he three anchors of the Nation's nutrition security strategy [are] the Child Nutrition Programs, the Special Supplemental Nutrition Program for Women, Infants, and Children (WIC), and the Food Stamp Program. Together, these programs form a network of food and nutrition assistance that ensures that every low-income American—regardless of who they are or where they live—has access to a nutritious diet."

After more than a decade of operation, however, the Food Stamp Act faced major criticisms concerning administrative practices and eligibility standards. Both Republicans and Democrats viewed the process of applying for and receiving benefits as limiting accessibility and delaying benefits; moreover, legislators disputed who was needy and who deserved to receive program benefits.

Prior to 1977, the law required individuals to purchase their food stamps, and this purchase requirement served as a barrier to participation for those without easy access to those government offices, and individuals with limited amounts of available cash—especially subsistence level farmers and other agricultural workers. The Food Stamp Act of 1977 eliminated the purchase requirement and allowed benefit delivery based upon eligibility standards. The 1977 legislation that created eligibility guidelines identified those with the right to obtain government assistance under the program. The early 1980s cutbacks in the food stamp programs were achieved by reducing eligibility and government funds available for use in the program; the mid- to late 1980s saw some restoration of benefits and increased resources made available. Currently, the food stamp program is implemented through a credit card distributed to eligible individuals. There is no longer an actual distribution of food stamps, and some argue that the credit card approach reduces stigma attached to these purchases and limits recipient abuse.

A young woman purchases food with food stamps in a New York City supermarket, 1970. (©BETTMANN/CORBIS)

Congress altered the structure of the Food Stamp Program again when it adopted the 1996 Personal Responsibility and Work Opportunity Reconciliation Act (PRWOR)—also known as Welfare to Work Program. PRWOR tightened the eligibility guidelines for food stamp assistance; legal immigrants were no longer entitled to receive food stamps, and the law allowed able-bodied adults with no dependent children to receive food stamps, but only for three months in any given three-year period. The Welfare to Work Program was a means to cut social welfare costs in the domestic budget and allow a broader scope of state initiatives in administering welfare programs.

The Farm Bill of 2002 enhanced program access in an effort to rectify a decline in program participation that had occurred over the previous five years. The decline in the use of food stamps caused a decrease in the demand for agricultural products, and this, in turn, decreased farmers' economic stability. The Food Security and Rural Investment Act of 2002 reauthorized the food stamp program and revised eligibility for several groups, particularly qualified aliens, immigrants, and children that the 1996 PRWOR excluded. Both pieces of legislation that Congress adopted in 2002 permitted states to increase access to the food stamp program by broadening the eligibility requirements. The Food Stamp Act and its alterations since 1964 have been—and remain—an important element in defining societal relationships with low-income individuals, federal-state administrative relationships, and economic support for the nation's agricultural sector.

See also: AID TO DEPENDENT CHILDREN ACT; MEDICAID ACT; PERSONAL RESPONSIBILITY AND WORK OPPORTUNITY RECONCILIATION ACT; SOCIAL SECURITY ACT OF 1935.

BIBLIOGRAPHY

Lemann, Nicholas. *The Promised Land: The Great Black Migration and How It Changed America.* New York: A. A. Knopf, 1991.

Schwartz, John. *America's Hidden Success: A Reassessment of Public Policy from Kennedy to Reagan.* New York: Norton, 1988.

FORCE ACT OF 1871

Ross Rosenfeld

The Force Act of 1871 provided for federal scrutiny of congressional elections. The act, passed during the Ulysses S. Grant administration, was intended to prevent election fraud in Southern states during the **Reconstruction** era. The Force Act was sandwiched between the Enforcement Act of 1870, which established criminal penalties for interfering with an election, and the Enforcement Act of 1871, which permitted the suspension of **habeas corpus**. Intended to enforce the Fourteenth Amendment, the Force Act of 1871 was described as "an Act to enforce the rights of citizens of the United States to vote in the several states of this union." If a town or city had "upward of twenty thousand inhabitants," any two citizens of that town who wished to have an election "guarded and scrutinized" could request the regional U.S. Circuit Court to oversee it. In such cases the court was instructed to choose two **bipartisan** supervisors, who,

Reconstruction: the political and economic reorganization of the South after the Civil War

habeas corpus: (Latin, "you should have the body") a written order to bring a prisoner in front of a judge, to determine whether his or her detention is lawful

bipartisan: involving members of two parties, especially the two major political parties

Jim Crow: the systematic practice of segregating and suppressing African Americans; the name is from a character in a nineteenth-century minstrel show

under the court's protection, could regulate the election. The three acts are sometimes referred to collectively as the Enforcement Acts or the Force Acts.

Southern bigots responded to the Force Act with a wave of discriminatory actions, known as **Jim Crow**. Such policies as literacy tests and poll taxes (taxes for voting) still kept many blacks from voting. Some Southern states included

The Force Act of 1871 provided for federal scrutiny of congressional elections.

measures prohibiting voting by blacks in their new constitutions. The Supreme Court did little to reverse this. In *Giles v. Harris* (1903) and *Giles v. Teasley* (1904), a black citizen challenged provisions such as these in the Alabama state constitution. The Supreme Court, however, ruled that it could not do anything about the provisions because they represented a "political question." It would take the Civil Rights movement, the Civil Rights Act, and the Voting Rights Act to put these matters to rest.

See also: CIVIL RIGHTS ACT OF 1964; VOTING RIGHTS ACT OF 1965.

BIBLIOGRAPHY

Hakim, Joy. *A History of U.S. Reconstruction and Reform.* New York: Oxford University Press, 1994.

The Force Acts of 1870–1871. Northern Virginia Community College. <http://www.nvcc.edu/home/nvsageh/Hist122/Part1/ForceActsEx.htm>.

FOREIGN ASSISTANCE ACT OF 1961

Antonio F. Perez

Cold War: a conflict over ideological differences carried on by methods short of military action and usually without breaking off diplomatic relations; usually refers to the ideological conflict between the U.S. and former U.S.S.R.

While Congress has constitutional authority over the spending of funds, the president as the nation's chief executive has independent foreign-affairs power. What happens when these two powers intersect? In the aftermath of World War II, in the context of the **Cold War** and the struggle between the United States and Soviet Union for influence around the globe, particularly in the new states emerging from decolonization, the Congress and executive branch needed to manage their policy differences concerning the provision of U.S. assistance. The Foreign Assistance Act of 1961 (FAA) (P.L. 87-194, 75 Stat. 424) has charted the course for this process of constitutional accommodation. Since its enactment, through annual appropriations acts (except for those years in which continuing resolutions or omnibus appropriations bills were necessary), the Congress has increased the level of its supervision—some would say micromanagement—of executive branch foreign policymaking through the imposition of a range of limitations, conditions, and certification requirements on the provision of U.S. aid.

checks and balances: the limiting powers that each branch of government has over the other two. (The government is divided into three branches: legislative, executive, and judicial, each with distinct powers.)

This article will describe the original context and purposes of the FAA, examine the administrative and legal regimes it established for the provision of various kinds of U.S. foreign assistance, and explore the legal and policy implications of subsequent developments in the annual appropriations process. The appropriations bills serve as compelling examples of the operation of the **checks and balances** between Congress and the president built into the U.S. Constitutional system of separation of power. Indeed, the congressional-executive conflict in this area has grown more complex in response to changing international circumstances and the internationalization of many new issues.

THE CONTEXT AND PURPOSES OF THE FAA

Prior to the FAA, statutory authority for the provision of U.S. foreign aid was located in a number of statutes, most prominently the Mutual Security Act of 1954. The principal goal of the FAA was to consolidate and rationalize these statutory authorities and programs under a regime, taking account of the new circumstances facing the United States during the Cold War in light of the dismantling of European colonial empires and the emergence of the Third World as an independent force in international politics. The FAA provided for nonmilitary assistance intended "to strengthen the forces of freedom by aiding peoples of less developed friendly countries of the world to develop their resources and improve their living standards, to realize their aspirations for justice, education, dignity, and respect as individual human beings, and to establish responsible governments" (section 102). Similarly, military assistance would be provided with the intention of "fostering an improved climate of political independence and individual liberty, improving the ability of friendly countries and international organizations to deter or, if necessary, defeat Communist or Communist-supported aggression, facilitating arrangement for individual and collective security, assisting friendly countries to maintain internal security, and creating an environment of security and stability in the developing friendly countries essential to their more rapid, social, economic, and political progress" (section 502).

In rationalizing these statutory regimes in terms of the ongoing international struggle between communism and market democracy, the FAA reflected the view that the struggle against communism would best be won through a campaign for the hearts and minds of the peoples of the Third World. Another important example of this new perspective was the Kennedy administration's Alliance for Progress in Latin America.

THE ADMINISTRATION AND LEGAL REGIME FOR FOREIGN ASSISTANCE

Although the FAA creates the basic scheme for the provision of foreign assistance by the United States, additional statutes also separately authorize appropriations of funds for activities related to foreign policy. These "authorization" bills originate in the congressional committees responsible for policy oversight, but they are not enacted every **fiscal year**. Accordingly, most congressional policy judgments on foreign assistance are found in annual appropriations legislation. Most appropriations policies are now established through the annual foreign-assistance appropriations acts, currently titled the Foreign Operations, Export Financing, and Related Programs Appropriations Act for a given fiscal year, which make appropriations for most forms of direct assistance. Also, the annual bills making appropriations for the operations of agencies, such as the Department of State, have become common

Since its enactment, through annual appropriations acts (except for those years in which continuing resolutions or omnibus appropriations bills were necessary), the Congress has increased the level of its supervision—some would say micromanagement—of Executive Branch foreign policymaking through the imposition of a range of limitations, conditions, and certification requirements on the provision of U.S. aid.

Although the FAA creates the basic scheme for the provision of foreign assistance by the United States, additional statutes also separately authorize appropriations of funds for activities related to foreign policy.

fiscal year: the term used for a business's accounting year; the period is usually twelve months which can begin during any month of the calendar year

vehicles for Congress to express its views on foreign-assistance policy. Under these bills, funds for U.S. participation in certain international organizations, such as the United Nations, are appropriated and are often subject to detailed conditions and certification requirements. These conditions and requirements largely reflect the fact that U.S. contributions to international organizations, which in turn use these funds to support purposes and policies in foreign countries, are viewed by the U.S. Congress as a form of indirect U.S. assistance to those countries.

The basic scheme created by the FAA, and its subsequent amendments, divided U.S. assistance into two categories. Part I of the FAA, titled the "International Development Act," focused on development loans, development grants and technical cooperation, and investment guarantees (to U.S. investors in foreign countries, which were deemed in effect to be assistance to those countries). Part II of the FAA, titled the "International Peace and Security Act," contemplated the provision of direct military assistance in the form of goods or services, foreign military sales on cash or credit terms, or through exchange for other defense articles or services. Part I assistance was under the direction and control of the Agency for International Development (AID), an agency created in 1961 to give an independent institutional voice to the essentially humanitarian objectives articulated in Part I of the FAA. Notably, however, AID was brought under more direct Department of State control by the Foreign Affairs Reform and Restructuring Act of 1998, adopted as part of the Omnibus Consolidated Emergency Supplemental Appropriations Act. Part II assistance, by contrast, was subject to political direction from the Department of State, subject to consultation with the Department of Defense. While most of the security-related assistance provided under Part II was in the nature of goods or services, chapter IV of Part II of the FAA was later added to authorize the appropriation of "Economic Support Funds." The provision of these funds to a foreign country was deemed to be security-, rather than development-, related and, therefore, not subject to the development criteria or under the control of the pro-development bureaucracy established under Part I of the FAA. In effect, this category straddled the line of policy separation initially drawn by the FAA in order to grant the executive branch the additional discretion Congress deemed to be prudent to advance the foreign- and security-related policies of the United States. The use of these discretionary authorities by the president, however, led to increased oversight by Congress through its investigative arm, the General Accounting Office (GAO), and directly by congressional committees with jurisdiction over foreign affairs and national security policy.

THE TWILIGHT STRUGGLE BETWEEN THE CONGRESS AND THE PRESIDENT

The path of congressional oversight of presidential foreign policymaking through the provision of foreign assistance has traversed what Justice Jackson in *Youngstown v. Sawyer* (1952) called a "zone of twilight" in the separation of powers between the branches, marked not by abstract theories but rather by "the imperatives of events." After Vietnam and **Watergate**, Congress enacted a series of measures to exercise greater control over executive discretion. Attempts to constrain the so-called **Imperial Presidency** included the War Powers Act, Arms Export Control Act, International Emergency Economic Powers Act, as well as amendments to the National Security Act of 1947 relating to covert activities. These efforts extended to the provision of foreign assistance.

Watergate: the scandal following the break-in at the Democratic National Committee headquarters located in the Watergate apartment and office complex in Washington, D.C. in 1972

Imperial Presidency: a powerful president who is being belligerent internationally, being intrusive domestically, and running roughshod over another branch of government

Pallets of humanitarian daily rations destined for Kosovo are ready to be loaded onto a cargo plane at Dover Air Force Base in Delaware, April 5, 1999. (© MICHAEL J. SANDERS/ USAF/GETTY IMAGES)

Because the major foreign-policy issue after the Watergate era and the election of Jimmy Carter as president was the morality of U.S. foreign policy, in particular the pursuit of international human rights affirmed in the Helsinki Protocols of 1975, the FAA was amended to require annual human rights reports on countries receiving U.S. assistance. In addition, a state engaging in a pattern of gross violations of internationally recognized human rights became disqualified from receiving U.S. assistance.

The FAA was amended to require annual human rights reports on countries receiving U.S. assistance.

Other amendments followed, such as the requirement that countries involved in the production or trade of illegal narcotics also would be the subject of annual reports, with the availability of foreign assistance predicated on compliance with U.S.-mandated antinarcotics efforts. A similar regime was created for countries supporting terrorism, and yet another set of triggers was enacted for countries engaging in nuclear, chemical and biological weapons proliferation (such as the "Glenn and Symington Amendments," which prohibited foreign assistance to countries engaging in certain weapons-related nuclear activities). As time progressed, congressional conditions on foreign aid in annual appropriations bills included prohibitions on assistance based on a broad range of criteria, including countries whose duly elected heads of government had been overthrown by military coup or countries in default on principal or interest payments due on loans by the U.S. government. Thus, congressional concern about domestic democracy and financial solvency in foreign countries led to explicit conditions on U.S. assistance. Finally, foreign-assistance programs began to address questions that were previously considered core issues of domestic policy, such as family planning, and the politics of international family-planning assistance in the annual foreign-assistance appropriations cycle became an extension of U.S. domestic political conflict over such issues.

These various statutory requirements imposed significant research and reporting responsibilities on the Department of State that compelled the department to become a source of information for members of Congress seeking to make such issues important components of U.S. foreign policy. Yet in deference to executive branch prerogatives in foreign policy, Congress ordinarily gave the president substantial discretion to make determinations, in the form of findings reported to Congress, that the foreign policy or security interests of the United States nonetheless required the provision of assistance to countries that were not in compliance with the requirements specified by Congress. Yet in special cases, such as the acquisition of nuclear weapons capability by Pakistan (the so-called Pressler Amendment), Congress made clear that a matter was so important that resumption of U.S. foreign assistance would require additional legislation rather than merely an express presidential judgment.

The Helsinki Final Act
Antonio F. Perez

As part of détente, a brief period of relaxation in Cold War tensions, in 1975 the Helsinki Final Act established the Conference on Security and Cooperation in Europe (the CSCE), a negotiating forum for mutual and balanced forced reductions between NATO and the Warsaw Pact. As part of the final document, NATO countries made a legally non-binding commitment to recognize the legitimacy of the territorial boundaries established in Eastern Europe after World War II, and the Warsaw Pact countries in turn made political commitments to respect internationally-recognized human rights. Although international human rights issues were always at the heart of the Cold War, international human rights issues achieved greater political salience as a result of the Helsinki Final Act, even though the Helsinki Final Act established no formal legal obligations. Through a formal treaty, concluded in 1995 after the end of the Cold War, the CSCE became the Organization for Security and Cooperation in Europe and many of the political commitments contained in the Helsinki Final Act became obligations under international law.

Congress sponsored a series of foreign assistance acts for Europe in the years following World War II, culminating in the Economic Cooperation Act of 1948 (Marshall Plan). In this political cartoon published in the Washington Evening Star *on December 2, 1947, Senators Robert Taft (R-Ohio) and Arthur Vandenberg (R-Mich.) are shown steamrolling an interim emergency aid act (S. 1774) through Congress. The Foreign Assistance Act of 1961 was created to limit such broad delegation of authority for foreign aid to the executive branch.* (US SENATE COLLECTION, CENTER FOR LEGISLATIVE ARCHIVES, US NATIONAL ARCHIVES AND RECORDS ADMINISTRATION)

Conflict between Congress and the executive branch may have peaked during the Reagan administration in the mid-1980s, when congressional supervision and control of foreign-assistance expenditures reached a level from which it has not since receded, yielding mammoth bills both authorizing and making appropriations for foreign assistance. By 1985 bills authorizing appropriations for State Department operations and for foreign assistance occupied fifty-two and ninety-three pages, respectively, in *United States Statutes at Large*. Similarly, the annual foreign-assistance appropriations acts now occupy sixty to seventy pages. The level and quality of congressional involvement grew as well, prompting a significant constitutional controversy involving the covert sale of U.S. arms to Iran, in possible violation of the Arms Export Control Act. This was a confrontation spawned directly by the executive branch's attempt to circumvent limitations on U.S. assistance, the "Boland Amendments," to insurgent forces in Nicaragua attempting to overthrow the pro-Communist Sandinista government. The zone of twilight, in this case, yielded a constitutional con-

> *Conflict between Congress and the Executive Branch may have peaked during the Reagan administration in the mid-1980s, when congressional supervision and control of foreign-assistance expenditures reached a level from which it has not since receded, yielding mammoth bills both authorizing and making appropriations for foreign assistance.*

frontation of the first magnitude and may have chastened the executive branch for a generation.

During the Bush (senior) and Clinton administrations, Congress continued to demand an equal, if not greater, level of participation in foreign policymaking—even when the stakes for the United States were at their greatest, such as the U.S. role in supporting pro-democracy developments in the newly independent states of the former Soviet Union and the new democracies of central and eastern Europe. Under the Freedom Support Act, Congress mandated a detailed set of reporting requirements and conditioned appropriations on executive branch monitoring and certification of compliance in specified areas. The national security implications of the dissolution of the former Soviet Union also received similarly intense congressional scrutiny, as so-called Nunn-Lugar funds were made available under strict conditions for nuclear weapons and materials stockpile security, weapons dismantling and related purposes.

CONCLUSIONS

Foreign assistance during the last half-century has marked not only the rise and fall of the Cold War, but also the rise and fall of the Imperial Presidency. The congressional reaction to broad delegation of authority to the president has resulted in an apparently permanent change in the degree of congressional supervision of the foreign-policy appropriations process. In sum, the study of the foreign-assistance appropriations process is not only an indispensable element in the study of the foreign relations of the United States, but also a central case study for students of American government.

See also: ECONOMIC COOPERATION ACT OF 1948 (MARSHALL PLAN); MUTUAL SECURITY ACT; UNITED STATES INFORMATION AND EDUCATIONAL EXCHANGE ACT.

BIBLIOGRAPHY

Fisher, Louis. *Constitutional Conflicts between Congress and the President,* 4th ed. Lawrence: University Press of Kansas, 1997.

Fisher, Louis. *The Politics of Shared Power: Congress and the Executive,* 4th ed. College Station: Texas A&M University Press, 1998.

Koh, Harold Hongju. *The National Security Constitution: Sharing Power after the Iran-Contra Affair.* New Haven, CT: Yale University Press, 1990.

INTERNET RESOURCES

George Washington University. *National Security Archive.* <http://www.gwu.edu/ ~nsarchiv>.

U.S. Agency for International Development Homepage. <http://www.usaid.gov>.

FOREIGN CORRUPT PRACTICES ACT (1977)

Jonathan S. Berck

A series of corruption scandals in the early 1970s led to the Foreign Corrupt Practices Act of 1977 (FCPA) (P.L. 95-213 91 Stat. 1494), which prohibits bribery of foreign officials by American and certain other companies. The act has been controversial since its enactment, with some critics attacking it as ineffective and the American business community complaining that it places U.S. enterprises at a competitive disadvantage abroad. Since the late 1990s, however, it has become a model for international efforts to stamp out corruption and improve the business climate in the developing world.

> *The act has been controversial since its enactment, with some critics attacking it as ineffective and the American business community complaining that it places U.S. enterprises at a competitive disadvantage abroad.*

BACKGROUND

In the 1970s a complex of scandals collectively known as **Watergate** consumed both government and public attention. Misdeeds committed during the administration of President Richard M. Nixon prompted investigations, including scrutiny of the conduct of major American corporations with close ties to the administration. Investigators learned of hidden slush funds and substantial payments of bribes by over 400 U.S. companies to foreign officials or political parties to obtain major contracts or other advantages. Following extensive hearings, Congress enacted the FCPA in 1977. Significant amendments followed in 1988 and in 1998. The 1998 amendments incorporated technical changes required by the anticorruption treaty of the Organization of Economic Cooperation and Development (OECD) that went into effect in 1999.

Watergate: the scandal following the break-in at the Democratic National Committee headquarters located in the Watergate apartment and office complex in Washington D.C. in 1972

In addition to the anticorruption fervor that swept the United States in the post-Watergate period, the major justification for enacting the FCPA was the belief that bribery is also an economic evil. In this view, bribery is a hidden cost of doing business, and the award of business for other than economic reasons distorts competition. Those most concerned about bribery believed that contracts should be awarded only on the basis of the merits of products and services as well as fully disclosed prices.

MAJOR PROVISIONS

There are three significant parts to the FCPA: prohibitions on activities, reporting requirements, and an exception for small "grease," or facilitating payments.

Prohibitions. The FCPA bars U.S. companies from "corruptly" offering, paying, promising to pay or authorizing the payment of money or other things of value to any foreign official in order to (1) influence any act or decision by the official, (2) persuade the official to do anything contrary to his or her duty, (3) secure any "improper advantage," or (4) induce the official to use his or her influence with a foreign government to influence its acts or decisions, in each case for the purpose of "obtaining or retaining business" or directing business to any person. A parallel section covers the same acts when made to political parties or candidates. Penalties include fines of up to $2 million against the company and up to $100,000 against officers or directors, as well as prison terms of up to five years. The U.S. Department of Justice generally is responsible for prosecuting violations of these provisions.

> *In addition to the anticorruption fervor that swept the United States in the post-Watergate period, the major justification for enacting the FCPA was the belief that bribery is also an economic evil.*

quid pro quo: (Latin, "something for something") an equal exchange or substitution

For a company to be found guilty of violating these prohibitions, there must be some sort of "**quid pro quo**"—some exchange of value for advantage. The "corrupt" requirement makes guilty intent an element of the crime. In short, it is very hard to violate the FCPA inadvertently.

The FCPA provides two primary defenses to an accusation of bribery: a company can claim (1) that the offending act was in fact legal under the written laws of the foreign country, or (2) that the act was a "reasonable and bona fide" expenditure directly related to promotional activities or to the execution or performance of a contract with a foreign government.

Reporting requirements were a reaction to the revelations about secret slush funds maintained by companies involved in the bribery scandals, as well as bribes disguised to look like legitimate transactions.

Reporting Requirements. The FCPA also has provisions requiring publicly held companies to fully record and report to investors and the Security and Exchange Commission (SEC) all expenditures made in violation of the prohibitions described above. In addition, such companies must have policies in place to ensure that all transactions comply with management's directions and are recorded in accordance with generally accepted accounting procedures. The SEC generally enforces these provisions. Civil liability to company shareholders is also possible. The penalty for violation of the reporting requirements is civil fines. There are no criminal penalties unless the violation was knowing or willing.

These requirements were a reaction to the revelations about secret slush funds maintained by companies involved in the bribery scandals, as well as bribes disguised to look like legitimate transactions. Given the intent requirement of the prohibitions described above, it is generally easier to prove misrepresentation in the financial statements than that an actual "quid pro quo" transaction has occurred. Put another way, these requirements provide a basis for prosecuting a wrongdoer even if the basic crime cannot be proved, much as the gangster Al Capone was finally jailed for tax evasion rather than for more blatant criminal activities like gang shootings.

"Grease" or Facilitating Payments. The 1988 amendments to the FCPA responded to businessmen's complaints that minor officials in many underdeveloped countries demanded small payments, known as "grease"—whether in the form of fees, tips, or gifts—for the provision of routine services such as the issuance of visas, licenses, and permits, as well as for speedy service. These payments, no matter how minor, were illegal under the FCPA as originally enacted. As a practical matter, American business interests were having trouble even getting into countries where petty corruption was common. Congress therefore loosened the FCPA slightly, to permit such payments for the provision or expedition of "routine government action," so long as the payments were not made for the purpose of influencing the award or retention of business.

CRITICISM

A major rationale for the FCPA was the notion that eliminating corruption would create a level playing field for free competition. American businessmen, though, complained bitterly that in fact the opposite was created: U.S.

business was placed at a competitive disadvantage as only U.S. companies were barred from paying bribes, whereas no such restrictions were in place for companies from other countries. The result, these critics charged, is that major contracts went to foreign companies willing to engage in graft.

Other critics attacked the FCPA as being ineffective. They charged that open bribery is prohibited, whereas more sophisticated forms of exerting influence continue to be perfectly legal. For example, payments of charitable contributions or the tacking on of extraneous goods and services outside the economic scope of a contract often serve the same purpose of a corrupt appeal for business. Similarly, the defense of expenditures for bona fide promotional activities can easily be abused. In this cynical view, all the FCPA requires is that companies act in a more refined way than handing over a suitcase filled with cash.

> *Building on the Organization of Economic Cooperation and Development Convention, many programs for the provision of aid in the form of grants or loans from developed countries to the developing world insist that the latter put reforms in place to prevent corruption, so that the aid reaches its targets and goes to the purposes earmarked by the donors rather than into the pockets of corrupt officials.*

THE OECD ANTIBRIBERY CONVENTION

The complaint that the FCPA created a competitive disadvantage for American businessmen was addressed through the adoption of the Convention on Combating Bribery of Foreign Public Officials in International Business Transactions of the OECD, which went into effect on February 15, 1999.

This convention, ratified by thirty-four countries as of 2003, requires participating countries to make it a crime to offer, promise, or give a bribe to a foreign public official to obtain or retain international business deals, and is based in large part on the FCPA. A related text effectively puts an end to the practice according tax deductibility for bribe payments made to foreign officials—a practice that used to be accepted in many major trading countries, such as Germany.

Building on the OECD Convention, many programs for the provision of aid in the form of grants or loans from developed countries to the developing world insist that the latter put reforms in place to prevent corruption, so that the aid reaches its targets and goes to the purposes earmarked by the donors rather than into the pockets of corrupt officials. In this way, developed countries seek to further create a level playing field for open competition for international contracts in an increasingly globalized world.

See also: BRIBERY ACT.

BIBLIOGRAPHY

Goldbarg, Andrea. "The Foreign Corrupt Practices Act and Structural Corruption." 18 *Boston University International Law Journal* 273 (fall 2000).

Johnson, J. Lee. "A Global Economy and the Foreign Corrupt Practices Act: Some Facts Worth Knowing." 63 *Missouri Law Review* 979 (fall 1998).

INTERNET RESOURCE

Transparency International. Business Principles for Countering Bribery. <http://www.transparency.org/building_coalitions/private_sector/business_principles.html>.

FOREIGN INTELLIGENCE SURVEILLANCE ACT (1978)

William Banks

In 1972 the Supreme Court first confronted the tensions between unmonitored executive surveillance and individual freedoms in the national security setting. *United States v. United States District Court* (1972) arose from a criminal proceeding in which the United States charged three defendants with conspiracy to destroy government property—the dynamite bombing of a Central Intelligence Agency (CIA) office in Ann Arbor, Michigan. During pretrial proceedings, the defendants moved to compel disclosure of electronic surveillance. The government admitted that a wiretap had intercepted conversations involving the defendants. However, the executive had acted alone in placing the wiretap, without meeting, to the satisfaction of a magistrate, the usual Fourth Amendment requirement of probable cause, or reason to believe that a crime had been or would soon be committed.

The Supreme Court found authority for national security surveillance implicit in the president's Article II Oath Clause, which includes the power to protect the government against those who would subvert, or undermine, it by unlawful means. Nonetheless, the Court was especially wary of possible abuses of the national security power because of the "privacy values at the core" of the Fourth Amendment and the convergence of First and Fourth Amendment values in national security wiretapping cases. Waiving the Fourth Amendment probable cause requirement could lead the executive to "yield too readily to pressures to obtain incriminating evidence and overlook potential invasions of privacy and protected speech."

Although the Court ruled against the government, the Court implicitly invited Congress to develop a set of standards for domestic intelligence surveillance. Congress did not react immediately, but Justice Lewis F. Powell's opinion provided an important impetus for the development of what became the Foreign Intelligence Surveillance Act (FISA) of 1978 (P. L. 95-511, 92 Stat. 1783). Like the Supreme Court, Congress recognized that surveillance by the executive branch without a warrant and not controlled by specific laws could undermine important constitutional values contained in the First and Fourth Amendments. At the same time, Congress came to appreciate that the nature and purpose of intelligence investigations differs considerably from criminal law enforcement investigations. For that reason, the traditional warrant requirement as practiced by law enforcement might not be the best model for assuring that national security investigations strike the right balance of security and liberty.

Article II Oath Clause

The "Oath Clause" in Article II of the Constitution states: "Before he enter on the Execution of his Office, he shall take the following Oath or Affirmation: 'I do solemnly swear (or affirm) that I will faithfully execute the Office of President of the United States, and will to the best of my Ability, preserve, protect and defend the Constitution of the United States'."

Like the Supreme Court, Congress recognized that surveillance by the executive branch without a warrant and not controlled by specific laws could undermine important constitutional values contained in the First and Fourth Amendments.

STRUCTURE OF THE ACT

FISA defines many categories of electronic surveillance that may be conducted, some of which go beyond conventional telephone taps and hidden microphones. Wiretaps may be used in the United States (so long as at least one party is in the United States) to obtain voice communications, teleprinter, telegraph, facsimile, and digital communications. In 1994, Congress amended FISA to authorize submission of applications for an order approving a physical search in the United States.

The FISA standards are far easier to meet than the standard for obtaining a traditional law enforcement search warrant, which requires evidence that the individual whose property is searched was involved in a crime. Once approved, a search may be conducted at any time within forty-five days. Notice need not be given if the attorney general determines that national security requires secrecy or if the target is not a "United States person" as defined in FISA—a citizen, permanent resident alien, or an association of such persons.

The FISA authorizes the attorney general to approve applications for warrants to conduct electronic surveillance or physical searches within the United States for the purposes of foreign intelligence, if the target is a "foreign power" or "agent of a foreign power." If the attorney general approves an application for a warrant pursuant to FISA, the request is then submitted to any of the judges who sit on a specially constituted court, created by FISA. The Foreign Intelligence Surveillance Court (FISC) consists of eleven United States district court judges designated by the chief justice. These judges meet in secret and are empowered to hear applications for and grant orders approving electronic surveillance and searches anywhere within the United States under the procedures set forth in FISA. Similarly, FISA allows the chief justice to designate three district or court of appeals judges to sit as a special court of appeals to hear appeals by the government from denial of an application by one of the district judges. The government may then appeal to the Supreme Court.

The FISC may permit surveillance of an official foreign power—a foreign government, or a terrorist or political group or organization controlled by a foreign government. A request for such surveillance need not describe the communications sought, the means for accomplishing the surveillance, or the surveillance devices to be employed. Targeting an "agent of a foreign power" is easier for the government to accomplish if an individual is not a "United States person." FISA expressly states that no "United States person" may become a target of FISA surveillance "solely upon the basis of activities protected by the first amendment."

A FISC judge must find probable cause, on the basis of the application, that the target is a foreign power or agent of a foreign power, and that the facilities where the surveillance is directed are or will be used by the target. For "United States persons," the FISC judge must find probable cause that one of four conditions has been met: (1) the target knowingly engages in clandestine intelligence activities on behalf of a foreign power that "may involve" a criminal law violation; (2) the target knowingly engages in other secret intelligence activities on behalf of a foreign power pursuant to the direction of an intelligence network, and his activities involve or are about to involve criminal violations; (3) the target knowingly engages in **sabotage** or international terrorism or is preparing for such activities; or (4) the target knowingly aids or **abets** another who acts in one of the above ways.

THE WAR ON TERRORISM

One question unresolved by FISA is the extent to which the FBI can use FISA surveillance to obtain evidence for criminal prosecution. Ordinarily, law enforcement investigations have this purpose from the start. In contrast, FISA

Fourth Amendment to the Constitution

The Fourth Amendment guarantees "the right of the people to be secure in their persons, houses, papers, and effects, against unreasonable searches and seizures, shall not be violated, and no warrants shall issue, but upon probable cause, supported by oath or affirmation, and particularly describing the place to be searched, and the persons or things to be seized."

sabotage: the destruction of property or obstruction of an action intended to hinder the normal operations of a company or government

abet: to actively, knowingly, and intentionally, assist another in the committing (or attempting) of a crime

One question unresolved by FISA is the extent to which the FBI can use FISA surveillance to obtain evidence for criminal prosecution.

surveillances must have an intelligence purpose. Before 2001, courts that allowed evidence gathered during the surveillance to support a criminal conviction required that intelligence be the "primary" purpose of the surveillance.

After September 11 and enactment of the Patriot Act, the Department of Justice sought approval from the FISC to implement new information-sharing procedures that permit criminal prosecutors or investigators to participate actively in FISA proceedings, even to the extent of initiating and controlling the surveillances approved by the FISC. The government's theory was that enforcing the criminal laws against those accused of terrorist activities also served a foreign intelligence objective. The FISC accepted most of the Department's proposal for information-sharing, but rejected the portion that would permit the criminal division to direct or control FISA procedures. Following the limited rejection by the FISC, the government appealed for the first time in the history of FISA to the special Court of Review, a never-before-constituted appellate court made up of three senior federal judges appointed by the chief justice of the Supreme Court. After a closed hearing, in November 2002 the Court of Review reversed the FISC and upheld the Department of Justice procedures, based on its reading of FISA, as amended by the Patriot Act. The Court of Review decision permits the government to use the FISA procedures for law enforcement objectives so long as there remains a "significant" foreign intelligence purpose for the surveillance or search.

APPLICATION REQUIREMENTS

For potential targets of surveillance, an application must include the following information:

- The name of the officer making the application
- Statements showing the attorney general's approval of the application and identifying and describing the surveillance target and supporting an affirmation that the target is an agent of a foreign power
- A description of the information sought and types of communications to be monitored
- The "minimization" procedures that will be employed to confine the boundaries of the surveillance
- A statement by the National Security Advisor that the information sought is foreign intelligence information that is not obtainable through normal investigative means
- A description of any past applications involving the target
- The surveillance devices to be employed and the means of installation (including whether physical entry will be required)
- The period of time for conducting the surveillance

In emergency circumstances, the president is permitted, through the attorney general, "[n]otwithstanding any other law," to authorize electronic surveillance without a court order for periods up to a year upon a written certification that such surveillance is "solely directed" at communications between or among foreign powers, or a technical intelligence from property or premises "under the open and exclusive control of a foreign power." These emergency powers may be exercised only where (1) there is "no substantial likelihood" that a communication involving a United States person will be acquired, and (2) the attorney general meets minimization requirements and reports these requirements to the intelligence committees and transmits his or her certification of such surveillance under seal to the FISC.

UNSETTLED ISSUES

Although the Supreme Court has not considered the constitutionality of FISA, the lower courts have uniformly followed *United States v. Duggan* (1984) in upholding the FISA procedures. (That ruling stated that FISA is a "constitutionally adequate balancing of the individual's Fourth Amendment rights against the nation's need to obtain foreign intelligence information.") In addition, the extent to which the government may rely on FISA to gain information for the purposes of prosecuting suspected terrorists remains unclear, although the November 2002 Court of Review decision settled the matter for the near term.

See also: ANTITERRORISM AND EFFECTIVE DEATH PENALTY ACT; USA PATRIOT ACT.

BIBLIOGRAPHY

Dycus, Stephen, et al. *National Security Law.* 3d ed. Boston: Aspen Law and Business, 2002.

Maas, Peter. *Killer Spy: The Inside Story of the FBI's Pursuit and Capture of Aldrich Ames, America's Deadliest Spy.* New York: Warner, 1995.

Polmar, Norman, and Thomas B. Allen. *Spy Book: The Encyclopedia of Espionage.* New York: Random House, 1998.

FOREIGN SERVICE ACT OF 1946

Shahla F. Maghzi

The Foreign Service Act of 1946 (P.L. 79-724) is a reorganization initiative established to develop professional opportunities to attract foreign service officers and to train them to become a "disciplined corps" of civil servants. Prior to the passage of the Foreign Service Act, there was little control over the selection of diplomatic and consular personnel representing the United States. After World War I, it became clear that the Foreign Service required restructuring. The first initiative was the Rogers Act of May 24, 1924, which established a career service combining the diplomatic and consular branches of the Foreign Service. Selection of officers was based on an examination and successful completion of a period of service. The second initiative was the Moses-Linthicum Act of February 23, 1931. This act revised the Rogers Act and attempted to address concerns regarding the need to coordinate the diplomatic and consular branches and regularize the promotion policy. These two initiatives contributed substantially to the development of the Foreign Service.

Prior to the passage of the Foreign Service Act, there was little control over the selection of diplomatic and consular personnel representing the United States.

Following America's period of isolation in the early part of the twentieth century and as the demands made on the Foreign Service during the Second World War began to exceed its traditional functions, efforts continued to focus on means of ensuring the comprehensive reorganization of the Foreign

Service. Following President Franklin Roosevelt's second Reorganization Plan, effective July 1, 1939, the Department of State became responsible for the foreign activities of the Departments of Agriculture and Commerce. It also became responsible for ascertaining the "welfare and whereabouts" of American nationals in dangerous zones abroad. In March 1944, the *American Foreign Service Journal* announced an essay contest open to Foreign Service officers for the purpose of presenting criticisms of the operation of the Service and making recommendations for improvements. On the basis of its own studies, the Department of State drafted a proposal for reorganization.

> *The Foreign Service Act was passed by unanimous consent and without lengthy debate on August 13, 1946.*

The Foreign Service Act was passed by unanimous consent without lengthy debate on August 13, 1946. The act undertakes "to improve, strengthen, and expand" the existing Foreign Service organization. It also addresses concerns regarding lack of representation of the American people as a whole by including the objective of eliminating "conditions favorable to inbred prejudice and caste spirit." In addition, according to Alona E. Evans, the major areas of change included administrative organization, personnel structure, and training. The introduction to the act reads:

> *Be it enacted by the Senate and House of Representatives of the United States of America in Congress assembled,* That the President is authorized under the provisions of this Act to appoint, by and with the advice and consent of the Senate, not to exceed two hundred and fifty persons to positions as Foreign Service officers. Each such appointment shall be made by commission to a classified grade and shall be in addition to all other appointments of Foreign Service officers.

> *The act also called for the training of Foreign Service officers in the political and economic policies of other countries so as to enable Foreign Service officers to act, according to Alona Evans, with "objectivity and understanding" abroad.*

The Foreign Service Act of 1946 contributed to increasing the organization of the Foreign Service, the attractiveness of the career aspects of the service, and the regularization of promotions within the service. The number of classes within the career service was reduced from eleven to seven, a new post of Career Minister was introduced, and promotions followed the pattern of "promotion-up or selection-out" which provides for a designated maximum time in which a foreign service officer can remain in a post without being promoted. It also called for the training of Foreign Service officers in the political and economic policies of other countries so as to enable Foreign Service officers to act, according to Alona Evans, with "objectivity and understanding" abroad.

BIBLIOGRAPHY

Evans, Alona E. "The Reorganization of the American Foreign Service." *International Affairs* 24, no. 2 (April 1948): 206–217.

Harrington, J. P. "How the Legislation Developed." *American Foreign Service Journal,* no. 23 (1946): 8.

Ravndal, C. M. "The New Duties of Our Foreign Service." *American Foreign Service Journal,* no. 19 (1942): 357–59.

FREEDMEN'S BUREAU ACTS (1865 AND 1868)

Elizabeth Regosin

During the **Reconstruction** period following the Civil War, Congress enacted two major pieces of legislation, the first to create the Bureau of Refugees, Freedmen, and Abandoned Lands, or Freedmen's Bureau, and the second (getting past two presidential **vetoes**) to sustain the Freedmen's Bureau. The history of the bureau's fate at the hands of legislators and the president reflects the history of Reconstruction itself, a history of good intentions, cross purposes, and promises both fulfilled and unfulfilled.

Reconstruction: the political and economic reorganization of the South after the Civil War

veto: when the president returns a bill to Congress with a statement of objections

BACKGROUND

Congress passed the first piece of legislation, "An Act to establish a Bureau for the Relief of Freedmen and Refugees," on March 3, 1865 (13 Stat. 507), as the American Civil War neared its end. As the historian Eric Foner explains, the idea for such an agency had been brewing since 1863, when the three-man American Freedmen's Inquiry Commission reported to Congress on its fact-finding mission about the condition of African Americans in the South. According to the report, former slaves would need temporary assistance as they made the transition from slavery to freedom. Designed to grant material aid, to supervise and redistribute abandoned land in "insurrectionary states," and to address any subject relating to the freedpeople, the initial plan for the Freedmen's Bureau was proposed for "freedmen" alone. In the debates around the bill in both houses of Congress, legislators raised the question of including those loyal whites in the South who might have needed assistance at the war's end. Other areas of concern included where in the government the bureau would be housed and what the bureau's role would be in the maintenance and distribution of abandoned lands to freedpeople.

FEATURES OF THE ACT

The act of March 3, 1865, provided that the Bureau of Refugees, Freedmen, and Abandoned Lands would operate "during the present war of rebellion, and for one year thereafter," offering freedpeople and loyal white Southerners material aid and access to land. The bureau was to be housed in the War Department and placed under the control of a commissioner who was to be appointed by the president and to work under the president's direction. The act authorized the secretary of war to "direct such issues of provisions, clothing, and fuel, as he may deem needful for the immediate and temporary shelter and supply of destitute and suffering refugees and freedmen and their wives and children...." In addition, it provided that the commissioner could set aside "tracts of land within the insurrectionary states as shall have been abandoned ... and to every male citizen, whether refugee or freedman ... there shall be assigned not more than forty acres of such land, and the person to whom it was so assigned shall be protected in the use and enjoyment of the land for the term of three years...." The provision for land also allowed freedmen and refugees to purchase the land, although the language of the statute was vague as to how that might come about and whether the federal government actually had the authority to do so.

Leadership of the Freedmen's Bureau fell into the hands of Union General Oliver Otis Howard, who was named commissioner in May 1864. Howard and his agents were busy that first year. Much of their work was devoted to helping former slaves make the transition from slavery to freedom not just economically, as perhaps originally conceived, but also socially and politically. Among their many responsibilities, Freedmen's Bureau agents doled out clothing, food, and other provisions. They registered freedpeople's marriages and spoke to them about "proper" familial relationships. They also helped freedpeople locate family members from whom they had been separated under slavery, and they assisted freedpeople in relocating. Agents helped black communities to establish schools. As the historian Donald G. Nieman explains, bureau agents soon discovered that facilitating the transition from slavery to freedom required attention to the relationships between freedpeople and their employers and protection of freedpeople's legal rights. Before long, bureau agents were negotiating labor contracts and even setting up courts to **arbitrate** disputes among freedmen and between blacks and whites. One of the agents' more challenging tasks was protecting freedpeople from discrimination in local courts and by local officials.

arbitrate: to resolve disagreements whereby parties choose a person or group of people familiar with the issues in question to hear and settle their dispute

EXTENDING THE BUREAU'S SERVICES

Originally, legislators saw the creation of the bureau as an extraordinary wartime measure, necessary to protect and support those innocent victims of slavery and the war. Since the bureau's existence was only temporary, a means of helping freedpeople and refugees get on their feet, the original act had not even provided for a budget outside of what already existed in the War Department. As the bureau's expiration date drew near, it was obvious to many that its services were still desperately needed in the South, in spite of the fact that the war was over. In fact, to many it seemed that the end of the war produced a greater need for a government agency to watch over the freedpeople. In addition to violence and prejudice, emancipation brought

The Impeachment of Andrew Johnson

Andrew Johnson, who was vice president under Abraham Lincoln, assumed the presidency in 1865 when Lincoln was assassinated. Johnson supported a modified version of Lincoln's plan for Reconstruction, but he faced strong opposition from those who felt his policies did not adequately protect the newly won rights of former slaves. Three members of Johnson's cabinet resigned because they disagreed with his positions, and one of the remaining four members, Secretary of War Edwin M. Stanton, also opposed Johnson. In 1866 Johnson vetoed the Freedmen's Bureau Act, which provided for temporary aid to former slaves making their transition to freedom, and Congress passed the bill over his veto. The following year Johnson vetoed the Tenure of Office Act, which Congress had designed to keep Stanton in office as his disagreements with Johnson escalated—and Congress once again passed the law over his veto. The Tenure of Office Act stipulated that individuals could only be dismissed from Senate appointments with the consent of the Senate, and that a president seeking to remove such an individual was guilty of a "high misdemeanor." Despite increasing pressure from Johnson, Stanton refused to resign, and Johnson ultimately removed him and appointed Lorenzo Thomas in his place. Three days later, the House of Representatives voted to impeach Johnson for "high crimes and misdemeanors" in defiance of the Tenure of Office Act. Johnson based his defense on the idea that the Constitution allowed the president to remove cabinet members from office and that the Tenure of Office Act was unconstitutional. The trial and vote were dramatic, with Senator James W. Grimes of Iowa, who had suffered a stroke, carried into the chamber to cast his vote for acquittal. Johnson was acquitted by one vote. He remained in office until 1869, but his battles with Congress rendered him ineffective for the remainder of his term. Johnson was elected to the Senate by Tennessee shortly before his death in 1875.

discriminatory laws, known as Black Codes, in many southern states. Provisions of these laws limited freedpeople's mobility, undermined their civil rights, and gave them stiffer penalties than whites for crimes.

In January 1866 Illinois senator Lyman Trumbull introduced into Congress a new Freedmen's Bureau bill (S. 60) designed not only to extend the life of the bureau but also to expand the scope of its responsibilities. S. 60 initially proposed that the bureau "continue in force until otherwise provided by law." New provisions in the 1866 bill included a broader jurisdiction, the division of those parts of the country where freedpeople resided into twelve districts, three million acres of public land set aside for freedpeople to buy or settle upon, the validation of claims to confiscated lands granted to freedpeople during the war by General Sherman, provisions for schools and asylums, and military protection and jurisdiction over cases where the rights and immunities of freedpeople had been denied in the courts or by state and local laws.

LEGISLATIVE DEBATE

Debates around the expanded scope of the bureau as outlined in S. 60 focused on issues such as the bureau's term and jurisdiction, the federal government's responsibilities, and the power of the legislative branch to extend the bureau during peacetime. Some Democrats objected to what they saw as the permanent nature of this provision. One main question was where the bureau should operate. Initially the bill provided that the bureau would operate wherever there were freedpeople and refugees in the United States. Some legislators proposed that the jurisdiction be limited to those states that were in rebellion, in other words, those states that had seceded from the Union. Others argued against such limitations, pointing to a need for the Freedmen's Bureau in the border states where many freedpeople resided.

Those who objected to the bill raised questions about the authority of the different branches of government to enact and enforce such legislation. They asked whether the material needs of freedpeople and refugees were the concern of the states or of the federal government. They challenged the legislature's authority to enact such legislation during peacetime. Opponents claimed that the creation of a permanent, peacetime bureau to protect freedpeople's rights would, in essence, be the creation of a separate judiciary for them.

VETO, REVISION, AND OVERRIDE

In the end, both houses of Congress passed S. 60, but President Andrew Johnson vetoed it. Among the concerns raised in his veto message, Johnson claimed that what had originally been a wartime measure would have "no limitation in point of time, but will form a part of the permanent legislation of this country." He argued that the bill would give the Freedmen's Bureau too much power and that it would be too expensive to maintain it. In keeping with his lenient policy of restoring land to white Southerners, Johnson claimed that the bill's land provisions violated the Fifth Amendment right to property. Ultimately, Johnson argued that the Freedmen's Bureau was unnecessary because freedpeople were protected under the Constitution and in the courts of the states and of the nation.

Congress did not **override** Johnson's veto that day, but six months later, when he vetoed the revised bill (H.R. 613), Congress overrode his veto and

override: if the President vetoes a bill passed by Congress, the bill can still become law if two-thirds of each House of Congress votes to override the veto

passed the law extending the bureau's tenure and expanding its scope. Enacted on July 16, 1866, the new Freedmen's Bureau Act (14 Stat. 173) extended the life of the bureau for two years, provided for the creation of schools, authorized the secretary of war to "issue such medical stores or other supplies and transportation, and afford such medical or other aid," and defined ineligible those who could "find employment, and could, by proper industry or exertion, avoid such destitution, suffering, or dependence." Addressing concerns voiced in both houses of Congress and by the president, the new law did not divide the South into districts, greatly reduced its land provisions, and lowered the cost of the bureau by minimizing its structure.

According to the new law, bureau agents would continue their work to protect from discrimination the freedpeople's "right to make and enforce contracts, to sue, be parties, and give evidence, to inherit, purchase, lease, sell, hold, and convey real and personal property, and to have full and equal benefit of all laws and proceedings concerning personal liberty, personal security, and the acquisition, enjoyment, and disposition of estate, real and personal, including the constitutional right to bear arms." In addition, the act extended military protection and jurisdiction in states where judicial proceedings had been interrupted by the war only until those states were fully restored in their constitutional relationship to the government and were again represented in Congress.

EFFECTIVENESS

Although its structure and function were pared down to the barest minimum by the end of 1868, the Freedmen's Bureau operated until June 1872. Historians have long debated the extent to which it was successful and what ultimately was the reason for its failure to fully protect and provide for freedpeople. Some point to President Johnson's explicit efforts to undermine the bureau as well as his lenience toward Southern landowners. Others point to divisions in Congress and concessions that led to legislation inadequate to the task of supporting, funding, and staffing the Freedmen's Bureau and providing freedpeople with access to land. Still others claim that the bureau's downfall was in its day-to-day operations. As these historians see it, the fault rests either with Howard, or with the other employees of the bureau, who in their ambivalence or outright racism did not help freedpeople as much as they could have.

Historians have long debated the extent to which it was successful and what ultimately was the reason for its failure to fully protect and provide for freedpeople.

What is clear is that the bureau's potential was great and the tasks it was charged with of great importance. Although it made significant efforts on behalf of freedpeople, when its doors were closed the work of the Freedmen's Bureau remained largely undone.

See also: CIVIL RIGHTS ACTS OF 1866, 1875; FORCE ACT OF 1871; KU KLUX KLAN ACT.

BIBLIOGRAPHY

Foner, Eric. *Reconstruction: America's Unfinished Revolution*. New York: Harper and Row, 1988.

Litwack, Leon. *Been in the Storm So Long: The Aftermath of Slavery*. New York: Vintage Books, 1979.

McFeely, William S. *Yankee Stepfather: General O.O. Howard and the Freedmen.* New Haven: Yale University Press, 1968.

Moreno, Paul. "Racial Classifications and Reconstruction Legislation." *Journal of Southern History* 61, no. 2 (May 1995): 271–304.

Nieman, Donald G. *To Set the Law in Motion.* New York: KTO Press, 1979.

Nieman, Donald G. "Andrew Johnson, the Freedmen's Bureau, and the Problem of Equal Rights, 1865–1866." In *The Freedmen's Bureau and Black Freedom,* ed. Donald G. Nieman. New York and London: Garland Publishing, 1994.

FREEDOM OF ACCESS TO CLINIC ENTRANCES ACT (1994)

Lucinda Finley

The Freedom of Access to Clinic Entrances Act (P.L. 103-259), passed on May 26, 1994 and codified at 18 U.S.C. § 248), popularly known by its acronym, FACE, makes it a federal crime intentionally to use force, threats of force, or physical obstruction in order to intimidate or interfere with a person because that person is providing or obtaining reproductive health services. The definition of prohibited physical obstruction includes making **ingress** to or egress from a facility impassable, but it goes further also to prohibit rendering passage in or out "unreasonably difficult or hazardous." FACE also prohibits actual or attempted property vandalism of reproductive health clinics.

ingress: a means or place for entering

In addition to its criminal penalties, which vary with the degree of force or obstruction and with the number of prior offenses, FACE also authorizes those affected by these acts, or the federal or state attorneys general, to bring civil lawsuits to recover monetary damages and to get injunctions that prohibit identified people from continuing to do these prohibited acts of obstructing access to reproductive health facilities. Although FACE was passed in response to a growing national problem of obstruction and vandalism and violence aimed at abortion clinics and individual abortion providers, the statutory definition of protected reproductive health services is much broader than abortion. Protected services "includes medical, surgical, counseling or referral services relating to the human reproductive system, including services relating to pregnancy or the termination of a pregnancy." Under this broad definition, the law would equally apply to someone who tried to block access to a Planned Parenthood facility that provides prenatal care and birth control but not abortions, and to someone who tried to block and interfere with staff or patients at a Crisis Pregnancy Center that ardently lobbies against abortion.

> *FACE makes it a federal crime intentionally to use force, threats of force, or physical obstruction in order to intimidate or interfere with a person because that person is providing or obtaining reproductive health services.*

LEGISLATIVE HISTORY

In the late 1980s, there was a noticeable increase in obstructive protests and vandalism at abortion clinics, as well as increased acts of violence aimed at abortion providers. The group Operation Rescue National formed to engage in what it called "rescues" at abortion clinics, which consisted of large numbers of people sitting or lying in front of clinic doors and driveways so that no one could get in or out. Some of these blockades degenerated into pushing, shoving, and harassment of people trying to get into clinics. In the summer of 1991, in an event it dubbed "the Summer of Mercy," Operation Rescue brought thousands of people to Wichita, Kansas, and for almost a month laid siege to the streets surrounding Dr. George Tiller's Women's Health Care Services clinic. The increasingly chaotic and dangerous situation, with impassable city streets, some stranded patients facing medical emergencies, hundreds of arrests and an overwhelmed local police force that had to be bolstered by a federal court injunction and federal marshals, garnered national media attention.

The Wichita event, and Operation Rescue's emboldened pronouncements that it would hold more large scale "rescue" sieges of other cities in the next year, led pro-choice organizations to call for national legislation with strengthened criminal penalties to respond to what was clearly not just a localized problem. In 1991, Congressman Mel Levine from the Los Angeles area introduced a bill he called the "Freedom of Access to Clinic Entrances Act," to make it a federal crime to blockade a medical facility. This bill began to gain co-sponsors and interest in Congress in the spring of 1992, when Operation Rescue tried to reproduce its Wichita event in Buffalo, New York, in an action it called "the Spring of Life." For two weeks several hundred protestors from around the nation came to Buffalo and clogged the streets and blocked access in front of several Buffalo area clinics. The local police again were reinforced by federal marshals and over 600 people were arrested.

In addition to the widely publicized massive blockades in Wichita and Buffalo, from 1991 to 1992 there were over 150 other blockade events at abortion clinics in all parts of the country. Death threats against doctors and clinic staff also increased, as did destructive acts of vandalism including spraying clinics with butyric acid, a hazardous noxious chemical whose putrid fumes render an area unfit for occupancy. This escalating climate of blockades and violence aimed at abortion clinics created a growing sense of urgency among pro-choice advocacy groups for a federal response.

On May 6, 1992, a few days after Operation Rescue ended the Buffalo "Spring of Life" blockades, the House Subcommittee on Crime and Criminal Justice of the Judiciary Committee convened oversight hearings to consider the growing problem of clinic blockades and the necessity for—and constitutionality of—federal legislation to criminalize blockading reproductive health facilities. Rep. Charles Schumer from New York, who became New York's senator a few years later, chaired the hearings and soon became a leading cosponsor of FACE along with Representative Connie Morella from Maryland. Another key active co-sponsor was Representative Louise Slaughter, also from New York. At these hearings, members of Congress heard from three women who had been patients trying to get into blockaded clinics, including a woman who had been trapped in her car outside the Wichita clinic, and a Michigan woman who could not get into her gynecologist's office for an urgent prenatal appointment to monitor her high risk pregnancy. A Virginia police chief also testified that his small department could not handle the large–scale protests and needed the additional resources and reinforcement of federal authorities. Keith Tucci, then the head of Operation Rescue, who had come to Washington directly from the streets of Buffalo, testified that their peaceful **civil disobedience** was akin to that

civil disobedience: nonviolent protest

of the abolitionists, women's suffrage activists, and civil rights advocates of the 1950s. He warned that legislating against the passive resistance of blockades would escalate violent confrontation at abortion clinics.

There was no further action on clinic blockade legislation until the spring of 1993. Three events combined to create both a sense of urgency and enhanced political prospects for a federal response. The pro-choice Bill Clinton became president in January 1993, and appointed a pro-choice attorney general, Janet Reno, who promised that the problem of violence targeted at clinics would become a top priority for the Justice Department. The U.S. Supreme Court, however, dealt a serious blow to available legal avenues for a federal role, when in January 1993 it ruled in the case of *Bray v. Alexandria Women's Health Clinic* that the federal civil rights statute known as the Klu Klux Klan Act did not apply to protestors obstructing access to abortion. This statute had been the basis for several federal court suits and injunctions against clinic blockaders, including the federal intervention in Wichita and Buffalo. After the *Bray* decision, Attorney General Reno and members of Congress concluded that new legislation was essential for federal law enforcement and federal courts to have any authority to

Police arrest antiabortion protesters blockading the entrance to the Water Street abortion clinic in Milwaukee, Wisconsin, June 20, 1992. (© AP/WIDE WORLD PHOTOS)

Sensitive to the first amendment issues involved when responding to a protest movement that used both legitimate and illegitimate tactics, they modeled the bill after a provision of the federal civil rights law that prohibits using force or threats of force to willfully injure, intimidate, or interfere with people engaging in a variety of federally protected activities, including voting.

deal with a problem that obviously was national in scope. The final impetus that made FACE inevitable happened in March 1993, when an antiabortion protestor named Michael Griffin, who had previously limited himself to blockades and picketing, murdered a Florida physician, Dr. David Gunn, as Gunn tried to enter the clinic where he worked. Arguments that the antiabortion protest movement was just peaceful civil disobedience became much harder to sustain.

Shortly after the confirmation of newly elected President Bill Clinton's attorney general, Janet Reno, staff attorneys from the Department of Justice met with staff from the Senate Labor and Human Resources Committee chaired by Senator Kennedy of Massachusetts, to draft a bill, S. 636, that with some modifications became the FACE law. Sensitive to the first amendment issues involved when responding to a protest movement that used both legitimate and illegitimate tactics, they modeled the bill after a provision of the federal civil rights law that prohibits using force or threats of force to willfully injure, intimidate, or interfere with people engaging in a variety of federally protected activities, including voting. S. 636 prohibited using force, threats of force, or physical obstruction to injure, intimidate, or interfere with people obtaining or helping to obtain abortion services. Representatives Schumer and Morella introduced a companion House version, H.R. 796.

In March 1994 the House voted to adopt S. 636 as a substitute for its bill but insisted on a conference committee to iron out a few differences. In early May 1994 each chamber adopted the conference committee final version, and on May 26, 1994, President Clinton signed FACE into law. Unfortunately, the enhanced federal criminal penalties soon had to be invoked, when, shortly after FACE became law, antiabortion protestor Paul Hill murdered Dr. Brittain and John Barrett, who was helping to escort him into a Pensacola, Florida, clinic.

FACE IN THE COURTS

The Justice Department immediately began bringing criminal prosecutions against those who blockaded clinics, and in federal courts in all parts of the country defendants challenged the constitutionality of FACE. They contended that FACE exceeded Congress's power under the Commerce Clause because they were engaged in political protest, not economic activity, and that FACE violated the First Amendment. Courts have routinely rebuffed these constitutional challenges, and the U.S. Supreme Court has consistently refused to hear any challenges to FACE. Within less than a decade after it became law, FACE's constitutionality under the First Amendment and Commerce Clause was considered a settled legal issue.

Courts that have upheld FACE as consistent with the First Amendment have emphasized that the statute targets the prohibited acts of force, threats, and obstruction, not protected speech.

Courts that have upheld FACE as consistent with the First Amendment have emphasized that the statute targets the prohibited acts of force, threats, and obstruction, not protected speech. To the extent that some expressive activities may fall into these definitions, the act does not single out speech because of its content and government's compelling interest in public safety and ensuring safe access to health care justifies any incidental effects on protected speech. Courts have also rejected the argument that FACE discriminates against the antiabortion viewpoint, noting that it applies equally to acts directed at staff or patients of antiabortion health care facilities.

Rejecting Commerce Clause challenges, courts have reasoned that the Act prohibits activities that are aimed at interfering with businesses that are substantially engaged in interstate commerce. Many patients and doctors have traveled interstate to obtain or provide services, and clinics purchase their equipment in interstate commerce. Even after the Supreme Court in 2000 adopted stricter limits on the scope of Congress's Commerce Clause power, courts have still ruled that FACE is a valid exercise of the Commerce power.

IMPACT OF FACE ON BLOCKADES AND CLINIC VIOLENCE

Since FACE's passage and its initial enforcement, antiabortion protestors have largely abandoned the tactic of large scale blockades. Operation Rescue and similar groups such as the Lambs of Christ claim that they have been deterred from this tactic by the federal criminal penalties. In those civil FACE cases that have resulted in buffer zone injunctions, protest activity and obstruction has decreased significantly. While individual or smaller scale instances of picketing, driveway interference, and harassment still occur, FACE has been credited by national abortion rights organizations with reducing the climate of obstruction and harassment at clinics.

While no law can completely stop violence, FACE has proved to be an important tool for clinics to protect themselves against obstruction and threats, and for the federal government to investigate and levy serious penalties against the most extreme acts of violence against reproductive health providers.

The most dedicated extreme proponents of violence, however, have not been deterred, just as they told Congress that no "man's law" would keep them from following what they regard as a higher command. After September 11, 2001 and the real anthrax attacks on the Senate and media outlets, abortion clinics around the country received a wave of letters purporting to contain anthrax and had to undergo full decontamination. The person accused of committing these attacks, who was branded a domestic terrorist by the attorney general, is at the time of this printing awaiting trial on federal FACE charges. Clinic bombings continue, and when the alleged perpetrators are apprehended, FACE is also used to levy serious penalties against them. Another abortion provider, Dr. Barnett Slepian, was murdered in 1998 in Buffalo, New York, and the man convicted of his murder is also facing a federal criminal trial under FACE. While no law can completely stop violence, FACE has proved to be an important tool for clinics to protect themselves against obstruction and threats, and for the federal government to investigate and levy serious penalties against the most extreme acts of violence against reproductive health providers.

BIBLIOGRAPHY

Campbell, Regina. "'FACE'ing the Facts: Does the Freedom of Access to Clinic Entrances Act Violate Freedom of Speech?" 64 *University of Cincinnati Law Review* 947 (1996).

Franco, Helen R. "Note & Comment: Freedom of Access to Clinic Entrances Act of 1994: The Face of Things to Come." 19 *Nova Law Review* 1083 (1995).

Risen, James, and Judy L. Thomas. *Wrath of Angels: The American Abortion War.* New York: Basic Books, 1998.

Tepper, Arianne K. "Comment: In Your F.A.C.E.: Federal Enforcement of the Freedom of Access to Clinic Entrances Act." 17 *Pace Law Review* 489 (1997).

Wainwright, Jessica. "The Evolutionary War on First Amendment Rights and Abortion Clinic Demonstrations." 36 *New England Law Journal* 231 (2001).

FREEDOM OF INFORMATION ACT (1966)

Robert G. Vaughn

The Freedom of Information Act (P.L. 89-554, 80 Stat. 383) asserts the public's right to know about the activities of government. That right to know is the foundation of accountability in a democracy and in fact preserves democratic government. The First Amendment right of free speech draws power from the availability of information, because knowledge enables people to identify government misconduct or incompetence and challenge government actions. Lacking access to information about government weakens the right to speak and the right to associate with others to advocate for change. Criticism without information is less powerful; ignorance dulls outrage and reduces the incentives to organize for democratic change. The supporters of the act often quote James Madison, the fourth president of the United States: "Knowledge will forever govern ignorance. And a people who mean to be their own governors, must arm themselves with the power knowledge gives. A popular government without popular information or the means of acquiring it is but a prologue to a farce or a tragedy or perhaps both."

> *The right to know is the foundation of accountability in a democracy and in fact preserves democratic government.*

"ANY-PERSON" ACCESS

Before passage of the act, the existing administrative provisions required people seeking government documents to state why they wanted them and allowed government officials to decide whether the interests in disclosure outweighed the interests in secrecy. Not surprisingly, these officials usually denied access to requested documents. Government officials also withheld rulings and standards used to exercise governmental authority, thereby creating a type of "secret law." The act amended these provisions to require that certain types of records be made available for public inspection. These documents include statements of policy and interpretations of rules and policies not published in the *Federal Register*, final opinions resulting from agency adjudications, and manuals that are not offered for sale but that affect a member of the public.

Federal Register: a newspaper published daily by the National Archives and Records Administration to notify the public of federal agency regulations, proposed rules and notices, executive orders, and other executive branch documents

Other documents and records are to be available on request to "any person." Requesters do not have to explain why they want the documents. Any-person access and the policy that government documents and records are public strengthens the public's right to know and reduces the discretion of governmental officials.

> *Some documents and records are to be available on request to "any person." Requesters do not have to explain why they want the documents.*

The law also establishes detailed procedures for requests and provides for administrative appeals of denials of requests. These procedures also address issues such as the time limits for responding to requests, the fees that may be charged (as well as the possibility of waivers or reductions of fees), and other obligations of the agency. One crucial provision requires that the agency segregate documents that can be withheld from ones that should be disclosed. Most important, a requester who has unsuccessfully sought documents from a government agency may ask a federal district court to order an agency to disclose these documents. In this suit, the federal court is bound neither by an agency's determinations of fact nor by its interpretation of the act. The federal courts have often ordered the disclosure of withheld documents, and judicial decisions have interpreted and given effect to many parts of the law.

EXEMPTIONS

The act, however, permits government officials to withhold documents that fall under one of nine exemptions contained in the law. These exemptions address documents:

(1) Properly classified in the interests of national defense or foreign policy
(2) That are internal guides discussing enforcement strategies, the release of which would risk evasion of the law
(3) The disclosure of which is specifically prohibited by other laws
(4) Containing confidential or privileged commercial or financial information
(5) Protected by litigation privileges, including the attorney-client, work product and deliberative process privileges
(6) The release of which would constitute a clearly unwarranted invasion of personal privacy
(7) Compiled for law-enforcement purpose, the release of which would, or in some instances could reasonably be expected to, create the risk of certain harms
(8) Contained in or related to oversight of financial institutions by an agency charged with regulation or supervision of such institutions
(9) Containing geophysical and geological information regarding oil wells

Generally, these exemptions allow government officials only to withhold documents but do not require them to do so. However, other laws, such as those protecting personal privacy, controlling the dissemination of classified

What Types of Information Have Been Requested?

The following have been requested under the Freedom of Information Act:

- Documents relating to underground nuclear testing.
- CIA records on whether the agency played a role in the assassination of John F. Kennedy or obstructed its investigation.
- Documents on Richard Nixon's use of the FBI to dig up "dirt" on political opponents.
- CIA files about sightings of unidentified flying objects (UFOs).

- Payroll reports submitted by nonunion contractors (requested by an electricians' union).

- CIA documents about the Bay of Pigs invasion of Cuba.

- Records of the Environmental Protection Agency about the agency's compliance with its federally mandated duties.

- Reports on Vietnam-era prisoners of war and soldiers listed as missing in action.

In the amendments of 1974 and 1976 Congress signaled its continuing support of the principle of open government and its willingness to address bureaucratic opposition to the law.

information, or specifically requiring withholding are exceptions to this general rule.

Much of the litigation under the act has focused on the meaning of the exemptions. The exemptions addressing national security, the deliberative process within and among federal agencies, the protection of business records, personal privacy, and law enforcement records have generated the most litigation. The Supreme Court has emphasized that the exemptions to the act must be "narrowly construed." A narrow interpretation of the scope of the exemptions prevents them from swallowing the general principles of the act requiring access to government documents.

AMENDMENTS

Although the act has been amended on a number of occasions, the most important amendments occurred in 1974 and in 1996. The 1974 amendments responded to agency practices thought to demonstrate an unwillingness to apply the right-to-know principle underlying the law. These amendments strengthened deadlines for agency responses, regulated fees and fee waivers, and provided for personal sanctions against federal officials who acted arbitrarily in withholding requested documents. These amendments also revised the exemption regarding national security information: they reversed an interpretation by the Supreme Court that denied federal judges the authority to determine whether classified documents were in fact properly classified. The amendments also responded to decisions that had expanded the scope of the law enforcement exemption. In these amendments Congress signaled its continuing support of the principle of open government and its willingness to address bureaucratic opposition to the law.

The Electronic Freedom of Information Act of 1996 (EFOIA) also changed procedures under the act to address the problem of agency delay in responding to requests. EFOIA expands the time that agencies have to respond to an initial request in an attempt to create more realistic standards for agencies. It also directs agencies to create categories of requesters whose requests can be considered on other than a first-come, first-served basis. These categories include requesters who can demonstrate that failure to obtain quickly requested records would endanger the life or physical safety of a person, and also requesters primarily involved in the dissemination of information to the public, if their requests are ones urgently requiring that the public be informed about "actual or alleged Federal Government activity." EFOIA allows agencies to create different avenues for processing requests, such as by considering large and small requests in different groups. It also limits the ability of agencies to use "exceptional circumstances" as an excuse for delay resulting from agencies' ordinary backlogs.

Many users of the act are private parties rather than newspapers, television stations, and other media.

EFOIA modifies the act for an electronic age. It broadly defines electronic records, includes library and reference materials within the definition of record, increases the ability of requesters to obtain documents in electronic form, directs agencies to conduct electronic searches, and considers how agencies should treat computerized removal of exempt information from request documents.

Most important, EFOIA imposes greater responsibilities on agencies to disseminate information rather than simply respond to requests. Now, agencies are required to make available any documents that "have become or are likely to become the subject of subsequent requests for substantially the same records." These records must be provided online in virtual reading rooms that a person can access without physically appearing at an agency. Agencies are also required to publish indices and guides that will help in framing a request. These changes shift the standard procedure from a request-and-respond model of access to one that relies more heavily on dissemination of information by the government.

REQUESTS BY PRIVATE PARTIES

Many users of the act are private parties rather than newspapers, television stations, and other media. The government holds not only information that it has created but also information that has been submitted to it. Much of this information does not directly concern the performance of government officials. For example, businesses seek documents from the government about their competitors, and consumers seek documents relating to health and safety information concerning consumer products or information about consumer frauds or other illegal business practices. In this sense, the act has helped to support competition among firms and to provide consumers with information to participate efficiently in the market.

Requests by private parties also support the principle of government accountability. For example, government contractors can acquire information about successful bidders. This not only serves the contractors' own commercial interests but also helps to ensure that the contracting process operates fairly. Government documents about risks to public health and safety also reinforce the responsibility of the government to attend to those risks.

The United States Freedom of Information Act is not the oldest in the world, but it has been one of the most influential. Dozens of countries, including ones with a reputation for bureaucratic secrecy, such as Great Britain and Japan, have adopted freedom of information laws. Countries throughout the world, including many nations in Eastern Europe and countries that were once part of the Soviet Union, have adopted such laws as an important step in their transition to democratic government.

See also: FEDERAL ADVISORY COMMITTEE ACT; GOVERNMENT IN THE SUNSHINE ACT; PRIVACY ACT OF 1974.

BIBLIOGRAPHY

Leahy, Patrick, et al. "Recent Developments: Electronic Freedom of Information Act." *Administrative Law Review* 50 (1998): 339–458.

O'Reilly, James T. *Federal Information Disclosure.* Colorado Springs, CO: Shepard's, 1977.

FUGITIVE SLAVE ACTS (1793, 1850)

Arthur G. LeFrancois

By the middle of the nineteenth century, the issue of slavery had caused a deep division between North and South. Slavery was an important part of the Southern way of life, and slave labor was a significant aspect of the Southern states' economy. Northerners opposed slavery yet were concerned that the political, economic, and ideological conflict with the South over slavery could threaten a civil war between the two sides.

The conflict intensified over the issue of fugitive, or escaped, slaves. Because slaves were treated as property in the South, slave owners felt it was their right to seek out and recapture slaves who had escaped to free Northern states. Northerners tended to view this practice as kidnapping. Many wondered if officials in the free states had a duty not to interfere with the slave owner or in fact had the power to declare the slave a free person. Article 4, section 2 of the Constitution stated that slaves who escaped to free states had to be surrendered to their owners upon demand. But although the Constitution recognized the institution of slavery and the rights of slave owners, it was still unclear just what the law required of the people and officials in free states in regard to the matter of fugitive slaves. In other words, enforcement of the Constitution on this matter was a gray area decades before the Civil War.

> *Although the Constitution recognized the institution of slavery and the rights of slave owners, it was still unclear just what the law required of the people and officials in free states in regard to the matter of fugitive slaves.*

THE FUGITIVE SLAVE ACT OF 1793

The Fugitive Slave Act of 1793 (1 Stat. 302) was an effort to provide a means to enforce the constitutional clause concerning escaped slaves. The act allowed a slave owner to seize an escaped slave, present the slave before a federal or local judge, and, upon proof of ownership, receive a certificate authorizing the slave to be retaken. It also established a penalty of 500 dollars for obstructing an owner's efforts to retake a slave, or for rescuing, harboring, or concealing a fugitive slave.

Slave Reparations

Many people believe that the descendents of slaves should be compensated, or paid "reparations," for the injustices that their ancestors endured. Reparations have been paid to other groups who were treated unjustly, such as Japanese Americans interned during World War II. While some believe that reparations should be paid by the U.S. government, others have begun seeking compensation by filing lawsuits against corporations that benefited from slavery. Opponents of reparations argue that many black Americans are not descended from slaves, and that it would be difficult to establish who would be eligible for reparations. Furthermore, many white Americans are descended from people who immigrated to the United States after the Civil War, and so should not be blamed for slavery or made responsible for paying reparations. Proponents of reparations, on the other hand, argue that black Americans as a group continue to suffer from the legacy of slavery, regardless of their particular lineage. Some propose that reparations be paid into a fund that would finance education, health care, and economic opportunities for black Americans rather than be paid to individuals.

Some Northerners saw the act as providing an excuse for the kidnapping of free blacks. Others resented the ability of slave owners to reclaim slaves who might have escaped many years ago and who had new lives in the North. As a result, Northern states responded to the act by passing "personal liberty" laws, which protected alleged fugitive slaves in various ways. Southerners saw these laws as objectionable efforts to get around the act and the Constitution.

In 1842, in *Prigg v. Pennsylvania*, the Supreme Court held that Pennsylvania's personal liberty law of 1826 was unconstitutional. Edward Prigg had been convicted of kidnapping for taking a black woman and her children from Pennsylvania (a free state) to Maryland (a slave state). The Supreme Court overturned his conviction, holding that state laws could not permissibly interfere with the rights of slave owners reclaiming fugitive slaves. In 1847 the Court reaffirmed the constitutionality of the 1793 act in *Jones v. Van Zandt*.

The Fugitive Slave Act of 1850 (9 Stat. 462) was an important part of the Compromise of 1850.

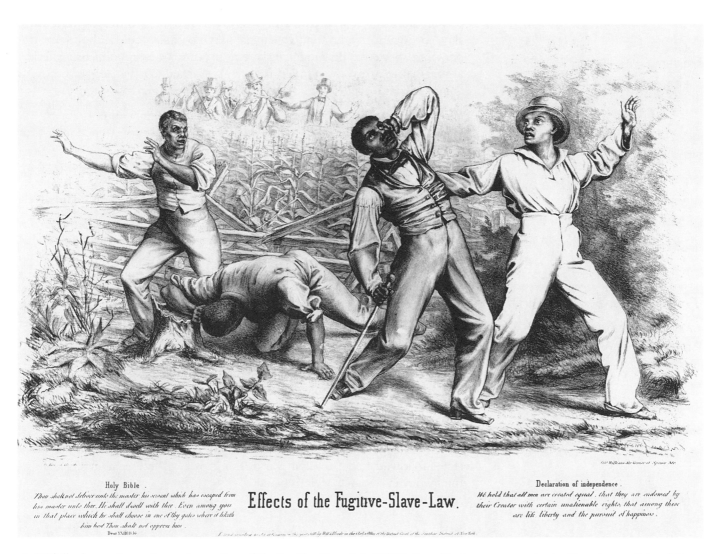

Effects of the Fugitive-Slave-Law.

Holy Bible.
Thou shalt not deliver unto the master his servant which has escaped from his master unto thee. He shall dwell with thee. Even among you in that place which he shall choose in one of thy gates where it liketh him best. Thou shalt not oppress him.
Deut XXIII.15.16

Declaration of independence.
We hold that all men are created equal, that they are endowed by their Creator with certain unalienable rights, that among these are life liberty and the pursuit of happiness.

A skillfully drawn dramatic condemnation of the Fugitive Slave Act of 1850. Four black men are ambushed by a posse of six white men. Below the drawing are quotations from the Bible (Deuteronomy; on the left) and the Declaration of Independence (right).
(LIBRARY OF CONGRESS, PRINTS AND PHOTOGRAPHS DIVISION)

Opponents of slavery resented these decisions, which sparked protest, resistance, and new laws and policies making the retaking of fugitive slaves more difficult and costly. **Abolitionists** effectively used the 1793 act and the court decisions upholding it to call attention to the evils of slavery. Southerners grew ever angrier and pressed for legislation that would more strongly protect their right to reclaim fugitive slaves.

THE FUGITIVE SLAVE ACT OF 1850

The Fugitive Slave Act of 1850 (9 Stat. 462) was an important part of the Compromise of 1850. On one side, Southerners sought to strengthen the fugitive slave law. On the other side, Northerners sought to respect the Constitution's fugitive slave clause and thereby preserve the Union by accommodating Southern anger over the fugitive slave issue. The act represented this effort to hold the country together.

Much longer than its 1793 predecessor, the 1850 act provided for federal commissioners to conduct hearings to grant or deny certificates permitting slave owners to retake fugitive slaves. Slave owners could either seize the person suspected to be a fugitive slave or procure a warrant directing a federal marshal to arrest the alleged fugitive before taking the person before a commissioner for a hearing. Under the act:

- The alleged fugitive was not allowed to testify at the hearing.
- Commissioners received twice as much compensation (ten dollars) for granting certificates as for denying them.
- Federal marshals were financially liable for not trying to execute the warrants and for allowing fugitives to escape.
- Penalties were increased for obstructing slave owners or helping fugitives, and included imprisonment.

Northerners saw this act as substantially more intrusive than the act of 1793, and their reaction was swift. Many people resisted and defied the law. In 1851, for example, Frederick Wilkins, known as Shadrach, a fugitive slave from Virginia, was rescued from a Boston courtroom and helped to escape to Canada. In some areas it was difficult to find people willing to do the duties required of commissioners under the act. Juries ignored evidence and acquitted people accused of violating the act. In June 1851 Harriet Beecher Stowe began publishing her influential antislavery novel, *Uncle Tom's Cabin,* in weekly installments in the *National Era* magazine. Shortly afterward it was published in book form and sold widely, increasing Northerners' opposition to slavery.

The Civil War began in 1861. Three years later, in 1864, the Fugitive Slave Acts were repealed.

In 1860 South Carolina seceded from the Union, and within months other states followed suit. The Civil War began in 1861. Three years later, in 1864, the Fugitive Slave Acts were repealed.

AN UNSUCCESSFUL ACCOMMODATION

The acts of 1793 and 1850 highlighted the uneasy accommodation between North and South on the issue of slavery. The acts offended Northern sensibilities that had turned against slavery. Northern social and legal reactions against the acts were threatening and insulting to Southerners. Southerners felt that

CAUTION!!

COLORED PEOPLE

OF BOSTON, ONE & ALL,

You are hereby respectfully CAUTIONED and advised, to avoid conversing with the

Watchmen and Police Officers of Boston,

For since the recent ORDER OF THE MAYOR & ALDERMEN, they are empowered to act as

KIDNAPPERS

AND

Slave Catchers,

And they have already been actually employed in KIDNAPPING, CATCHING, AND KEEPING SLAVES. Therefore, if you value your LIBERTY, and the *Welfare of the Fugitives* among you, *Shun* them in every possible manner, as so many *HOUNDS* on the track of the most unfortunate of your race.

Keep a Sharp Look Out for KIDNAPPERS, and have TOP EYE open.

APRIL 24, 1851.

A warning to fugitive slaves. (© AP/WIDE WORLD PHOTOS)

some abolitionists in the North—and even some Northern legislatures—were encouraging slaves to revolt, a possibility that many Southerners greatly feared.

The Fugitive Slave Acts failed as part of an effort to hold the Union together. Instead, they highlighted differences on the issue of slavery. The acts also raised important issues about what it means to follow the rule of law and pursue justice under a Constitution that both promoted freedom and allowed slavery.

The acts raised important issues about what it means to follow the rule of law and pursue justice under a Constitution that both promoted freedom and allowed slavery.

See also: COMPROMISE OF 1850; KANSAS NEBRASKA ACT OF 1854; MISSOURI COMPROMISE.

BIBLIOGRAPHY

Cover, Robert M. *Justice Accused*. New Haven, CT: Yale University Press, 1975.

Fehrenbacher, Don E. *Slavery, Law, and Politics*. New York: Oxford University Press, 1981.

Fehrenbacher, Don E. *The Slaveholding Republic*. New York: Oxford University Press, 2001.

Finkelman, Paul. *An Imperfect Union*. Chapel Hill: University of North Carolina Press, 1981.

Hall, Kermit L. *The Law of American Slavery*. New York: Garland Publishing, 1987.

Wiecek, William M. *The Sources of Antislavery Constitutionalism in America, 1760–1848*. Ithaca, NY: Cornell University Press, 1977.

G

GLASS-STEAGALL ACT (1933)

Michael P. Malloy

Many economic and political factors led to the financial crisis that began in 1929, but the general breakdown of the U.S. banking system during the period from 1929 to 1932 certainly played a significant role in the crisis. It was this systemic failure that led Congress to review and reform the Federal Reserve System and the national banking system as well. In particular, the Banking Act of 1933, known as the Glass-Steagall Act (GSA) (48 Stat. 162), made several significant changes in the federal regulation of banks. Primary among these was the separation of commercial banking from investment banking.

Congress accomplished this separation through the application of several techniques. First, it applied direct prohibitions to the activities of certain commercial banks. Congress narrowly limited the types of investment activities in which national banks and state-chartered banks that were members of the Federal Reserve System (member banks) could engage. The law permitted the banks to act as agents for their customers in the purchase and sale of securities without recourse, but the law generally prohibited banks from dealing in (purchasing or selling) securities for their own accounts. The law also banned banking institutions from underwriting (distributing to the public) any issue of securities.

These prohibitions were not absolute, even as originally enacted. While the law prohibited the banks from purchasing any shares of stock of any corporation, they could purchase "investment securities" (high-quality debt securities) for their own account under certain limitations administered by the comptroller of the currency pursuant to GSA. The banks could also purchase, deal in, and underwrite obligations of the federal government and general obligations of states and their political subdivisions.

Many economic and political factors led to the financial crisis that began in 1929, but the general breakdown of the U.S. banking system during the period from 1929 to 1932 certainly played a significant role in the crisis.

The second major regulatory technique GSA adopted was the elimination of legal affiliations between member banks (national and state) and investment banking firms. The GSA banned national banks and state member

133

banks from maintaining affiliations with any organization engaged principally in the issuance, underwriting, or distribution of securities. Congress later repealed this prohibition, however, in the 1999 Gramm-Leach-Bliley Act (GLBA). Similarly, GSA prohibited corporations engaged in the issuance, underwriting, or distribution of securities from receiving deposits. Third, GSA prohibited interlocking directorates between member banks and any organizations engaged primarily in the securities business. (GLBA also repealed this provision in 1999.)

These provisions were intended to build a wall between commercial and investment banking. To understand why this position was taken, one must consider a number of factors, including: (1) the expansion of commercial bank involvement in the securities business during the 1920s; (2) the early legislative and regulatory responses to this development, ultimately unsuccessful; (3) the apparent effects of this extension of commercial banking into the securities field; and (4) the reaction of Congress when these effects became apparent during congressional hearings from 1931 to 1933.

The provisions were intended to build a wall between commercial and investment banking.

EARLY BANKING REGULATION AND ACTIVITY

Two approaches to banking, broadly conceived, have been apparent throughout American banking history. The first is the English model, based on a sharp division between those institutions engaged in commercial banking and those engaged in investment banking. From this perspective, the law views investment banking as a risky, speculative venture and consequently as an inappropriate activity for an institution devoted to the care of deposits from the public.

In contrast, the German model views combining investment and commercial activities in a single enterprise as appropriate. Experts defend this approach on two grounds: efficiency and security. The efficiency of the German model is premised on the fact that the information sources and the business skills necessary for success in the investment banking business are similar to those needed in commercial banking as well. Further, the German model supposedly provides a more secure investment strategy because it provides a bank with a more diverse portfolio.

By 1865, Americans had accepted the English model of banking, and some commentators say that this is evidenced by the National Bank Act (NBA), which arguably required the separation of commercial and investment banking. The act defined the general powers of national banking associations to include "all such incidental powers as shall be necessary to carry on the business of banking," but did not explicitly allow banks to deal in securities. In *California Bank v. Kennedy* (1896), the U.S. Supreme Court held that national banks cannot exercise any powers except those the NBA expressly granted or that are incidental to carrying on a banking business. A national bank therefore did not possess the power to deal in equity securities, since that power was not granted by the act.

Despite the clear limitation found in the NBA, the U.S. banking system moved slowly toward the German model. Several factors explain this: increasing competition within the commercial banking industry; the development of the trust company after the Civil War (1861–1865); and the continuing competition between state and national banks. The typical trust company, authorized under state corporate law to engage in securities activities, soon became a full-service institution that could offer its customers both banking and investment services.

In response to the growing competition from trust companies, state-chartered commercial banks demanded additional powers from the state legislatures. By the early 1900s, legislatures granted most state banks many of the same powers to engage in investment activities already possessed by trust companies. National banks, however, were left out, and they sought justification for securities activities under the NBA. One of the first national banks to engage in underwriting activities was the First National Bank of New York. In 1908, in response to criticism from the comptroller concerning its securities dealings, the bank formed a securities affiliate, the First Security Company. The affiliate was incorporated under state law and was arguably free to conduct investment activities. In 1911 a second affiliate, National City Company, was organized, and by 1916 that affiliate was actively engaged in origination, underwriting, wholesaling, and retailing.

> *In response to the growing competition from trust companies, state-chartered commercial banks demanded additional powers from the state legislatures.*

Eventually, a large number of securities affiliates of banks sprang up. By 1922, sixty-two commercial banks were actively engaged in investment banking, and ten others had formed securities affiliates. By 1932, there were approximately 300 securities affiliates of commercial banks in the United States. National banks owned two hundred of these affiliates, state-chartered member banks owned seventy, and nonmember banks owned thirty such affiliates.

THE GROWTH OF SECURITIES AFFILIATES AND THE GSA

The growing involvement of commercial banks in investment banking drew criticism from legislative and regulatory quarters of the federal government. As early as 1913, a House Special Investigating Subcommittee known as the Pujo Committee (named after its chair, Representative Arsene Paulin Pujo, also the chair of the House Banking and Currency Committee), which investigated the institutional concentration of money and credit, denounced the extension of commercial banks into investment banking. The earliest extensive criticism from a regulatory authority came in a 1920 report of the comptroller of the currency, which questioned the legality of the securities affiliate system. It also noted functional problems with the use of affiliates, including conflicts of interest between management of the commercial bank and management of the affiliate, and the impropriety and risk of using bank deposits to fund speculative activities.

> *The growing involvement of commercial banks in investment banking drew criticism from legislative and regulatory quarters of the federal government.*

Despite these criticisms, Congress took no action to curtail the securities activities of commercial banks and their securities affiliates. During the 1920s even the comptroller's position eventually metamorphosed into a permissive one. Congress codified this position in the McFadden Act of 1927, amending the GSA by expressly extending the corporate powers of national banks to include the "buying and selling without recourse marketable obligations evidencing indebtedness ... in the form of bonds, notes and/or debentures commonly known as investment securities." The McFadden Act authorized the comptroller to determine what types of securities investments were sufficiently marketable to be appropriate. Thus, the only limiting principle was the "marketability" of these securities. The comptroller gave the term "marketable" a broad interpretation, so broad that virtually any public issue of bonds would qualify as a proper investment for a national bank.

From 1927 to 1929 commercial banks and their securities affiliates became even more significantly involved in the investment banking business. In 1929 J. W. Pole, then comptroller of the currency, proudly noted that the McFadden Act had added impetus to the movement to make commercial banks the distributors of the best type of investment securities. He stressed that the trust and securities fields were likely to be the area of greatest future expansion in commercial banking. The banks and the government discarded the English model. No doubt to Pole's embarrassment, soon after his statement the stock market panic of 1929 began, and by 1933 nearly 9,000 commercial banks in the United States had failed.

The banking disasters set the stage for definitive congressional action with respect to the securities activities of commercial banks.

This series of disasters set the stage for definitive congressional action with respect to the securities activities of commercial banks. However, it took three years of contentious congressional investigation and debate (from the June 1930 introduction of Senator Carter Glass's first bill on the subject, until the enactment of the GSA in June 1933) before federal law decisively excluded banks and other financial institutions from the investment banking business.

A NEW ERA

The GSA and its prohibitions on banking activities remained stable until the 1960s, when banks began to seek regulatory and statutory justifications for competitive incursions into the securities business once again. As competitive pressures intensified on the banks' traditional, core businesses both from domestic nonbanking firms like mutual funds and from foreign banking and nonbanking competitors, the banks sought to widen their involvement in the securities business through favorable regulatory rulings and through litigation.

At the same time, federal courts began to limit the scope of GSA. In a 1971 case, *Investment Company Institute v. Camp*, the U.S. Supreme Court expressed skepticism of bank involvement in the securities business, particularly in light of the "subtle hazards" presented by such involvement, hazards the GSA had intended to eliminate in 1933. As late as 1984, in *Securities Industry Association v. Board of Governors,* the Supreme Court still emphasized the important prohibitions found in the GSA. However, as experts began to view the GSA as obsolete in light of the complex competition between banking and securities firms, the Supreme Court and the lower federal courts gradually began to interpret the scope of the act narrowly and technically, and to defer more to the judgment of the bank regulators. This narrowness was particularly evident in cases in which a holding company affiliate of a bank conducted the securities activities, rather than within the bank itself, as in *Board of Governors v. Investment Company Institute* (1981). In this case, the Supreme Court allowed a bank holding company to operate a closed-end investment company. And in *Securities Industry Association v. Board of Governors* (1984), the court allowed a bank holding company to operate a discount brokerage firm.

Nevertheless, it took Congress until 1999 to set new limits on GSA. Congress approved the GLBA, and President Bill Clinton signed it into law on November 12, 1999. This financial services reform legislation is one of the most significant pieces of federal banking legislation since the GSA itself. Among other things, it works a fundamental change in the scheme of regulation of securities activities of depository institutions. The GLBA eliminates prohibitions on affiliations between commercial and investment banking enterprises and on interlocking directorates between such enterprises, by repealing various GSA provisions. It also requires as a general rule that federal and state securities regulators, not bank regulators, supervise securities activities—whether undertaken by securities firms or banking enterprises. Whether this realignment of financial services regulation will prove to be effective awaits the judgment of future events.

It took Congress until 1999 to set new limits on GSA.

President Franklin D. Roosevelt signs the Glass-Steagall Act, June 16, 1933. Behind the president (left to right) are: Senator Allen Barkley; Senator Thomas Gore; Senator Carter Glass; Comptroller of Currency J. F. T. Connors; Senator William G. McAdoo; Representative Henry S. Steagall; Senator Duncan U. Fletcher; Representative Alan Goldsborough; and Representative Robert Luce.
(©BETTMANN/CORBIS)

See also: FEDERAL DEPOSIT INSURANCE ACTS; FEDERAL RESERVE ACT; SECURITIES ACT OF 1933; SECURITIES EXCHANGE ACT OF 1934.

BIBLIOGRAPHY

Kennedy, Susan. E. *The Banking Crisis of 1933.* Louisville: University of Kentucky Press, 1973.

Malloy, Michael P., ed. *Banking and Financial Services Law: Cases, Materials, and Problems.* Durham, NC: Carolina Academic Press, 1999 & 2002-2003 Supp.

Malloy, Michael P. *Banking Law and Regulation*, 3 Vols. New York: Aspen Law & Business, 1994 & Cum. Supps.

Malloy, Michael P. *Bank Regulation Hornbook.* 2d ed. St. Paul, MN: West Group, 2003.

McCoy, Patricia A., ed. *Financial Modernization after Gramm-Leach-Bliley.* Newark, NJ: LexisNexis, 2002.

Perkins, Edwin J. "The Divorce of Commercial and Investment Banking: A History." 88 *Banking Law Journal* 483 (1971).

GOLD RESERVE ACT OF 1934

Lawrence H. Officer

The gold standard is a monetary standard that ties a unit of currency, or money, to a stated amount of gold. Under this system, both banks and the government stand ready to redeem their note and deposit liabilities in gold at the stipulated rate. In September 1931 the United Kingdom abandoned the gold standard, and many countries followed. The United States held on to the gold standard until 1933, when both foreign and domestic demand for gold led to runs on U.S. banks (with depositors and note-holders rushing to cash in their assets for gold). The fear was that a large number of banks would fail due to insufficient gold to cover demand, and that the U.S. official gold stock would be depleted. This economic danger occurred just as President Herbert Hoover's term was ending and Franklin Delano Roosevelt's had not yet begun. Moreover, there was no cooperation between the president and **president-elect**. Rumors were spreading that the new president might terminate U.S. adherence to the gold standard. While this would be the most obvious policy response to the problem, the rumors worsened the runs on banks. (An end to the gold standard would mean that gold would no longer be available; the public wanted to get gold while it could.) To solve the problem, abandonment of the gold standard had to be done quickly. Roosevelt took office on March 4, 1933, and the process of taking the U.S. off the gold standard began three days later, and culminated with the Gold Reserve Act of 1934 (P.L. 73-87, 48 Stat. 337).

The United States held on to the gold standard until 1933, when both foreign and domestic demand for gold led to runs on U.S. banks (with depositors and note-holders rushing to cash in their assets for gold).

president-elect: one who has been elected president but has not yet begun his term of office

LEGISLATION AND PRESIDENTIAL ACTION

To deal with the economic crisis, on March 6 President Roosevelt declared a national bank holiday until March 9 and specifically forbade banks from paying

Official Dollar Price of Gold

| Authorizing Act | Price of Gold (dollars per fine troy ounce[a]) | |
	Exact	Rounded
1792, P.L. 2–16, 1 Stat. 246	1913/33	19.39
1834, P.L. 23–95, 4 Stat. 699	2020/29	20.69
1837[b], P.L. 24–3, 5 Stat. 136	20260/387	20.67
1933, P.L. 73–10, 48 Stat. 31; 1934, P.L. 73–87, 48 Stat. 337	35	35.00
1972, P.L. 92–268, 86 Stat. 116	38	38.00
1973, P.L. 93–110, 87 Stat. 152	422/9	42.22

[a]One troy ounce = 117/175 = 1.0971 avoirdupois (customary) ounces.
[b]Reauthorized in 1873, P.L. 42–131, 17 Stat. 424 and 1900, P.L. 56–41, 31 Stat. 45.

out any gold coin or bullion (gold that is not yet formed into coin). Although it was peacetime, he claimed authority for this proclamation under the wartime Trading with the Enemy Act of 1917. Some doubted that his action was legal. Also on March 6, the Treasury Department stopped transacting in gold or gold certificates (currency representing gold deposited with the Treasury). These actions suspended the gold standard but did not formally end it.

In **special session** called by the president, Congress passed the Emergency Banking Relief Act on March 9. This act established that the presidential powers to regulate transactions in foreign exchange, gold, silver, and currency under the 1917 act applied to any emergency, thus eliminating any doubts as to the legality of Roosevelt's actions of March 6. The Emergency Banking Relief Act also authorized the secretary of the treasury, at his discretion, to require the delivery to the Treasury of all gold coin, bullion, and certificates. Now claiming authorization under the new act, on March 9 Roosevelt extended the measures of March 6 through March 12 (a Sunday).

special session: an extraordinary or special session of congress is called to meet in the interval between regular sessions

On March 10 the president issued an **executive order** authorizing the reopening of banks but prohibiting all gold payments by banks and other financial institutions (except under license by the secretary of the treasury). On April 5, stating authority under the acts of 1917 and 1933, Roosevelt required that all bank and other owners of gold coin, bullion, or certificates deliver all present and future holdings, with minor exceptions, to a Federal Reserve Bank (U.S. central bank institution) directly or via commercial banks. This was the beginning of nationalization (the process of government becoming the sole owner and holder of gold), with payment at face value ($20.67 per fine ounce, where "fine" denotes pure gold and the "ounce" is slightly greater than the customary measure. See the Official Dollar Price of Gold table above).

executive order: an order issued by the president that has the force of law

On August 29, by executive order, the secretary of the treasury was to receive all newly mined gold of domestic origin. On August 28, by another executive order, anyone other than a Federal Reserve Bank was forbidden from acquiring or holding gold in the United States or exporting gold (except under license). Finally, on December 28, 1933, the secretary of the treasury ordered that all gold be delivered to it at the official price of $20.67 per ounce. The process of nationalization of gold was complete.

On April 5, 1933, stating authority under the acts of 1917 and 1933, Roosevelt required that all bank and other owners of gold coin, bullion, or certificates deliver all present and future holdings, with minor exceptions, to a Federal Reserve Bank (U.S. central bank institution) directly or via commercial banks.

FURTHER LEGISLATION ON COINAGE AND CURRENCY

Other legislation at this time contributed to the termination of the gold standard. The Agricultural Adjustment Act of May 12, 1933, included the Thomas Amendment (named for its sponsor, Senator Elmer Thomas), which had two pertinent provisions. First, all U.S. coins and currencies were made full legal tender (money for payment of an obligation in any amount). This meant in particular that silver coins had the same status as gold. Second, the president was given authority to fix the weight of the gold dollar to stabilize domestic prices or protect foreign commerce. This was an unprecedented transfer of congressional power over coinage and currency to the president. However, the present weight of the dollar could not be reduced by more than 50 percent. This meant that the price of gold could be set no higher than $41.34 per ounce.

All gold coin was to be withdrawn from circulation and formed into bars. Redemption of any U.S. currency in gold was forbidden. Thus the gold standard was legally terminated.

The Gold Reserve Act of January 30, 1934, now enters the picture. The president had specifically requested this legislation to end the coinage of gold. All gold coin was to be withdrawn from circulation and formed into bars. Redemption of any U.S. currency in gold was forbidden. Thus the gold standard was legally terminated. Also, a provision supplementing the Thomas Amendment stated that the weight of the gold dollar could not be fixed at more than 60 percent of its present weight. This meant that the price of gold could be set at no less than $34.45 per ounce.

The next day, the president established a fixed dollar price of gold at $35 per ounce. The complete legislative history of the official price of gold is shown in the official Dollar Price of Gold table.

The series of acts and proclamations over 1933 to 1934 had several effects. First, there was a large inflow of gold into the United States, in part because of the fixed, high price of gold. Second, the Treasury made a huge profit—almost $3 billion—by acquiring gold at $20.67 prior to its revaluation to $35.00. Third, the United States readopted the gold standard, but of a limited kind. From January 31, 1934, to August 15, 1971, the Treasury purchased gold from all sellers at $34.9125, but sold gold *only* to foreign monetary authorities and licensed industrial users at $36.0875. However, from 1973 onward, the official gold price has significance only for valuation of the U.S. official gold stock. Fourth, with holdings of gold forbidden to U.S. residents, Americans could not readily invest in the metal or **speculate** on the gold price. Removal of all restrictions on private ownership of gold did not occur until December 31, 1974.

speculate: to engage in the buying or selling of a commodity with the expectation (or hope) of making a profit

See also: Coinage Act of 1792; Coinage Acts; Gold Standard Act of 1900.

BIBLIOGRAPHY

Friedman, Milton, and Anna Jacobson Schwartz. *A Monetary History of the United States, 1867–1960.* Princeton, NJ: Princeton University Press, 1963.

Nussbaum, Arthur. *A History of the Dollar.* New York: Columbia University Press, 1957.

Officer, Lawrence H. *Between the Dollar-Sterling Gold Points.* Cambridge, U.K.: Cambridge University Press, 1996.

Officer, Lawrence H. "What Was the Price of Gold Then? Importance, Measurement, and History." EH.Net. <http://www.eh.net/hmit/goldprice/Interpretation.pdf>.

Yeager, Leland B. *International Monetary Relations.* New York: Harper and Row, 1976.

GOLD STANDARD ACT OF 1900

Jerry W. Markham

The Gold Standard Act of 1900 (31 Stat. 45) was the culmination of an epic political battle over monetary policy in the United States. But it also reflected an age-old debate over whether gold or silver should control monetary measurements. The act set the value of gold at $20.67 per troy ounce (troy weight is based on a pound of twelve ounces). The act further states that:

> the dollar consisting of twenty-five and eight-tenths grains of gold nine-tenths fine ... shall be the standard unit of value, and all forms of money issued or coined by the United States shall be maintained at a parity of value with this standard, and it shall be the duty of the Secretary of the Treasury to maintain such parity.

BACKGROUND

Gold and silver have long served as monetary standards throughout the world, but debate raged as to their relative values and whether one of those precious metals should be preferred over the other in the monetary system. The introduction of paper currency complicated this debate because it usually promised to pay gold or silver upon demand. Such specie payments, or payments in coin, were often suspended in times of monetary stress. The Civil War was one such event.

After the war the question of whether the country should return to a specie-based monetary system was hotly contested. A populist movement sought to inflate farm prices through the increased use of paper currency and called for the use of silver, which was more plentiful than gold, as backing for that currency. The high point of that movement was the "Cross of Gold" speech, given by the lawyer and politician William Jennings Bryan to the Democratic convention in 1896. Bryan became the Democratic candidate for president but lost in the general election, and the United States went onto a gold standard in 1900 with the adoption of the Gold Standard Act.

The **Great Depression** in the 1930s resulted in the abandonment of the gold standard by the United States. President Franklin Roosevelt changed the valuation of gold to $35 per ounce of gold as an inflationary measure, where an increase in the valuation of gold tends to increase price levels in general. Farmers, for example, will get more dollars for their grain, but they will have to pay more for the goods purchased with the inflated grain sale proceeds. The Gold Reserve Act of 1934 also withdrew all gold from circulation, and Congress nullified clauses in public and private contracts that provided for payment in gold. In 1935 the U.S. Supreme Court considered the constitutionality of the ban on gold in the so-called Gold Clause Cases, where the court upheld the statute's negation of gold clauses: *Perry v. United States*, *Nortz v. United States*, and *Norman v. Baltimore & O.R.R.*

THE INTERNATIONAL MONETARY FUND

At the conclusion of World War II, the United States and Great Britain created the International Monetary Fund (IMF). That body set a "value" of $35 per

Gold and silver have long served as monetary standards throughout the world, but debate raged as to their relative values and whether one of those precious metals should be preferred over the other in the monetary system.

Great Depression: the longest and most severe economic depression in American history (1929–1939); its effects were felt throughout the world

ounce for gold. Other countries participating in the IMF were required to maintain their currencies at a specified parity against the dollar, thereby tying much of the world to a dollar standard that was in turn tied to a gold standard.

That system, however, fell apart after debilitating inflation in the 1960s caused a run—as countries began exchanging dollars for gold from the U.S. Treasury when world gold prices exceeded the $35.00 value set under the IMF agreement—on U.S. gold stocks. President Richard Nixon announced on August 15, 1971, that the United States would no longer exchange dollars for gold under the IMF standard. Within two years, currency exchange rates were allowed to float against each other. These floating currency rates are set by market forces rather than the artificial parity rates set by the IMF, and change constantly in foreign exchange transactions conducted through banks and currency dealers. In 1975 the IMF eliminated gold as the basis for internation-

Campaign poster for William McKinley and Theodore Roosevelt (c. 1900), advocating for the gold standard, among other things. The Gold Standard Act of 1900 was passed during McKinley's first term as president (1897–1901). He was assassinated about six months after beginning his second term in 1901. (LIBRARY OF CONGRESS, PRINTS AND PHOTOGRAPHS DIVISION)

al monetary standards, and two years later, the prohibition against gold clauses was repealed, allowing private sales of gold.

See also: BLAND-ALLISON ACT; COINAGE ACT OF 1792; COINAGE ACTS; GOLD RESERVE ACT OF 1934.

BIBLIOGRAPHY

Markham, Jerry W. *A Financial History of the United States.* Armonk, NY: M.E. Sharpe, 2002.

GOVERNMENT IN THE SUNSHINE ACT (1976)

Gary J. Edles, Richard K. Berg, and Stephen H. Klitzman

Excerpt from the Government in the Sunshine Act

The Government in the Sunshine Act is based on the policy that "the public is entitled to the fullest practicable information regarding the decisionmaking processes of the Federal Government." The purpose of the act is "to provide the public with such information while protecting the rights of individuals and the ability of the Government to carry out its responsibilities."

The Government in the Sunshine Act (P. L. 94-409, 90 Stat. 1241) requires that meetings of federal agencies with multiple members—agencies headed by a collegial body, a majority of whose members are appointed by the president with the advice and consent of the Senate—must be open to public observation. More than sixty agencies, such as the Federal Communications Commission and the Securities and Exchange Commission, are subject to the law. But key government entities headed by a single individual, such as the cabinet departments, are not.

EXEMPTIONS

The act sets forth ten specific grounds, called "exemptions," on which meetings may be closed and information regarding such meetings withheld from the public. Six of these exemptions were derived from, and are similar to, those contained in the Freedom of Information Act (FOIA). For example, agencies may close meetings that address classified information, that would invade an individual's personal privacy, or that involve law enforcement information. An important exemption is for meetings held to discuss **adjudication** of particular cases within the agency or pending or anticipated court litigation.

adjudication: the act of settling something judicially

PROCEDURES

The statute also prescribes specific procedures that agencies must follow in announcing and changing meetings, closing meetings, and withholding substantive information regarding meetings. When meetings are closed, the agency must maintain a transcript, electronic recording, or minutes of the meeting. The right of observation granted by the act does not include any right to participate in the agency's deliberations.

Members of the public can enforce the statute's requirements by bringing an action in a federal court.

Members of the public can enforce the statute's requirements by bringing an action in a federal court. A court can order release of the transcript, recording, or minutes of a meeting that was improperly closed. The act also allows a court to award "reasonable attorneys fees and other litigation costs" from the government if a party "substantially prevails" in the action.

BACKGROUND

The constitutional basis of the act is Congress's right to control the procedures of the agencies it has created. Beyond that, the House Committee on Governmental Operations observed that "the basic premise of the Sunshine legislation is that, in the words of [the] Federalist [Papers] No. 49, 'the people are the only legitimate foundation of power, and it is from them that a constitutional charter ... is derived. Government is and should be the servant of the people and it should be fully accountable to them for the actions which it supposedly takes on their behalf'" (H.R. Rep. No. 94-880 [Part 1], 94th Cong., 2d Sess. 2 [1976]).

The Government in the Sunshine Act was the last in a quartet of "open government" statutes that included the Freedom of Information Act in 1966, the Federal Advisory Committee Act in 1972, and the Privacy Act in 1974. A bill that evolved into the Government in the Sunshine Act was first introduced in Congress by Senator Lawton Chiles of Florida in 1972. After extensive consideration in one Senate committee, two House committees, and a Senate-House Conference committee, the bill was passed with near unanimity and signed into law on September 13, 1976.

EXPERIENCE UNDER THE ACT

Agencies now follow the act's requirements as a matter of course. They have implemented the statute in ways that have not seriously compromised their ability to manage their business. At the same time, the segments of the public most affected by the act—primarily the media, public interest organizations, and the regulated sector—find that they can monitor agency operations and understand the agency decision-making process more easily than they could in the pre-Sunshine Act era.

Agencies now follow the act's requirements as a matter of course.

However, two aspects of the act's implementation have remained controversial. The first is the definition of the term "meeting," because the law requires that only "meetings" must be open to public observation. The definition of "meeting" consists of three elements. First, a meeting must include at least the number of agency members required to take action on behalf of the agency, in other words, a **quorum**. Second, the required number of members must be in a position to exchange views. The use of the word "joint" in the act is intended to exclude instances, for example, where an agency member gives a speech concerning agency business and other members are in the

quorum: the number of members required to be present for a vote to take place

audience. Finally, a meeting must consist of "deliberations [that] determine or result in the joint conduct or disposition of official agency business." This is an ambiguous concept. On one hand, it is clear that not every mention of agency business turns a gathering of members into a meeting. On the other hand, the term "meeting" applies to more sessions than the one at which the collegial body finally and formally resolves an issue or makes a decision.

The definition of "meeting" was squarely at issue in *FCC v. ITT World Communications* (1984), the one case in which the U.S. Supreme Court interpreted the language of the statute. The Court determined that a "meeting" occurs only where a quorum of members actually conducts or disposes of (resolves) official agency business. So informal background discussions that simply clarify issues or expose varying views do not rise to the level of a "meeting." Similarly, discussions designed only to implement decisions already reached do not constitute a meeting subject to the act.

The second controversial aspect of the act's implementation concerns the collegiality that is supposed to be the cornerstone of the decision-making process at multimember agencies. Critics charge that the act has compromised that collegiality. A study by the Administrative Conference of the United States found that "one of the clearest and most significant results of the Government in the Sunshine Act is to diminish the collegial character of the agency decisionmaking process" (Recommendation 84-3, *Improvements in the Administration of the Government in the Sunshine Act,* 49 Fed. Reg. 29937 [July 25, 1984]).

Finally, the act does not increase or decrease the public's access to records under the FOIA. In fact, access to the actual documents or other written matter discussed or referred to at a meeting subject to the Government in the Sunshine Act is expressly governed by the FOIA.

> *Finally, the act does not increase or decrease the public's access to records under the FOIA.*

See also: FEDERAL ADVISORY COMMITTEE ACT; FREEDOM OF INFORMATION ACT; PRIVACY ACT OF 1974.

BIBLIOGRAPHY

Berg, Richard K., Stephen H. Klitzman, and Gary J. Edles. *An Interpretive Guide to the Government in the Sunshine Act,* 2d ed. Washington, DC: American Bar Association Section of Administration Law and Regulatory Practice, 2003.

Senate Committee on Governmental Affairs, *Government in the Sunshine Act: History and Recent Issues.* 101st Congress, 1st session, 1989.

Skrzycki, Cindy. "Getting a Little Burned Up About the Sunshine Act." *Washington Post,* (April 18, 1995) F-1.

Vitello, Paul. "They Want the Public Shut Out." *Newsday* Nassasu/Suffolk ed. (October 17, 1996) A-8.

GRAMM-RUDMAN-HOLLINGS ACT

See BALANCED BUDGET AND EMERGENCY DEFICIT CONTROL ACT

GUN CONTROL ACT OF 1968

Keith Rollins Eakins

After three decades of quiescence in the arena of gun control politics, the turmoil of the 1960s unleashed a wave of demand for new gun control legislation. The assassination of President John F. Kennedy in Dallas on November 22, 1963, prompted the country to focus on the regulation of firearms. Then the urban riots beginning in 1964 and the 1968 assassinations of Reverend Martin Luther King, Jr. and Senator Robert F. Kennedy fueled an inferno of outrage that demanded congressional action. In the wake of these acts of violence the U.S. Congress enacted the Gun Control Act (P.L. 90-618, 82 Stat. 1213) which President Lyndon B. Johnson signed in 1968. Although the Gun Control Act did not contain the owner licensing and gun registration provisions that President Johnson desired, the act, along with the Safe Streets and Crime Control Act passed by Congress months earlier, contained the most significant restrictions on firearms since Congress enacted the National Firearms Act (NFA) in 1934.

> *Although the Gun Control Act did not contain the owner licensing and gun registration provisions that President Johnson desired, the act, along with the Safe Streets and Crime Control Act passed by Congress months earlier, contained the most significant restrictions on firearms since Congress enacted the National Firearms Act (NFA) in 1934.*

THE DEVELOPMENT OF GUN CONTROL LEGISLATION IN THE 1960s

A highly controversial bill that precipitated emotional debate and ferocious political battles, the Gun Control Act traveled quite a convoluted path prior to its ultimate approval by Congress. It started down its torturous road in 1963 when Senator Thomas J. Dodd, Democrat of Connecticut, championed legislation geared specifically at tightening restrictions on the sale of mail-order handguns. After President Kennedy was murdered with a military-style rifle obtained through the mail, Senator Dodd extended the reach of the legislation to include "long guns," including rifles and shotguns. The legislation met an early demise when it was held up in the Commerce Committee and not allowed out for a vote on the Senate floor. Interestingly, the National Rifle Association (NRA) leaders initially supported the measures and even engaged in drafting Dodd's bill. Yet the NRA leadership did not wish to alienate its more radical rank and file, so they neglected to divulge this to their members. Instead, in a letter to each of its affiliates, the NRA claimed its executive vice-president testified against the bill and prevented it from being voted out of Committee. The NRA publication *The Rifleman* criticized the bill as a product of "irrational emotionalism," and the first four issues of *The Rifleman* in 1964 dedicated more than thirty columns to firearms legislation, never telling its members of the NRA leadership's support of the bill. These publications provoked the grass roots members to send off a great number of angry letters opposing the bill to Congress.

> *In 1965 President Johnson aggressively undertook the cause of fighting crime and regulating firearms by spearheading a new, strict gun control measure that Senator Thomas J. Dodd introduced in the Senate.*

In 1965 President Johnson aggressively endorsed the cause of fighting crime and regulating firearms by spearheading a new, strict gun control measure that Dodd introduced in the Senate. But the Johnson administration's proposal suffered a string of defeats over the next three years because of heavy pressure from the NRA, key congressional leaders who supported them, the American Legion, and gun importers, manufacturers, and dealers. Adding to the administration's difficulties was the lack of an organized pro–gun control lobby to check the relentless onslaughts against the legislation by the NRA.

In 1968 President Johnson and his administration intensified their efforts. Johnson began using the bully pulpit of the presidency to chide Congress publicly to enact his gun control policy. In his 1968 State of the Union address, Johnson exhorted Congress to pass a gun control law that would stop "mail order murder." And months later, President Johnson conveyed to Congress, in no uncertain terms, his desire for crime legislation that required national registration of every gun in America and licenses for all gun owners. Both the House of Representatives and the Senate responded to the president's admonishment in short order. Congressional representatives carefully, and often vociferously, argued about the provisions of the president's crime legislation. The measure, titled the Safe Streets and Crime Control Bill, received stiff resistance from gun control opponents.

NRA OPPOSITION TO THE ACT

By 1968 the leadership of the NRA was fully against any and all gun regulations. The group undertook a mass-mailing **lobbying** effort to undermine the legislation. Their organized lobbying efforts proved successful in wiping out much of the support for gun licensing and registration restrictions. Congress eventually enacted the Safe Streets and Crime Control Act, a watered-down version of the Johnson administration's anticrime and gun control proposal. The act prohibited the interstate shipment of pistols and revolvers to individuals, but it specifically exempted rifles and shotguns from any regulations.

lobby: to try to persuade the legislature to pass laws and regulations that are favorable to one's interests and to defeat laws that are unfavorable to those interests

With the assassination of Robert F. Kennedy on June 5, 1968, the groundswell of support for tough gun control laws reached unprecedented levels. On June 6, the day after the Kennedy assassination, Johnson signed the Safe Streets and Crime Control Act, but lamented the law's weak provisions. President Johnson, who had proposed gun control measures every year since becoming president, appeared on national television imploring Congress to pass a new and tougher gun control law that banned mail-order and out-of-state sales of

With the assassination of Robert F. Kennedy on June 5, 1968, the groundswell of support for tough gun control laws reached unprecedented levels.

long guns and ammunition. Reading a letter he sent to Congress, Johnson pleaded to Congress "in the name of sanity... in the name of safety and in the name of an aroused nation to give America the gun-control law it needs." On June 24, President Johnson again addressed the country, calling for mandatory national gun registration and licenses for every gun owner. Around this time, polls showed that approximately 80 percent of Americans favored gun registration laws. The public flooded members of Congress with letters demanding greater regulation of guns. Protestors picketed the Washington headquarters of the NRA. Even many members of Congress who had been staunch adversaries of strict firearms regulation crossed over to the other side and rallied in favor of a tough gun control bill.

ORGANIZED GUN CONTROL EFFORTS

Pro–gun control advocates mobilized and constructed an effective pro–gun control pressure group called the Emergency Committee for Gun Control.

bipartisan: involving members of two parties, especially the two political parties

The **bipartisan** organization was headed by Colonel John H. Glenn, Jr., a former astronaut and friend of Senator Robert Kennedy. The Committee, comprising volunteer staffers who had worked for Senator Kennedy before he was assassinated, received extensive support from a variety of organizations such as the American Bankers Association, the AFL-CIO, the Conference of Mayors, the International Association of Chiefs of Police, the National Association of Attorneys General, the American Civil Liberties Union, and the U.S. Chamber of Commerce. Riding a wave of support, the Committee sought to counteract the highly organized and resource-laden NRA. Their efforts proved somewhat effective, but ultimately fell short of the group's goal of a comprehensive scheme of gun registration and gun owner licensing.

Facing this unprecedented, widespread push for gun control, the NRA became highly energized and rallied against the president's proposed regulations. National Rifle Association executive vice-president Franklin L. Orth argued publicly that no law, existing or proposed, could have prevented the murder of Senator Kennedy. On June 15, 1968, the NRA mailed a letter to its members calling for them to write their members of Congress to oppose any new firearms laws. Using hyperbole and emotionally charged rhetoric, NRA President Harold W. Glassen wrote that the right of sportsmen to obtain, own, and use firearms for legal purposes was in grave jeopardy. Furthermore, Glassen wrote, the clear goal of gun control proponents was complete abolition of civilian ownership of guns. Senator Joseph D. Tydings, Democrat of Maryland, who had introduced the provisions requiring licensing of gun owners and registration of firearms, responded to this accusation in a press conference calling the letter "calculated hysteria" and saying no bill would prevent law-abiding citizens from having guns. Nevertheless, Glassen's tactic effectively energized the membership of the NRA, then 900,000 strong, just as the public outcry calling for more firearms regulations was dissipating. Whereas Congress had encountered overwhelming support for more gun control measures in the week after Senator Kennedy's death, by late June and early July they reported the majority of the letters from constituents indicated opposition to any new gun control provisions.

The battle over the president's proposals continued in the halls of Congress in typical fashion, featuring emotionally charged debates and supporters split along specific demographic and ideological lines. In the House, opponents argued against a registration provision claiming it would be costly and ineffective in preventing crime. In the Senate, Dodd attacked the NRA, decrying its tactics of "blackmail, intimidation and unscrupulous propaganda." The licensing and registration provisions, backed solidly by northern liberals, were easily defeated in both the House of Representatives and Senate by a conservative coalition of Republicans and southern Democrats. However, the provisions banning mail-order and out-of-state sales of long guns and ammunition fared better, passing both the House and Senate. Eastern and Midwestern members of Congress overwhelmingly supported these measures, while those from the South and West were much less supportive. Members of Congress representing urban areas staunchly supported the bill, whereas those from rural sections of the country voted against it in significant numbers.

On October 22, President Johnson signed into law the Gun Control Act of 1968—an instrument which, just months earlier, was considered a lost cause because of staunch opposition.

PROVISIONS OF THE GUN CONTROL ACT

On October 22, President Johnson signed into law the Gun Control Act of 1968—an instrument which, just months earli-

Senator Robert F. Kennedy (D-N.Y.), urges the Senate Judiciary Subcommittee to "save lives and spare thousands of families grief and heartbreak," by passing a gun control bill, May 1965. A significant gun control act would not be passed, however, until after Robert Kennedy's assassination in 1968. (©BETTMANN/CORBIS)

er, was considered a lost cause because of staunch opposition. The signing of the legislation represented a significant political win for the president, Senator Dodd, and other gun control advocates who had struggled for years to pass a gun control bill that would effect real change. Enacted pursuant to the Congress's constitutional authority to regulate interstate **commerce**, the legislation had three major features. First, it prohibited interstate traffic in firearms and ammunition. Second, it denied guns to specific classes of individuals such as felons, minors, fugitives, drug addicts, and the mentally ill. Third, it prohibited the importation of surplus military weapons into the United States as well as guns and ammunition not federally certified as sporting weapons or souvenirs.

As is usually the case in American politics, the statute did not signify a complete victory for either side. Advocates of gun control failed to get provisions requiring owner licensing and firearms registration, yet gun control opponents, typically NRA members, suffered another setback to their goal of removing governmental regulation of firearms. This partial defeat for the NRA served as the group's wake-up call, energizing and expanding the member-

commerce: the large-scale exchange of goods, involving transportation from one place to another

A woman places a shirt with a picture of her grandson, who was fatally shot, on a memorial outside the Massachusetts State House during an anti-gun rally, July 16, 2002. (© AP/WIDE WORLD PHOTOS)

ship of the NRA who suddenly felt politically vulnerable. Yet unlike the NRA, the pro–gun control advocates were not organized for long-term pressure politics, and their political influence began to wane. Thus in 1986 the NRA successfully weakened the provisions of the 1968 act by spearheading the passage of the Firearms Owners Protection Act.

The Gun Control Act of 1968 received its first challenge in the Supreme Court in *Lewis v. United States* (1980). In that case the Court addressed whether the provision banning the possession of firearms by convicted felons was constitutional. The Court held that the right to bear arms was not a fundamental right and deemed the act's provisions constitutional because they had a rational basis and had relevance to the purpose of the statute. The Court also restated its earlier holding in *United States v. Miller* (1939): "[T]he Second Amendment guarantees no right to keep and bear a firearm that does not have 'some reasonable relationship to the preservation or efficiency of a well regulated militia.'" The political debate about gun ownership remains rigorous.

See also: BRADY HANDGUN VIOLENCE PREVENTION ACT.

BIBLIOGRAPHY

Congressional Quarterly 1968 Almanac. Washington, DC: CQ Press, 1968.

Davidson, Osha Gray. *Under Fire: The NRA and the Battle for Gun Control.* New York: Holt, 1993.

Patterson, Samuel C., and Keith R. Eakins. "Congress and Gun Control." In *The Changing Politics of Gun Control,* ed. John M. Bruce and Clyde Wilcox. Lanham, MD: Rowman & Littlefield Publishers, Inc., 1998.

Spitzer, Robert J. *The Politics of Gun Control.* Chatham, NJ: Chatham House Publishers, Inc., 1995.

Sugarmann, Josh. *National Rifle Association: Money, Firepower and Fear.* Washington, DC: National Press Books, 1992.

Brady Campaign Online. "Waiting Periods and Background Checks." July 2003. <http://www.bradycampaign.com/>.

H

HARRISON ACT

See NARCOTICS ACT

HATCH ACT (1939)

William V. Luneburg

The Hatch Act of 1939 (53 Stat. 1147) restricted the ability of federal, or civil service, employees to participate in partisan political life. The goal of the act was to ensure that the civil service would remain politically neutral and efficient. However, many believed that the restrictions infringed on the constitutional rights of federal employees. In 1993 Congress adopted amendments to the act: "It is the policy of Congress that employees should be encouraged to exercise fully, freely, and without fear of penalty or reprisal, and to the extent not expressly prohibited by law, their right to participate or to refrain from participating in the political processes of the Nation." Those amendments are the latest in a series of attempts to respect the constitutional rights of government employees, in particular the rights to speak, organize, and act peacefully to carry out their personal political views, while at the same time ensuring that the public administration of government is carried out in a neutral and efficient manner.

> *The goal of the act was to ensure that the civil service would remain politically neutral and efficient.*

HISTORICAL BACKGROUND

As early as the presidency of Thomas Jefferson, the political activities of federal employees were restricted in the name of effective government. By executive order, the officers of government could not attempt "to influence the votes of others [or] take any part in the business of electioneering." Later administrations adopted similar restrictions in an effort to foster political neutrality. The Civil Service Act of 1883 (known as the Pendleton Act) limited the influence of party politics in the appointment of federal employees. That act was designed to ensure that the civil service was not used for political purposes.

In the years following the Pendleton Act, many continued to see political activity by federal employees as a problem. In 1907 President Theodore Roosevelt required that civil service rules be adopted to prevent anyone in the civil service from using his or her official authority or influence to interfere with an election. Such rules also forbid employees appointed to their positions on the basis of examinations (such employees were called the "classified" service) from taking part "in political management or in political campaigns." Employees could, however, express "privately" their own political opinions.

In thousands of cases decided over the next thirty years, the Civil Service Commission (established by the Pendleton Act) developed a body of law that attempted to distinguish between, on the one hand, prohibited political activ-

Senator Carl A. Hatch (D-N. Mex.) is depicted in this October 1938 cartoon as a hen nesting over her chicks, which represent provisions of the Hatch Act. Attorney General Frank Murphy looks on with approval. (LIBRARY OF CONGRESS, PRINTS AND PHOTOGRAPHS DIVISION)

ity by federal employees and, on the other, the permissible expression of political opinions.

The experience over this same period, including the 1938 election, when it was alleged that President Franklin Roosevelt exploited certain government workers for political purposes, persuaded Congress in 1939 to adopt the 1907 civil service rule as the Hatch Act. The Hatch Act (named after Senator Carl A. Hatch of New Mexico) extended the rule to apply to the entire civil service other than high policy-making officials. Removal from office was the designated penalty for violation. In 1940 the act's restrictions were extended to state and local employees whose jobs were funded by federal money (54 Stat. 767). The Civil Service Commission was designated to enforce the Hatch Act restrictions. In 1950 and 1962, the penalty for violations was reduced from removal from office to a thirty-day suspension without pay.

COURT CHALLENGE

In two cases, *United Public Workers of America v. Mitchell* (1947) and *United States Civil Service Commission v. National Association of Letter Carriers* (1973), the Supreme Court rejected constitutional challenges to the Hatch Act. The Court found that Congress could reasonably believe that the restrictions were necessary to ensure neutral and effective public administration. In doing so, it noted that executive branch employees "should administer the law in accordance with the will of Congress, rather than in accordance with their own or the will of a political party."

The Court also noted that the immediate reason for the enactment of the Hatch Act was the fear that a large federal workforce unrestrained in its political activity could become "a powerful, invincible, and perhaps corrupt political machine."

The Court also noted that the immediate reason for the enactment of the Hatch Act was the fear that a large federal workforce unrestrained in its political activity could become "a powerful, invincible, and perhaps corrupt political machine." (In fact such a prospect struck fear into Republicans during the Roosevelt administration.) Finally, the Court emphasized the concern that, without the Hatch Act restrictions, advancement in government service might occur less because of excellence on the job and more because of the political views of employees. Critics faulted the Court for its apparent failure to put enough weight on the First Amendment right to political speech, a right that is afforded the highest of protections outside the context of government employment.

1993 AMENDMENTS

In 1974 Hatch Act restrictions on state and local government were watered down, and in 1993 the advocates for removing or reducing restrictions on the political activities of federal employees carried the day. The Hatch Act Reform Amendments of 1993 (107 Stat. 1001) removed the prohibition on participation in "political management or political campaigns." Federal employees are still forbidden, however, to use their authority to affect the results of an election. They are also forbidden to run for office in a partisan election, to solicit or receive political contributions, and to engage in political activities while on duty or on federal property. The Merit Systems Protection Board and its Office of Special Counsel are responsible for enforcement of the Hatch Act.

In 1974 Hatch Act restrictions on state and local government were watered down, and in 1993 the advocates for removing or reducing restrictions on the political activities of federal employees carried the day.

See also: CIVIL SERVICE ACTS.

BIBLIOGRAPHY

Eccles, James R. *The Hatch Act and the American Bureaucracy.* New York: Vantage Press, 1981.

Emerson, Thomas I. *The System of Freedom of Expression.* New York: Vintage Books, 1971.

Rosenbloom, David H. *Federal Service and the Constitution.* Ithaca, NY: Cornell University Press, 1971.

INTERNET RESOURCE

U.S. Office of Special Counsel. "Political Activity (Hatch Act)." <http://www.osc.gov/hatchact.htm>.

HAWLEY-SMOOT TARIFF

See SMOOT-HAWLEY TARIFF

HAZARDOUS AND SOLID WASTE AMENDMENTS OF 1984

Eugene H. Robinson, Jr.

Excerpt from the Hazardous and Solid Waste Amendments

The Congress hereby declares it to be the national policy of the United States that, wherever feasible, the generation of hazardous waste is to be reduced or eliminated as expeditiously as possible. Waste that is nevertheless generated should be treated, stored, or disposed of so as to minimize the present and future threat to human health and the environment.

The Hazardous and Solid Waste Amendments of 1984 (HSWA) (P.L. 98-616, 98 Stat. 3221) became law on November 8, 1984, when signed by President Ronald Reagan. The HSWA amended the Solid Waste Disposal Act of 1965 (SWDA), as amended by the Resource Conservation and Recovery Act of 1976 (RCRA). In general, both the scope and requirements of the SWDA, as amended by RCRA, were significantly expanded and reinforced.

Proponents maintained that the HSWA was needed due to various **loopholes** in the SWDA, as amended by RCRA. For example, loopholes allowed approximately forty million metric tons of hazardous waste to escape control annually through the unregulated burning and blending of hazardous waste for energy recovery and allowed small-quantity generators (up to 1,000 kilo-

loophole: a means of evading or escaping an obligation or enforcement of a law or contract

grams per month) of hazardous waste to dispose of their wastes in municipal landfills and city sewer systems.

The debate on the HSWA lasted over two-and-a-half years. Much of that debate centered on several provisions that required the U.S. Environmental Protection Agency (EPA) to take certain action by specific dates, which, if not met, would require remedies crafted by Congress to take effect. Although the bill that passed was introduced by a Democrat, the final product was the result of work by members of both major political parties and in both houses of Congress who were frustrated with the EPA's slow pace in implementing RCRA. The work focused on section-by-section changes rather than another complete revision, as had been done with RCRA. The extensive legislative history reflects the amount of detail—and compromise—that went into formulating the HSWA.

Loopholes allowed approximately forty million metric tons of hazardous waste to escape control annually through the unregulated burning and blending of hazardous waste for energy recovery and allowed small-quantity generators (up to 1,000 kilograms per month) of hazardous waste to dispose of their wastes in municipal landfills and city sewer systems.

The HSWA was enacted largely in response to the public's vocal opposition to existing hazardous waste disposal practices that were perceived as being harmful to human health and the environment. Accordingly, the HSWA, like the SWDA as amended by RCRA, strives to engage the entire socio-economic spectrum in the regulatory process. Of the more than seventy major provisions, over fifty required EPA action within the first year of enactment. Some of the changes brought about through HSWA include:

- Creation of the Land Disposal Restrictions Program
- Establishment of RCRA Corrective Action requirements
- Establishment of permitting deadlines for hazardous waste facilities
- Regulation of small-quantity generators of hazardous waste
- Requirement for a nationwide survey of the conditions at solid waste landfills

The changes required by HSWA led to such things as:

- Establishment of treatment standards to prevent disposal of untreated wastes into and onto the land
- Permitting of more than 900 hazardous waste management facilities
- Establishment of a strong criminal enforcement program
- The closing of substandard landfills and incinerators

The HSWA was enacted largely in response to the public's vocal opposition to existing hazardous waste disposal practices that were perceived as being harmful to human health and the environment.

No significant amendments to the HSWA have been adopted. The HSWA remains incorporated within the SWDA, as amended by RCRA, and the three combined acts are generally referred to as RCRA.

See also: Comprehensive Environmental Response, Compensation, and Liability Act; Solid Waste Disposal Act; Toxic Substances Control Act.

BIBLIOGRAPHY

Hall, Ridgeway M., Jr.; Robert C. Davis, Jr.; Richard E. Swartz, et al. *RCRA Hazardous Wastes Handbook,* 12th ed. Rockville, MD: Government Institutes, Inc., 2001.

U.S. Environmental Protection Agency. "25 Years of RCRA: Building on Our Past to Protect Our Future." July 2003. <http://www.epa.gov/>.

HAZARDOUS MATERIALS TRANSPORTATION ACT (1975)

Arthur Holst

In the 1970s many landfills throughout the United States began to refuse to accept hazardous materials, and few cheap disposal alternatives existed. As a result, illegal dumping became common. Enforcement of antidumping laws was weak. In response to the need for better regulations and enforcement, Congress passed the Hazardous Materials Transportation Act (HMTA) (P.L. 93-633, 88 Stat. 2156) in 1975. Its stated purpose is "to provide adequate protection against the risks to life and property inherent in the transportation of hazardous material in commerce by improving the regulatory and enforcement authority of the Secretary of Transportation."

The HMTA sets extensive guidelines for carriers of hazardous materials. They must classify, package, and label materials appropriately, use specific hazardous material placards for shipments, and have suitable shipping papers at all times. They must follow Department of Transportation (DOT) rules, maintain rapid response plans for emergencies, undergo safety training programs, and comply with packaging standards.

The HMTA gives enforcement authority to the DOT. Under delegated authority from the secretary of the DOT, the Federal Highway Administration (FHWA) enforces motor carrier regulations, the Federal Railroad Administration (FRA) enforces rail carrier regulations, the Federal Aviation Administration (FAA) enforces air carrier regulations, and the U.S. Coast Guard enforces maritime shipping regulations. Considerable hazardous waste regulation authority is given to the Environmental Protection Agency (EPA) as well, under the Resource Conservation and Recovery Act (RCRA) of 1976, which requires the EPA to set guidelines for the management of hazardous and nonhazardous waste in an environmentally friendly manner.

> *The HMTA sets extensive guidelines for carriers of hazardous materials.*

Even with these guidelines addressing hazardous material transportation, confusion about federal, state, and local hazardous material regulations arose. In 1990 Congress passed the Hazardous Materials Transportation Uniform Safety Act (HMTUSA). This act addressed the confusion by encouraging uniformity throughout the levels of government concerning guidelines for hazardous material transportation. Also, states are advised to designate certain highways and roads that are acceptable for hazardous material transportation.

The DOT's Office of Hazardous Materials Safety has published the Federal Hazardous Materials Regulations, which is a complete guide to hazardous material guidelines and interpretations. Knowingly violating these guidelines subjects carriers to a range of penalties. Violations result in fines in amounts from $250 to $25,000. If violations occur over numerous days, each day is subject to a separate fine. Also, one who tampers with or defaces a hazardous material label, container, truck, placard, or other object is guilty of a criminal offense, punishable by up to five years in prison.

Many fines and prison sentences have been assessed for violations of the HMTA. In one particular case, a man had packed fireworks in his luggage for

Prosecutions of violations are of heightened concern following the rise of terrorist threats to the United States, emphasizing the importance of strict enforcement of the HMTA.

a flight to San Francisco on the weekend of July 4, 1994. Airline employees came upon the items in the bag and alerted FAA officials, who levied a $1,250 fine on the individual. The man appealed the fine, but it was affirmed since the man knowingly acted in violation of the HMTA. Prosecutions of violations are of heightened concern following the rise of terrorist threats to the United States, emphasizing the importance of strict enforcement of the HMTA.

See also: HAZARDOUS AND SOLID WASTE AMENDMENTS OF 1984; NUCLEAR WASTE POLICY ACT; SOLID WASTE DISPOSAL ACT.

BIBLIOGRAPHY

"Hazardous Materials Transportation Act." Department of Energy: Office of Environment, Safety and Health. <http://tis.eh.doe.gov/oepa/law_sum/HMTA.HTM>.

"Resource—Hazardous Materials Transportation Act." Department of the Interior: Bureau of Land Management. <http://www.ntc.blm.gov/learningplace/res_HMTA.html>.

Wagner, Travis P. *The Hazardous Waste Q & A: An In-Depth Guide to the Resource Conservation and Recovery Act and the Hazardous Materials Transportation Act.* Indianapolis, IN: John Wiley and Sons, 1997.

INTERNET RESOURCES

Department of Transportation. <http://www.dot.gov>.

Environmental Protection Agency. <http://www.epa.gov>.

Federal Aviation Administration. <http://www.faa.gov>.

HIGHER EDUCATION ACT OF 1965

Lawrence Schlam

With the goal of strengthening American colleges and universities, the Higher Education Act of 1965, or HEA, provides financial assistance and other resources for students pursuing postsecondary and higher education. Title I of the act provides funding for extension and continuing education programs. Title II allocates funds to increase library collections and the number of employed qualified librarians. Title III focuses on strengthening "developing institutions" that have not yet met minimum standards for accreditation by means of, for example, faculty exchange programs, joint use of learning facilities, and training programs for developing more capable faculties.

Title IV assists students by supporting undergraduate scholarships, loans with reduced interest rates, and work-study programs. Title V concentrates on improving the quality of teaching (supporting, for example, teacher preparation programs designed to attract recent graduates into the teaching field, and advanced training for experienced teachers). Title VI provides financial assistance to improve undergraduate instruction (by, for example, providing assistance to those institutions that are unable to afford modern teaching materials).

Proponents of the act had voiced concern about the rising costs of college at a time when a college education had clearly become necessary for young adults seeking employment opportunities. Rising costs were especially problematic for students from low- and middle-income families. There was also concern over the lack of adequate staffing in emerging areas of study, such as Latin American and Asian studies, and the need for expanded library collections and more specialized librarians to keep pace with the changing educational environment. The U.S. Commissioner of Education at that time warned that all existing institutions are integral to the country's educational development. He pointed out that allowing only "survival of the fittest" might result in "assembly-line" institutions, thereby decreasing the diversity of fields of study and choices in universities. President Lyndon B. Johnson, who signed the act on November 8, 1965, at his alma mater, Southwest Texas State College, stated that American universities "can offer expert guidance in community planning; research and development in pressing educational problems; economic and job market studies; continuing education of the community's professional and business leadership; and programs for the disadvantaged."

Proponents of the act had voiced concern about the rising costs of college at a time when a college education had clearly become necessary for young adults seeking employment opportunities.

The act has undergone several amendments since 1965. In 1991 Congress eliminated any statute of limitations for the collection of student loans made under the act (see *United States v. Smith,* a 1992 Alabama state ruling). As a result of several academic institutions having closed midsemester, the act was modified in 1992 to allow for a number of additional protections for students in such situations. Those attending a school that had suddenly closed its doors could now fully discharge their student loans, as could those students who did not hold a high school diploma but were erroneously assured by the university that they were eligible to begin a course of study. Students were also offered the opportunity to "rehabilitate" their loans in order to remove themselves from default status.

The 1991 amendment also created a Program Integrity Triad, a group composed of accrediting agencies, the states, and the Department of Education, that would be authorized to control access to the financial aid programs. In 1998 the act was reauthorized and amended to include a decrease in student loan interest rates, loan "forgiveness" programs for teachers in inner-city schools, increased Pell Grants, and early intervention programs for eligible low-income students.

The act was preceded by several other laws intended to have a similar impact on higher education. The GI Bill, for example, was designed to make it easier for returning World War II soldiers to obtain a higher education. The National Science Foundation Act and the National Defense Education Act encouraged students to enter the fields of science and mathematics. The Higher Education Facilities Act of 1963 had already attempted to support higher education by authorizing assistance in financing the construction, rehabilitation, or improvement of facilities at undergraduate and graduate institutions.

Since its passage, the act has complemented several other laws. It joins the Elementary and Secondary Education Act in articulating a strong commitment to state and local control over education, and an Office of Migrant Education was established to accomplish goals envisioned by both of these laws.

HEA joins the Elementary and Secondary Education Act in articulating a strong commitment to state and local control over education, and an Office of Migrant Education was established to accomplish goals envisioned by both of these laws.

nonprofit: an organization whose business is not conducted or maintained for the purpose of making a profit, but is usually aimed at providing services for the public good

The courts have also construed the HEA in conjunction with other laws. For example, the Federal Debt Collection Procedures Act allows stoppage of wages to repay consumer debt. The courts have ruled that this act must defer to the HEA, which independently allows for stoppage of wages to collect financial aid debt. (See *United States v. George* [2000]). The act has also been construed so as to not allow the discharge of student loans in bankruptcy proceedings unless the debtor will face undue hardship, defined narrowly.

Benefits under the HEA may only be received by "institutions of higher education," defined as those that admit students holding a high school diploma (or equivalent), are certified to provide higher education pursuant to state regulations, are accredited (or are likely to be accredited) by a nationally recognized accrediting agency, and provide an educational program that awards a bachelor's degree (or have a two-year program that awards credit toward such degree), and qualify as a public or nonprofit institution. Other schools may qualify for benefits if they provide at least a one-year program to prepare students for gainful employment, enjoys status as a public or **nonprofit** institution, and are properly accredited. The act may also cover a "combination of institutions of higher education," defined as a group of institutions of higher education that have entered into an agreement to carry out a common objective.

See also: ELEMENTARY AND SECONDARY EDUCATION ACT OF 1965.

HIGHWAY ACT OF 1956

Mary-Beth Moylan

Excerpt from the Highway Act

It is the intent of the Congress that the Interstate System be completed as nearly as practicable over a thirteen-year period and that the entire system in all States be brought to simultaneous completion.

Focusing on concerns of national security and economic prosperity, President Dwight D. Eisenhower made the construction of a national interstate highway system a priority of his administration. The Highway Act of 1956 (P.L. 83-627, 70 Stat. 374) was the first comprehensive plan for the construction and financing of the National System of Interstate and Defense Highways.

While as early as the 1930s, government officials were concerned about the development of a national system of roadways, the interests of farmers, truckers, engineers, and average Americans concerning the construction and funding of the massive federal project were not in accord. At the time President Eisenhower won election in 1952 there was general agreement that a national highway system would promote traffic safety, convenience to travelers, national defense and economic opportunities in a post–World War II America.

Once in office, President Eisenhower appointed several committees to consider a national highway system. Some advisers suggested funding the system with toll roads, while others advocated user taxes on trucks, gasoline and associated industry needs. A federal highway bill drafted by Lucius Clay, a retired general, was defeated during the 1955 congressional session. Drawing on the failed 1955 legislation, Representatives George H. Fallon of Maryland and Hale Boggs of Louisiana introduced legislation the following year. Representative Fallon wrote the portion of the legislation relating to appropriations for the construction of the interstate system. Representative Boggs is credited with creating the Highway Trust Fund. With success of the Fallon-Boggs legislation in the House, Senator Albert Gore, Sr., of Tennessee introduced companion legislation in the Senate. On June 29, 1956, President Eisenhower signed the act into law.

Significant provisions of the act included the appropriation of millions of dollars to states for building an interstate highway system, the directive for the project to be completed "as nearly as practicable over a thirteen-year period" and that it be completed simultaneously in all states. The act also provided that the federal government would generally provide between 90 percent and 95 percent of the funds for interstate roadways. Oversight of funding requests, the creation of standards for roadways, and the administration of the interstate system were vested in the secretary of commerce, who was directed to report back to Congress periodically. Critical to the act's success was the creation of the Highway Trust Fund and the provisions that directed a number of specific categories of taxes, including all gasoline taxes, diesel and special motor fuel taxes, and tread rubber taxes, to be deposited into that Fund. Without the money derived from these taxes, the interstate highway system could not have been built.

The interstate system was not completed in the thirteen years contemplated by the act. However, Congress repeatedly extended the deadline for completion and ordered additional appropriations for the massive network of roads that now make up the interstate highway system. Cities have sprung up all across the country along these highway routes, and more cities are blossoming as Americans seek more convenience and more services with jobs and housing readily accessible to the highway system. In 1990 the Interstate was designated the "Dwight D. Eisenhower System of Interstate and Defense Highways" in recognition of President Eisenhower's leadership role in its construction.

See also: HIGHWAY BEAUTIFICATION ACT; HIGHWAY SAFETY ACT OF 1966; NATIONAL TRAFFIC AND MOTOR VEHICLE SAFETY ACT.

BIBLIOGRAPHY

Eisenhower Birthplace State Historical Park. "Federal-Aid Highway Act of 1956." July 2003. <http://www.eisenhowerbirthplace.org>.

Garreau, Joel. *Edge City: Life on the New Frontier.* New York: Doubleday, 1991.

Rose, Mark H. *Interstate: Express Highway Politics, 1941–1956.* Lawrence, KS: Regents Press of Kansas, 1979.

Weingroff, Richard F. "Federal-Aid Highway Act of 1956: Creating the Interstate System." *U.S. Department of Transportation Federal Highway Administration.* July 2003. <http://www.fhwa.dot.gov/infrastructure/history.htm>.

HIGHWAY BEAUTIFICATION ACT (1965)

Craig J. Albert

Excerpt from the Highway Beautification Act

Federal-aid highway funds apportioned ... to any State which ... has not made provision for effective control of the erection and maintenance along the Interstate System and the primary system of outdoor advertising signs, displays, and devices which are within six hundred and sixty feet of the nearest edge of the right-of-way and visible from the main traveled way of the system ... [or] ... located outside of urban areas, visible from the main traveled way of the system, and erected with the purpose of their message being read from such main traveled way, shall be reduced by amounts equal to 10 per centum of the amounts which would otherwise be apportioned to such State....

Great Society: broad term for the domestic programs of President Lyndon B. Johnson, in which he called for "an end to poverty and racial injustice"

The Highway Beautification Act of 1965 (P.L. 89-285, 79 Stat. 1028) was the first major environmental legislation of President Lyndon B. Johnson's **Great Society** program, paving the way for the Clean Water Act and the Clean Air Act. It sought to improve the appearance of the nation's roads by controlling the size, number, and placement of billboards and by screening off junkyards. Road construction and maintenance have traditionally been (with a few exceptions) state functions, but the federal government took an interest in road conditions when it began to subsidize a large portion of highway construction beginning in 1916. The act's strategy was to create a federal financial incentive for the states to take action.

The act sought to improve the appearance of the nation's roads by controlling the size, number, and placement of billboards and by screening off junkyards.

The act followed decades of efforts by state and local governments to regulate billboards on their own by exercising their general police power. That power is the core authority of states to enact regulations promoting the health, safety, and welfare of their residents. Because the federal government has no police power, it needed to adopt legislation through its conditional spending power. Under that power, Congress may attach a condition to its spending. For example, the federal government can tell states they will be given funds for certain purposes only on the condition that they improve their highways. States voluntarily agree to enact the policies expressed in the federal government's conditions.

The act was the brainchild of the First Lady, Lady Bird Johnson. Shortly after the 1964 presidential election, she assembled a conference to discuss ways to make Washington, D.C., more beautiful. Her efforts and her travels through the country led her naturally to question whether the aesthetics of daily American life could be improved. Billboard and junkyard blight were constant reminders of the work that needed to be done.

The act was the brainchild of the First Lady, Lady Bird Johnson.

In the congressional debate over the issue, an important question was whether the regulation of roadside advertising would harm the interests of businesses and government because motorists would have less information about local services and attractions. Another question was how (if at all) the owners of billboards would be compensated for the business that they lost. In a compromise, Congress required the states that adopted the federal restrictions to pay the billboard owners immediately, in cash, with the payments being subsidized by the federal government.

EXPERIENCE UNDER THE ACT

The act has been a disappointment to those who wanted to reduce billboard blight. In fact, it has been a boon for the outdoor advertising industry. First, the federal government allocated only a tiny fraction of the funds that it promised for billboard removals, so few removals ever occurred. Second, the act prevented the states from controlling the billboards on their own through a mechanism called amortization, which offered a phase-out period in lieu of cash. Third, the outdoor advertising industry simply found other billboard locations. The industry recognized that its investment could not be lost, as governments were required to pay full cash compensation for removals. Fourth, the act led to billboards bigger than any previously seen and placed strategically outside the corridor regulated by the act. The act's secondary goal—screening junkyards from roadside view—has largely been achieved.

Lady Bird Johnson plants flowers as part of her mission to beautify America, March 9, 1965. She was the impetus behind the Highway Beautification Act. (©CORBIS)

See also: HIGHWAY ACT OF 1956; HIGHWAY SAFETY ACT OF 1966.

BIBLIOGRAPHY

Albert, Craig J. "Your Ad Goes Here: How the Highway Beautification Act of 1965 Thwarts Highway Beautification." *University of Kansas Law Review* 48 (2000): 463–544.

Cunningham, Roger A. "Billboard Control Under the Highway Beautification Act of 1965." *Michigan Law Review* 71 (1973): 1296–1371.

Gould, Lewis A. *Lady Bird Johnson and the Environment.* Lawrence: University Press of Kansas, 1988.

HIGHWAY SAFETY ACT OF 1966

Todd Olmstead

Excerpt from the Highway Safety Act

Each State shall have a highway safety program approved by the Secretary, designed to reduce traffic accidents and deaths, injuries, and property damage resulting therefrom. Such programs shall be in accordance with uniform standards promulgated by the Secretary.... Such uniform standards shall be promulgated by the Secretary so as to improve driver performance ... and to improve pedestrian performance. In addition such uniform standards shall include ... provisions for an effective record system of accidents ... , accident investigations ... , vehicle registration, operation, and inspection, highway design and maintenance ... , traffic control, vehicle codes and laws, surveillance of traffic for detection and correction of high or potentially high accident locations, and emergency services.

The Highway Safety Act of 1966 (P.L. 89-564, 80 Stat. 731) established a coordinated national highway safety program to reduce the death toll on the nation's roads. The act authorized states to use federal funds to develop and strengthen their highway traffic safety programs in accordance with uniform standards promulgated by the secretary of transportation.

The act authorized states to use federal funds to develop and strengthen their highway traffic safety programs in accordance with uniform standards promulgated by the secretary of transportation.

The act was motivated primarily by growing public concern over the rising number of traffic fatalities in the United States. Between 1960 and 1965, the annual number of traffic fatalities increased by nearly thirty percent. As President Lyndon B. Johnson stated at the signing of the act on September 9, 1966, " ... we have tolerated a raging epidemic of highway death ... which has killed more of our youth than all other diseases combined. Through the Highway Safety Act, we are going to find out more about highway disease—and we aim to cure it."

During its early years, the act required the secretary of transportation to establish uniform performance standards for the state highway safety programs. To be eligible for federal funds, states were required to formulate comprehensive highway safety programs to implement the federal standards. The initial thirteen (later eighteen) standards promulgated by the secretary touched on many aspects of highway traffic safety, including driver education, driver licensing, vehicle registration, vehicle inspection, highway design and maintenance, and traffic control devices. The National Highway Traffic Safety Administration (NHTSA) and Federal Highway Administration (FHWA) jointly administered the standards, with NHTSA taking responsibility for the "driver and vehicle" standards and FHWA overseeing the "roadway" standards.

Administration during the early years focused primarily on ensuring state compliance with the uniform performance standards. By 1976, however, state highway safety programs had matured considerably, and Congress amended the act to give states more flexibility in implementation. In essence, the standards became more like guidelines, and administration of the act "shifted from enforcing standards to using the standards as a framework for problem identification, countermeasure development, and program evaluation."

The National Highway Safety Administration (NHTSA) was created in 1970 to implement the safety programs prescribed by the National Traffic and Motor Vehicle Safety Act of 1966 and the Highway Safety Act of 1966. NHTSA is responsible for reducing deaths, injuries, and economic losses resulting from motor vehicle crashes. As part of this mission, the agency performs and reports results of a series of crash tests to inform consumers of the relative safety of specific vehicles in front-end collisions. (©TIM WRIGHT/CORBIS)

constraint: a restriction

The act was amended in 1987 to formally change the standards to guidelines. Another amendment stipulated that only projects belonging to one of nine National Priority Program areas (e.g., speed control, alcohol and other drug countermeasures, emergency medical services) were eligible for certain types of funding under the act. In 1998, however, this **constraint** was relaxed by another amendment requiring only that "States 'consider' the National Priority Program areas when developing their highway safety programs."

The act was amended in 1987 to formally change the standards to guidelines.

The Highway Safety Act of 1966 has undoubtedly improved traffic safety in the United States by providing leadership, guidance, and financial assistance to state highway safety programs. However, it is difficult to estimate with certainty the act's precise impact. Although between 1966 and 2001 traffic fatalities and the fatality rate (measured in fatalities per million vehicle miles traveled) declined 17 percent and 71 percent, respectively, at least some of the improvement in traffic safety is due to changes in other factors that contribute to motor vehicle crashes. These include the promulgation of federal motor vehicle safety standards (see the National Traffic and Motor Vehicle Safety Act of 1966), and improvements in medicine.

See also: NATIONAL EMISSIONS STANDARDS ACT; NATIONAL TRAFFIC AND MOTOR VEHICLE SAFETY ACT OF 1966.

BIBLIOGRAPHY

US Department of Transportation. National Highway Safety Bureau. *1969 Report on Activities Under the Highway Safety Act.* Washington DC: The Bureau, 1969.

National Highway Traffic Safety Administration, Federal Highway Administration, US Department of Transportation. "Uniform Procedures for State Highway Safety Programs." <http://www.nhtsa.dot.gov>.

HILL-BURTON ACT (1946)

Roger K. Newman

Depression and war had taken their toll on hospitals by the end of World War II. Many hospitals had become obsolete, and over 40 percent of the nation's counties had no hospital facilities at all. In early 1945 Senators Lister Hill of Alabama and Harold H. Burton of Ohio introduced a bill to construct new hospitals throughout the nation. Hill, a progressive Democrat whose father was the first American to suture a human heart, was the driving force. Their proposal languished in the Senate Education and Labor Committee until November 1945 when President Harry S. Truman announced a comprehensive, prepaid medical insurance program for all Americans, tied to Social Security.

Suddenly, to deflect Truman's plan, the bill emerged, rewritten by the American Hospital Association. Its centerpiece was a five-year program authorizing $75 million annually for hospital construction according to a formula devised by Ohio Senator Robert A. Taft, based on population and per capita income, which favored poorer rural and Southern states. When some senators from larger states objected that the bill ignored the needs of low-income patients, its sponsors stated that facilities agreed to promote a "reasonable" amount of medical services for free or at reduced charges for persons unable to pay in return for federal funds. This program, by default, established the first provision for the uninsured in American law.

In order to secure Southern votes Senator Hill added a provision permitting hospitals to segregate patients and doctors according to the "separate but equal" formula. This was the only time in the twentieth century that racial segregation had been codified in federal legislation, and it remained so until 1963 when a federal court ordered desegregation of facilities. Notwithstanding, compared to the political explosiveness and high cost of national health insurance, it seemed relatively risk-free and inexpensive. The bill passed with little fanfare, becoming law on August 13, 1946.

The law introduced the concept of state and local cost sharing-matching funds. Federal "seed money" and "joint tithing," Hill later said, was in keeping with the biblical injunction "where your treasure is, there will your heart be also." By 1968 it had helped to finance 9,200 new medical facilities, with a total of 416,000 new beds. By 1975 when expenditures ended under the act, the federal government had assisted in financing almost one-third of all hospital projects in the nation, contributing about 10 percent of the annual costs of all hospital construction. The act's standard of 4.5 beds per 1,000 people was nearly double the average twenty years earlier. Many rural areas had access to hospital care for the first time.

The law grew to address other needs. A 1954 amendment added long-term facilities, rehabilitation centers, and outpatient departments. Amendments in 1964 established a precedent for the use of public funds to subsidize planning by voluntary health agencies. The act provided a model for federal and state standards for the design, regulation, and financing of facilities that nursing homes later used.

By 2000 the Hill-Burton Act dispensed more than $4.6 billion as well as $1.5 billion in loans to nearly 6,800 healthcare facilities in over 4,000 communities, which in turn provided free or reduced charged services to persons unable to pay for them.

> *This program, by default, established the first provision for the uninsured in American law.*

> *By 2000 the Hill-Burton Act dispensed more than $4.6 billion as well as $1.5 billion in loans to nearly 6,800 healthcare facilities in over 4,000 communities, which in turn provided free or reduced charged services to persons unable to pay for them.*

BIBLIOGRAPHY

Hamilton, Virginia V. *Lister Hill: Statesman from the South.* Chapel Hill: University of North Carolina Press, 1987.

Perlstadt, Harry. "The Development of the Hill-Burton Legislation: Interests, Issues and Compromises." *Journal of Health and Social Policy* 6, no. 3 (1995): 77–96.

HOBBS ANTI-RACKETEERING ACT (1946)

Barry L. Johnson

Excerpt from the Hobbs Anti-Racketeering Act

Whoever in any way obstructs, delays, or affects commerce or the movement of any article or commodity in commerce, by robbery or extortion or attempts or conspires to do so ... shall be fined under this title or imprisoned not more than twenty years, or both.

T he Hobbs Anti-Racketeering Act of 1946 (P.L. 79–486, 60 Stat. 420), passed as an amendment to the Anti-Racketeering Act of 1934, was part of Congress's efforts to combat labor racketeering and the activities of organized crime. Like its predecessor, the Hobbs Act prescribes heavy criminal penalties for acts of robbery or **extortion** that affect interstate commerce. The courts have interpreted the Hobbs Act broadly, requiring only a minimal effect on interstate commerce to justify the exercise of federal jurisdiction, and interpreting the concept of extortion to cover receipt of bribes by public officials. As a result, the Hobbs Act has been used as the basis for federal prosecutions in situations not apparently contemplated by Congress in 1946, including intrastate robberies and public corruption.

extortion: the obtaining of money (or other concessions) by force or intimidation

JUDICIAL REVIEW AND CONGRESSIONAL RESPONSE

The Hobbs Act was passed in direct response to the United States Supreme Court's 1942 decision in *United States v. Teamsters Local 807*, a case involving prosecution of members of a New York City truck drivers union. Prosecutors accused union members of violating the Anti-Racketeering Act by using threats of force to obtain payments from out-of-town trucking companies in return for permission for their trucks to enter the city. The evidence showed that union members' assistance was not requested by the out-of-town truckers, and that in many cases no actual work was performed by union members in exchange for the payments. The prosecution contended that the union activity was a classic labor extortion racket. The Supreme Court disagreed, holding that the union activities were not illegal under the Anti-Racketeering Act because the act exempted wage payments to employees from coverage by that law. The Court viewed as wages the payments that the truckers' union was demanding.

loophole: a means of evading or escaping an obligation or enforcement of a law or contract

With this ruling, the Court had created a **loophole** in the law. Shortly after the *Teamsters Local 807* decision, members of Congress introduced several bills designed to eliminate that loophole. One of these bills, introduced by Representative Samuel F. Hobbs (D-Alabama), ultimately was enacted in 1946. According to one congressman, the Hobbs bill was "made necessary by the amazing decision of the Supreme Court in the case of the United States against Teamsters' Union 807 [which] practically nullified the anti-racketeering bill of 1934" (91 *Congressional Record* 11900, remarks of Congressman Hancock).

A key provision of the Hobbs Act eliminated the wage exception that had been the basis for the Court's decision in *Teamsters Local 807*. Another provision deleted language in the Anti-Racketeering Act of 1934 that had instructed courts not to interpret that statute in a way that would "impair, diminish, or in any manner affect the rights of bona-fide labor organizations in lawfully carrying out" their legitimate objectives. Representative Hobbs explained that this language was eliminated so that courts could not use it to resurrect the *Teamsters Local 807* decision.

The major controversy over the Hobbs Act involved complaints by its opponents that it was antilabor. These opponents felt that the act could be used to prosecute strikers, frustrating legitimate activities of organized labor. Supporters of the bill insisted that it did not apply to legitimate labor activity, including strike activity that led to violence. In its 1973 decision in *United States v. Enmons*, the Supreme Court emphasized that the Hobbs Act prohibited only personal payoffs, or "wages" for unwanted or fictitious labor services. Thus in *Enmons* the Court held that violent strike activity by members of an electrical union seeking higher wages and benefits from a utility company did not violate the Hobbs Act.

EXTENDING THE ACT

For many years, prosecutions under the Hobbs Act involved the activities of organized crime and labor racketeering. However, judges have been aggressive in interpreting the act's language to apply to a broader range of actions. These judicial opinions have permitted federal prosecutors to apply the act to ordinary robberies and corruption by state and local public officials. The courts have, for example, interpreted certain language in the Hobbs Act as evidence that Congress intended for the statute to reach to the outer limit of Congress's constitutional authority to regulate commerce. As a result, courts have upheld use of the Hobbs Act even where there is no direct and immediate obstruction of the movement of goods in interstate commerce. This permits federal prosecution for simple robberies of businesses. These crimes have traditionally been prosecuted under state law. But courts have held that these crimes also fall under the federal Hobbs Act, because such robberies will have at least some minimal effect on customer traffic or on the businesses' purchases of goods from out-of-state suppliers. This extension of the reach of federal criminal law into areas traditionally policed by the states has been controversial.

Also controversial has been the use of the Hobbs Act in corruption cases against state and local public officials. The legislative history of the Hobbs Act shows no intent on the part of Congress to apply this law to corrupt demands by state or local officials for the payment of bribes. Nevertheless, federal prosecutors have successfully argued that such activities do constitute extortion, a crime covered by the Hobbs Act.

Labor racketeering activity has declined over the years, and the concerns that motivated Congress to pass the Hobbs Act have lessened in importance. In the 1970s and 1980s other federal laws were passed to combat organized crime (including the Organized Crime Control Act, or RICO, of 1970 and anti-money laundering provisions).Yet the Hobbs Act continues to be a vital and controversial tool for federal prosecutors.

See also: BRIBERY ACT; FEDERAL BLACKMAIL STATUTE; ORGANIZED CRIME CONTROL ACT OF 1970.

BIBLIOGRAPHY
Lindgren, James. "The Elusive Distinction Between Bribery and Extortion: From the Common Law to the Hobbs Act." 35 *UCLA Law Review* 815 (1988).

Ruff, Charles F.C. "Federal Prosecution of Local Corruption: A Case Study in the Making of Law Enforcement Policy." 65 *Georgetown Law Journal* 1171 (1977).

Whitaker, Charles N. "Federal Prosecution of State and Local Bribery: Inappropriate Tools and the Need for a Structured Approach." 78 *Virginia Law Review* 1617 (1992).

HOMESTEAD ACT (1862)

James L. Huston

Excerpt from the Homestead Act

That the person applying for the benefit of this act shall, upon application to the register of the land office in which he or she is about to make such entry, make affidavit before the said register or receiver that he or she is the head of a family, or is twenty-one years or more of age, or shall have performed service in the army or navy of the United States, and that he has never borne arms against the Government of the United States…, and that such application is made for his or her exclusive use and benefit, and that said entry is made for the purpose of actual settlement and cultivation…; and upon filing the said affidavit with the register or receiver, and on payment of ten dollars, he or she shall thereupon be permitted to enter the quantity of land specified …

egalitarian: marked by a belief in human equality

Throughout American history, various individuals have dreamed of certain laws that when enacted would transform society and make us a more **egalitarian** and just nation. The Homestead Act (12 Stat. 392) was one of these visions, but, unlike other schemes, the homestead ideal was actually put into practice. Its results proved far different from the hopes that promoted its passage.

The homestead ideal was that each head of a family—in the nineteenth century, this person was almost always a man—should possess a small farm of some 100 acres to support a family. By having land of their own, the farmers could be independent of the bullying of others and thus could act as objective citizens, making wise choices between good legislators and poor ones. These farmers could not be threatened with dismissal from jobs (as could wage-earners, people hired to work for owners of wealth). They valued hard work, by which they fed themselves and their families, and distrusted luxury and leisure. Indeed, the ideal of the independent farmer formed the basis of Thomas Jefferson's political philosophy—he hoped the nation would always be guided by the yeoman farmer (a farmer who owned his own land), and he purchased the territory of Louisiana partly to ensure the United States would forever remain a small farmer nation.

> *The homestead ideal was that each head of a family—in the nineteenth century, this person was almost always a man—should possess a small farm of some 100 acres to support a family.*

THE HOMESTEAD IDEAL AND CLASS CONFLICT

By the 1830s the country had experienced urban development and industrialization, changes unforeseen by Jefferson. Small farmer life was not possible

Thirty-seventh

Congress of the United States,

At the Second Session

BEGUN AND HELD AT THE CITY OF WASHINGTON

in the District of Columbia

on Monday the second day of December one thousand eight hundred and sixty-one

AN ACT to secure homesteads to actual settlers on the public domain.

Be it Enacted by the Senate and House of Representatives of the United States of America in Congress assembled.

That any person who is the head of a family, or who has arrived at the age of twenty-one years, and is a citizen of the United States, or who shall have filed his declaration of intention to become such, as required by the naturalization laws of the United States, and who has never borne arms against the United States government or given aid and comfort to its enemies, shall from and after the first January, eighteen hundred and sixty-three be entitled to enter one quarter section or a less quantity of unappropriated public lands, upon which said person may have filed a pre-emption claim, or which may, at the time the application is made, be subject to pre-emption at one dollar and twenty-five cents, or less, per acre; or eighty acres or less of such unappropriated lands, at two dollars and fifty cents per acre; to be located in a body, in conformity to the legal subdivisions of the public lands, and after the same shall have been surveyed: Provided, That any person owning and residing on land may, under the provisions of this act, enter other land lying contiguous to his or her said land, which shall not, with the land so already owned and occupied, exceed in the aggregate, one hundred and sixty acres.

Sec. 2. And be it further enacted, That the person applying

A handwritten copy of the Homestead Act, 1862. (US National Archives and Records Administration)

in the large cities, and of course factories employed wage-earners. Thus the United States began to acquire a working class. But the new working class received miserable wages and battled employers over their pay and working hours. Leaders among the working men usually sought to establish labor unions by which they could bargain with employers for better conditions, but some sought a more general solution. Such reformers turned to the supply of land in the West and believed that the nation could be saved severe class conflicts between employers and workers by reserving that land for small farmers. Thus, workingmen from the East could travel to the West, obtain a small farm (about 100 to 200 acres) for free from the federal government, and preserve the small independent farmer quality of American political life.

Two New York working-class leaders vigorously promoted the homestead ideal. George Henry Evans, who founded the Land Reform Association in the 1840s, and John Commerford, a trade unionist who headed the National Reform Association in the 1850s, received great aid and publicity from the New York City newspaper publisher Horace Greeley. Greeley's paper, the *New York Tribune,* had the greatest circulation of all newspapers prior to the Civil War. However, others became attracted to the homestead plan for reasons other than rejuvenating American society with more farmers. Rather, they reasoned that by using the West to siphon off some workers—not all of them—a labor shortage would be created in the East, thereby raising wages and dispelling class conflict. This latter view became popular among politicians.

POLITICAL UPS AND DOWNS

By the late 1840s the homestead proposal attracted politicians who brought the subject before Congress, the most prominent being Andrew Johnson of Tennessee. Until this time the government had auctioned off public lands to the highest bidder, thereby allowing speculators to buy vast tracts of land and hold it off the market until the price rose so they could make handsome profits. The small farmer was effectively excluded from such land sales. However, by 1841 pressure on Congress to make lands available to common folk had produced the Preemption Act, by which settlers on government land could buy 160 acres for $1.25 per acre before the land was auctioned off. The Preemption Act was popular, but it soon was displaced in public sentiment by the homestead agitation. The House of Representatives passed a homestead bill in 1852, but the Senate would not agree to it. A somewhat similar proposal was actively considered in 1854, and a plan by Pennsylvania Representative Galusha A. Grow was actually passed by Congress in 1860, only to be vetoed by then President James Buchanan.

Originally, the homestead ideal received general approval from both the Whigs (the precursor of the Republicans) and Democrats. But in the 1850s questions about slavery came into prominence that emphasized regional differences connected with the question of free western land. Southern politicians increasingly saw the homestead ideal as a means of increasing the number of free states so as to diminish the power of the South in national councils. Republicans, on the other hand, saw the homestead plan as a way to attract Northern voters and stop what they feared was the burgeoning influence of the slave states.

The controversy over slavery's expansion into the territories brought about the secession of South Carolina, Georgia, Mississippi, Alabama, Florida,

Manifest Destiny

The term "manifest destiny" expressed the belief that the expansion of the United States across North America was both right and inevitable. The term was first used in 1845 in the Democratic Review by John L. O'Sullivan, who wrote that it was "our manifest destiny to overspread the continent allotted by Providence for the free development of our yearly multiplying millions." O'Sullivan was referring in particular to the annexation of Texas, but his phrase was quickly adopted by those advocating annexation of the Oregon Territory, parts of Mexico, and even Cuba. Believers in manifest destiny felt that American abilities and institutions were inherently superior to those of other peoples, and that it was therefore their "mission" to spread American values across the continent. During the 1890s, the concept was revived and used to justify the annexation of Hawaii and islands taken from Spain in the Spanish-American War.

Louisiana, and Texas in 1860 to 1861, and soon plunged the country into Civil War. That circumstance led to the passage of the Homestead Act. When the states that formed the Confederacy seceded, they also withdrew their senators and representatives from Congress, thereby giving the Republicans a commanding majority. Senator Justin S. Morrill of Vermont picked up the Grow Homestead Bill of 1860 and with little dissent marshaled it through the House of Representatives on February 28, 1862. It passed the Senate on May 6, and Abraham Lincoln signed the bill into law on May 20.

UNINTENDED RESULTS

And so the homestead vision took actual legislative form and became law. But its results were hardly anything its promoters intended. Indeed, at least four important factors hindered the achievement of the homestead dream:

A family poses in front of their wagon in Loup Valley, Nebraska, on their way to their new homestead in 1886. (© HULTON/ARCHIVE BY GETTY IMAGES)

First, the public land available for homesteading was in the Great Plains, an area not well suited to small farming. Much of the land was more adapted to cattle ranches and mining, operations that required much more than the 160 acres allowed by the Homestead statute. In short, the Homestead law might have worked better had it passed in 1790 or 1800, when the land available for habitation would support small farms. But by 1862 public lands were those in a climate that did not fit the agriculture practiced in the East.

Second, national legislators saw in the public lands not only a chance to help small farmers but to stimulate the national economy by giving portions of the region to enterprises and to eastern states. In the 1850s Congress began (with the Illinois Land Grant of 1850) the practice of giving land to railroads to assist in the completion of these vital arteries of transportation. The most famous of these land grants came during the Civil War in the Pacific Railway Acts of 1862 and 1864. Then, Congress thought it wise to stimulate the creation of agricultural and mechanical colleges in the nation. In 1862 Congress passed the Land Grant College Act, the handiwork of Justin Morrill, and offered states funds from the sale of certain amounts of western land. Congress also passed a batch of land laws to achieve various objectives in development of the West: the Timber Culture Act of 1873, the Desert Land Act of 1877, and the Timber and Stone Act of 1878. All these actions removed western land available to homesteaders.

Third, Congress constantly amended the Homestead Act so as to allow settlers less time to claim their land. This opened the door for fraud. By letting settlers file for land titles early—settlers then paying a small price per acre—Congress encouraged them to make momentary improvements in order to obtain the land and settle their title to a speculator or monopolist. Congress did not encourage settlers to establish permanent farms for themselves.

Fourth, the federal government in the nineteenth century lacked the personnel to adequately run the land offices. Enforcement officials were overwhelmed. This of course gave rise to cheating. Speculators, monopolists, and others used the land laws to create giant farms. So instead of the Homestead Act promoting small farms, it ended up promoting the large western ranch. Of the some 1 billion acres of public land that the government owned in the nineteenth century, 183 million acres went to railroad corporations; 140 million acres to the states; 100 million acres to Indian tribes; and 100 million acres to free farmers (the total acreage given out in cash sales). (One half of the land had not been sold because it had been reserved for national parks or was totally unsuited for agricultural development.)

Only one acre in five that the government released out of its hands went to small farmers—certainly not the vision of the Homestead Act promoters.

So only one acre in five that the government released out of its hands went to small farmers—certainly not the vision of the Homestead Act promoters. And to show how irrelevant the policy actually was to the social condition of the United States, class relations grew even more violent in the years between 1873 and 1896, as capitalists and workers fought bitterly over control of the factory floor, working conditions, and wages. Indeed, the period has been called the "Great Upheaval." As it turned out, the homestead ideal was no solution to the nation's social problems stemming from the Industrial Revolution.

BIBLIOGRAPHY

Bronstein, Jamie L. *Land Reform and Working-Class Experience in Britain and the United States, 1800–1862.* Stanford, CA: Stanford University Press, 1999.

Gates, Paul Wallace, and Robert W. Swenson. *History of Public Land Law Development.* Washington, DC: U.S. Government Printing Office, 1968.

Richardson, Heather Cox. *The Greatest Nation of the Earth: Republican Economic Policies during the Civil War.* Cambridge, MA: Harvard University Press, 1997.

Robbins, Roy M. *Our Landed Heritage: The Public Domain, 1776–1936.* Lincoln, NE: Bison Books, 1962.

Shannon, Freed A. *The Farmer's Last Frontier: Agriculture, 1860-1897.* New York: Harper and Row, 1945.

HOSPITAL SURVEY AND CONSTRUCTION ACT

See HILL-BURTON ACT

HOUSING AND URBAN DEVELOPMENT ACT OF 1965

Charles E. Daye

The Housing and Urban Development Act of 1965 (P.L. 89-117, 79 Stat. 451) was the most ambitious federal housing effort undertaken since the Housing Act of 1949. The 1965 act extended the urban renewal programs set in motion by the 1949 act, which provided various forms of federal assistance to cities for removing dilapidated housing and redeveloping parts of downtowns. The act also extended the code enforcement program, which required that cities enact a code specifying minimum standards for housing before they could participate in the urban renewal program. In addition, the act initiated or extended Federal Housing Administration mortgage-insurance programs, which enabled more American families to purchase a home. The basis for the act is Congress's taxing and spending power as stated in the U.S. Constitution, article I, section 8, which authorizes the legislature to provide for the general welfare.

> *The basis for the act is Congress's taxing and spending power as stated in the U.S. Constitution, article I, section 8, which authorizes the legislature to provide for the general welfare.*

The most controversial and innovative part of the act, however, created a rent-supplement program. Under this program, qualified tenants paid 25 percent of their income in rent, and the program paid the balance directly to the housing provider. The supplement ceased when the occupant was able to pay the full rent. To qualify, a person's income had to be within the limits set for eligibility for public housing, and the person had to be either elderly, physically handicapped, displaced by a public-improvement program, living in substandard housing, or occupying housing damaged by a natural disaster. Only private, **nonprofit** (or, in some cases, limited-profit) corporations were eligible housing sponsors.

nonprofit: an organization whose business is not conducted or maintained for the purpose of making a profit, but is usually aimed at providing services for the public good

In 1973 President Nixon halted funding for the rent-supplement program. Ultimately, it was replaced by other federal programs, including those known as the section 8 programs. These programs were enacted by the Housing and Community Development Act of 1974 to assist tenants living in privately-owned housing in paying their rent.

PROS AND CONS

New Deal: the legislative and administrative program of President Franklin D. Roosevelt designed to promote economic recovery and social reform (1933–1939)

Great Society: broad term for the domestic programs of President Lyndon B. Johnson, in which he called for "an end to poverty and racial injustice"

President Franklin Roosevelt's **New Deal** legislation and the Housing Act of 1949 reflected the view that the federal government had a responsibility to help provide for decent housing. After Congress adopted these programs, housing advocates and social reformers demanded more attractive, well-planned cities and better housing for individuals of limited means. President Lyndon B. Johnson submitted a bill to Congress in March 1965 proposing the rent-supplement program as part of his **Great Society** program. In his message on housing accompanying the bill transmitted to congress, President Johnson argued that "the most crucial new instrument in our effort to improve the

A homeless man pulls two crates of empty bottles and cans down Madison Avenue in New York City on November 20, 2001. On this day, President George W. Bush announced that the Department of Housing and Urban Development would administer $1 billion in grants to non-governmental organizations that help the homeless. (© AP/WIDE WORLD PHOTOS)

American city is the rent supplement." He proposed the program to assist low- and moderate-income renters whose incomes were above the initial limits set for those who sought public housing.

The legislative debate on the bill centered on the rent-supplement proposal, with specific attention to income limitations. Opponents argued that rent supplements would take away renters' incentives to seek homeownership, impose extraordinary costs on government, and encourage socialism. To gain enough votes for passage of the bill, President Johnson accepted the restriction of supplements to individuals who qualified for public housing.

EXPERIENCE AND RELATIONSHIP WITH OTHER LAWS

In 1965 the Department of Housing and Urban Development (HUD) was established to consolidate federal agencies that dealt with urban housing. These agencies included the Public Housing Administration, the Federal Housing Administration (which operates extensive mortgage-insurance programs), and the Federal National Mortgage Association (popularly known as "Fannie Mae," which buys and sells bank mortgages). The Housing and Urban Development Act of 1968 continued the shift of federal subsidies away from publicly owned housing toward private housing. The Housing and Community Development Act of 1974 enacted the section 8 program that replaced the rent-supplement program.

See also: FEDERAL NATIONAL MORTGAGE ASSOCIATION CHARTER ACT; NATIONAL HOUSING ACT; UNITED STATES HOUSING ACT OF 1837 (WAGNER-STEAGALL HOUSING ACT).

BIBLIOGRAPHY

Bratt, Rachel G. *Rebuilding a Low-Income Housing Policy*. Philadelphia: Temple University Press, 1989.

Keith, Nathaniel S. *Politics of the Housing Crisis Since 1930*. New York: Universe Books, 1973.

Wilson, James Q., ed. *Urban Renewal: The Record and the Controversy*. Cambridge, MA: MIT Press, 1966.

FHA and Fannie Mae
Charles E. Daye

The Federal Housing Administration (FHA), created in the Housing Act of 1934, insures mortgages that banks offer to qualified borrowers who cannot afford to make large down payments ordinarily required by the bank. Insurance protects the bank against loss if the buyer defaults (that is, fails to make the mortgage payments).

The Federal National Mortgage Association (Fannie Mae) was originally a government-chartered corporation created in 1938 to assist housing lenders by buying mortgages from or selling mortgages to them. In 1954 Fannie Mae's ownership changed when private stockholders became part owners.

I

IMMIGRATION AND NATIONALITY ACT (1952)

Bo Cooper

The Immigration and Nationality Act (P.L. 82-414, 66 Stat. 163) mirrors the American public and policy attitude toward immigration; it is complex, its pieces do not always fit well with one another, and Congress tinkers with it endlessly. Even immigration experts are hard pressed to master it, and most affected by its provisions find it a difficult riddle. Executive branch agencies administering it have never approached full success, and courts interpreting it commonly reach dramatically different conclusions from one another. For all of its faults, though, the Immigration and Nationality Act provides a dense, rich record of our country's struggle to make the right decisions about who should be able to come to this country as guests and as permanent members of the American community.

> *For all of its faults, the Immigration and Nationality Act provides a dense, rich record of the United States' struggle to make the right decisions about who should be able to come to this country as guests and as permanent members of the American community.*

The immigration debate is sparked continually by dramatic events that crowd the newspapers and television: waves of Cubans coming to the shores of Florida in the *Mariel* boatlift of 1981; tens of thousands of Haitians plying the straits of Florida in crowded, rickety vessels after the military overthrew Haiti's first elected president in 1991; bitter public disputes over whether visas available to foreign workers are contributing to the country's economy or displacing their American counterparts; a months-long standoff over the fate of a small Cuban boy dramatically rescued at sea on Thanksgiving Day in 1999, after a marine accident left his mother drowned; colossal backlogs of applications; and the September 11, 2001 attacks on the World Trade Center and the Pentagon, carried out by hijackers who navigated in very sophisticated ways the tangled immigration process to gain entry to this country, some of them even learning here the flying skills that equipped them to execute the attacks.

These are only modern examples of the continuing American immigration controversies. Throughout its history, the United States has struggled with its proper cultural composition, the economic benefits or losses from immigration, its role to provide refuge, and the way to administer the complex rules that have evolved.

Uncle Sam puts an immigration quota in place in this 1921 cartoon. A 1921 act, made permanent in the National Origins Act of 1924, limited annual immigration to 3 percent of the number of foreign-born nationals from each country residing in the United States, as measured by the 1910 census. (© HULTON/ARCHIVE BY GETTY IMAGES)

HISTORICAL CONTEXT

No significant federal restrictions on immigration existed until the late nineteenth century. Up to that time, Congress allowed free migration into America, and the volume of that traffic was immense. About a quarter-million immigrants are believed to have entered the country between the end of the Revolutionary War and 1819. Between 1820 and 1840, just over 750,000 immigrated here, and another 4,300,000 came between 1840 and 1860. The total from 1860 to 1880—over 5,100,000—roughly equaled the entire number that had immigrated to this country previously. By far, most who immigrated before 1880 were from Great Britain, Germany, and Ireland.

No significant federal restrictions on immigration existed until the late-nineteenth century.

Public attitudes during this period varied. Many welcomed the notion of an immigrant nation. Herman Melville romanticized this sentiment: "There is something in the contemplation of the mode in which America was settled, that ... should forever extinguish the prejudices of national dislikes. Settled by people of all nations, all nations may claim her for their own." Disquiet over the huge immigration flow, rooted partly in anti-Catholicism, was represented by Samuel Morse: "How is it possible that foreign turbulence imported by shiploads, that riot and ignorance in hundreds of thousands of human priest-controlled machines, should suddenly be thrown in our society and not produce turbulence and excess? Can one throw mud into water and not disturb its clearness?" Associations and political parties, like the Know-Nothing Party, emerged, dedicated to forming immigration policy that would preserve the ethnic composition of the country.

Nevertheless, there prevailed during this time a strong sentiment toward this country as a land of freedom (despite the persistence of slavery); and perhaps an even stronger set of labor and economic needs for substantial immigration as the country pushed westward, built railroads, developed urban centers, and fueled the early stages of industrialization. Federal immigration policy continued to adhere to this idea as late as 1864, as evidenced by the Republican Party platform, to which Abraham Lincoln was a contributor: "Foreign immigration which in the past has added so much to the wealth, resources, and increase of power to this nation ... the asylum of the oppressed of all nations ... should be fostered and encouraged by a liberal and just policy."

Patriotic organizations such as the Daughters of the American Revolution and conservatives argued that the law was needed to protect the nation from radicals and to keep out immigrants who might lower the U.S. standard of living. Similarly, they saw the national-origins quotas as a way to select immigrants most able to assimilate in U.S. society.

The last two decades of the nineteenth century marked an important turn. As the rate of immigration continued to increase, its patterns changed. Immigrants came increasingly not from northern and western Europe, but from southern and eastern Europe. Public attitudes likewise began to change. While resistance to a perceived dilution in the national cultural strength had been evident throughout the country's history, it was now heightened as the religious, cultural, and physical characteristics of the changing stream of immigrants began to differ more obviously, and as their number rose further. Perhaps predictably, federal lawmaker's position on immigration changed at about this time as well.

EARLY STATUTORY EVOLUTION

The first federal statutes restricting immigration into America appeared in 1875 and 1882. The Act of 1875 barred the entry of convicts and prostitutes. The Act of 1882, the first general federal immigration statute, forbade the entry of idiots, lunatics, and paupers. In addition, the Act of 1882 imposed a head tax of fifty cents per immigrant. In 1891, Congress began work on an immigration bill that seemed specifically aimed at the "new" immigrants from southern and eastern Europe. Henry Cabot Lodge, a key voice in the debate, urged reform to "separate ... the chaff from the wheat" and to address "a decline in the quality of American citizenship." That year Congress easily passed new categories of exclusion for those bringing "loathsome or contagious diseases" or who had been convicted of "crimes involving moral turpitude," a bar to admission that, in an only slightly evolved version, remains a significant part of the law today.

Also in 1882, there appeared the first legislation limiting entry on the basis of national origin. The two prior decades had witnessed a 250 percent increase in the rate of immigration from China. This had first been welcomed to meet mining and railroad-building needs, but the completion of the cross-country railroad project and an economic decline coincided with the growth of vocal sentiment against Chinese immigration. The Chinese Exclusion Act would remain a part of U.S. law for more than sixty years.

As immigration numbers rose further in the early twentieth century, national opinion against free admission into America solidified as well. New control strategies focused on whether to impose a literacy test as a condition of admission, a measure aimed specifically at limiting immigration from southeastern Europe. Three times between 1896 and 1915, Congress passed literacy provisions that the presidents vetoed. Vetoing the 1915 bill, President Wilson decried the proposed shift away from the American tradition of asylum and broad admission of those not medically or criminally threatening to the country's well-being: "the new tests [based on literacy] are not tests of quality or of character or of personal fitness, but tests of opportunity. Those who come seeking opportunity are not to be admitted unless they have already had one of the chief of the opportunities they seek, the opportunity of education. The object of such provisions is restriction, not selection." After the United States entered World War I, Congress finally overrode a

President Lyndon B. Johnson signs the Immigration and Nationality Amendments of 1965 at a ceremony on Liberty Island, New York, October 3, 1965. The 1965 amendments repealed the nationality quotas set in the 1952 act and replaced them with a system based on family reunification and job skills. (© YOICHI R. OKAMOTO, LYNDON BAINES JOHNSON LIBRARY)

fourth presidential veto, and in 1917 a literacy requirement for immigration became U.S. law.

In 1921, Congress passed, and President Harding signed, the first legislation setting forth the notion of a national origins quota, imposing what were for the most part the first quantitative, rather than qualitative, limits.

In 1921, Congress passed, and President Harding signed, the first legislation setting forth the notion of a national origins quota, imposing what were for the most part the first quantitative, rather than qualitative, limits. These limits, temporary in 1921, were made permanent in 1924 in the National Origins Act. This structure (which did not apply to the Western Hemisphere) was designed to preserve the racial and ethnic content of the country's population, by permitting a larger flow of immigration from those northern and western European countries already most strongly represented in the U.S. population. Between these legislative restrictions and the economic effects of the Great Depression, immigration in the 1930s fell to its lowest level in a century.

Three consequences of World War II further shaped U.S. immigration policy. First, partly as a result of wartime alliances, the Chinese Exclusion Act was repealed. Second, wartime labor needs were filled through the negotiation with Mexico of the "bracero" program, admitting large numbers of temporary Mexican workers over the next two decades. Third, the Displaced Persons Act of 1948 marked the first refugee legislation in American history, following the tragic consequences for large numbers of people refused entry into this country from Nazi Germany.

THE IMMIGRATION AND NATIONALITY ACT AND ITS CONTINUING EVOLUTION

In 1952, the passage of the Immigration and Nationality Act marked a major revision of existing law. It created a system of preferences for skilled workers and relatives of citizens and permanent residents. It also amplified security and screening requirements, consistent with the prevailing Cold War atmosphere. The 1952 Act retained, though, the national origins quota system. Congress overrode the veto of President Truman, who in his veto statement proclaimed his view that "[i]n no other realm of our national life are we so hampered and stultified by the dead hand of the past, as we are in this field of immigration."

Today's immigration law owes perhaps more to a far-reaching set of amendments in 1965 than to the 1952 law itself. In 1965, amid the American Civil Rights movement, Congress repealed the national origins quota with a regime based primarily on family reunification and skills. This regime, though substantially revised, remains today the basis of U.S. policy toward legal immigration. Eastern Hemisphere immigration would no longer be controlled through the national origins system, but according to an overall numeric limitation, a standard per-country limitation, and a seven-category preference system based principally on close family relationships and work abilities. Western Hemisphere immigration would be controlled according to an overall ceiling, without a preference system or per-country limitation. In the next decade, both hemispheres were made subject to a single overall limit and a common preference system. The sources of immigration were changing as well, principally now from Latin America and Asia rather than Europe.

Today's immigration law owes perhaps more to a far-reaching set of amendments in 1965 than to the 1952 law itself.

From 1980 to 1990, other major revisions followed. The Refugee Act of 1980 aligned the U.S. definition of refugee—previously referring to those fleeing persecution in communist or Middle East countries—with the more neutral international definition contained in the 1952 United Nations Refugee Convention. It also created a more orderly system for the admission and integration of refugees, who have since been admitted at a rate roughly of between 50,000 and 100,000 per year. In 1986 Congress passed the Immigration Reform and Control Act, designed to deal comprehensively with the problem of illegal immigration, by (1) providing "amnesty" to large categories of aliens already in this country unlawfully, but (2) eliminating job-related incentives to come to this country illegally by creating a system of penalties for those who employ people not eligible to work.

The Immigration Act of 1990 significantly revised the system for legal immigration. This act amended the Immigration and Nationality Act by raising overall limits, significantly increasing employment-based immigration, and creating a system to admit "diversity immigrants" from underrepresented countries. The 1990 Act also made important changes to the employment-related "nonimmigrant" categories, under which people are admitted to the country temporarily rather than as permanent residents. Finally, the 1990 Act rewrote the grounds for excluding or deporting aliens and enacted measures to ensure more effective removal of criminal aliens.

The Immigration and Nationality Act by 1990 had taken on the basic form it has today. A preference system, based mainly on family relationships and needed job skills, provides for "immigrant" visas, or permanent residence: these are commonly known as "green cards," though they have not been actually green for some time. There is a complex set of categories for "nonimmigrant" or temporary visas, ranging from short-term admissions for those coming as tourists to years-long admissions of those in "specialty occupations" such as computer programming. There are rules governing the acquisition of citizenship at birth and through naturalization. Complex grounds are set out for the exclusion of certain categories of persons seeking admission to the country, ranging from criminals, terrorists, those lacking entry documents, and polygamists. A similar set of rules provides for the deportation of those who commit certain acts after admission, ranging from crimes to violation of the terms of their admission (like staying longer than permitted, dropping out of school, or working without permission). A complex government bureaucracy, spanning many executive branch agencies and encircling the globe, administers the system.

Yet the pattern of constant change to the statute, today hundreds of pages long, has persisted. In 1996 the most far-reaching revisions in three decades focused on stricter enforcement against illegal immigration, particularly criminal aliens. In 2000 alone, Congress made changes relating to business visas, human trafficking, family-based immigration, and citizenship for children born to citizens outside the United States, and more. The September 11, 2001 terrorist attacks prompted a wholesale reevaluation of the system's security vulnerabilities. The demand for immigration to this country, both from inside and outside the United States, remains high: roughly one million people were given permanent residence in 2002, and about thirty-five million were admitted temporarily. Illegal immigration remains an issue, with the undocumented population estimated at roughly ten million. Immigration will

The pattern of constant change to the statute, today hundreds of pages long, has persisted.

continue to hover near the top of the national policy agenda, and the Immigration and Nationality Act will be wrung through many more changes, as the twenty-first century proceeds.

BIBLIOGRAPHY

Bennett, Marion T. *American Immigration Policies: A History.* Washington, DC: Public Affairs Press, 1963.

Congressional Research Service. *Brief History of United States Immigration Policy.* Report No. 91-141, January 25, 1991.

Mills, Nicolaus, ed. *Arguing Immigration: The Debate over the Changing Face of America.* New York: Simon & Schuster, 1994.

Neuman, Gerald R. "The Lost Century of Immigration Law (1776-1875)." 93 *Columbia Law Review* 1833 (1993).

Salyer, Lucy E. *Laws Harsh as Tigers: Chinese Immigrants and the Shaping of Modern Immigration Law.* Chapel Hill: University of North Carolina Press (1995).

Select Commission on Immigration and Refugee Policy. *U.S. Immigration Policy and the National Interest.* Staff Report, 1981.

INTERNET RESOURCES

Library of Congress. "American Memory" <http://www.memory.loc.gov>

IMMIGRATION REFORM AND CONTROL ACT OF 1986

Jennifer S. Byram

The Immigration Reform and Control Act of 1986 (IRCA) (P.L. 99-603, 100 Stat. 3359) amended the Immigration and Nationality Act of 1952 to better control unauthorized immigration. Many members of Congress felt immigration was "out of control" because legal and illegal immigration had come to account for approximately thirty to fifty percent of U.S. population growth.

Congress determined the best way to control immigration was to take away the incentive to enter the United States by preventing illegal immigrants from working or receiving government benefits.

Congress determined the best way to control immigration was to take away the incentive to enter the United States by preventing illegal immigrants from working or receiving government benefits. The Immigration Reform and Control Act provides sanctions for knowingly hiring an employee who is not legally authorized to work. It requires employers and states to check work authorization documents for every new employee or benefit applicant, including U.S. citizens, and to complete a related form.

Many people were concerned that employer sanctions would lead to discrimination against legal immigrants or U.S. citizens who appeared foreign. To prevent such discrimination, the IRCA imposed penalties on employers who discriminated in this manner. The new employer sanctions, however, could cause great hardships for illegal immigrants who had been living and working in the United States for many years. The IRCA provided a program for certain illegal immigrants who had lived in the United States since at least January 1, 1982, to apply to become legal residents with the right to work. A different program allowed seasonal agricultural workers to apply for legal residency. Newly legal residents could eventually become citizens.

Nonagricultural workers had to prove they had a continuous physical presence in the United States, except for brief, casual, and innocent travel abroad. The Immigration and Nationalization Service (INS) required advance permission for any travel abroad, or the immigrant would be ineligible for the legalization program. Several lawsuits contested this advance-permission regulation. The courts invalidated the regulation twelve days before the deadline to file applications for legal resident status. Many immigrants, however, had not been allowed to file applications for legalization, or had not tried to file because they had been told their travel disqualified them from the program.

Immigrants who had been prevented from filing, or had not tried to file because of the invalidated regulation sued to force the INS to accept their late applications. During this litigation Congress passed the Immigration Reform and Immigrant Responsibility Act of 1996, which removed the courts's jurisdiction to decide complaints from immigrants who had not "in fact" filed a legalization application before the deadline. The constitutionality of the provision is still being litigated in 2003.

Some economic sectors, particularly agriculture, have long relied heavily on labor supplied by illegal immigrants. The IRCA provided for an increase in temporary worker visas when employers could show there were not enough legal workers able, willing, and qualified to perform the work. These provisions have been used predominantly to allow additional seasonal agricultural workers to enter the United States, but they have also been used by employers in technology and other industries.

The IRCA affects every employee in America by requiring citizens and immigrants alike to provide proof of authorization to work before starting a new job. It gave many formerly illegal immigrants the right to live and work in the United States and to eventually become U.S. citizens.

The IRCA affects every employee in the United States by requiring citizens and immigrants alike to provide proof of authorization to work before starting a new job.

See also: IMMIGRATION AND NATIONALITY ACT

BIBLIOGRAPHY

Briggs, Vernon M., Jr., and Stephen Moore. *Still an Open Door?: U.S. Immigration Policy and the American Economy.* Washington, DC: The American University Press, 1994.

Lanham, Nicholas. *Ronald Reagan and the Politics of Immigration Reform.* Westport, CT: Praeger, 2000.

Montwieler, Nancy Humel. *The Immigration Reform Law of 1986: Analysis, Text, Legislative History.* Washington, DC: BNA Books, 1987.

INDIAN CIVIL RIGHTS ACT (1968)

Steve Russell

The Bill of Rights, (the first ten amendments to the Constitution) originally bound only the federal government, but after ratification of the fourteenth amendment portions of the Bill of Rights have also come to apply to state government. But for the over 550 American Indian nations currently recognized by the U.S. government, the Constitution and the Bill of Rights represent a social contract which was created without their representation long after their own social contracts. This is why, for example, federal courts had no power to try an Indian for a crime against another Indian on Indian land before the enactment of the Major Crimes Act.

> *Although all of the Bill of Rights applies to the federal government and most of it now applies to state government, it does not—and never has—applied to tribal governments.*

Although all of the Bill of Rights applies to the federal government and most of it now applies to state government, it does not—and never has—applied to tribal governments. As a result, the Constitution would allow tribal governments to shut down newspapers, search tribal members without cause, and lock up tribal members without a fair trial.

EVENTS LEADING TO THE ACT

Historically, the idea of "rights" as something possessed by individuals and enforceable against governments is foreign to most tribal traditions. Traditional governments had established methods for dealing with disputes among individuals or disputes among clans, but an individual who was unhappy with a tribal decision had the choice of living with the decision or leaving the tribe. In modern times, leaving is no longer an option except in the sense of assimilating completely into the United States, away from the tribe. Intratribal disagreements have developed in recent years, such as friction between traditional religions and Christianity, or divisions over whether to operate casinos, and if so whether to serve alcohol and what to accomplish with the money, as well as environmental issues. The combination of these disagreements and dispute resolution tools unsuited to the modern world have led to many scandals in tribal governments and unfair treatment of dissenters by those tribal governments.

> *The problem with meeting corrupt and dictatorial tribal governments head-on is that in order to assert rights against tribal governments, individual Indians would have to come to federal courts, and the empowerment of individual Indians comes at the expense of what is left of tribal sovereignty.*

U.S. Supreme Court decisions have given Congress power to limit the actions of tribal governments. However, the problem with meeting corrupt and dictatorial tribal governments head-on is that in order to assert rights against tribal governments, individual Indians would have to come to federal courts, and the empowerment of individual Indians comes at the expense of what is left of tribal sovereignty.

These competing values (the value of clean government and the value of self-government without outside interference) led to the Indian Civil Rights Act of 1968 (P.L. 90-284, 82 Stat. 77), which is designed to accomplish clean government by applying parts of the Bill of Rights to Indians against their own governments but also minimizes outside interference by limiting the remedy for a violation to a writ of **habeas corpus** in case the conferred rights are denied. A writ of habeas corpus in this context is an order to bring the person who claims his or her rights have been denied to federal court to decide whether the person's rights have in fact been denied. If the denial of rights is proven, the federal court orders a release from custody (jail).

habeas corpus: (Latin, "you should have the body") a written order to bring a prisoner in front of a judge, to determine whether his or her detention is lawful

TRIBAL CIVIL RIGHTS AND LIBERTIES

The Indian Civil Rights Act does not allow a tribal member whose rights are violated to collect money damages against the tribal government. It does not even allow for an injunction (an order to quit violating the law). Because the only remedy is a writ of habeas corpus, a tribal member cannot even sue under the Indian Civil Rights Act unless he or she is being held in custody. One case decided under the Indian Civil Rights Act allows a writ of habeas corpus to challenge a banishment from the reservation. In that case, the "custody" is in the world outside the reservation rather than in a jail.

What the Indian Civil Rights Act is best known for is extending part of the Bill of Rights to individual Indians against tribal governments. The parts of the Bill of Rights not included in this extension are those that would make no sense in the Indian government context. For example, the free exercise of religion is protected to account for the conflict between Christians and traditional religions where such conflict exists, but there is no ban on establishment of religion, since some tribes had traditional theocracies (government by religious leaders). The right to a lawyer in a criminal case is absent because lawyers are absent from many reservations.

Section 202 of the Indian Civil Rights Act

No Indian tribe in exercising powers of self-government shall—

(1) make or enforce any law prohibiting the free exercise of religion, or abridging the freedom of speech, or of the press, or the right of the people peaceably to assemble and to petition for a redress of grievances;

(2) violate the right of the people to be secure in their persons, houses, papers, and effects against unreasonable search and seizures, not issue warrants, but upon probable cause, supported by oath or affirmation, and particularly describing the place to be searched and the person or thing to be seized:

(3) subject any person for the same offense to be twice put in jeopardy;

(4) compel any person in any criminal case to be a witness against himself;

(5) take any private property for a public use without just compensation;

(6) deny to any person in a criminal proceeding the right to a speedy and public trial, to be informed of the nature and cause of the accusation, to be confronted with the witnesses against him, to have compulsory process for obtaining witnesses in his favor, and at his own expense to have the assistance of counsel for his defense;

(7) require excessive bail, impose excessive fines, inflict cruel and unusual punishments, and in no event impose for conviction of any offense any penalty or punishments imprisonment for a term of one year and [or] a fine of $5,000, or both;

(8) deny to any person within its jurisdiction the equal protection of its laws or deprive any person of liberty or property without due process of law;

(9) pass any bill of attainder or ex post facto law; or

(10) deny to any person accused of an offense punishable by imprisonment the right, upon request, to a trial by jury of not six persons.

The Indian Civil Rights Acts goes farther than the language of the Bill of Rights in that it guarantees "equal protection of the law," something absent from the U.S. Constitution before the Fourteenth Amendment.

Section 203 of the Indian Civil Rights Act

The privilege of the writ of habeas corpus shall be available to any person, in a court of the United States, to test the legality of his detention by order of an Indian tribe.

The Second Amendment (right to keep and bear arms) is absent because whether to have gun control is left to tribal government except for weapons that are completely illegal to own off the reservation. The Third Amendment (quartering troops in private homes) does not apply because Indian tribes do not have professional armies, and the Tenth Amendment (reserving unenumerated powers to the states) does not apply because states have no power over Indian nations unless a particular power explicitly is conferred on states by Congress.

However, the Indian Civil Rights Acts goes farther than the language of the Bill of Rights in that it guarantees "equal protection of the law," something absent from the U.S. Constitution before the Fourteenth Amendment. It also denies tribal governments the power to pass *ex post facto* laws and bills of attainder, provisions that are contained in the main body of the U.S. Constitution rather than the Bill of Rights, and the power to imprison tribal members for a term greater than six months. Traditional tribal governments did not practice imprisonment at all.

The Indian Civil Rights Act of 1968 also contains provisions directing the Secretary of the Interior to create a model code for courts of Indian offenses (courts on reservations not created by the tribal government) and requiring consent by tribal governments before states can assume and criminal or civil jurisdiction over Indians on Indian land.

See also: CIVIL RIGHTS ACTS; INDIAN GAMING REGULATORY ACT; INDIAN GENERAL ALLOTMENT ACT (DAWES ACT); INDIAN REMOVAL ACT.

BIBLIOGRAPHY

Prucha, Francis Paul, ed. *Documents of United States Indian Policy,* 2d edition. Lincoln, NE: University of Nebraska Press, 1990.

Wilkins, David E. and K. Tsianina Lomawaima. *Uneven Ground: American Indian Sovereignty and Federal Law.* Norman: University of Oklahoma Press, 2001.

Wunder, John R. *"Retained by the People": A History of American Indians and the Bill of Rights.* New York: Oxford University Press, 1994.

INDIAN GAMING REGULATORY ACT (1988)

Steven J. Gunn

Congress adopted the IGRA in 1988 and established a complex system to authorize and regulate the gaming and gambling enterprises of American Indian tribes.

Congress adopted the Indian Gaming Regulatory Act (IGRA) (P.L. 100-497, 102 Stat. 2475) in 1988 and established a complex system to authorize and regulate the gaming and gambling enterprises of American Indian tribes. The act divides Indian gaming into three classes— I, II, and III— and provides a different set of regulations for each class.

Class I gaming is defined by the act to include "social games solely for prizes of minimal value or traditional forms of Indian gaming engaged in by individuals as a part of, or in connection with, tribal ceremonies or celebrations." The operation and regulation of class I gaming activities is left to "the exclusive jurisdiction of the Indian tribes."

Class II gaming includes bingo, games similar to bingo (such as pull tabs, lotto, punch boards, tip jars, and instant bingo), and non-banking card games (such as poker and other card games in which players bet against each other rather than against the house). Expressly excluded from the scope of class II gaming are banking card games (such as blackjack, baccarat, and chemin de fer), electronic games of chance, and slot machines.

The IGRA allows an Indian tribe to engage in class II gaming only if the state in which the tribe is located "permits such gaming for any purpose by any person, organization or entity," and the "governing body of the Indian tribe adopts an ordinance or resolution which is approved by the Chairman" of the National Indian Gaming Commission (NIGC). This Commission, a government agency consisting of three members, was created by the Act to monitor the class II and class III gaming activities of tribes throughout the country. Under the act, tribes are primarily responsible for regulating their own class II gaming activities, with oversight by the commission.

Class III gaming includes all forms of gaming that are not included in classes I and II. Games commonly played at casinos, such as slot machines, black jack (and other banking card games), craps, and roulette, fall within the scope of class III. For this reason, class III gaming is often referred to as casino-style gaming. Wagering and electronic games of chance are also included in class III.

In order for a tribe to conduct class III gaming, three conditions must be met. First, the type of class III gaming that the tribe wants to conduct must be permitted, "for any purpose by any person, organization or entity," in the state in which the tribe is located. Second, the tribe and the state must have negotiated a compact, or agreement, concerning the nature and extent of the class III gaming the tribe may conduct and the manner in which that gaming will be regulated, and that compact must have been approved by the secretary of the interior. Third, the tribe must have adopted a tribal gaming ordinance that has been approved by the Chairman of the NIGC.

The IGRA imposes upon states a duty to negotiate in good faith with Indian tribes to form class III gaming compacts. The Act originally contained a provision allowing tribes to sue noncompliant states in federal court to force the states to negotiate in good faith. However, the U.S. Supreme Court struck down that provision in the case of *Seminole Tribe v. Florida* (1996), finding that Congress did not have the authority, in this context, to allow tribes to sue states in federal court without the states' consent. Now, if states do not negotiate in good faith, tribes must resort to other remedies, including petitioning the secretary of the interior to approve special regulations authorizing the tribes' class III gaming activities.

The IGRA represents a compromise between the competing interests and powers of Indian tribes, states, and the federal government. Before Congress adopted the act, tribes generally had the right to engage in all forms of gaming, including casino-style gaming, with little regard for state laws regulating the permissible types of gambling or the size of prizes. The U.S. Supreme Court affirmed this right in the case of *California v. Cabazon Band of Mission Indians* (1987). However, Congress has the power to outlaw all forms of American Indian gaming, and was under considerable pres-

> *The IGRA represents a compromise between the competing interests and powers of Indian tribes, states, and the federal government.*

sure from several states to do so in the mid-1980s. These states believed, among other things, that tribal gaming enterprises would become infiltrated by organized crime. Congress weighed the states' concerns against the tribes' interests in using gaming to promote economic development on their reservations. The IGRA, as adopted by Congress, allows tribes to engage in gaming, but it imposes restrictions on their ability to do so and it also gives the state and federal governments substantial authority to regulate tribal gaming activities.

Only federally recognized tribes have the right to operate casinos and to conduct other gaming activities under the IGRA. Indian groups that are not officially recognized by the United States government do not have rights under the IGRA, nor do individual Indians.

There are 562 federally recognized Indian tribes in the United States. Only 201 of these tribes operated class II or class III gaming enterprises in 2001, according to data from the NIGC. These tribes operated a total of 290 enterprises in twenty–nine states in 2001, generating over $12.7 billion in annual revenues. That amount, while significant for the tribes involved, was less than ten percent of the total revenues generated by the U.S. gaming industry in 2001.

Gamblers play the slots at the Harrah's Ak-Chin Casino on the Ak-Chin Indian Reservation in Arizona, July 1998. (© AP/WIDE WORLD

Tribes may use the revenues generated by their class II and III gaming enterprises only for purposes designated in the IGRA. The act states that such revenues must be used to fund tribal government operations and programs (such as hospitals, schools, police and fire departments, tribal courts, and the like), to provide for the general welfare of the tribe, to promote tribal economic development, to make donations to charitable organizations, and to help fund the operations of neighboring cities and counties. Once these obligations have been met, a tribe may petition the secretary of the interior to approve a Revenue Allocation Plan under which the tribe may make per capita payments to individual tribal members. Approximately one-third of the tribes engaged in class II and III gaming distribute per capita payments to their members. The size of these payments varies considerably from tribe to tribe, depending on the profitability of the gaming enterprises.

Not all tribes have benefited from Indian gaming. Some refuse to engage in gaming on the grounds that it is inconsistent with their traditional cultures and values. Other tribes are located in sparsely populated sections of the country in which it is not possible to operate lucrative bingo halls or casinos. A limited number of successful gaming tribes, located primarily along the east and west coasts, generate the vast majority of all Indian gaming revenues, and there is no requirement in the IGRA that these tribes share their wealth with the poorer tribes in the middle of the country.

See also: INDIAN CIVIL RIGHTS ACT; INDIAN GENERAL ALLOTMENT ACT (DAWES ACT); INDIAN REMOVAL ACT; INDIAN REORGANIZATION ACT OF 1934.

BIBLIOGRAPHY

Eisler, Kim Isaac. *Revenge of the Pequots: How a Small Native American Tribe Created the World's Most Profitable Casino*. New York: Simon and Schuster, 2000.

> *Tribes may use the revenues generated by their class II and III gaming enterprises only for purposes designated in the IGRA.*

INDIAN GENERAL ALLOTMENT ACT (DAWES ACT) (1887)

Steven J. Gunn

Excerpt from the Indian General Allotment Act

In all cases where any tribe or band of Indians has been or shall be located upon any reservation ... the President shall be authorized to cause the same or any part thereof to be surveyed ... whenever in his opinion such reservation or any part may be advantageously utilized for agricultural or grazing purposes by such Indians, and to cause allotment to each Indian located thereon to be made in such areas as in his opinion may be for their best interest not to exceed eighty acres of agricultural or one hundred and sixty acres of grazing land to any one Indian.

The Indian General Allotment Act of 1887 (24 Stat. 388), also known as the Dawes Act after its leading sponsor, Senator Henry L. Dawes of

Massachusetts, authorized the president to divide Indian reservations into separate tracts of land for individual tribal members. These tracts were to be used for farming and cattle grazing. The act was implemented without the consent or consultation of the tribes. Native-American heads of household received allotments of 160 acres, while single adults received 80 acres and minors 40 acres. Double those amounts were provided if the land was suitable only for grazing. Married Native women were ineligible to receive land. The act was amended in 1891 to treat all Native-American adults equally, regardless of their sex or familial status. However, the size of the allotments was cut in half.

The act also authorized the government to negotiate with Indian tribes for the sale of all tribal lands remaining after allotments were made to individual members. The government often paid less than $1.00 per acre for these so-called "surplus" lands, which it then sold to non-Native homesteaders and corporations.

The Dawes Act applied to most, but not all, tribes. Many tribes not covered by the act were subjected to allotment by later acts of Congress, such as the Curtis Act of 1898, which authorized the allotment of the Cherokee, Chickasaw, Choctaw, and Creek reservations in Oklahoma.

PURPOSES OF THE ACT

The Dawes Act had two primary purposes. The first was to "civilize" the Native peoples. Those sympathetic to the Indians, mainly philanthropists from the East, believed that the reservation system, in which most tribes held their lands communally, was preventing the economic and cultural development of the Native peoples. By the late nineteenth century most tribal economies were in dire straits, with indigenous people living in abject poverty. The Friends of the Indians, an influential group of philanthropists and reformers in the Northeast, believed that if individual Indians were given plots of land to farm, they would flourish and become integrated into the American economy and culture as middle-class farmers. In the *Report of the Secretary of the Interior* of 1886, Senator Dawes said he wanted the government to:

> put [the Indian] on his own land, furnish him with a little habitation, with a plow, and a rake, and show him how to go to work to use them .... The only way [to civilize the Indian] is to lead him out into the sunshine, and tell him what the sunshine is for, and what the rain comes for, and when to put his seed in the ground.

The forced allotment of tribal lands was consistent with other government policies to assimilate the Native peoples into American society, including the forced education of Indian children in off-reservation boarding schools and the suppression of Native religions, languages, and cultural practices.

The second major purpose of the Dawes Act was to gain use of Native-American lands for non-Natives. The act called for breaking up large tribal landholdings to enable settlement of the West by non-Natives. The act secured only a part of the tribes' lands to the Indians, opening the remainder to settlers.

IMPLEMENTATION OF THE ACT

Approximately 41 million acres of tribal reservation land were allotted under the Dawes Act. The act established a period of twenty-five years during

Reclamation of Tribal Lands

During the 1960s and 1970s, Native American activists began making efforts to reclaim native lands ceded as the result of the Dawes Act and individual treaties. The Cayuga Indians, for example, had ceded 64,000 acres of land to the State of New York in 1795 under the Cayuga Ferry Treaty. Because the treaty was not ratified by Congress, it was illegal, and in 1980 the tribe sued the State of New York for the return of the property. After a court battle that lasted a full twenty years, New York was finally ordered to pay the Cayuga tribe $248 million, which is the largest award ever in a case involving tribal land claims.

which the U.S. held title to the allotted lands in "trust" for the individual Indian owners. The government legally owned the lands, but it allowed the Native peoples to use them. The government's intention was to protect new Native landowners. During the trust period, states could not tax the Natives' lands, nor could the Indians sell them. The latter restriction protected Indians from exploitation by land-hungry settlers. Once the trust period expired, the government delivered title to the lands to the Native peoples. With a free and clear title, the Native peoples became citizens of the U.S. and of the states in which they resided. They were then subject to state law, and their lands were subject to state taxation.

Approximately 41 million acres of tribal reservation land were allotted under the Dawes Act.

Some of these provisions were later amended. For example, in 1906 Congress authorized the president immediately to give land titles to individual Indians who were deemed competent to manage their own lands. Further, in 1924 Congress enacted a law making all Native peoples U.S. citizens, regardless of whether or not they had been given title to their lands.

HISTORY OF THE ACT

The Dawes Act was one of the first acts of Congress to deal with nearly all tribes at once, and to alter their rights without their consent. Previously, the U.S. government dealt with tribes individually through treaties. In most treaties the tribes agreed to relinquish large sections of their territory while reserving portions of their lands for themselves. In exchange, the U.S. government promised to protect the tribes and to allow them to live permanently on their remaining lands, or reservations. (The term "reservation" comes from the treaty-based process in which Native-American tribes reserved a part of their land to themselves.) However, in 1871, Congress terminated this treaty-making process. In the 1880s it began enacting comprehensive legislation that applied to all tribes without their consent.

The term "reservation" comes from the treaty-based process in which Native-American tribes reserved a part of their land to themselves.

The Supreme Court explained the basis for this new approach to Indian policy when it ruled in the case of *Kagama v. U.S.* (1886) that Congress has complete power to regulate Native-American affairs. The Court stated that Indian tribes, "once powerful," were now "weak and diminished in numbers," economically and politically dependent on the United States. As a result, the Court said, the government had a duty to protect them, and with that duty came the power to regulate all aspects of their affairs. Historians have argued that most Native peoples opposed breaking up the tribal system but that the U.S. government was indifferent to the Natives' own wishes.

Other clauses in the U.S. Constitution have been used to justify the government's power over Indian tribes: Article 1, section 8, clause 3, giving Congress the power "to regulate commerce with ... the Indian tribes," and Article 2, section 2, clause 2, giving the president the power to make treaties.

RESULTS OF ALLOTMENT

Historians and other observers agree that the Dawes Act was disastrous for the Indians. Most allotted lands were not suitable for agriculture. The government made only minimal efforts to provide farming equipment to the indigenous peoples. Its annual appropriations for that purpose were often no more

The primary effect of the Dawes Act was a severe reduction in the quantity of Indian landholdings, from 138 million acres in 1887 to 48 million acres in 1934, the year Congress passed the Indian Reorganization Act, which ended allotment.

than $10.00 per Native. Many Indians with lands suitable for farming or grazing lacked the resources or training to succeed at those pursuits and so leased their land to non-Natives. The government often forced Indians to lease their lands, whenever in its judgment the Natives were not using lands productively. These leases were seldom lucrative for the Indians and thus did not help Natives to become self-sufficient.

The primary effect of the Dawes Act was a severe reduction in the quantity of Indian landholdings, from 138 million acres in 1887 to 48 million acres in 1934, the year Congress passed the Indian Reorganization Act, which ended allotment. Most lands were lost through the sale of "surplus" lands by the government to non-Native homesteaders. In addition, many Indians who had received title to their lands sold their allotments to non-Natives, often for less than market value. Others were unable to pay state property taxes and lost their allotments in tax foreclosures. In all, the Indians lost 90 million acres. Of the lands that remained, 20 million acres were desert or semidesert lands unfit for most profitable uses.

The Indian Reorganization Act sought to restore and protect the diminished land bases of Native-American tribes. The act extended indefinitely the trust period for existing Indian allotments. The government restored "surplus" lands that had not already been sold to homesteaders. The act also authorized the government to acquire other lands for the tribes. Today, tribal landholdings in the continental U.S. total over 54 million acres, the vast majority of which is communally owned by tribes, not individual Natives.

Although ownership of most Indian lands is now consolidated in tribal governments, allotment has had a lasting impact. Many reservations are checkerboards of Indian and non-Native lands. John Collier, former commissioner of Indian affairs, testified before Congress in 1934 that "on many reservations the Indian-owned parcels are mere islands within a sea of white-owned property" (73d Cong., 2d Sess., 16–18, 1934). This remains true today. Another legacy of allotment is the division of allotments among the many heirs of original allottees. Inherited shares are often less than one-hundredth of a single allotment, making it difficult for heirs to agree how to use allotments.

The lasting effects of the Dawes Act contribute to the difficulties many modern tribes face in managing their tribal lands, developing their economies, and maintaining their communities and cultures.

See also: INDIAN CIVIL RIGHTS ACT; INDIAN GAMING REGULATORY ACT; INDIAN REMOVAL ACT; INDIAN REORGANIZATION ACT OF 1934.

BIBLIOGRAPHY

Carlson, Leonard A. *Indians, Bureaucrats, and Land: The Dawes Act and the Decline of Indian Farming.* Westport, CT: Greenwood Press, 1981.

Deloria, Vine, Jr., and Clifford M. Lytle. *American Indians, American Justice.* Austin: University of Texas Press, 1983.

Hoxie, Frederick E. *A Final Promise: The Campaign to Assimilate the Indians, 1880–1920.* Lincoln: University of Nebraska Press, 1984.

Otis, Delos Sacket. *The Dawes Act and the Allotment of Indian Lands.* Norman: University of Oklahoma Press, 1973.

Prucha, Francis Paul, ed. *Americanizing the American Indian: Writings by the "Friends of the Indian" 1880–1900.* Cambridge, MA: Harvard University Press, 1973.

Washburn, Wilcomb E. *The Assault on Indian Tribalism: The General Allotment Law (Dawes Act) of 1887.* Philadelphia: Lippincott, 1975.

INDIAN REMOVAL ACT (1830)

Sara M. Patterson

Excerpt from the Indian Removal Act

It shall and may be lawful for the President solemnly to assure the tribe or nation with which the exchange is made, that the United States will forever secure and guaranty to them, and their heirs or successors, the country so exchanged with them.... Provided always, That such lands shall revert to the United States, if the Indians become extinct, or abandon the same.

With the Louisiana Purchase of 1803, thoughts of Native American removal became a very real possibility for the policy makers of the U.S. government. It appeared that the Purchase had given the government endless amounts of land, more than could ever possibly be put to use. Thomas Jefferson initiated discussion over whether portions of this land could be used to solve what some viewed as the "Indian problem"—Native Americans were occupying land that many European Americans believed could be put to better use. Jefferson proposed that unincorporated land west of the Mississippi River be exchanged for the more sought-after land occupied by Native Americans in the east. Debates over the removal of Native Americans grew more intense as the nineteenth century progressed and culminated in the passage of the 1830 Indian Removal Act (4 Stat. 411).

With the Louisiana Purchase of 1803, thoughts of Native American removal became a real possibility for the policy makers of the U.S. government.

In the act Congress authorized President Andrew Jackson to begin the process of removal. Allocated $500,000, Jackson vigorously pursued his plan and in 1835 was able to announce that removal was complete or near completion. The majority of Native Americans had been removed to regions west of the Mississippi. The Indian Removal Act stood at the intersection of numerous debates among European Americans over the fate of American Indians. Questions surrounding the controversy included: Would removal benefit or hinder efforts to civilize Native Americans? Were Native American groups going to be considered **sovereign** nations? Did Native American groups own the land that they occupied? How was the extinction of Native Americans going to be prevented?

The Indian Removal Act stood at the intersection of numerous debates among European Americans over the fate of American Indians.

sovereign: self-governing and independent

SUPPORTERS AND DETRACTORS

Supporters of Jackson's removal policy agreed with the arguments Jackson made in his 1830 Second Annual Message. Jackson stated that, "Humanity has often wept over the fate of the aborigines of this country, and Philanthropy has been long busily employed in devising means to avert it, but its progress has never for a moment been arrested, and one by one have many powerful tribes disappeared from the earth." Jackson and his supporters claimed that the "savage" Native American culture must inevitably give way to the onslaught of civilization. They believed that efforts to civilize Native Americans within European American culture had been entirely unsuccessful. The only hope for Native American survival, according to these supporters, was to be moved outside the reach of civilization. In the West, they argued, missionaries could continue their efforts at Christianizing and civilizing the Native American at a slower pace, away from the vices of more populated areas.

Jackson's approach to the question of sovereignty and land ownership supported his arguments for removal. He declared that Native Americans choosing to remain east of the Mississippi were subject to the laws and jurisdictions of the state and federal governments. Native American sovereignty and land ownership existed only insofar as it could be ceded to the U.S. government.

Opponents of Jackson's policy had quite different claims. Many of them, like Jackson, believed that Native Americans were in the process of becoming

Trail of Tears, *1838, by Robert Lindneux. This painting shows the Cherokee marching to Oklahoma after being forcibly removed from their native land in Georgia.* (THE GRANGER COLLECTION)

extinct. However, the solution in their eyes did not lie in segregation. Instead they insisted that the process of civilization had been successful. They turned to the Cherokee nation as their primary example. The Cherokee farmed, were Christian, had created a written language, supported their own newspaper, and in 1828 had written their own constitution. Jackson's opponents argued that this process would not occur in other groups without the encouragement and example of civilization. These opponents also claimed the U.S. government was obligated to recognize the sovereignty of Native American groups and their right to hold lands their ancestors had occupied.

The debates over whether removal offered the solution to the "Indian problem" continued after the passage of the Indian Removal Act. Although the act was meant to encourage Native Americans voluntarily to give up lands east of the Mississippi, the process of removal was one of misdeeds and corruption. Agents of the treaty-making process forged signatures of Native leaders, dealt with individuals unauthorized to cede land, and falsified records.

These actions led as well to the forced removal of several Native American groups who had not voluntarily ceded their land holdings. Soldiers and government officials forced several of the southern tribes, like the Cherokee, to Oklahoma on the infamous Trail of Tears. On this path many Native Americans faced starvation, freezing cold, and disease. Because of removal deadlines, 15,000 individuals were placed in detention camps where again they faced starvation and the spread of disease. Despite the claim that it would benefit Indians, the removal process hastened further seizure of Native American land and further disregard for Native American culture by the U.S. government.

See also: INDIAN GENERAL ALLOTMENT ACT (DAWES ACT); INDIAN REORGANIZATION ACT OF 1934.

Trail of Tears

In 1838 the U.S. Army forced approximately fifteen thousand Cherokees to relinquish their native land in Georgia and march more than 800 miles west to Indian Territory, where they were to be resettled. Supplies were short, winter was setting in, and it is estimated that more than four thousand people, or 25 percent of the Cherokee nation, died on the journey. Another thousand are said to have perished soon after their resettlement. The Cherokees' path, which is known as the Trail of Tears, became a national monument in 1987.

Although the act was meant to encourage Native Americans voluntarily to give up lands east of the Mississippi, the process of removal was one of misdeeds and corruption.

BIBLIOGRAPHY

Berkhofer, Robert F. *The White Man's Indian: Images of the American Indian from Columbus to the Present.* New York: Knopf, 1978.

Prucha, Francis Paul. *American Indian Policy in the Formative Years: The Indian Trade and Intercourse Acts, 1790–1834.* Cambridge, MA: Harvard University Press, 1964.

Rogin, Michael. *Fathers and Children: Andrew Jackson and the Subjugation of the American Indian.* New York: Knopf, 1975.

Satz, Ronald. *American Indian Policy in the Jacksonian Era.* Lincoln: University of Nebraska Press, 1975.

INDIAN REORGANIZATION ACT OF 1934

Lawrence Schlam

When Congress adopted the Indian Reorganization Act of 1934 (P.L. 73-383), in many respects it intended to allow Native Americans to resurrect their culture and traditions lost to government expansion and **encroachment** years earlier. The act replaced the Indian General Allotment Act

encroach: to infringe upon or violate

When Congress adopted the Indian Reorganization Act of 1934, in many respects it intended to allow Native Americans to resurrect their culture and traditions lost to government expansion and encroachment years earlier.

of 1887, known as the "Dawes Act," which broke up tribal lands and allotted them to individual members of tribes; traditionally the tribes held the land on reservations in a communal capacity. The Dawes Act also opened up surplus lands to non–American Indians. As a result of the Dawes Act, Native American lands totaling 138 million acres in 1887 had fallen to 48 million acres by 1934.

These losses virtually destroyed traditional tribal government on the reservations. In essence, the federal government replaced tribal councils and courts that had once given the tribes autonomy with its own legal structures.

In the early 1920s the secretary of the interior authorized the Institute of Government Research to conduct a survey of the social and economic status of Native Americans. One study conducted by the Institute, the Meriam Report, uncovered the destructive impact of the earlier federal policy of allotting to individual tribe members plots of tribal land. This policy, it found, resulted in extreme poverty and a substantial loss of tribal land due to sale to white settlers. As a result, the United States Senate, some members of which were skeptical about these conclusions, launched a thorough investigation, including field hearings on reservations. The Senate ultimately reached the same conclusion as the Meriam Report.

With the election of Franklin D. Roosevelt in 1932, John Collier, a staunch supporter of the Meriam Report, became Indian commissioner. He immediately began to work on legislation that incorporated the Meriam Report and several other ideas for the advancement of the Native American population proposed by members of tribal delegations. Although it was defeated, this bill led the way for the Indian Reorganization Act of 1934.

A NEW ERA

Also known as the Wheeler-Howard Act, the Indian Reorganization Act of 1934 terminated the Dawes Act's allotment system, extended limits on the sale of American Indian lands, and authorized the secretary of the interior to purchase additional lands or proclaim new reservations for Native American people. In addition, it provided definitions for "Indians" and "tribes" (through subsequent amendments, these terms now include Alaskans and Hawaiians), extended to tribes the right to form corporations, established a credit system for Native Americans, granted limited tribal sovereignty, and provided Native Americans with educational opportunities and funds for trade, vocational, elementary, and secondary schools.

Historians have regarded the Indian Reorganization Act of 1934 as marking a shift in policy away from assimilation and toward renewed recognition of Indian tribes. However, while it brought about the end of the policy of allotments, the act severely restricted the powers and autonomy of the new tribal governments.

Certain features of the act, however, tempered its benefits. The requirement that various actions of the tribal government needed the approval of the secretary of the interior limited the tribe's autonomy. Moreover, American Indian autonomy and success were also limited by the effects of previous laws. For example, earlier laws had consolidated several independent tribes on reservations, and thus former enemies were living and working together in a situation that led to much social and cultural unrest.

Courts have interpreted the term "Indians" to include all people of Native American descent who are members or descendants of any recognized American Indian tribe under federal jurisdiction and are residing within the boundaries of any Native American reservation. The word "tribe" refers to any organized band, pueblo, or Native American people residing on one reservation, including any group that meets the definition of "Indians" under the act. Finally, the federal government need not recognize American Indian people in order for them to be considered a tribe.

The goal of the act was to give greater independence to local tribes, not individual members.

Despite contrary policies enacted before 1934, this act has been construed in light of present federal policy, which is to strengthen tribal self-government. Part of Congress's intent was to help Native Americans achieve economic parity with white people, while not becoming dependent on state governments. The goal of the act, however, is to give greater independence to local tribes, not individual members.

Secretary of the Interior Harold L. Ickes hands the first constitution issued under the Indian Reorganization Act to delegates of the Confederated Tribes of the Flathead Indian Reservation (Montana), 1935. (LIBRARY OF CONGRESS, PRINTS AND PHOTOGRAPHS DIVISION)

The law did not retroactively change the individual allotments given out under the earlier Dawes Act. This is important because there are crucial differences between allotted and tribal lands. Allotted lands are grazing and agricultural lands, while tribal lands are the boundaries of the reservation. Moreover, allotted lands are not under tribal jurisdiction as are tribal lands. For example, if a crime is committed on tribal land, tribal courts would have the power to **adjudicate** the criminal case, but if the crime was on allotted land, it is under state court jurisdiction. With regard to ordinary civil cases, like contract or taxation disputes, tribes have jurisdiction over not only Native Americans but non–American Indians found on their reservations. They may tax the activities of non-tribal members who have agreements with the tribe through commercial dealing or other similar arrangements.

adjudicate: to settle something judicially

The act has been expanded since 1934 by amendments adding new territories and greater flexibility in the act's application.

See also: INDIAN CIVIL RIGHTS ACT; INDIAN GAMING REGULATORY ACT; INDIAN GENERAL ALLOTMENT ACT (DAWES ACT); INDIAN REMOVAL ACT.

BIBLIOGRAPHY

Casey, James A. *Sovereignty by Sufferance: The Illusion of Indian Tribal Sovereignty,* 79 *Cornell Law Review* 404, 413 (1994).

Cohen, Felix S. *Handbook of Federal Indian Law.* Charlottesville, VA: Michie, Bobbs-Merrill, 1982.

Deloria, Vine, Jr., and Clifford M. Lytle. *American Indians, American Justice.* Austin: University of Texas Press, 1983.

Taylor, Graham D. *The New Deal and American Indian Tribalism: The Administration of the Indian Reorganization Act, 1934–45.* Lincoln: University of Nebraska Press, 1980.

INDIVIDUALS WITH DISABILITIES EDUCATION ACT (1975)

Ruth Colker

The Individuals with Disabilities Education Act (IDEA) (P.L. 101–476.), formerly the Education For All Handicapped Children Act, (P.L. 94–142) requires all states receiving federal funds for education to provide individuals with disabilities between the ages of three and twenty-one a free appropriate public education (FAPE) that is designed to meet each child's unique needs and prepare them for employment and independent living.

The concept of educational rights for children with disabilities, embodied in the Individuals with Disabilities Education Act, is a relatively recent one.

THE CONCEPT OF EDUCATIONAL RIGHTS

The concept of educational rights for children with disabilities embodied in the IDEA is a relatively recent one. In 1958 the Illinois Supreme Court held that a provision of the state constitution calling on the state to provide a system of free schools so all children could receive a good education did not apply to a child described as "mentally deficient or feeble minded." Until 1969 a North Carolina statute made it a crime for parents to insist that a disabled child be allowed to attend school after the superintendent had determined the child should be excluded.

In the early 1970s, however, courts began to accept the principle that children with disabilities had a civil right to receive an education. In the 1971 case *Pennsylvania Association for Retarded Children (PARC) v. Pennsylvania*, a **class action** suit was brought on behalf of fourteen mentally retarded students and others similarly disabled, arguing that the state had violated their rights of due process and equal protection by excluding them from public education. In the resulting **judicial decree**, the United States District Court ordered the state to place every mentally retarded child in a "free public program of education and training appropriate to his capacities." In 1972 the United States District Court in *Mills v. Board of Education* held that all children with disabilities have a right to an education, that excluding them while providing able-bodied children with public education denies equal protection, and that cost is not a justifiable reason for denying children with disabilities an education.

class action: a lawsuit brought by a representative member of a large group of people who have suffered the same injury or damages

judicial decree: the ruling of a court

The *PARC* and *Mills* suits were not unique, and by June 1975 forty-six right-to-education cases had been filed on behalf of disabled children in twenty-eight states. The decisions in *PARC* and *Mills,* the pending litigation in other states, and statistics documenting the large number of students with disabilities excluded from public education prompted Congress to pass the Education for All Handicapped Children Act (EAHCA) in 1975. The EAHCA's significance is often compared with that of *Brown v. Board of Education*, the 1954 Supreme Court decision that barred racial segregation in schools.

The Rehabilitation Act of 1973 called for better physical access and opportunities for handicapped people. EAHCA, enacted in 1975, reinforced parental involvement in special education, increased and hastened both the financial commitment and the move to include handicapped children in mainstream schools.

JUDICIAL REVIEW AND CONGRESSIONAL ACTION

In the 1984 case *Smith v. Robinson*, the Supreme Court concluded that, for claims involving issues covered under the EAHCA, that act "is the exclusive avenue through which the child and his parents or guardian can pursue their claim." Thus it denied a request for attorney's fees in a proceeding to secure a free, appropriate education for a child with cerebral palsy.

Congress viewed this ruling as a judicial misinterpretation of the law's intent. It responded quickly and decisively by passing the Handicapped Children's Protection Act of 1986 (HCPA). Among other things, this act specifically provided that the parents or guardians of disabled children were entitled to reasonable attorney's fees if they succeeded in making claims based on EAHCA.

In 1990 the EAHCA was renamed the Individuals with Disabilities Education Act (IDEA) to reflect the preference for the term "disability" over "handicap." This is also the language used in the Americans with Disabilities Act (ADA).

FEATURES OF THE ACT

The IDEA governs the public schooling of all children with disabilities who require special education services and are

The IDEA governs the public schooling of all children with disabilities who require special education services and are therefore classified as "educationally disabled."

therefore classified as "educationally disabled." The IDEA generally defines a child with a disability as:

> a child (i) with mental retardation, hearing impairments (including deafness), speech or language impairments, visual impairments (including blindness), serious emotional disturbance, ... orthopedic impairments, autism, traumatic brain injury, other health impairments, or specific learning disabilities; and (ii) who, by reason, thereof, needs special education and related services.

The IDEA has three primary purposes:

(1) To assure that all children with disabilities receive a free appropriate public education that emphasizes special education and related services designed to meet their unique needs.
(2) To protect the rights of children with disabilities and their parents and guardians.
(3) To assist the states in providing for the effective education of all children with disabilities.

A boy, 8, with physical disabilities is one among several students with learning disabilities and physical handicaps that attended this regular kindergarten class in Troy, Pennsylvania, in 1995. Behind the Individuals with Disabilities Education Act is the idea that children with disabilities have a civil right to education. (© AP/WIDE WORLD PHOTOS)

At the heart of the IDEA is Part B, which establishes a set of procedural safeguards to protect the interests of individuals with disabilities from three to twenty-one years of age. Among the most significant of those protections is the requirement that school districts, with the assistance of parents, prepare an Individualized Education Plan (IEP) for each student with a disability. Furthermore, the IDEA:

- Requires that parents be involved in planning an appropriate educational program for their child with a disability
- Specifies that a child with a disability is to be removed from the regular educational environment only when "the nature or severity of the disability of a child is such that education in regular classes with the use of supplementary aids and services cannot be achieved satisfactorily."

Also under the IDEA, states can receive grants from the federal government to develop and implement statewide systems to provide early intervention services for infants and toddlers (from birth to age three) with disabilities.

For children who are between the ages of three and nine, the IDEA provides that a state or local educational agency may broaden the definition of a child with a disability to include a child:

> (i) experiencing developmental delays, as defined by the State and as measured by appropriate diagnostic instruments and procedures, in one or more of the following areas: physical development, cognitive development, communication development, social or emotional development, or adaptive development; and (ii) who, by reason thereof, needs special education and related services.

States have typically responded to this invitation by providing a broader definition only for preschoolers.

THE IDEA TODAY

As a result of the passage and enforcement of the IDEA, nearly all children with disabilities do receive a free public education. The courts have heard cases dealing with questions such as the content of that education, whether services should be offered in a segregated or integrated setting, and whether school districts can exclude children who pose disciplinary problems. Each time that Congress has reauthorized funding for the IDEA, it has tinkered with the discipline rules. The IDEA was reauthorized in 2003, giving school districts additional latitude to exclude students with disabilities who presented significant discipline problems.

As a result of the passage and enforcement of the IDEA, nearly all children with disabilities do receive a free public education.

See also: AMERICANS WITH DISABILITIES ACT.

BIBLIOGRAPHY

Colker, Ruth, Adam Milani, and Bonnie Poitras Tucker. *The Americans with Disabilities Act,* 4th ed. Anderson Press, 2003.

INTERNAL IMPROVEMENTS ACTS

Chandra Miller Manning

In the nineteenth century Congress passed many acts for the purpose of creating *internal improvements,* a term that refers to federally funded public works such as building roads or digging canals. Such improvements were an important point of political debate in the early nineteenth century, when the survival of the American Republic depended on its ability to govern itself effectively and flourish economically. Efficient government and economic prosperity relied in part on adequate transportation networks, to enable both the exchange of information indispensable to competent government and the transport of goods to market, where they could be sold for cash that could be pumped back into the economy. Advocates of internal improvements argued that transportation networks constructed by the government achieved these ends and therefore protected republican government. Yet the issue of internal improvements provoked controversy about the power of the federal government, relations between states and the federal government, and the interaction between private interests and public authority.

> *Efficient government and economic prosperity relied in part on adequate transportation networks, to enable both the exchange of information indispensable to competent government and the transport of goods to market, where they could be sold for cash that could be pumped back into the economy.*

ECONOMIC AND OTHER BENEFITS

A nationalistic economic plan called the American System, which matured between 1816 and 1828, consisted of a national bank, **tariff**, and internal improvements. Roads were particularly important. The chief architect of the American System was Henry Clay of Kentucky, who served in both the Senate and the House of Representatives. Clay and other advocates believed that roads opened areas for settlement and allowed goods and people to travel between various parts of the nation, binding the United States closer together as they did so. The entire nation benefited from the boost that roads gave to national unity and economic prosperity. Thus federal involvement in road building was a matter of national interest and a contributor to the success of the nation's experiment in republican government.

tariff: a tax imposed on goods when imported into a country

The American System is identified with Henry Clay's political party, the Whigs, in the 1830s and 1840s. Precedent for government sponsorship of transportation projects emerged earlier with the Act Admitting Ohio to the Union (1802). This act allotted a portion of the proceeds of federal land sales in Ohio to road building. In 1806 Congress passed an Act to Regulate the Laying Out and Making of a Road from Cumberland, in the State of Maryland, to the State of Ohio. This act enabled the survey, construction, and maintenance of a road, at federal expense, from the Potomac River to the Ohio River. In 1808 Secretary of the Treasury Albert Gallatin outlined a plan for a comprehensive national transportation network in his *Report on Roads and Canals.*

The War of 1812 stalled government appropriation (allotting money for specific purposes) for internal improvements, but it also convinced more Americans that the national interest required reliable transportation networks. In 1818 Speaker of the House Henry Clay observed that good roads led to military victory and prosperity, whereas the lack of good roads compromised national security and prosperity. The Bonus Bill, passed by Congress in March 1817, earmarked federal funds for a system of roads and canals, and an 1822 measure proposed additional plans to construct roads and maintain them through the collection of tolls.

POLITICAL DEBATE

Both the 1816 and the 1822 measures were vetoed for reasons that reveal some of the complications surrounding internal improvements. Strict constructionists, or people who believed that the federal government could claim only those powers explicitly described in the Constitution, opposed internal improvements for fear that they gave the federal government more power than the Constitution intended. No article in the Constitution explicitly says that Congress may build canals or collect tolls on roads. Far from shoring up republicanism, opponents argued, federal involvement in internal improvements threatened republicanism by dangerously enlarging federal power, and by upsetting the balance of power between the federal government and the states.

Southerners especially worried that internal improvements would pave the way for increased federal interference with state institutions such as slavery. North Carolina Senator Nathaniel Macon wrote in an 1818 letter to a friend, "if Congress can make canals they can ... **emancipate**," and he staunchly resisted internal improvements on these grounds. Others objected to internal improvements because they believed that federal aid to one state or section was unfair to the rest of the nation. Still others believed that competition among private companies for federal contracts would breed corruption.

Despite opposition, from 1816 to 1824 congressional interest in roads and canals escalated. The General Survey Act of 1824, which empowered Army engineers to survey lands for potential road and canal routes, represented a key

Far from shoring up republicanism, opponents argued, federal involvement in internal improvements threatened republicanism by dangerously enlarging federal power, and by upsetting the balance of power between the federal government and the states.

emancipate: to free from another's control, restraint, or bondage

The National Road

At the turn of the nineteenth century, overland travelers in the United States relied on country roads, many of which were developed from Indian trails or farming tracks. These roads were maintained by county governments, with local farmers working off their "road tax" by contributing time to repairs and construction. As the need for travel and trade with the West increased, so did support for a major East-West highway funded by the federal government. In 1815 construction began on a project known as the Cumberland Road, or, particularly in its western stretch, the National Road. Running west from Cumberland, Maryland, the highway reached Wheeling, West Virginia, in 1818 and its terminus in Vandalia, Illinois, twenty years later. The project faced strenuous opposition, with many detractors arguing that the federal government was not authorized by the Constitution to fund "internal improve-ments," and that it would take a Constitutional amendment to authorize such activity. Using this reasoning, in 1822 President James Monroe vetoed a bill establishing the collection of tolls on the National Road, which were to be used for maintenance. The federal government turned the highway over to the states and backed away from further efforts to develop a national network of roads. Nevertheless, as a major route to the West, the National Road was a huge boon to the development of the Ohio and upper Mississippi valleys; indeed, a traveler on the National Road in the 1840s wrote, "it looks as if the whole earth is traveling this way." After 1850 the highway was supplanted by the railroad as the major westward artery, and the importance of the National Road faded. With the development of automobile traffic in the twentieth century, the National Road became U.S. Route 40.

Perhaps even more significant, the tradition of political wrangling over federal transportation projects continues, as perennial debates over issues like federal highway funding make clear.

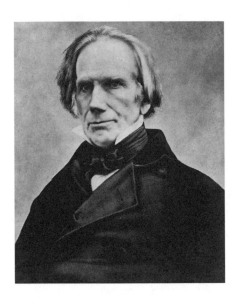

Henry Clay (1777–1852), a major force behind internal improvements in the antebellum period. (LIBRARY OF CONGRESS, PRINTS AND PHOTOGRAPHS DIVISION)

victory. Meanwhile, work on the National Road continued. By 1833 it reached Columbus, Ohio, and by mid-century it stretched to Vandalia, Illinois. Between 1824 and 1828 Congress funded approximately ninety internal improvements projects, including canal construction, river and harbor development, and especially road construction. Throughout the Union, particularly in the West, federal funds and the labor of federal troops built roads between states.

DECLINING MOMENTUM

Momentum for internal improvements declined in the 1830s, especially after President Andrew Jackson vetoed the Maysville Road Bill in May 1830. The Maysville Road Bill sought funds to improve sixty-four miles of road from Lexington, Kentucky, to Maysville, Kentucky, a town on the Ohio River. By connecting to the National Road on the opposite shore of the Ohio River, the Maysville Road would offer Kentuckians access to the National Road. Jackson vetoed the bill on the grounds that it unduly expanded federal authority, cost too much, and unfairly favored one state, Kentucky. In addition to the Maysville Road veto, growing sectional tensions between Northern and Southern states further undermined internal improvements in the 1830s and 1840s.

As Congress faced issues such as the expansion of slavery into the Western territories, increasing numbers of Southerners resisted internal improvements for fear that expanded federal power could undercut slavery. Yet, the internal improvements issue did not vanish. Henry Clay's last speech in the Senate in 1851 concerned waterway improvements. Still, because of waning enthusiasm and mounting regional tensions, states increasingly undertook transportation projects one at a time rather than as part of a systematic federal program.

Clay's American System did not survive the 1840s, but it remains pertinent. The National Road still exists as U.S. Highway 40. Perhaps even more significant, the tradition of political wrangling over federal transportation projects continues, as perennial debates over issues like federal highway funding make clear.

BIBLIOGRAPHY

Baxter, Maurice. *Henry Clay and the American System.* Lexington: University Press of Kentucky, 1995.

Jordan, Philip D. *The National Road.* New York: Bobbs-Merrill Company, 1948.

Larson, John Lauritz. "Jefferson's Union and the Problem of Internal Improvements." In *Jeffersonian Legacies,* ed. Peter S. Onuf. Charlottesville: University of Virginia Press, 1993.

Remini, Robert. *Henry Clay: Statesman for the Union.* New York: Norton, 1991.

Taylor, George R. *The Transportation Revolution.* New York: Holt, Rinehart and Winston, 1951.

INTERNAL REVENUE ACT OF 1954

Steven A. Bank

The Internal Revenue Act of 1954 (P.L. 83-591) was the first comprehensive revision of the federal income tax system since its origin in 1913. It is significant, however, not for its important changes, but for the process by which reform was achieved. In less than two years, representatives from various groups, including Treasury, Congress's Joint Committee on Taxation, and the House Office of Legislative Counsel, coordinated a massive information-gathering and legislative drafting process that culminated in the enactment of the Internal Revenue Code of 1954. While the income tax was codified in 1939, the 1954 code fundamentally altered its organization and for the first time addressed many of the deficiencies that had plagued the income tax for years. The 1954 code remained the standard for more than thirty years, until a new code was adopted as part of the Tax Reform Act of 1986, and many of the features introduced in 1954 survive to this day.

The act is significant, not for its important changes, but for the process by which reform was achieved.

The decision to pursue fundamental reform was a long time coming by the early 1950s. Years of experience with the internal revenue laws had revealed many **loopholes**, weaknesses, and inequities, but the relatively low pre–World War II rates had helped stem any pressure for revision. After the war, however, the top marginal rate jumped to 91 percent, and minor irritations became grave problems. The expansion of the tax base to include lower socioeconomic groups, the advent of such employer-provided benefits as pensions and health insurance, and the increased complexity of corporations and partnerships, all necessitated a more sophisticated system. With the 1952 election of Dwight Eisenhower, the first Republican president in twenty years, the time was ripe for fundamental reform.

loophole: a means of evading or escaping an obligation or enforcement of a law or contract

Even prior to Eisenhower's election, Congress had begun laying the groundwork for reform in the summer of 1952. The Republican leader of the House Ways and Means Committee, Representative Daniel A. Reed of New York, demanded simplification and indicated his intent to block any tax legislation until revision was accomplished. At his insistence, the Joint Committee on Taxation, which was composed of members of the Senate Finance Committee and the House Ways and Means Committee, developed and distributed to taxpayers all over the country a questionnaire requesting suggestions for reforms of the income tax laws. In January 1953 the Joint Committee and Treasury staffs started holding informal meetings with over 200 taxpayer groups. That spring, based on the input it gathered in these meetings, as well as in the 17,000 responses it received to the questionnaire, the 25,000 private letters it received regarding tax revision, and the preliminary reports of an American Law Institute project on income taxation, the Joint Committee and Treasury personnel created a 150-page "bible" of suggestions and problem areas for discussion.

Once this information was collected, work began on the task of developing specific recommendations. The Joint Committee staff organized the law into fifty major areas and appointed various formal and informal working groups to address each. In the summer of 1953 the Ways and Means Committee

Even prior to Eisenhower's election, Congress had begun laying the groundwork for reform in the summer of 1952.

The act included literally thousands of technical changes to the tax laws and took hundreds of pages in committee reports to explain. In most cases, the changes were not considered radical.

held public hearings on forty topics. During these hearings 504 witnesses testified, and 1,000 statements were submitted. As tentative conclusions were reached toward the end of 1953, the working groups began drafting proposed legislation with the assistance of the House Office of Legislative Counsel.

By January 7, 1954, President Eisenhower was able to make a set of twenty-five specific recommendations in his State of the Union address, which included support for a variety of special relief provisions and a comprehensive technical revision of the code. Over the next two months the Committee held a series of closed-door meetings with Treasury officials to discuss the proposals. This secrecy was designed to block any pre-submission lobbying by special interests that would delay the process.

The streamlined legislative process proved successful. On March 9, 1954, H.R. 8300 was introduced in Congress, and within nine days it passed in the House. While the bill spent a little more time in the Senate, including a few weeks of public hearings before the Senate Finance Committee, interest groups had only limited time to speak. Even this limited input was sufficient to affect the final legislation, though, and many sections were partially or completely reworked as a result. By July 29, 1954, the final bill passed in Congress and was signed into law.

The act included literally thousands of technical changes to the tax laws and took hundreds of pages in committee reports to explain. In most cases, the changes were not considered radical. A variety of individual or job-related tax benefits were provided, such as exclusions for employer-provided lodging and retirement benefits as well as college scholarships and prizes, deductions for certain child care and medical expenses, and liberalized rules on accident recoveries. Other changes reflected the development of business entities by providing a new simplified system for small corporations. Perhaps the most controversial change was a four percent credit for dividends to individual shareholders. The legacy of the 1954 act, however, is not the individual changes it included, but its modernization of the code and the speed and efficiency with which this was accomplished.

See also: CORPORATE INCOME TAX ACT OF 1909; FEDERAL INCOME TAX ACT OF 1913; TAX REFORM ACT OF 1986.

BIBLIOGRAPHY

Ratner, Sidney. *Taxation and Democracy in America.* New York: John Wiley & Sons, 1967.

Witte, John F. *The Politics and Development of the Federal Income Tax.* Madison: University of Wisconsin Press, 1985.

INTERNATIONAL EMERGENCY ECONOMIC POWERS ACT (1977)

Michael P. Malloy

Congress passed the International Emergency Economic Powers Act (IEEPA) (P.L. 95-223, 91 Stat. 1626) in 1977 as a refinement of the Trading with the Enemy Act (TWEA), which at the time provided a source of presidential emergency authority, as well as wartime authority. Subject to requirements that the president consult with and report periodically to Congress, IEEPA authorizes the president "to deal with any unusual and extraordinary threat, which has its source in whole or substantial part outside the United States, to the national security, foreign policy, or economy of the United States, if the president declares a national emergency with respect to such threat." Under this authority the president may "investigate, regulate, or prohibit any transaction in foreign exchange," and "investigate, regulate, direct and compel, nullify, void, prevent or prohibit, any ... exportation of ... any property in which any foreign country or a foreign national thereof has any interest." IEEPA gives the president broad authority over financial transactions and property in which any foreign country, any citizen or national of a foreign country, or any other person aiding the foreign country, has any interest, provided that the president first declares a national emergency under the act.

Such cases as the Supreme Court's decision in *Dames & Moore v. Regan* (1981), the First Circuit's decision in *Chas. T. Main Int'l v. Khuzestan Water & Power Auth.* (1981), and the D.C. Circuit's decision in *American Int'l Group v. Islamic Republic of Iran* (1981) have recognized that the power given to the president by IEEPA is "sweeping and broad."

IEEPA essentially recodifies, for peacetime emergency use, the wartime economic powers available to the president under Section 5(b) of TWEA. The two statutory authorities differ in that IEEPA does not contain the following TWEA powers still available to the president during time of war:

- the power to "vest" (i.e. expropriate) property in which foreign states or their nationals have an interest;
- the power to regulate purely domestic transactions;
- the power to regulate gold or silver coin or bullion;
- the power to seize records.

In addition, IEEPA contains new restrictions on certain powers that were otherwise available to the president under TWEA. Thus, under the new authority, the president does not have power to: regulate or prohibit personal communications not involving the transfer of anything of value; or regulate uncompensated transfers of articles for humanitarian aid, unless he determines that transfers of this type would either seriously impair his ability to deal with the emergency situation; respond to coercion against the potential donor or recipient; or endanger U.S. armed forces. In *Veterans Peace Convoy, Inc. v. Schultz* (1988), the Southern District of

> *Subject to requirements that the president consult with and report periodically to Congress, IEEPA authorizes the president "to deal with any unusual and extraordinary threat, which has its source in whole or substantial part outside the United States, to the national security, foreign policy, or economy of the United States, if the president declares a national emergency with respect to such threat."*

> *In addition, IEEPA contained new restrictions on certain powers that were otherwise available to the president under TWEA.*

Texas interpreted the humanitarian aid exception very broadly, to include even the donation of trucks carrying humanitarian goods.

Unlike the original version of TWEA, IEEPA explicitly excludes any authority to regulate or prohibit, directly or indirectly:

> any postal, telegraphic, or other personal communication, which does not involve a transfer of anything of value; ... or the importation from any country, or the exportation to any country, whether commercial or otherwise, regardless of format or medium of transmission, of any information or informational materials, including but not limited to, publications, films, posters, phonograph records, photographs, microfilms, microfiche, tapes, compact disks, CD ROMs, artworks, and news wire feeds.

However, this exemption is only available for exports that are not otherwise controlled under the national security and foreign policy provisions of the Export Administration Act, such as exports of goods and technology that may have a military use.

In the Senate Report accompanying the passage of IEEPA, the Senate Foreign Relations Committee added that IEEPA also did not apply to donations and humanitarian contributions, so long as such transfers did not subvert the effective exercise of emergency authority. An amendment of IEEPA, enacted in 1988 and amended in 1994, broadened and strengthened the exemption for informational materials. According to the House Conference Report, the amendment adopted in 1988 was intended to ensure "that no **embargo** may prohibit or restrict directly or indirectly the import or export of information that is protected under the First Amendment to the U.S. Constitution. The language was explicitly intended ... to have a broad scope." However, overly narrow interpretations of the exception by the Treasury Department prompted the 1994 amendment to "facilitate transactions and activities incident to the flow of information and informational materials without regard to the type of information, its format, or means of transmission, and electronically transmitted information."

embargo: a prohibition on commerce with a particular country for political or economic reasons

IEEPA is the broadest statute available to the president to impose economic sanctions.

The first use of IEEPA by the president occurred during the 1979–1981 crisis involving Iran's holding U.S. diplomatic and consular personnel stationed in Teheran as hostages. Since then, IEEPA has frequently been invoked by the president against Libya, Iran (beginning again in 1985 and unrelated to the previous hostage crisis), Iraq (from 1990 to 2003), international terrorists and countries supporting terrorism, and the former Taliban regime in Afghanistan, among many other targets. IEEPA is the broadest statute available to the president to impose economic sanctions. In contrast, for example, the United National Participation Act of 1945 requires a mandate from the U.N. Security Council before sanctions can be imposed. The Iran and Libya Sanctions Act of 1996 is limited to those two countries and makes only specific limited powers available to the president. The Cuban Liberty and Democratic Solidarity Act of 1996 (known as the Helms–Burton Act) applies only to Cuba and imposes only specific limited sanctions against that country.

See also: TRADING WITH THE ENEMY ACT.

BIBLIOGRAPHY

Carter, Barry E. *International Economic Sanction.* Cambridge, U.K.: Cambridge University Press, 1988.

Hufbauer, Gary C. and Jeffrey J. Schott. *Economic Sanctions Reconsidered.* Washington, DC: Institute for International Economics, 1985.

Malloy, Michael P. *United States Economic Sanctions: Theory and Practice.* The Hague, The Netherlands: Kluwer Law International, 2001.

INTERSTATE COMMERCE ACT OF 1887

Ross Rosenfeld

The Interstate Commerce Act (ICA) of 1887 (24 Stat. 379) targeted unfair practices in the railroad industry by attempting to eliminate discrimination against small markets, outlawing pools and rebates, and establishing a "reasonable and just" price standard. To ensure the overall purpose of the act and avoid favoritism in the industry, railroad companies were to publish their rates for all to see. The Interstate Commerce Commission (ICC) was created by the act to enforce these regulations and investigate allegations of fraud, deception, and discrimination.

> *To ensure the overall purpose of the act and avoid favoritism in the industry, railroad companies were to publish their rates for all to see.*

For years railroad tycoons such as J. P. Morgan and Jay Gould had been milking the public. Taking advantage of area transportation monopolies, these "robber barons" often charged unreasonable rates to farmers, small businessmen, and individual passengers for branch service rides, while providing sweet deals to large companies that shipped across the nation. Since large companies represented greater business potential than small ones, they were given "rebates," wherein they received undisclosed sums in consideration of their patronage.

Initially states had tried to combat these unscrupulous business practices by enacting their own railroad laws. But the Constitution granted only Congress the power to control interstate commerce, and states were limited to within their own borders. Political organizations tried to get around this by pushing for regulatory laws in various states. These efforts, while not universal, were somewhat successful nonetheless. Proponents of regulation would, however, receive a setback in 1886. In *Wabash, St. Louis, and Pacific Railway v. Illinois*, the Supreme Court ruled that Illinois had exceeded its Constitutional authority when it attempted to regulate the railroads. This was a power reserved to Congress, the Court said. If Congress wanted to get involved, it could; but states had no power to regulate interstate businesses. This left Congress no choice but to take action on its own and the ICA was the result.

> *The result was utter disregard for ICC findings; the ICC was quickly becoming little more than a public support group.*

"All charges made for any [rail] service ... shall be reasonable and just," the act declared, "and every unjust and unreasonable charge for such service is prohibited and declared to be unlawful." Unfortunately, the five board members of the ICC (later seven, then eleven) had little power to enforce this goal. The authority given to them was ambiguous at best, and further weakened by the Supreme Court. In the *Maximum Freight Rate* case (1897), the Supreme Court denied the ICC's ability to set standards for future rates and undermined its ability to question rates in general. In the *Alabama Midland Railway Company* case of the same year, the Supreme Court again decided against the ICC, ruling that companies could conduct their own investigations to counter the ICC inquiries. The result was utter disregard for ICC findings; the ICC was quickly becoming little more than a public support group.

Yet the strong voices of changing times would not go unheard. The people were anxious for reform and they would find it in the presidency of Theodore Roosevelt. With Roosevelt's induction into office in 1901, a new era of governmental regulation began. The Roosevelt Administration sought to enforce and strengthen the ICA, and Congress was obliged to review its weaknesses.

Congress addressed these weaknesses by passing the Elkins Act of 1903, the Hepburn Act of 1906, and the Mann-Elkins Act of 1910. The Elkins Act strengthened the ICA's antirebate initiative by making it illegal to receive rebates as well as to give them. The Hepburn Act enabled the ICC to put a cap on rate charges, to determine adequate accounting procedures, and to alter unfair rates to ones it deemed "just and reasonable." The Mann-Elkins Act empowered the ICC to suspend proposed rate increases pending an investigation of the potential effects.

Other acts intent on assuring the integrity of the railroads followed, expanding the role of the ICC. The Valuation Act of 1913 required the ICC to verify the value of railroad properties, while the Transportation Act of 1920 gave the ICC authority over railroad pooling and enabled it to regulate railroad securities. The 1935 Motor Carrier Act brought the ICC into the new territory of trucking, though regulation in this area did not nearly approach the amount prescribed for the railroad industry. Many railroad executives complained that they were being singled out.

Railroad companies were losing their grip on transportation. What had once been the fastest way to travel was no longer the fastest nor the most convenient. Trucking and air travel had knocked the rails from their place of prominence, and, along with shipping, relegated it to a lesser role. Railroad companies were justified in declaring the old travel monopolies extinct. Perhaps in a nod toward this opinion, Congress passed the Transportation Act of 1958 which allowed the ICC to guarantee loans to railroad companies for capital, equipment, and main-

Gilded Age
Alfred L. Brophy

The years between the end of the Reconstruction (in 1877) and the Progressive Era at the beginning of the Twentieth Century are often called the "Gilded Age." It was the periods of the growth of great industries—like railroads and oil—and of excesses that went along with wealth. The term "gilded Age" refers to the opulent displays of wealth that characterized the era. It was also an era of political sandal, such as the Credit Mobilier scandal in which Congressmen were given stock in return for favorable government contracts. The Pendelton Act was designed to curb political patronage. Other acts increased government regulation of the growing industries. The Interstate Commerce Commission was formed in 1888 and the Sherman Antitrust Act was passed in 1890. Throughout the era, Congress struggled with currency and tariff regulations.

There was also increasing legislation over issues of race, such as the Chinese Expulsion Act of 1882 and the Dawes Act. Unlike the Reconstruction Era, when legislation was aimed at protecting minorities, in the Gilded Age Congress was more concerned with controlling and excluding them.

tenance. The goal had turned from one of regulation to both regulation and support. The 1976 Railroad Revitalization and Regulatory Reform Act allowed railroad companies to lower their prices for competitive purposes. In addition, two major acts of 1980 gave the industry some breathing room: the Staggers Rail Act relaxed government control over rates, mergers, and line abandonment; and the Motor Carrier Act began the process of ending rate regulation.

Despite the fall of the industry, railroad employment still represented a major sector of the economy. At the time of the ICA, the government had feared the effects of railroad domination. Less than a hundred years later, the government was ready and willing to rescue the industry, even if it had to join in as a partner, as it did with Amtrak, taking on a substantial financial risk to retain jobs. The need for the ICC, meanwhile, gradually became obsolete. It was finally dissolved by act of Congress on December 31, 1995. Most of the surviving functions of the ICC were assigned to the Surface Transportation Board of the Department of Transportation, which began operation on January 1, 1996. These functions included the oversight of railroad rates and service issues, rail mergers, and labor disputes within the industry.

See also: MOTOR CARRIER ACT; STAGGERS RAIL ACT OF 1980.

BIBLIOGRAPHY

Bryant, Keith L., and Henry C. Dethloff. *A History of American Business.* Englewood Cliffs, NJ: Prentice-Hall, Inc., 1983.

Galambos, Louis, and Joseph Pratt. *The Rise of the Corporate Commonwealth: United States Business and Public Policy in the Twentieth Century.* New York: Basic Books, Inc., 1988.

Pusateri, Joseph C. *A History of American Business.* Arlington Heights, IL: Harlan Davidson, Inc., 1984.

J

JONES ACT

See MERCHANT MARINE ACT OF 1920

JUDICIARY ACT OF 1789

Wythe W. Holt, Jr.

When the First Congress gathered in the spring of 1789, eleven of the thirteen states had recently agreed to the Constitution. Although the Constitution provided important details for the legislative and executive branches, it did not flesh out the judicial branch of the new national government. For example, no one knew whether there would be any federal courts other than the "one Supreme Court" mandated by the Constitution, or how many judges would sit on the Supreme Court, or what sorts of jurisdiction any lower federal court might have. So, one of the First Congress's first and most important duties was to establish the federal judiciary. After a summer of heavy debate, the Judiciary Act of 1789 (1 Stat. 73) was signed into law in September.

Although the Constitution provided important details for the legislative and executive branches, it did not flesh out the judicial branch of the new national government.

THE POWER OF THE NATIONAL GOVERNMENT

The Framers of the Constitution, and even more so the citizens of the United States, were sharply divided on the issue of **federalism**. Debate raged as to how much power should be delegated by the previously independent states to the newly centralized national government—which, because of that centralized power was threatening to the powers and privileges of the states.

Federalists, including most of the Framers, wanted to increase the power of the central government, while "anti-Federalists" either desired no such increase or were afraid that the Constitution increased national power too much.

The issue of federal power versus states' power extended to the idea of a national judiciary. Under the loose alliance established by the Articles of Con-

federalism: a system of political organization; a union formed of separate states or groups that are ruled by a central authority on some matters but are otherwise permitted to govern themselves independently

federation, there had been no national court structure. Some saw no need for a national court system even in 1787 to 1789, when the Constitution was drafted, debated, and adopted, arguing that the existing state courts would be good enough. Some thought that only a few federal judges would be needed to deal with issues such as the interpretation of the Constitution, controversies between states, cases involving the official representatives of other nations, and perhaps admiralty cases concerning commerce on the high seas. Others thought that national courts should essentially replace the state courts, at least for much important litigation over debts, contracts, and commerce.

THE PROBLEM OF DEBTS

At the Constitutional Convention in 1787, the Framers were seriously upset at many actions taken by the state legislatures and courts during the six years since England had surrendered at Yorktown. Most of the offending actions concerned debts, since state courts were the usual debt collection agency for creditors (people to whom a debt is owed). The 1780s were depression years, as the Revolution had drained off to Europe all of the hard money (coin) in circulation in the former colonies. Paper money was manufactured to fill the gap, but its worth generally declined rapidly. Bad crop years in the middle of the decade made times even tougher, for most Americans were farmers. States also increased taxes to pay off their own war debts. The common people and many in the elites found that they could not pay their debts, especially millions of dollars owed to British merchants since before the Revolution broke out. Many people thought that winning the war with England meant these debts were canceled, and many were so angry at British depredations throughout eight bloody years of war that repaying them seemed out of the question in any case.

State courts were flooded with debt cases, and sympathetic or frightened judges ruled according to the prevailing winds of Democratic public opinion. Juries openly forgave debts. The people demanded relief in the forms of paper money, debt moratoria, tax relief, and the closing of courts. Legislatures obliged in many states, by making other things besides "gold and silver

> *At the Constitutional Convention in 1787, the Framers were seriously upset at many actions taken by the state legislatures and courts during the six years since England had surrendered at Yorktown.*

Articles of Confederation

In June 1776, while Thomas Jefferson worked with a committee to draft the Declaration of Independence, a second committee developed the nation's first constitution. Called the Articles of Confederation, this document took five years to complete and be ratified, as arguments arose over how much power should be delegated to the central government, whether small states should have the same vote as large states, and whether the western lands should be controlled by the collective or by states on the western border. The finished document established a weak central government, with each state retaining its independence and sovereignty.

States maintained authority over taxation, raising troops, and regulating trade, while Congress, the lawmaking body of the central government, was responsible for foreign affairs, Indian affairs, war, coining money, and maintaining a postal service. Because Congress had no authority to raise money or troops, the system depended on the cooperation of the states to provide funds and, as necessary, soldiers, and by 1786 there was widespread agreement that the arrangement was not effective. The following year a convention met in Philadelphia to develop the U.S. Constitution, which replaced the Articles of Confederation in 1789.

Coin a Tender in Payment of Debts" and otherwise passing "Law[s] impairing the Obligation of Contracts" (to quote two prohibitions placed on the states in article I, section 10 of the 1787 Constitution), as well as delaying taxes due. When legislatures or courts balked or matters got worse, popular antidebt protests or marches occurred in at least eight states from 1785 to 1787. In five states these protests temporarily closed some courts, Shays' Rebellion in Massachusetts in 1786–1787 being only the largest and longest of them.

The "British debts," or the prewar debts that Americans owed to British merchants, proved even more difficult to deal with. Six states closed their courts to British creditors. Every state enacted some legislation suspending, lowering, or otherwise impairing (that is, making less collectible) these debts, and most allowed juries to deduct interest accrued during wartime. Owing to British pressure, the 1783 Peace Treaty provided that "Creditors ... shall meet with no lawful Impediment to the Recovery of the full value in Sterling Money of all bona fide debts heretofore contracted." But, faced with debtor upset and the popular hatred of "British debts," state legislatures continued to enact legislation against those debts. Courts and juries from New York to Georgia, especially those below the **Mason-Dixon line**, where more than 80 percent of such debts rested, continued to refuse to enforce them.

Mason-Dixon line: the boundary line between Pennsylvania on the north and Maryland on the south which, before the end of slavery, was the line between the slave and the free states

The "scales of justice," outside a courthouse in Alexandria, Virginia. A major responsibility of the First Congress was to establish the federal judiciary, provisions for which were left vague in the Constitution. (©ALAN SCHEIN PHOTOGRAPHY/CORBIS)

THE CONSTITUTIONAL CONVENTION

Popular debtor representatives by and large refused the seats offered to them at the Constitutional Convention, so that it was dominated by those who favored creditors interests and wealthy planters. Such Framers continually expressed outrage against debtor interests and against the state courts that enforced them. James Madison asked bluntly, "What was to be done after improper Verdicts in State tribunals obtained under the biased directions of a dependent Judge, or the local prejudices of an undirected jury?" But even many convention delegates opposed a system of lower federal courts, and it was clear that popular opposition to national courts would be great. Because of this controversy and opposition, the article of the Constitution concerning the judiciary was short and vague.

The Constitution specified only a Supreme Court, allowing Congress to decide whether to create other courts and how many judges would sit on each. It gave the Supreme Court jurisdiction over:

- Suits involving foreign citizens
- Suits between citizens of two states
- All suits arising under the Constitution, the laws of Congress, and treaties
- Cases in equity (in which jurors did not sit)
- Appellate jurisdiction over questions of fact (enabling the Supreme Court to override jury verdicts on appeal)
- All admiralty cases and instances involving the United States as a party

These provisions, though broadly stated, seemed to sweep into federal court all the troublesome debt issues. While the Supreme Court was given trial jurisdiction over suits between states and suits involving the public ministers of other nations, and appellate jurisdiction over all others, Congress could make "exceptions" and "regulations." Some terms were even vaguer. No one knew, for example, what constituted a suit "arising under" the Constitution or a treaty.

When the newly drafted Constitution was disclosed, it was met by raging anti-Federalist opposition. The judiciary provisions in particular provoked much antagonism. To many, the broad and vague jurisdictional language undermined the state courts, especially in instances of debt. The fight over adoption was fierce, and the Consti-

Thanks to the wise leadership of Senator Oliver Ellsworth of Connecticut, the Judiciary Act of 1789 put forth a compromise plan that established a strong national judiciary (though there were some surprises).

Shays's Rebellion

After the Revolutionary War, the United States suffered from an economic depression and the almost complete collapse of paper currency, which made it difficult, if not impossible, for farmers to pay their debts. In addition, state governments imposed high taxes to pay for the war. As farmers began to lose their farms because of debt, unrest spread. The most significant revolt was led by Revolutionary War veteran Daniel Shays, who rallied farmers in Western Massachusetts to forcibly shut down courts to prevent foreclosures. The rebellion was crushed in January 1787, but was an influence on those who elected to abandon the Articles of Confederation in favor of a stronger federal government under the Constitution, which was adopted in 1789. Reformers sought both to prevent such rebellions and to establish an economy strong enough that they would not occur. The new federal government assumed the states' war debts, which they paid off with the proceeds from land sales in the West.

tution was barely accepted in such large key states as Massachusetts, Virginia, and New York. It apparently passed in Pennsylvania and New Hampshire only because of political shenanigans, and North Carolina and Rhode Island at first rejected it outright. Some anti-Federalist opponents were elected to the First Congress. With so much controversy, Congress, facing the crucial issue of the judiciary, would have to find a compromise.

CONGRESSIONAL COMPROMISE: A THREE-TIERED FEDERAL COURT

Thanks to the wise leadership of Senator Oliver Ellsworth of Connecticut, the Judiciary Act of 1789 put forth a compromise plan that established a strong national judiciary (though there were some surprises). Ellsworth developed an acceptable structure for the judicial branch that, with three major exceptions, has endured to the present day.

Contrary to those who wished for a minimal judicial presence, the act established three tiers of federal courts: the Supreme Court, district courts, and circuit courts:

The Supreme Court was to sit at the place of government, primarily as an appeals court, and was staffed by a Chief Justice and five associates.

Single-judge district courts were placed in each state. These courts, with trial jurisdiction over admiralty, revenue collection, and petty crimes, had very little to do with the matters that divided Federalists and anti-Federalists, and they established a localized, nonconfrontational presence of the national government.

Circuit courts would sit twice a year in each of the states and would handle most of the trials in matters of contention between the Federalists and anti-Federalists: debt cases involving British creditors, suits between citizens of different states, and important criminal trials. Supposedly to cut costs, but more likely to enable judges of national reputation to handle the tough issues of the day, the circuit courts were staffed with two Supreme Court judges, plus the local district judge.

To calm the opposition, the Judiciary Act gave trial jurisdiction over suits arising under the Constitution, federal laws, and treaties to state courts. Decisions could be appealed to the Supreme Court only when the ruling was against the national interest. Over the strong objection of Great Britain, only debt cases worth more than 500 dollars (at the time a large sum) could be brought to federal court. The Supreme Court was prevented from overturning facts found by juries.

State legislation in favor of creditors was quickly overturned. Nevertheless, no great anti-Federalist explosion occurred over the judiciary structure as set up by the act. Prosperity returned, helping to calm the populace, and continuing upset over British debt cases was finally settled diplomatically. After about a century, with anti-Federalist fears long forgotten, later acts made some changes to the judiciary: they established federal trial jurisdiction over federal questions, stopped the practice of Supreme Court justices ceased serving in circuit courts, and made circuit courts exclusively appellate. Otherwise, the Judiciary Act of 1789 is with us still.

The Judiciary Act of 1789 is with us still.

See also: JUDICIARY ACT OF 1801.

BIBLIOGRAPHY

Holt, Wythe. "'To Establish Justice': Politics, the Judiciary Act of 1789, and the Invention of the Federal Courts." *Duke Law Journal* 1421 (1989): 1421–1531.

Ritz, Wilfrid J. *Rewriting the History of the Judiciary Act of 1789: Exposing Myths, Challenging Premises, and Using New Evidence.* Norman: University of Oklahoma Press, 1990.

Warren, Charles. "New Light on the History of the Federal Judiciary Act of 1789." 37 *Harvard Law Review* (1923) 49–132.

JUDICIARY ACT OF 1801

L. A. Powe, Jr.

The Judiciary Act of 1801 (2 Stat. 69), an act "for the more convenient organization of Courts of the United States," cured major defects in the federal judicial system. It ended the practice of Supreme Court justices sitting as circuit judges, which had been established under the Judiciary Act of 1789. This practice had created two separate problems. First, a justice would sit on appeal at the Supreme Court to hear a case he had already decided as a circuit court judge. Second, justices found it a huge burden to "ride" the circuit, literally traveling from one court to another, often on bad roads and in inclement weather. Riding circuit caused some to avoid serving on the Court. To replace the Supreme Court justices as circuit judges, the act created sixteen new judgeships to fill the courts. Finally, it expanded the jurisdiction of the federal courts by giving them, for the first time, power to decide all cases involving federal questions.

> *The act ended the practice of Supreme Court justices sitting as circuit judges, which had been established under the Judiciary Act of 1789.*

The problems with the federal courts were well known by 1801, and legislative action to correct them had been debated since 1798. President John Adams greeted the Sixth Congress when it convened in December 1799 with a call for a judicial bill. Yet just twelve months after the Judiciary Act of 1801 passed, it was repealed by the Judiciary Act of 1802 (known as the Repeal Act).

PARTY POLITICS AND THE JUDICIARY

What made a meritorious, largely uncontroversial bill so objectionable that it was quickly repealed? Timing. Had the Judiciary Act of 1801 been passed

Repeal Act of March 8, 1802

Sec. 1. That the act of Congress passed on the thirteenth day of February one thousand eight hundred and one, intituled [sic] "An act to provide for the more convenient organization of the courts of the United States" ... shall be, and is hereby repealed.

Sec. 3. That all the acts, and parts of acts, which were in force before the passage of the aforesaid act, and which by the same were either amended, explained, altered, or repealed, shall be, and hereby are ... revived, and in as full and complete force and operation, as if the said act had never been made.

The statute was passed at a time when the effects of two-party politics—at that time, the Federalists and the Republicans—had become clear.

either twelve months earlier or twelve months later, it would have been safe. But the statute was passed at a time when the effects of two-party politics—at that time, the Federalists and the Republicans—had become clear. Neither party trusted the other. The Federalists had controlled the executive and legislative branches up till 1800, and they had appointed only Federalist judges. The presidential election of 1800 was about to deliver a Republican, Thomas Jefferson, into the White House for the first time, as well as a Republican majority to Congress. The election, however, was still being settled in the House of Representatives. The Federalists were considering placing Aaron Burr, Jefferson's Republican vice-presidential running mate, in the presidency instead of Jefferson, and Jefferson and his followers were furious.

If the presidential stalemate was not sufficient to make the Republicans believe the Federalists were trying to steal the government, Chief Justice Oliver Ellsworth offered another reason. After the Federalist defeat in the November 1800 elections became clear, Ellsworth retired so that President Adams would be able to nominate a Federalist to replace him before the Republicans took over. After John Jay turned the post down, in large part because of circuit riding, Adams selected his secretary of state, John Marshall, for the post.

The Judiciary Act passed the House on January 20, 1801, by a partisan 51–43 margin. It passed the Senate, without amendments, on February 11 by a 16–11 vote. Adams signed the Judiciary Act into law on February 13, with less than three weeks remaining in his presidency. Four days later the House deadlock on who would be president was broken, and Jefferson was selected.

Jefferson initially believed the Federalist Congress would not pass the Judiciary Act, because the appointment of judges to the new judgeships created by the act would be made by Republicans, who were about to take control of the government. Then Jefferson realized that the Federalists were pushing the bill with the intent of filling the new positions with their own judges before he took office. He was correct. Adams quickly nominated sixteen Federalists, and the Senate confirmed them all.

The politician and diplomat Gouverneur Morris observed that the Federalists were "about to experience a heavy gale of adverse wind; can they be blamed for casting many anchors to hold their ship through the storm?" Jefferson's answer was yes. On the eve of the inauguration James Monroe, then governor of Virginia and later to become president, wrote to Jefferson, noting that the Federalist "party has retired into the judiciary, in a strong body where it lives on the treasury, & therefore cannot be starved out. While in possession of that ground it can check the popular current which runs against them, & seize the favorable occasion to promote reaction." In other words, the Federalists had made a power grab by means of the judiciary. Thus Jefferson made repeal of the Judiciary Act his first legislative priority. When the Congress finally convened in December 1801, Jefferson sent a message "urging reconsideration of the [February] 1801 legislation." He privately wrote that "lopping off the parasitical plant engrafted at the last session on the judicial body" was necessary because "from that battery all the works of Republicanism are to be beaten down and erased."

In other words, the Federalists had made a power grab by means of the judiciary. Thus Jefferson made repeal of the Judiciary Act his first legislative priority.

CONSTITUTIONAL ISSUES

In the congressional debates and in the partisan press, Federalists claimed that repeal of the Judiciary Act was unconstitutional, because the Constitution provided for judges' life tenure (dependent on good behavior). They claimed that repeal was an attack on the independence of the judiciary. Republicans responded that the power to create includes the power to abolish. And since the Constitution provides only for salaries "during their Continuance in Office," stripping them of the office would end the need for payment.

The Repeal Act of 1802 barely passed the Senate but was solidly supported in the House. The votes, 16–15 and 59–32, reflected the party makeup in the new Seventh Congress. The *National Intelligencer,* a Republican publication, exulted: "Judges created for political purposes, and for the worst of purposes under a republican government, for the purpose of opposing the national will, from this day cease to exist." An editorial in the Federalist press lamented the repeal, fearing the worst: "The fatal bill has passed and our Constitution is no more."

Federalists believed that now only the judiciary could save the country from the Republicans, and many were anxious for the constitutional fight. Some Republicans, too, relished a fight, which they believed the unpopular Federalist party could not hope to win. Federalists had frequently warned that the Supreme Court would declare the Repeal Act unconstitutional, but they were wrong. In the case *Stuart v. Laird,* the Court wrote a three-paragraph opinion that sustained the Repeal Act (although it did not mention it by name) by deciding the case according to its terms. The Court held that circuit riding by Supreme Court justices was so established as to be beyond question and that removing a case from a court created by the 1801 act (and abolished by the Repeal Act) to a court existing under the Judiciary Act of 1789 gave the latter jurisdiction.

Stuart was decided just one week after the famous case *Marbury v. Madison* and is barely known today. Yet *Stuart* underscores the genius of

> *At this stage in the young republic, executive decisions to ignore judicial rulings could have been fatal to the development of an independent judiciary.*

Marbury v. Madison

Marbury v. Madison (1803) was the first case in which the Supreme Court asserted its authority to decide whether a law passed by Congress is constitutional. Before Thomas Jefferson assumed the presidency in 1801, his predecessor, John Adams, hurried to stock public offices with members of his own Federalist party. He appointed his secretary of state, John Marshall, to the position of Chief Justice of the Supreme Court; he also appointed forty-two new justices of the peace, including William Marbury. The commissions for the latter offices were signed by Marshall in his capacity as secretary of state; however, they were not all delivered by the time Jefferson took office on March 4th, and Jefferson directed his own secretary of state, James Madison, to consider them invalid. Marbury petitioned the Supreme Court to order Madison to deliver his commission. The Court's opinion was written by Chief Justice Marshall, who found that Marbury was indeed entitled to his commission. However, he maintained, the Court did not have the right to issue such an order. While the Judiciary Act of 1789 included provisions granting the Court that right, the act was in conflict with the Constitution, which stipulated that unless a state was a party to the case, the Supreme Court had only appellate jurisdiction—in other words, Marbury would have to take his case to a federal district court, and appeal to the Supreme Court only if he lost. In finding the Judiciary Act of 1789 invalid, Marshall established the principle of judicial review, whereby the Supreme Court could overturn congressional legislation that was in conflict with the Constitution.

Justice Marshall's reasoning in *Marbury*. In *Marbury* Marshall's ruling protected and asserted judicial power while simultaneously avoiding a direct challenge to Jefferson. *Marbury* concerned the ability of the judiciary to order the executive to do something. If the Court had issued an order to James Madison, then secretary of state, to deliver Marbury's commission that entitled him to a position as a justice of the peace, Madison would have refused and the Court would have looked and been impotent because its order would not have been obeyed. The same would have been true in *Stuart* if the Court had held the Repeal Act unconstitutional. The sixteen judges would have been entitled to their payment, and the Treasury would not have paid them. At this stage in the young republic, executive decisions to ignore judicial rulings could have been fatal to the development of an independent judiciary.

The Court avoided a fight with Jefferson in *Marbury* by concluding that Congress could not add to the Supreme Court's original jurisdiction. By contrast, *Stuart* was an attack on the independence of the judiciary, and the constitutional issue was whether life-tenured judges could lose their jobs via the expedient of abolishing their courts. At a glance, the Repeal Act seems more clearly unconstitutional than the provision that added to the original jurisdiction of the Court. But unlike *Marbury, Stuart* did not hold a statute unconstitutional because that was a fight it could not win. That, too, reflects Marshall's genius.

See also: JUDICIARY ACT OF 1789.

BIBLIOGRAPHY

Simon, James F. *What Kind of Nation*. New York: Simon and Schuster, 2002.

Smith, Jean Edward. *John Marshall*. New York: Henry Holt and Company, 1996.

JUVENILE JUSTICE AND DELINQUENCY PREVENTION ACT OF 1974

Eric J. Miller

The Juvenile Justice and Delinquency Prevention Act of 1974 (P.L. 93-415, 88 Stat. 1109) was the first major federal legislation to shape the content of state policy on the juvenile court system. It was enacted in response to sustained criticism of the juvenile court system that reached its peak in three Supreme Court decisions in the late 1960s and early 1970s. Through this act Congress created federal standards for the treatment of juvenile offenders and provided financial incentives for state systems to comply with those standards.

The act had two main goals: (1) to remove juveniles from adult jails and prisons, and (2) to end the practice of using the juvenile court system as a means of sending both criminal and noncriminal minors to prisonlike institutions for rehabilitation. The theory of rehabilitation holds that people's behavior, especially young people's behavior, can be changed so that individuals can reenter and function normally in society. How-

Through this act Congress created federal standards for the treatment of juvenile offenders and provided financial incentives for state systems to comply with those standards.

ever, putting that theory into practice through the juvenile court system actually had a negative effect both on individuals and society.

HISTORY OF JUVENILE COURTS

Juvenile courts first appeared in Chicago, Illinois, in 1899. The goal of the juvenile court was not to punish but to "cure" the delinquent child. In undertaking this mission, the juvenile court system broke with the traditional practice of criminal justice. The central feature of the juvenile court system was the belief that crimes were committed by pathological characters who were inadequately socialized, and that therapy could cure such individuals. (Someone who is not *socialized* has trouble fitting into social groups or functioning in social situations.)

Experts in **penal** policy believed that children were less set in their characters, attitudes, and behavior and therefore more open to intervention and reform. The juvenile court system therefore attempted to identify behavior that appeared to predict criminal behavior, such as **truancy**, running away from home, or spending time in pool halls. Children showing such "precriminal" behavior were characterized as "delinquent" in the same manner as juvenile burglars and thieves. The juvenile court could then treat the precriminal delinquent in the same manner as those juveniles charged with a crime.

penal: having to do with punishments or penalties

truancy: skipping out of school

The juvenile court process was based on a technique of intervention and diversion (directing juveniles away from adult courts and prisons). A variety of state officers (not only the police) could identify children as "at risk" or delinquent and refer them to juvenile court, where the child would come under the "protection" of both judge and probation officer in the role of surrogate parent. To emphasize its **nonpunitive** orientation, the juvenile courts' proceedings were not criminal but civil in nature. Because rehabilitation programs rely on individualized treatment, the rules of court procedure, evidence, and proof were more relaxed than in an adult environment. Instead of the passive role assumed by the judge in adult court, the juvenile court judge was supposed to get to know and become more involved with his or her charge. Thus many of the due process protections available in adult court were absent in juvenile court.

nonpunitive: not having the character of punishment or penalty

In practice, however, the juvenile judge rarely spent sufficient time engaging with the child to tailor treatment to the offense. Judges could and would sentence juvenile offenders to long periods of incarceration in juvenile institutions or transfer juveniles to adult prisons. They did so without providing the minimal attention required by the due process protections available in adult courts.

CRITICISM OF THE SYSTEM AND SUPREME COURT REVIEW

Critics began to expose judges' decisions and recommendations in juvenile courts as arbitrary. Furthermore, academics in various fields, led by Francis Allen, called the ideal of rehabilitation into question. By 1970 three Supreme Court cases transformed the juvenile justice system by requiring that the traditional criminal protections of due process and proof beyond a reasonable doubt be applied in juvenile court. The Court's decisions in

By 1970 three Supreme Court cases transformed the juvenile justice system by requiring that the traditional criminal protections of due process and proof beyond a reasonable doubt be applied in juvenile court.

Kent v. United States (1966), *In re Gault* (1967), and *In re Winship* (1970) attacked the juvenile courts' lack of uniformity in sentencing and rejected the idea of "the delinquent." As Justice Abe Fortas wrote in *Gault,* this label carried "only slightly less stigma than the term 'criminal' applied to adults."

By 1974, as a result of the Supreme Court's rulings, the juvenile court system was regarded as a failure. The idea that criminal and precriminal behaviors could be identified by judges and others in the court system was discredited. Juvenile courts had failed to divert enough children away from adult court (where they did not belong), failed to pay enough attention to the needs of the children referred to the courts, and employed an arbitrary set of procedures to determine what should be done with children who had passed through the system.

The act defined a juvenile as someone under the age of eighteen, and juvenile delinquency as a violation of the law by a juvenile (which if committed by an adult would be treated as a crime).

LEGISLATIVE ACTION

Congress passed the Juvenile Justice and Delinquency Prevention Act to overhaul the failing practice of intervention and rehabilitation. State juvenile justice systems would no longer institutionalize juveniles for supposedly "precriminal" offenses. The act defined a juvenile as someone under the age of eighteen, and juvenile delinquency as a violation of the law by a juvenile (which if committed by an adult would be treated as a crime). The act established a system for diverting juveniles away from adult prison through "grants to states and local governments to assist them in planning, establishing, operating, coordinating, and evaluating projects ... for the development of more effective education, training, research, prevention, diversion, treatment, and rehabilitation programs in the area of juvenile delinquency and programs to improve the juvenile justice system."

EFFECTIVENESS

The act has had mixed results in achieving uniform sentences for juvenile offenders. Many states have attempted to avoid diverting youth from adult prisons by permitting prosecutors to choose whether to try minors in the juvenile or adult justice systems. Other states exclude serious criminal offenses

Trying Juveniles as Adults

Those in favor of trying juveniles as adults argue that strict punishment is a deterrent against crime. And simply from the perspective of justice, they argue, brutal crimes should not receive lighter sentences just because the perpetrator is under eighteen. Those opposed to the practice argue that young people are the most likely candidates for rehabilitation, but that those held in adult prisons are more likely to be assaulted or commit suicide than those held in juvenile facilities, and upon their release they are much more likely to become repeat offenders. Studies have shown that the process is applied unfairly, as minority youths are much more likely to be tried as adults than are white youths convicted of similar crimes. Furthermore, many feel that it is inhumane to impose adult punishments on young people who have not had time to develop the complex moral judgments expected of adults. In twenty-three U.S. states, a juvenile tried as an adult may be executed, although the United Nations Convention on the Rights of the Child prohibits execution for crimes committed by minors. The United States is one of only a handful of countries in the world that allows this practice.

from juvenile court. The emphasis on trying juveniles as adults has undermined the act's goal of keeping juveniles out of adult prisons, and in fact has greatly increased the number of juveniles tried in adult courts and present in the general prison population. In relative terms, however, diversion has worked. Through the 1980s and 1990s, the juvenile prison population grew at one-quarter the rate of the young adult population.

The act's greatest legacy may be the humane treatment of young offenders through diversion from prison and supervision in the community.

In the late twentieth century the ideal of rehabilitation gave way to an emphasis on punishment of crime in general, and youth crime was increasingly viewed simply as crime. The act was part of this shift in attitudes, but it is unclear whether it was directly responsible for the trend. Accordingly, the act's greatest legacy may be the humane treatment of young offenders through diversion from prison and supervision in the community.

BIBLIOGRAPHY

Allen, Francis A. "The Juvenile Court and the Limits of Juvenile Justice." In *The Borderland of Criminal Justice: Essays in Law and Criminology.* Ed. Francis A. Allen. Chicago: University of Chicago Press, 1964.

Allen, Francis A. *The Decline of the Rehabilitative Ideal: Penal Policy and Social Purpose.* New Haven, CT: Yale University Press, 1981.

Fagan, Jeffrey, and Franklin E. Zimring, eds. *The Changing Borders of Juvenile Justice: Transfer of Adolescents to the Criminal Court.* Chicago: University of Chicago Press, 2000.

Platt, Anthony M. *The Child Savers: The Invention of Delinquency.* Chicago: University of Chicago Press, 1969.

Roberts, Albert R., ed. *Juvenile Justice: Policies, Programs and Services,* 2d ed. Chicago: Nelson-Hall, 1998.

Ryerson, Ellen. *The Best-Laid Plans: America's Juvenile Court Experiment.* New York: Hill and Wang, 1978.

Watkins, John C., Jr. *The Juvenile Justice Century: A Sociolegal Commentary on American Juvenile Courts.* Durham, NC: Carolina Academic Press, 1998.

K

KANSAS NEBRASKA ACT OF 1854

James L. Huston

Excerpt from the Kansas Nebraska Act of 1954

That the Constitution, and all Laws of the United States which are not locally inapplicable, shall have the same force and effect within the said Territory of Nebraska as elsewhere within the United States, except the eighth section of the act preparatory to the admission of Missouri into the Union ... which, being inconsistent with the principle of non-intervention by Congress with slavery in the States and territories, as recognized by the legislation of eighteen hundred and fifty,..., is hereby declared inoperative and void; it being the true intent and meaning of this act not to legislate slavery into any Territory or State, nor to exclude it therefrom, but to leave the people thereof perfectly free to form and regulate their domestic institutions in their own way....

Each year Congress passes thousands of laws, but only a few truly shape the course of national life. One such law was the Kansas Nebraska Act of 1854 (10 Stat. 282). This act produced terrible consequences and perhaps deserves the title of the most ill-conceived and wretched piece of congressional handiwork in the nation's history. More than any other single action, this law put the United States on the path to Civil War.

The Kansas Nebraska Act was the consequence of three forces: the spirit of Manifest Destiny, the conflict between Northern and Southern states over slavery's expansion into the Western territories acquired after the Mexican War, and the expansionist visions of Illinois Senator Stephen A. Douglas.

Each year Congress passes thousands of laws, but only a few truly shape the course of national life.

SLAVERY AND THE WESTERN TERRITORIES

From 1846 to 1850, Congress had wrestled with the question of slavery's expansion into the Western territories and finally devised a somewhat unsatisfactory solution in the Compromise of 1850. The previous Missouri Compromise of 1820 had established a line (at 36 degrees 30 minutes) below which slavery was permitted and above which it was prohibited. The Compromise of 1850 did not extend that line to the Pacific Ocean. Instead, California was to enter as a free state and, in terms the compromise left very vague, settlers in the other territory acquired from Mexico would decide for themselves whether to establish slavery.

Senator Stephen Douglas, one of the strong men of the Democratic Party and the outstanding leader in the Great Lakes region, was an ardent expansionist who desired to turn the territories between Iowa and California into states. He sought statehood for this area partly because he wanted a transcontinental railroad to San Francisco to originate from Chicago rather than from a rival city (such as St. Louis or New Orleans). No railroad could be built unless the lands of the West were on their way toward statehood, because only then would law enforcement be brought to the region.

Douglas immediately ran into Southern opposition concerning the organization of areas beyond Iowa and Missouri into territories. Still smarting from the debates over the Compromise of 1850, Southerners wanted assurance that slave property would be looked upon as any other type of property. In 1853 Douglas tried to organize the territory of Nebraska and was bluntly told by Senator David Atchison of Missouri that the South would never support such an organization as long as the 36 degree 30 minute line of the Missouri Compromise prohibited slavery in the Nebraska region. The Missouri Compromise marked out slave property as different from ordinary property and therefore subject to different rules. For many Southerners, after the political crisis from 1846 to 1850, this discrimination (as they saw it) against slave property was no longer acceptable.

CONGRESSIONAL CONTROVERSY

A frustrated Douglas was determined to set the land between Iowa and the Rocky Mountains on the path to eventual statehood. As chairman of the Sen-

Stephen A. Douglas

A prominent Democratic leader and U.S. senator, Stephen A. Douglas was an important figure in national politics during the period preceding the Civil War. Born in Vermont in 1813, Douglas moved to Illinois in 1833 and became involved in politics, helping to build and organize the state Democratic party. Over the next thirteen years he moved quickly through a succession of offices including state attorney-general, secretary of state for Illinois, state supreme court justice, U.S. congressman, and U.S. senator. Douglas was a gifted legislator and excellent orator whose Senate speeches drew capacity crowds, and he soon became a leader of the northern Democrats. A proponent of territorial expansion, Douglas advocated allowing the voters of the Western territories to rule on whether or not slavery would be permitted in the West—a controversial position that was incorporated into the Kansas Nebraska Act and which eventually helped instigate the Civil War. After the Supreme Court's 1857 Dred Scott decision, in which the court ruled slaveholders could bring their human property into any federal territory, Douglas antagonized Southern voters by arguing that settlers in the territories could indeed keep slavery out by refusing to allocate the police protection necessary to sustain it. In 1858 Douglas held a famous series of debates with Abraham Lincoln, a Republican candidate challenging Douglas for his Senate seat, in which the two powerful thinkers and orators debated the issue of slavery before passionately partisan audiences. Although Douglas won reelection, Lincoln rose to national stature as a result of the debates and won the Republican nomination for president in 1860. Lincoln defeated Douglas in the election, in part because the Democratic party had split over Douglas's positions on slavery and nominated two candidates. Douglas pledged his support to Lincoln and the Union, but he was exhausted, discouraged, in ill health, and he died the following year.

ate Committee on Territories in the first session of the Thirty-Third Congress, he proposed to organize the Territory of Nebraska and let the question of slavery be settled at its eventual constitutional convention. This proposal did not satisfy Southerners. Kentucky Senator Archibold Dixon of the Whig Party offered an amendment that specifically repealed the Missouri Compromise line of 36 degrees 30 minutes. Douglas took his bill back into committee and consulted with his peers. He then came back to the Senate on January 23, 1854, with a new bill that repealed the Missouri Compromise line and divided the land into the new territory of Kansas and Nebraska.

The critical question of slavery was to be settled by the settlers themselves, by the doctrine of popular sovereignty. This concept was devised by Michigan Senator Lewis Cass in December 1847 and then picked up by the Democrats in the presidential election of 1848. The act stated that its intent was "to leave the people [of Kansas and Nebraska] perfectly free to form and regulate their domestic institutions in their own way." Popular sovereignty became the grand touchstone of truth for Douglas thereafter, and the rest of his life (he died in April 1861) was devoted to championing its righteousness.

Douglas's new bill tore Congress into battling halves and eventually destroyed the Whig-Democrat two-party system that had ruled the nation since the 1830s.

Douglas's new bill tore Congress into battling halves and eventually destroyed the Whig-Democrat two-party system that had ruled the nation since the 1830s. Douglas and many of the Northern Democrats adopted popular sovereignty and insisted on its validity in overcoming arguments about slavery. In effect they agreed that the Missouri Compromise line demeaned Southerners. Southerners agreed about the injustice done to them by the Missouri Compromise but hesitated to accept popular sovereignty, for they believed that settlers could not determine the existence of slavery at any time other than when they framed their state constitutions.

Northern Whigs and many Northern Democrats exploded in wrath at the repeal of the venerable Compromise of 1820. For them, the Missouri Compromise had virtually become a part of the Constitution. What possible reason could there be to repeal the compromise line—especially at a moment when there was no public agitation about slavery—except to allow Southerners to expand slavery into places where it had been prohibited? The aristrocratic slaveholders of the South were called the "Slave Power." Northern congressional leaders feared that the Slave Power had become aggressive, intending to gain more slave states, would overwhelm Congress with slave-state representatives and senators, destroy civil liberties, convert free states into slave states, enslave all workingmen regardless of color, and transform the United States from a republic into a slaveholding despotism.

The debate over the bill raged for three months. President Franklin Pierce applied pressure on Northern Democrats to accept it, and on May 22, 1854, the House passed the Kansas Nebraska Act (the Senate had passed it on March 3). Pierce signed the bill into law on May 30.

A DISASTROUS MISCALCULATION

No congressional member had so badly miscalculated the consequences of his actions as had Douglas. He believed that, besides getting a transcontinental railroad terminating in Chicago, he had removed the slavery issue from national life. By putting discussion of slavery in the hands of settlers and taking it away from members of Congress, Douglas believed, as did many others, that the national agitation over slavery's expansion would cease. This prediction was proven miserably wrong. Many Northerners fiercely resisted any possibility of slavery's extension into the Louisiana Purchase area or in the states of Wisconsin and Michigan, and out of the ashes of the Whig Party soon rose the Republican Party. In the congressional elections of 1854, the Democratic Party suffered the greatest defeat in its history. At the beginning of Congress in December 1853, Northern Democrats had ninety-one members; after the elections of 1854, they had twenty-five. Only seven out of forty-four Northern Democrats who had voted for the Kansas Nebraska Act were reelected. It took the Northern Democrats twenty years to recover from this disaster.

BLEEDING KANSAS

Kansas territory became a running sore on the national political body that only inflamed hostility between North and South. Northerners who advocated a free state, known as "free soilers," streamed into Kansas Territory, only to be met by proslavery Southerners and Missourians. These Missourians were

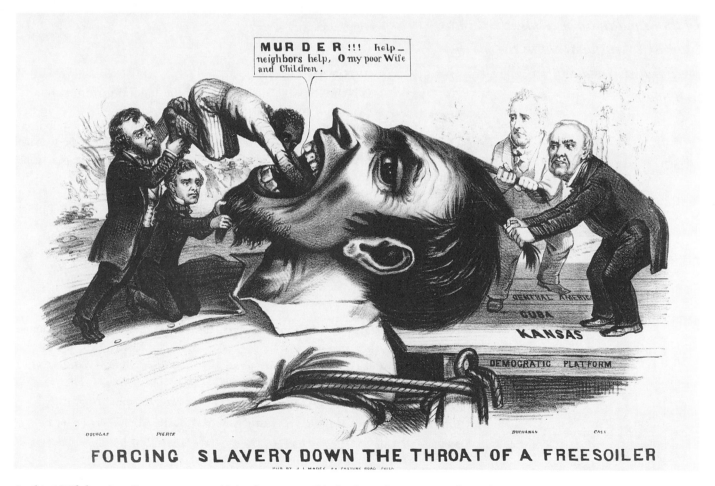

In this 1856 drawing, Democrats are criticized as responsible for the violence against freesoilers in Kansas. The freesoiler is bound to the "Democratic Platform"; presidential nominee James Buchanan and Senator Lewis Cass restrain him; and Senator Stephen Douglas and President Franklin Pierce force a black man into his mouth. (LIBRARY OF CONGRESS, PRINTS AND PHOTOGRAPHS DIVISION)

Kansas territory became a running sore on the national political body that only inflamed hostility between North and South.

called "Border Ruffians" because they lived in Missouri but then traveled to Kansas to vote illegally in Kansas elections. By 1856 the controversy between these two factions was so intense as to be called "Bleeding Kansas." Two rival legislatures existed, one in Topeka (the free soil capital) and one in Lecompton (the proslavery capital). By fraudulent election tactics, the proslavery faction took over the territorial legislature and wrote a constitution making Kansas a slave state. This constitution was then ratified under fraudulent conditions by a vote of the settlers, with most free soilers abstaining.

Douglas considered the actions of the proslavery faction in Kansas a perversion of the doctrine of popular sovereignty, so he refused to vote for it and joined the Republicans in opposition. The Lecompton Constitution was rejected by Congress in 1858, making Southern leaders furious at Douglas. Meanwhile, all this deceitful activity designed to make Kansas a slave state convinced a majority of Northerners that a Slave Power did in fact intend to convert the United States into a slaveholding despotism. In response, the power of the Republican Party swelled. In the election of 1860, the Democratic Party, polarized by the Kansas Nebraska Act, broke into Northern and Southern fragments, enabling the Republicans to stride to victory.

In the actual chain of events, the Kansas Nebraska Act stands out as the one that precipitated armed conflict between North and South.

CIVIL WAR

With the Republicans controlling the federal government and because of their evident dislike of slavery, Southerners in the plantation states (Georgia, South Carolina, Florida, Alabama, Mississippi, Louisiana, and Texas) decided to leave the Union. The stage was set for the Civil War. Other events probably would have triggered the reactions which led to secession and civil war, for the antagonism of Northern society to slavery was not simply going to vanish. But in the actual chain of events, the Kansas Nebraska Act stands out as the one that precipitated armed conflict between North and South.

See also: COMPROMISE OF 1850; MISSOURI COMPROMISE.

BIBLIOGRAPHY

Gara, Larry. *The Presidency of Franklin Pierce.* Lawrence: University Press of Kansas, 1991.

Gates, Paul Wallace. *Fifty Million Acres: Conflicts over Kansas Land Policy, 1854–1890.* Ithaca, NY: Cornell University Press, 1954.

Holt, Michael F. *The Political Crisis of the 1850s.* New York: Hill and Wang, 1978.

Johannsen, Robert W. *Stephen A. Douglas.* New York: Oxford University Press, 1973.

McPherson, James M. *Ordeal by Fire: The Civil War and Reconstruction,* 2d ed. New York: Knopf, 1992.

Potter, David M. *The Impending Crisis, 1848–1861.* Completed and edited by Don. E. Fehrenbacher. New York: Harper and Row, 1976.

KEATING-OWEN ACT OF 1916

William G. Ross

The Keating-Owen Act of 1916 (P.L. 249, 39 Stat. 675), was the first federal statute to impose restrictions on child labor. Under the act, the products of mines that employed children under age sixteen and factories employing children under age fourteen could not be transported by means of interstate commerce. The law also prohibited interstate shipment of products from factories that employed children under age sixteen for more than eight hours a day, for more than six days any week, or at night. Violation of the law constituted a criminal misdemeanor for which factories could be fined.

The Keating-Owen Act eliminated or restricted employment for approximately a quarter of a million children. The law did not affect the far larger number of children who labored on farms, usually under conditions that were less harsh than those endured by children who worked in factories or mines.

The statute was part of a long campaign waged by social reformers and progressive activists, who had achieved significant victories in most states even before enactment of the federal law. By 1916 approximately thirty-six states prohibited industrial employment of children under aged fourteen, and eighteen states limited the working hours of children ages fourteen to sixteen. Opponents of child labor believed a federal law was needed because the states that lacked child labor laws were unlikely to enact such laws during the foreseeable future. The lack of a federal law also gave competitive economic advantages to those states, mostly Southern, that lacked child labor laws. Various business interests outside the South forged a coalition with social reformers to ensure the statute's enactment.

Carried along by the tide of the progressive reform movement, the Keating-Owen bill passed the House by a vote of 337 to 46 and received Senate approval by a margin of 50 to 12. President Woodrow Wilson signed it into law with great enthusiasm, regarding it as a centerpiece of his social and economic reform program (his New Freedom program), recognizing that it could help win votes in the upcoming presidential election.

Under the act, the products of mines that employed children under age sixteen and factories that employed children under age fourteen could not be transported by means of interstate commerce.

CONSTITUTIONAL ISSUES

The statute encountered vigorous opposition by Southern textile manufacturers. In 1918 the U.S. Supreme Court invalidated it in a five-to-four decision in *Hammer v. Dagenhart* on the grounds it exceeded Congress's power, as stated in the Constitution, to regulate interstate commerce. The Court's decision surprised many opponents of child labor, as the Court in 1913 had unanimously sustained a state child labor law as an appropriate exercise of the state's inherent power to promote the welfare of its citizens in *Sturges & Burns Manufacturing Co. v. Beauchamp*. Moreover, in other decisions the Court had seemed to reject the distinction between manufacturing and commerce which it now revived in the 1918 ruling.

Although the Court acknowledged that child labor was a social evil, Justice William R. Day's opinion contended that any relief, or elimination of that evil, must come from the states not from a federal law.

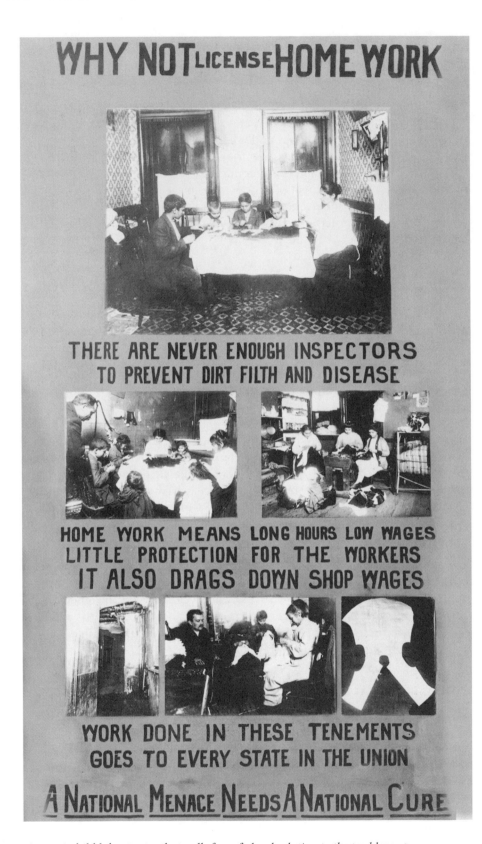

An anti-child labor poster that calls for a federal solution to the problem. (LIBRARY OF CONGRESS, PRINTS AND PHOTOGRAPHS DIVISION)

Although the Court acknowledged that child labor was a social evil, Justice William R. Day's opinion contended that any relief, or elimination of that evil, must come from the states not from a federal law. He argued that the child labor law would practically destroy **federalism**, emphasizing that Congress lacked power to regulate the conduct of local manufacturing enterprises.

federalism: a system of political organization; a union formed of separate states or groups that are ruled by a central authority on some matters but are otherwise permitted to govern themselves independently

In a stinging dissent, Justice Oliver Wendell Holmes argued that earlier Supreme Court decisions had established that Congress enjoyed broad powers to regulate interstate commerce and that the statute did not impinge on any right of the states to regulate their own internal affairs. Holmes also chided the Court for reading its own "moral conceptions" into the Constitution.

One year after the *Dagenhart* case, Congress tried to avoid the Court's objections by enacting a law that imposed taxes rather than fines on employers of children. The Court struck down this statute in *Bailey v. Drexel Furniture Co.* (1922), an eight-to-one decision holding that this statute exceeded Congress's constitutional power to impose taxes.

Although both houses of Congress overwhelmingly approved a child labor amendment in 1924, intense opposition by business interests prevented its ratification by the required three-quarters of the states.

After these Supreme Court decisions, opponents of child labor concluded it was futile to push for further federal legislation. Their next step was an attempt to amend the Constitution. Although both houses of Congress overwhelmingly approved a child labor amendment in 1924, intense opposition by business interests prevented its ratification by the required three-quarters of the states.

Widespread political support for reform measures returned during the **New Deal** of President Franklin D. Roosevelt. Congress included restrictions on child labor in the Fair Labor Standards Act of 1938. The Supreme Court sustained the constitutionality of this statute in *United States v. Darby* (1941), which overruled *Dagenhart* by holding that child labor was a proper subject for regulation under the **commerce clause**.

New Deal: the legislative and administrative program of President Franklin D. Roosevelt designed to promote economic recovery and social reform (1933–1939)

commerce clause: the provision of the U.S. Constitution (Article I, section 8, clause 3) which gives Congress exclusive powers over interstate commerce—the buying, selling or exchanging of goods or products between states

See also: FAIR LABOR STANDARDS ACT.

BIBLIOGRAPHY

Tratter, Walter I. *Crusade for the Children: A History of the National Child Labor Committee and Child Labor Reform in America.* New York: Crown, 1970.

Wood, Stephen B. *Constitutional Politics in the Progressive Era: Child Labor and the Law.* Chicago: University of Chicago Press, 1968.

KU KLUX KLAN ACT (1871)

Julie Davies

The Enforcement Act (17 Stat. 13), commonly known as the Ku Klux Klan Act or the Civil Rights Act of 1871, was a response to extraordinary civil unrest during the **Reconstruction** period. This unrest threatened the lives and the political and economic rights of all newly freed slaves. Although closely

Reconstruction: the political and economic reorganization of the South after the Civil War

Although closely tied to the era in which it was enacted, portions of the statute remain extraordinarily important to modern civil rights enforcement.

tied to the era in which it was enacted, portions of the statute remain extraordinarily important to modern civil rights enforcement.

MAJOR FEATURES OF THE ACT

Section 1 of the act (now codified at 42 U.S.C. § 1983, and called in this entry "section 1983"), provided that any person deprived of rights conferred by the Constitution by someone acting "under color" of law (i.e., a state or local official acting with legally granted authority, or, through purporting to act within such limits, an official may be misusing authority) or custom could bring suit in federal court and recover damages or equitable relief. Section 2 (now codified at 42 U.S.C. § 1985, and called in this entry "section 1985") of the act provided criminal sanctions and a civil damages action for conspiracy to commit a range of offenses. These offenses included attempting to overthrow the government, intimidating witnesses or parties to legal action, using threat or force to influence jurors, or going on the highway in disguise to deprive others of the exercise of constitutional rights guaranteed by the Fourteenth and Fifteenth Amendments. The section is used less frequently than section 1, but is still a relevant and powerful piece of civil rights legislation.

Section 3 of the act authorized the president to use the U.S. armed forces to put down rebellions, and section 4 permitted the suspension of the writ of **habeas corpus**. Section 5 provided that jurors in U.S. courts must not be parties to combinations or conspiracies and that they must swear, on penalty of **perjury**, that they did not have any allegiances to groups dedicated to the overthrow of the government or denial of constitutional rights. Section 6 (now 42 U.S.C. § 1986), provided that persons with knowledge of a conspiracy who failed to take reasonable actions to prevent wrongful acts from occurring could be named as a defendant and be held liable for any death caused by failure to intercede.

habeas corpus: (Latin, "you have the body") a written order to determine whether one's detention or imprisonment is lawful

perjury: lying under oath or otherwise breaking an oath by not doing what was promised

HISTORICAL CIRCUMSTANCES LEADING TO THE ACT

Knowing the act's background is essential to understanding its place in history and its contemporary relevance. The United States Supreme Court, in its interpretation of the act, has taken that historical background extremely seriously.

The act was intended to enforce the Fourteenth Amendment.

The act was intended to enforce the Fourteenth Amendment. The motivation for its passage really begins with events that took place near the end of the Civil War in 1863. At the time, President Abraham Lincoln issued a simple statement called the Emancipation Proclamation. This document freed the slaves in the states that had seceded from the Union. Because the Emancipation Proclamation was a presidential order, Congress was concerned it might be overridden by subsequent legislation. Congress then passed the Thirteenth Amendment, which abolished slavery and involuntary servitude and gave Congress the power to enforce its provisions.

It soon became clear that the Thirteenth Amendment was insufficient to end the conditions of servitude in which the freed slaves found themselves. Many states enacted "Black Codes." These were laws that so closely regulated the lives of the former slaves as to be just short of slavery. For example, unemployed African Americans could be fined as vagrants or imprisoned. To enter some states, they had to post bond. As a result, African Americans found themselves limited to working for their former masters, and still ostracized and inhibited from enjoying any fruits of freedom.

Congress passed several historic civil rights acts in an effort to remedy the limitations of the Thirteenth Amendment. The Act of April 9, 1866 gave the former slaves citizenship and some basic economic and legal rights. Doubts as to the constitutional validity of this law led to the adoption of the Fourteenth Amendment to the Constitution in 1868. Like the 1866 act, the Fourteenth Amendment bestowed citizenship as a national birthright, overruling the Dred Scott Decision of 1857. It contained broader prohibitions against discrimination than those in the 1866 act. It guaranteed that no state would make laws to abridge "the privileges and immunities of citizens" or deprive any person of "life, liberty or property without due process of law," or "deny any person within its jurisdiction the equal protection of the laws." Section 5 of the Fourteenth Amendment gave Congress the power to enforce its provisions.

The Southern states initially refused to **ratify** the Fourteenth Amendment. In response, Congress instituted military, or radical, reconstruction, in the South. Congress's efforts to exert greater control were successful in reconstituting the state **electorates**, but unsuccessful in stemming the rebelliousness of state officials and the citizenry. Evidence of the brutal lynchings of former slaves and the destruction of property began to emerge. These attacks were the work of a number of white supremacy groups, the most notorious of which was the Ku Klux Klan. Their acts were intended to deter African Americans from exercising any of the basic rights granted to them by the Civil Rights Act of 1866 or the Fourteenth and Fifteenth Amendments. Even worse, there was evidence that state officials were encouraging this **vigilante** action and were deliberately unresponsive to pleas they utilize law enforcement power to stop it. Even if perpetrators were apprehended, there was no com-

ratify: to formally approve; three-fourths of all states in the Union must approve an amendment for it become part of the Constitution

electorate: the body of people qualified to vote

vigilante: a member of a self-appointed group of citizens who undertake law enforcement in their community without legal authority

Apartheid

The term apartheid, which is the Afrikaans word for "apartness," refers to the South African policy of strict racial segregation. The term was first used in the 1930s and the practice of apartheid became law in 1948 when nonwhites were put under the domination of the white minority. South Africans were identified by one of four racial categories: white, Bantu (black), Coloured (which referred to people of mixed race), or Asian (mostly Indians and Pakistanis). Education and public facilities were segregated, and social contact between the races was prohibited. Nonwhites were allowed to live only in designated areas and during the 1950s, blacks were relegated to ten distinct, self-governing states called "Bantustands." The Bantustands had few resources or economic opportunities and quickly became slums. White police harassed those suspected of association with black nationalist groups, and civil rights leaders were jailed. Nelson Mandela, leader of the opposition African National Congress, was sentenced to life in prison on the charge of attempting to overthrow the South African government. During the 1970s and 1980s strikes and riots in the Bantustands helped bring the situation to the attention of the world. International firms began pulling out of the country, neighboring African countries increased political pressure, and the United States and the United Kingdom imposed economic sanctions. Amid extreme violence and turmoil, the South African government finally abandoned apartheid during the 1990s and free elections were held for the first time in history. In 1994 Nelson Mandela, released in 1990, was elected president.

mitment within the state legal systems to bringing them to justice or mete out punishment.

In March 1871 President Ulysses S. Grant came to Congress and requested emergency legislation to stem what he described as virtual anarchy in the South.

In March 1871 President Ulysses S. Grant came to Congress and requested emergency legislation to stem what he described as virtual anarchy in the South. He told Congress the states would not and could not control the violence. The legislative response to this plea was the Civil Rights Act of April 20, 1871. It was known as the Ku Klux Klan Act because of that group's prominent participation in the violence.

LEGISLATIVE HISTORY OF THE ACT

Section 5 of the Fourteenth Amendment gave Congress the power to address the problem President Grant described. Representative Samuel Shellabarger, a Republican from Ohio, introduced "a bill (H.R. No. 320) to enforce the provisions of the fourteenth amendment to the Constitution of the United States, and for other purposes." Section 1, the civil remedy for violation of the Fourteenth Amendment, was derived from the 1866 Civil Rights Act. It generated little debate among the representatives. The controversial portion of the act was section 2, which imposed its penalties on "any person" conspiring to do certain acts. Opponents argued that the provision would be unconstitutional because it was not limited to those acting under color of state law. This meant it could potentially reach purely private parties. The sections granting the president the power to suspend habeas corpus and to use armed force to suppress violence were also argued to be beyond the scope of the Fourteenth Amendment's protection. First the House, and then the Senate, passed the bill. The chair of the Senate Judiciary Committee, Lyman Trumbull, a Republican from Illinois, was a proponent of the act though he interpreted it rather narrowly. One controversial amendment, known as the Sherman Amendment, sought to make cities and counties liable for violence occurring within their borders. The House refused to concur, and legislators held a conference committee meeting. The Sherman Amendment was rewritten to impose liability only for persons who knew of a conspiracy to violate civil rights and who could have prevented it. Finally both Houses agreed and the Ku Klux Klan Act became law on April 20, 1871.

HISTORY OF THE ACT FROM 1871 TO 1961

If you try to find the Klu Klux Klan Act among current United States statutes, you will be unsuccessful. In 1874 the statutes were revised in what was to be merely a procedural reorganization. Sections 1, 2, 3, 5, and 6 were scattered throughout the Revised Statutes. Section 4, permitting the suspension of habeas corpus, provided its own expiration date (after the end of the next regular section of Congress) and so did not make it into the Revised Statutes. A modern reader encounters only remnants and revisions of the original Act located in several places in the United States Code.

The various provisions of the Ku Klux Klan Act were not used frequently after their enactment. One reason was that the Supreme Court gave an extremely narrow interpretation to the privileges and immunities clause of the Fourteenth Amendment in the *Slaughterhouse Cases* (1873). In these cases, the Court held that only privileges and immunities of national citizenship were protected by the provision. Most civil rights were deemed to be privileges of state citizenship and fell outside the protection of the Fourteenth Amendment. This interpretation meant that states, not the federal government, would be the primary protectors of civil rights. Since the Ku Klux Klan Act was designed to enforce the Fourteenth Amendment, the result was that there was not much left to enforce. Subsequent decisions further narrowed the Fourteenth Amendment by ruling that it applied only to state action (*United States v. Cruikshank* [1876]; *Virginia v. Rives* [1879]). The Court's decision in *United States v. Harris* (1882) invalidated the criminal conspiracy section of the act for the same reason.

The result of these decisions was that states were once again primarily responsible for protecting the rights of their citizens, and Black Codes reappeared and melded with a system of social apartheid that became known as "Jim Crow." Congress, which had lost any political will to protect and enforce the Reconstruction Amendments and legislation, was content to see the statutes fall into disuse. Consequently, discriminatory laws affected not only African Americans but many other racial minorities.

Most civil rights were deemed to be privileges of state citizenship and fell outside the protection of the Fourteenth Amendment.

KEY PROVISIONS AND THEIR CURRENT RELEVANCE

Of the many sections of the Ku Klux Klan Act, the most influential today is the little debated section 1983. The section provides in part:

> Every person who, under color of any statute, ordinance, regulation, custom, or usage, of any State or Territory or the District of Columbia, subjects, or causes to be subjected, any citizen of the United States or other person within the jurisdiction thereof to the deprivation of any rights, privileges, or immunities secured by the Constitution and laws, shall be liable to the

The Ku Klux Klan

The Ku Klux Klan is a brutal white supremacy organization that has gone through several distinct incarnations since the Civil War. Founded in Tennessee as a social fraternity in 1866, the Klan evolved into a vigilante organization of former Confederates who opposed the Republican state government and sought to keep blacks "in their place." Klan members disguised in white robes, masks, and tall hats terrorized blacks and their Republican supporters with floggings, lynchings, and the destruction of property. Congress retaliated with the Civil Rights Acts, and the Klan was effectively suppressed by 1872. A second incarnation of the group appeared in 1915, when the patriotism prompted by World War I combined with a wave of Southern romantic nostalgia about the lost Confederacy. The Klan's members—who numbered more than three million by the early 1920s—found it a bastion not only against blacks, but also against immigrants, Jews, Catholics, and Communists. Positioned as the guardian of American institutions and Protestant values, the Klan became a significant political influence, helping to elect more than two dozen senators and governors. As reports of lynching, mutilation, rape, and other violence by the Klan began to emerge, however, the group's broad, mainstream base was alienated. Weak organization and corrupt leadership contributed to a rapid drop in membership, and by the late 1920s the Klan had faded once again. It was legally disbanded in 1944 in lieu of payment of back taxes. The Klan reemerged after World War II in response to the civil rights movement. In the early 1960s the Klan attacked freedom riders, killed four children in a Birmingham church bombing, and murdered three civil rights workers in Mississippi. In 1964 the FBI began to infiltrate the Klan in order to suppress it and by 1975 membership had dropped from 50,000 to 6,500. The Klan as it exists today is small and fragmented.

party injured in an action at law, suit in equity, or other proper proceeding for redress....

The language of the statute is much the same as it was in 1871. Interestingly, the 1874 revisions resulted in the apparently inadvertent insertion of the words "and laws," which has resulted in a large expansion of the statute's coverage. Reference to the District of Columbia and to territories was added in 1979.

Section 1983 allows people to sue for state and local violations of the Constitution and federal law. It enables private citizens to affirmatively enforce these rights. Lawsuits may be brought in federal or state court, and the remedies available for violations include damages and **injunctive relief.** A key to Section 1983's revitalization was when the Supreme Court breathed new life into the Fourteenth Amendment. The Court developed an extensive theoretical framework for the due process and equal protection clauses, under which it recognized a wide variety of federally protected rights. Also, in *Monroe v. Pape* (1961), the Supreme Court interpreted Section 1983's "under color of law" requirement to cover cases in which state and local officials were not acting in accordance with state law but in violation of it. This was the beginning of a series of interpretations that loosened the judicial stranglehold on civil rights legislation that had been passed during the Reconstruction era.

More recently, a vast number of Supreme Court decisions relate to Section 1983. They cover issues such as the conditions under which governmental entities can be held liable for acts of their various employees, immunities that can be asserted to preclude suits against particular officials, the requirements for awards of damages and injunctive relief, circumstances in which federal courts should abstain from deciding a Section 1983 claim, and more. The rights litigated under Section 1983 are extremely varied, including not only equal protection and due process, but constitutional rights made applicable to the states by the Fourteenth Amendment and many federal statutes.

injunctive relief: a court order that requires a person to refrain from doing something; the order guards against future damages rather than remedies past damages

> *Monroe was the beginning in a series of interpretations that loosened the judicial stranglehold on civil rights legislation passed during the Reconstruction era.*

Section 1985 provides a civil action for those injured by conspiracies formed to prevent an officer of the United States from performing official duties, to obstruct justice, or "for the purpose of depriving, either directly or indirectly, any person or class of persons of the equal protection of the laws, or of the equal privileges and immunities under the laws." Unlike Section 1983, the statute was interpreted to apply to the actions of private parties in *Griffin v. Breckenridge* (1971). This interpretation is consistent with the statute's original goal of reaching Ku Klux Klan conspirators. Although it applies to private individuals, the statute has a narrow scope because the Supreme Court has sought to ensure that it does not encompass ordinary civil wrongs or crimes. To confine the type of private behavior covered by section 1985, the Court wrote in the *Griffin* case that "there must be some racial or perhaps other class-based invidiously discriminatory animus behind the conspirators' action."

Bray v. Alexandria Women's Health Clinic (1993) illustrates this limitation. In *Bray,* a group of plaintiffs who provided abortions or wished to use abortion clinics sought unsuccessfully to use section 1985 against members of Operation Rescue for their organization and coordination of demonstrations blocking access to abortion clinics. Justice Antonin Scalia, writing for the Court, rejected arguments that the conspiracy was against women as a class, or that it was designed to defeat exercise of the right to travel guaranteed in the Constitution. He concluded that "women seeking abortion" was not a qualifying class.

Although the criminal counterpart to section 1985 was found unconstitutional, a very similar criminal conspiracy statute derived from the Civil Rights Act of 1870 survived, and was interpreted to reach private conspiracies. Another viable, but rarely used provision, section 1986 (42 U.S.C. Section 1986), permits an action for neglecting to prevent a conspiracy. Courts have found that plaintiffs seeking to establish a violation of section 1986 must also establish a violation of Section 1985. An example of a potentially valid claim stems from a case where African American motorists alleged that the attorney general of New Jersey had conspired with members of his office staff to conceal the existence of racial profiling from the judiciary and Justice Departments, and that, despite his knowledge of racially motivated conspiracies among the state police, he did nothing to stop the conspirators.

President Ulysses S. Grant signs the Ku Klux Klan Act in the President's room at the Capitol, April 20, 1871. Also shown in this illustration, published in Frank Leslie's Illustrated Newspaper, *May 13, 1871, are Secretary of the Navy George M. Robeson, seated, and General Horace Porter.* (LIBRARY OF CONGRESS, PRINTS AND PHOTOGRAPHS DIVISION)

Another provision grants the president the power to utilize the armed forces of the United States to combat insurrections. Although it has not been used frequently, it was invoked by President Dwight Eisenhower to order federal troops to Little Rock in 1957 when the governor of Arkansas had ordered the Arkansas National Guard to block school desegregation.

In conclusion, though the Klu Klux Klan Act was a response to a unique threat to the exercise of constitutional rights, the act was drafted broadly enough that portions of it, particularly section 1983, are vital to modern enforcement of constitutional and federal statutory rights.

See also: CIVIL RIGHTS ACTS OF 1866, 1875, 1957, 1964; FAIR HOUSING ACT; FORCE ACT OF 1871; VOTING RIGHTS ACT OF 1965.

BIBLIOGRAPHY

Kluger, Richard. *Simple Justice: The History of* Brown v. Board of Education *and Black America's Struggle for Equality.* New York: Vintage, 1977.

Schwartz, Bernard, ed. *Statutory History of the United States: Civil Rights, Part 1.* New York: Chelsea House, 1970.

Smith, Carter, ed. *One Nation Again: A Sourcebook on the Civil War.* Brookfield, CT: Millbrook Press, 1993.

Stampp, Kenneth M. *The Era of Reconstruction 1865–1877.* New York: Vintage, 1965.

Woodward, C. Vann. *The Strange Career of Jim Crow,* 3d ed. New York: Oxford University Press, 1974.

Ziff, Marsha. *Reconstruction Following the Civil War in American History.* Berkeley Heights, NJ: Enslow Publishers, 1999.

LABOR MANAGEMENT RELATIONS ACT

See TAFT-HARTLEY ACT

LEGAL SERVICES CORPORATION ACT (1974)

Travis McDade

Excerpt from the Legal Services Corporation Act

The Congress finds and declares that—

(1) there is a need to provide equal access to the system of equal justice in our Nation for individuals who seek redress of grievances;

(2) there is a need to provide high quality legal assistance to those who would be otherwise unable to afford adequate legal counsel and to continue the present vital legal services program;

(3) providing legal assistance to those who face an economic barrier to adequate legal counsel will serve best the ends of justice;

(4) for many of our citizens, the availability of legal services has reaffirmed faith in our government of laws;

In 1964, in an effort to combat poverty in the United States, Congress passed the Economic Opportunity Act. Though there were no specific provisions in the act relating to legal services, the Economic Opportunity Amendments of 1967 specifically added a legal services program to "further the cause of justice among persons living in poverty by mobilizing the assistance of lawyers and legal institutions." The program was unique in that it offered federal resources to people otherwise unable to afford help in civil litigation. Situated within the Office of Economic Opportunity, the executive branch would administer legal services.

In its general aim, the Legal Services Corporation was similar to that of the Legal Services program that had existed under the Office of Economic Opportunity: to provide quality legal help in the civil justice arena to people otherwise unable to afford it.

In 1971 the president recommended that, rather than retaining the Legal Services program within the executive branch, Congress charter an independent, nonprofit corporation to assume the program's duties. For two years Congress considered legislation to create the Legal Service Corporation (LSC), but members disagreed about its structure. Finally, in 1974, Congress passed the Legal Services Corporation Act (LSCA) (P.L. 93-355, 88 Stat. 378) and the president signed it into law.

In its general aim, the LSC was similar to the Legal Services program that had existed under the Office of Economic Opportunity: to provide quality legal help in the civil justice arena to people otherwise unable to afford it. In its practical details, however, the 1974 law was much different. There were two important differences in the LSC as created by the 1974 act.

First, the LSC was to be an independent corporation. The Legal Services program had been subject to the political exigencies of the day. Depending on the director, the program could have a radically different agenda from administration to administration. This politicization was detrimental to a consistent and uniform functioning of the program. The new LSC was to be insulated, as much as possible, from political concerns. The president, with advice and consent of the Senate, appointed the eleven members of the board of directors. Each board member could serve for no more than two consecutive three-year terms. Also, no more than six members of the board could be from one political party.

Second, the LSCA enjoined the LSC from engaging in political conduct. What this meant was that no employee of LSC, in his or her official capacity, was to encourage or engage in public dissent or picketing, civil disobedience, or striking. Nor could the LSC attempt to influence the passage or defeat of legislation—or campaign for any measure, initiative, referenda, or candidate.

Amendments in 1977 required the LSC to establish procedures for determining service priorities, taking into account the needs of clients eligible for assistance, including people with disabilities and other individuals facing special difficulties in accessing legal services.

In 1977 the LSCA was amended to address deficiencies in the original law. The amendments required the LSC to establish procedures for determining service priorities, taking into account the needs of clients eligible for assistance, including people with disabilities and other individuals facing special difficulties in accessing legal services.

See also: ECONOMIC OPPORTUNITY ACT OF 1964.

BIBLIOGRAPHY

Auerbach, Jerold S. *Unequal Justice*. New York: Oxford University Press, 1976.

George, Warren E. "Development of the Legal Services Corporation." 61 *Cornell Law Review* 681–692, 1976.

Moliterno, James E., and John M. Levy. *Ethics of the Lawyer's Work*. St. Paul, MN: West Publishing, 1993.

INTERNET RESOURCE

Legal Service Corporation. <http://www.lsc.gov/index2.htm>.

LEND-LEASE ACT (1941)

Warren F. Kimball

Excerpt from the Lend-Lease Act

The President may ... , when he deems it in the interest of national defense, ... sell, transfer title to, exchange, lease, lend, or otherwise dispose of, to any such government [whose defense the President deems vital to the defense of the United States] any defense article.... The terms and conditions ... shall be those which the President deems satisfactory.

The Lend-Lease Act of 1941 (55 Stat. 31) initiated a program of military aid by which the United States provided goods and services to its allies in the fight against Germany, Italy, and later Japan during World War II. Under the terms of "lend-lease," these allies would repay the United States not in money but by returning the goods or using them in support of the cause, or by a similar transfer of goods.

OPPOSITION TO FOREIGN AID

President Franklin Roosevelt wanted to aid the Western democracies in their fight against the Nazi and Fascist threat, but political and public opinion was opposed. For one thing, World War I had left a legacy of postwar debts. In addition, in the 1920s Americans were critical of the squabbling and colonial expansion of the European powers and were not inclined to aid even friendly nations. Then the **Great Depression** and the international economic collapse of the 1930s increased American uneasiness about doling out precious resources. In response to growing threats from Nazi Germany and Fascist Italy in the 1930s, Congress passed a series of legislative barriers, particularly the Neutrality Acts, designed to prevent the nation from being drawn into another European war by trade and investment ties with belligerent nations. Americans blamed such ties for U.S. involvement in World War I.

When war broke out in September 1939, Congress modified the prohibitions on arms trading with nations at war. But arms purchasers like Great Britain and France still had to pay cash (gold or dollars), which was in short supply as their economies moved from producing exports to arms production. In November 1940 the British Ambassador to the United States told reporters that "Britain's broke." Then, in early December, Prime Minister Winston Churchill sent President Roosevelt an eloquent plea for help, warning that "the moment approaches when we shall no longer be able to pay cash."

ROOSEVELT'S PLAN

Even before Churchill's message arrived, Roosevelt was ready to act. The German invasion of Britain had been postponed as Hitler began to look to the East. Large scale American aid held out the promise of a successful war effort against Germany without the participation of American ground troops in Europe. On December 17, 1940, Roosevelt suggested a way to give Britain the aid it needed without creating postwar debts. His new idea, he said,

Great Depression: the longest and most severe economic depression in American history (1929–1939); its effects were felt throughout the world

would get "rid of the silly, foolish old dollar sign." As he put it, the United States would lend its garden hose to help its neighbor put out the fire, with the understanding that the neighbor would repay in kind rather than receive an invoice for the dollar amount. The United States should become the "Arsenal of Democracy," Roosevelt said, and Americans seemed comfortable with the concept of paying for security while someone else fought for it. Only the so-called "isolationists" objected that Britain alone, even with American aid, could not defeat Hitler. But these isolationists were already seen as unrealistic appeasers (those willing to make concessions to an aggressor, sacrificing principles) or even as pro-Nazi.

Roosevelt had a two-part plan for translating his garden hose concept into legislation. First, the debate in and out of Congress was to *appear* full and unrestricted, though he himself might not be fully candid about how much aid he planned to give. Only a "Great Debate" would give him the mandate (an authorization to act) that he sought. Second, Roosevelt wanted a bill that gave him the widest possible latitude to decide which nations to aid, what goods to send, and what to ask for as repayment.

The bill that came under debate in Congress was called H.R. 1776, a number chosen by the Parliamentarian of the House so as to make it sound more patriotic. It was long and full and served to heighten public awareness of the geopolitical crisis in Europe. Congress did require lend-lease be carried out through annual appropriations (funds set aside for a specific purpose) and that it should receive regular reports to establish some semblance of oversight. But administration spokesmen refused to discuss certain awkward issues that seemed to move the nation toward war, especially the convoys needed to protect aid shipments from attack by German U-boats. On March 11, 1941, Roosevelt signed the Lend-Lease Act, which had passed easily in votes that generally followed party lines, as Democrats overwhelmingly supported the president.

SUCCESS OF THE PROGRAM

It took nearly two years for America's industrial potential to reach its peak, but lend-lease was a rousing success. Initially it boosted morale amongst the major U.S. allies, but it quickly began to provide the supplies they needed to fight the war. Wartime estimates, including the value of services and technological transfers, came to between $43 and $50 billion (1945 dollars) of aid to America's wartime allies. Some $8 billion of "reverse" lend-lease— mainly technology transfers and raw materials from the British and French empires— came back to the United States.

Even while lend-lease functioned as an aid and exchange program, it took on its second life as a political program. Almost as soon as the bill became law, State Department officials began to use it as a lever to force broad changes in the world's political economy. The negotiation in 1942 of a Master Lend-Lease agreement with the British included requirements for the United Kingdom to open its empire to free trade—later called free markets. American leaders had deep suspicions that Great Britain remained a major economic rival and so lend-lease was not extended into the immediate postwar period.

During the lend-lease debate, opponents had tried to exclude the Soviet Union from the program. But American strategists knew that only the Red Army could defeat Hitler on the ground, and lend-lease would help do just

The GOP elephant is torn between opposing opinions of the Lend-Lease bill held by two prominent Republicans, Senate minority leader Charles R. McNary (Oreg.) and House minority leader Joseph W. Martin (Mass.). This cartoon was published in the Washington Evening Star, *March 8, 1941.* SENATE CURATOR'S OFFICE. REPRODUCED BY PERMISSION.)

that. U.S. aid constituted only about 7 percent of what the Soviet Union itself produced during the war, but it did allow the Soviets to concentrate their production in the most efficient manner. Lend-lease to Russia was, for Roosevelt, much more than just a wartime aid program. It could demonstrate the benefits of the American system and promote mutual trust, all key elements in Roosevelt's postwar plans. It was, therefore, presidential policy to promise to give the Russians almost everything they requested. Misunderstandings and resentment resulted when supply requirements to other theaters made it impossible to deliver. The **Cold War** prevented a formal lend-lease settlement with the Russians until June 1990, when, with the Soviet system on the verge of collapse, a repayment agreement (for nonmilitary goods) was reached.

Lend-lease, what Churchill had called "the most unsordid act," was an immensely successful wartime aid program, one that set the stage for the U.S. foreign aid programs that followed. Lend-lease was designed to help win the war without leaving behind a residue of war debts and recriminations, and it did just that.

See also: NEUTRALITY ACTS.

Cold War: a conflict over ideological differences carried on by methods short of military action and usually without breaking off diplomatic relations; usually refers to the ideological conflict between the U.S. and the former U.S.S.R.

BIBLIOGRAPHY

Dobson, Alan P. *US Wartime Aid to Britain, 1940–1946*. New York: St. Martin's, 1986.

Herring, George C. *Aid to Russia, 1941–1946*. New York: Columbia University Press, 1973.

Kimball, Warren F. *The Most Unsordid Act: Lend-Lease, 1941*. Baltimore: Johns Hopkins Press, 1969.

LOBBYING DISCLOSURE ACT (1995)

Thomas Susman

A part of national politics since the beginning of the Republic, lobbying is a paid activity designed to influence decision making by government officials through some form of communication. The Lobbying Disclosure Act (LDA) of 1995 (P.L. No. 104-65, 109 Stat. 691), which replaced an inadequate and unenforceable 1946 statute, made accessible to the public, the media, and Congress information on who lobbies for whom, what issues are involved, and how much is being paid or received by the lobbyist in the process. Although the new statute continues to have shortcomings, it strikes a balance between, on the one hand, the need to encourage and foster vigorous advocacy in fulfillment of the public's right to petition the government and, on the other, the need to inhibit unethical behavior and promote transparency in what has long been viewed as an easily corrupted system.

HISTORY OF LOBBYING AND FEDERAL REGULATION OF LOBBYISTS

Historically, lobbying has too often been associated with corruption and special interests. The poet Walt Whitman wrote of "bribers, compromisers, lobbiers, spongers ... the freedom-sellers of the earth." The Crédit Mobilier scandal of the 1870s was a classic example of corrupt lobbying during the Ulysses S. Grant administration. The scandal involved a member of Congress, on the payroll of the Union Pacific Railroad, who gave shares of the railroad's stock to legislators and cabinet members to protect the company's interests in the transcontinental project.

Public outcry soon called for regulating lobbyists. Whereas state regulation of lobbying dated back to the 1870s, efforts by Congress to regulate lobbying began in the 1850s but did not reach fruition until 1946. States have used three approaches to regulating lobbying. One involved defining and prohibiting abusive lobbying practices; a second was to require registration of lobbyists. The third, used in tandem with registration, involves disclosure of expenditures, subject matter, and targets of lobbying.

The 1946 Federal Regulation of Lobbying Act attempted to incorporate the latter two approaches, but its weaknesses were exposed by a 1953 Supreme Court opinion, *United States v. Harriss*. That ruling upheld the constitutionality of the act but construed it in such a way as to render implementation meaningless and enforcement impractical. Most significant was the Court's imprecise and overly narrow definition of "lobbying" activities, which included only direct communications with members of Congress and excluded preparation, research, and all forms of grassroots activities (indirect lobbying to mobilize

Core Principles
Thomas Susman

The core principles of the Lobbying Disclosure Act can be found in the congressional findings accompanying that statute in section 2:

The Congress finds that—

(1) responsible representative Government requires public awareness of the efforts of paid lobbyists to influence the public decision-making process in both the legislative and executive branches of the Federal Government;

(2) existing lobbying disclosure statutes have been ineffective ... ; and

(3) the effective public disclosure of the identity and extent of the efforts of paid lobbyists to influence Federal officials in the conduct of Government actions will increase public confidence in the integrity of Government.

constituencies into pressuring government officials), as well as contacts with congressional staff and executive branch officials. It took Congress over forty years to replace the mortally wounded Lobbying Act with the LDA.

ENACTMENT OF THE LDA

From the 1950s through the mid-1990s, scores of bills and dozens of hearings were focused on reforming the inadequate and unenforceable 1946 statute. Following the **Watergate** scandals in the 1970s, both the House and Senate approved lobbying reform bills. Both bills were substantially stronger than the existing law but differed vastly from each other. Business, public interest, and civil liberties groups opposed them for being overly intrusive. The differences were never resolved, and the bills died in conference committee.

In 1994 history repeated itself, with both houses of Congress approving bills but none reaching the White House. (This time the House and Senate conferees resolved their differences, but the final product was killed by a Senate **filibuster**) A revised bill was introduced the following year and, principally through the efforts of Michigan Democratic Senator Carl Levin, was shepherded through Congress and onto the president's desk. It was signed by President Bill Clinton on December 19, 1995 to take effect the first day of 1996.

SCOPE AND COVERAGE OF LDA

The LDA requires registration with the Secretary of the Senate and the Clerk of the House of Representatives when a lobbyist is employed or retained to make lobbying contacts for a client if income earned or incurred expenses for lobbying activities exceed certain thresholds. A person does not become a "lobbyist," however, unless employed or retained by a client for compensation for services including more than one lobbying contact, where the lobbyist's activities for that client amount to 20 percent or more of the time that person spends on services for that client during a six-month period. Lobbying the executive branch, as well as Congress, is covered, and lobbyists must file semiannual reports detailing issues worked, agencies or houses of Congress lobbied, and money received or expended within certain ranges.

The statute establishes a number of significant exclusions and exceptions. Traditional legal representation before federal agencies is excluded, for example, as is lobbying by religious organizations and by state and local governments. The most glaring gap in coverage involves grassroots or indirect lobbying, which remains wholly outside the scope of the statute.

One method of LDA enforcement is through civil penalties of fines up to $50,000. This can occur only if a demand for compliance by one of the congressional offices where reports are filed, goes unheeded.

CONSTITUTIONAL ISSUES

When the Supreme Court upheld the constitutionality of the 1946 Lobbying Act through *Harriss,* it recognized that Congress had a need to know more about "special interest groups seeking favored treatment while masquerading as proponents of the public weal." The Court viewed the disclosure requirement of the 1946 act as a reasonable vehicle for obtaining "a modicum of

Watergate: the scandal following the break-in at the Democratic National Committee headquarters located in the Watergate apartment and office complex in Washington, D.C. in 1972

filibuster: a tactic involving unlimited debate on the floor of the House and Senate designed to delay or prevent legislative action

information from those who for hire attempt to influence legislation or who collect or spend funds for that purpose."

Two decades later, the Supreme Court in *Buckley v. Valeo* (1976) sustained the disclosure requirements of the Federal Election Campaign Act against the challenge that disclosure would unconstitutionally burden the exercise of free speech. The Court found sufficient governmental interests to overcome the constitutional challenge: the law was designed to provide the public with information, deter corruption, and gather data needed to detect violations.

Although the U.S. Supreme Court has never directly ruled that lobbying is a protected activity under the First Amendment, lower federal courts and state supreme courts in the 1970s, 1980s, and 1990s readily reached that conclusion. Restrictions on lobbying, therefore, would be subjected to a "strict scrutiny" standard. That standard demands both that a strong governmental interest be shown to justify any burden imposed on free speech and that the burden be related to the governmental interest to be served. The LDA, however, would surely meet that test under *Harriss* and *Buckley*.

EXPERIENCE UNDER THE LDA

The number of lobbyists registering under the LDA has climbed each year, surpassing 14,000 in 2002. Even so, because the law is narrowly focused, this number vastly underestimates the number of persons involved in activities designed to influence federal governmental decision making in the legislative and executive branches.

The number of lobbyists registering under the LDA has climbed each year, surpassing 14,000 in 2002.

The law has proved user-friendly for lobbyists, who may now submit registrations and reports to the relevant congressional offices electronically. Although occasional amendments have been proposed—especially ones designed to bring grassroots lobbying within the LDA's reporting requirements—none is likely to be approved soon.

The LDA is a rational, responsible tool for opening lobbying activities to public scrutiny. Despite the statute's absence of strong enforcement measures, there appears to be near universal compliance with the LDA among lobbyists in the nation's capital.

BIBLIOGRAPHY

Luneburg, William V., ed. *The Lobbying Manual: A Compliance Guide for Lawyers and Lobbyists,* 2d ed. Chicago: American Bar Association, 1998.

Potter, Trevor, ed. *Political Activity, Lobbying Laws and Gift Rules Guide,* 2d ed. Little Falls, NJ: Glasser Legal Works, 1999.

Vanderbeck, Mary Kathryn. Comment, "First Amendment Constraints on Reform of the Federal Regulation of Lobbying Act." 57 *Texas L. Rev.* 1219 (1979).

LOW-RENT HOUSING ACT

See UNITED STATES HOUSING ACT OF 1937 (WAGNER-STEGALL HOUSING ACT)

M

MAIL FRAUD AND FALSE REPRESENTATION STATUTES

Barry L. Johnson

Excerpt from the Mail Fraud and False Representation Statutes

Whoever, having devised or intending to devise any scheme or artifice to defraud ... for the purpose of executing such scheme or artifice or attempting to do so, places in any post office or authorized depository for mail matter, any matter or thing whatever to be sent or delivered by the Postal Service ... shall be fined not more than $1,000,000 or imprisoned not more than 30 years, or both.

The federal mail fraud statute, first enacted in 1872 (§ 301, 17 Stat. 323), and originally entitled "An Act to revise, consolidate, and amend the Statutes relating to the Post-office Department," makes it a federal offense to use the mails in connection with "any scheme or artifice to defraud." Together with the similar wire fraud statute, the Communications Act Amendment of 1952, which extends the mail fraud provisions to cover the use of interstate telephone lines, radio, or television to perpetrate a fraud, the mail fraud law serves as a broad and adaptable mechanism to deal with ever-changing varieties of fraud. Prosecutors have eagerly seized on this law to go after consumer frauds, investment scams, the filing of false insurance claims, election fraud, bribery, and other forms of public corruption.

THE ORIGINAL MAIL FRAUD STATUTE

The 1872 mail fraud statute was enacted as part of a larger act revising laws governing the post office. Because there was no congressional debate specifically about the mail fraud provision, it is not clear why Congress saw the law as necessary. The widespread rise of financial frauds following the Civil War may have provided the impetus for this novel extension of federal authority.

The U.S. Supreme Court's unanimous ruling in *Ex parte Jackson*, an 1877 case upholding the constitutionality of a federal antilottery law, left no doubt as to the constitutionality of the mail fraud statute. Yet some courts remained suspicious of the extension of federal law enforcement authority over crimes traditionally prosecuted by the states. The language in the statute emphasized that misuse of the post office was central to the definition of the crime, and the courts relied on this language in their narrow interpretations of the statute. This interpretation limited the law's application to frauds that could not have occurred without use of the mails. As one court explained, "not every fraudulent scheme in which mails may happen to be employed ... is made an offense against the federal law, but only such as are 'to be effected' through that medium as an essential part ...." (*United States v. Clark* 1903). An amendment to the mail fraud statute by Congress in 1909, however, rejected this narrow interpretation of the statute, setting the stage for a more expansive modern interpretation.

MODERN INTERPRETATION

Modern courts have interpreted each of the elements of the mail fraud statute broadly. For example, schemes involving virtually any use of the United States mails satisfy the statute's mailing requirement. As the 1989 ruling in *Schmuck v. United States* made clear, the mailing need not be essential to the scheme, or even support it, but may be merely incidental to the scheme. Similarly, courts have held that the wire fraud statute applies to schemes involving any interstate communication, including use of telephone lines, radio or television, fax machine or computer transmission.

In addition, for over 100 years courts have broadly interpreted the "scheme or artifice to defraud" language. For example, in its 1896 decision in *Durland v. United States*, the Supreme Court held that the statute encompassed new frauds even if they did not fit the original legal definition of fraud. Just under a century later, the Supreme Court opened the door to mail fraud prosecutions involving the fraudulent obtaining of information, extending the act's coverage beyond its traditional focus on money or goods. In the 1987 case *Carpenter v. United States*, the Court ruled that a *Wall Street Journal* reporter had engaged in mail fraud by using the newspaper's confidential information to defraud investors, trading in stocks on the basis of private information not available to the general public.

Even in rare situations in which courts have interpreted the statute narrowly, Congress has amended the law to achieve broader coverage. For example, in 1987 the Court held in *McNally v. United States* that the statute did not cover schemes to defraud citizens of their right to have officials conduct governmental affairs in an honest and impartial manner. Congress then amended the mail fraud statute to apply to honest services fraud. This amendment permits the use of the mail fraud law to prosecute public officials who accept bribes or otherwise act in a corrupt manner.

Judicial interpretation and congressional amendment have broadened the original narrow focus of the federal mail fraud statute. No longer applying solely to monetary fraud by means of the mail, it is a flexible provision that serves as federal prosecutors' first line of defense against newly invented frauds, and provides federal jurisdiction over a wide array of traditional frauds.

BIBLIOGRAPHY

Coffee, John C., Jr. "The Metastasis of Mail Fraud: The Continuing Story of the 'Evolution' of a White-Collar Crime." 21 *American Criminal Law Review* 1 (1983).

Kennedy, Shani S., and Rachel Price Flum. "Mail and Wire Fraud." 39 *American Criminal Law Review* 817 (2002).

Moohr, Geraldine Szott. "Mail Fraud Meets Criminal Theory." 67 *University of Cincinnati Law Review* 1 (1998).

Rakoff, Jed S. "The Federal Mail Fraud Statute (Part I)." 18 *Duquesne Law Review* 771 (1980).

MANN ACT (1910)

David J. Langum

The White Slave Traffic Act of 1910 (36 Stat. 825), is commonly called the Mann Act because of its congressional sponsorship by Representative James R. Mann of Illinois. Many factors led to its enactment, and once it became law it was enforced in a manner probably unforseen by its authors.

AN AGE OF ANXIETY

From 1880 to 1910, the old order of rural, largely Protestant, male-controlled America was rapidly fading. During this period immigration increased tremendously, mostly by Jews and Roman Catholics from southern and eastern Europe. Large scale urbanization was taking place, with movement from the countryside to the cities. Urbanization, together with the invention of the typewriter, the telephone switchboard, and the growth of the department store, made it possible for single women to support themselves in cities. Women could become free, for the first time in American history, from the control of a father or brother.

During this period of changes, the nation developed an anxiety over sexuality. Women did flock to the cities, shocking the older generation with their carefree dating and flirting in dance halls. Indeed, dating in the sense of a couple going off by themselves, was born in this period. Poorer families and single women in boarding houses lacked the front parlor that had been the focal point of the earlier style of courtship, where a male suitor called on a young woman and conversed with her in her own home. Traditional moralists feared the city provided a cover and an anonymity that shielded **licentious** behavior.

Another problem with cities, the rural moralists thought, was their red-light districts. America had a very **libertarian** attitude toward prostitution in the nineteenth century. Brothels were legal and openly available within segregated vice districts, and every city of even modest size had a vice district.

In the years 1907 to 1912, a moral panic developed in America. Suddenly people accepted as truth that women were being forced into prostitution, with large scale organizations mostly controlled by foreigners moving these women around the country. Lurid stories spread of young girls arriving at city train stations, only to be lured away by "cadets" who would befriend them and then drug them. The young women would wake up the next morning and find themselves raped and prisoners in a brothel. The term "white slave" came

licentious: lacking moral discipline or sexual restraint

libertarian: one who upholds the principles of absolute and unrestricted liberty and strongly opposes any government imposed restrictions

Dating in the sense of a couple going off by themselves was born in this period.

Even women already secure in the cities were thought to be in danger, and in the media nonsensical accounts multiplied of girls numbed by poison darts pushed into their legs on the subway or shot at them while walking, then kidnapped and forced into brothels.

The Department of Justice had not originally intended to prosecute the noncommercial interstate travel by boyfriends and girlfriends for the purpose of " consensual sex," yet it was led to that position by public opinion in the years 1910 to 1913.

from this scenario. Even women already secure in the cities were thought to be in danger, and in the media nonsensical accounts multiplied of girls numbed by poison darts pushed into their legs on the subway or shot at them while walking, then kidnapped and forced into brothels. Reflecting the country's general concern with business trusts, many people supposed that this enslavement of girls as prostitutes was a highly organized, almost corporate, activity. Irresponsible statements by public officials and the media fanned the hysteria.

GOVERNMENT RESPONSE TO HYSTERIA

There were two major state responses to this hysteria and one federal response. Numerous communities appointed vice commissions to investigate the extent of local prostitution, whether prostitutes participated in it willingly or were forced into it, and the degree to which it was organized by any cartel-type organizations. These commissions reported extensive prostitution, overwhelmingly locally organized without any large business structure, and willingly engaged in by the prostitutes. The second significant action at the local levels was to close the brothels and the red light districts. Brothels had always been legal nuisances and existed only by the tolerance of local officials. From 1910 to 1913, city after city withdrew this tolerance and forced the closing of their brothels. Of course, there was more to this story than the moral panic of 1907–1912. Opposition to openly practiced prostitution had been growing steadily throughout the last decades of the nineteenth century.

The federal response to the moral panic was the Mann Act. The legislative committee reports and the discussion on the floor of the Senate and House clearly indicate that the chief purpose of the act was to make it a crime to coerce transportation of unwilling women. Congress, however, used broader language. The statute made it a crime to "transport or cause to be transported, or aid or assist in obtaining transportation for" or to "persuade, induce, entice, or coerce" a woman to travel "in interstate or foreign commerce, or in any Territory or the District of Columbia" if the travel was "for the purpose of prostitution or debauchery, or for any other immoral purpose ... whether with or without her consent."

This language went far beyond coerced prostitution and clearly targeted those, both pimps and madams, who moved quite willing prostitutes from state to state. But what about the vague language "any other immoral purpose"? The Department of Justice had not originally intended to prosecute the noncommercial interstate travel by boyfriends and girlfriends for the purpose of "consensual sex," yet it was led to that position by public opinion in the years 1910 to 1913.

JUDICIAL INTERPRETATION

In three famous cases that were reported and decided together (*Caminetti v. United States; Diggs v. United States*; and *Hayes v. United States*) in 1917, the U.S. Supreme Court held that illicit fornication, whether or not for the com-

James R. Mann (1856–1922), sponsor of the White Slave Traffic Act (Mann Act) of 1910. (LIBRARY OF CONGRESS, PRINTS AND PHOTOGRAPHS DIVISION)

mercial purpose of prostitution, was an "immoral purpose" under the Mann Act. Immediately after this ruling, prosecutions were undertaken against men transporting willing adult women into another state, even if the purpose was merely to continue a sexual relationship already begun. Complaints were lodged by fathers and husbands angry over their daughters or wives' departures, nosy neighbors upset over an unmarried couple living down the hallway, and even local law enforcement officials worried about a possibly unmarried couple who had just arrived in town. A morals crusade was underway in America. Interstate womanizers could expect a term in a federal prison of between one and two years.

One consequence of this interpretation of the statute was the development of a significant blackmail industry. Women would lure male conventioneers across a state line, say from New York to Atlantic City, New Jersey and then threaten to expose them to the prosecutors for violation of the Mann Act unless paid off. Another consequence of the Court's interpretation was that it limited the mobility of women. Since it was only the movement of women by men that was criminalized, a couple living in different states had to meet only by the man traveling to the woman. For a girlfriend to travel to a boyfriend risked a Mann Act prosecution. So the protected class of the statute became its chief victim, since it virtually forbade women to travel if such travel involved a male companion.

THE END OF THE MORALS CRUSADE

By the end of the 1920s, America had had enough of its morals crusade. Prosecutors in many federal districts reported to Washington that juries would simply not convict in noncommercial cases unless there were significant special factors. The government shifted its focus to violations of the Mann Act involving prostitutes or juveniles. Other noncommercial prosecutions were limited to select types. For Mann Act prosecutions the government now targeted its political opponents (actor Charlie Chaplin, who held radical political views, was prosecuted under the Mann Act as were many German sympathizers during World War II), black men (such as boxer Jack Johnson and singer Chuck Berry) who dared to have sexual relationships with white women, gangsters (the best known is Machine Gun McGauran, a hit man for Al Capone), and miscellaneous people who had become offensive to the federal government (such as Ku Klux Klan officials).

From 1930 to 1960, Mann Act prosecutions were primarily cases of prostitutes, juveniles, and the categories described above. The **Sexual Revolution** of the 1960s forced the redefinition of "immoral purpose," and many activities denounced as an immoral purpose in the 1920s, such as strip dancing, cohabitation of an unmarried couple, or even casual sex, were declared by courts as not covered by the act. Congress was called on to amend the statute. It was difficult, however, for federal politicians to be seen as supporting

Sexual Revolution: the liberalization of social and moral attitudes towards sex and sexual relations

The Progressive Era
Alfred L. Brophy

In the beginning of the twentieth century, a series of reformers became increasingly concerned with the excesses of the "gilded age"—the period of opulent displays of wealth and seeming disregard for the health and safety of workers and consumers. For example, muckraking journalist Upton Sinclair's book *The Jungle* described the unhealthy working conditions in meatpacking plants.

Reformers sought to harness the power of government to improve the lives of workers, children, women, and the poor. They used legislation at the state level to promote minimum wages, ensure safe working conditions, limit child labor, reform prisons, improve conditions at hospitals for the mentally ill and disabled, and to limit building factories near homes.

At the federal level, the major legislation of the Progressive era included the Federal Trade Commission Act; Clayton Antitrust Act; Keating-Owen Act; Food, Drug, and Cosmetic Act; National Park Service Act; and the Mann Act, as well as four constitutional amendments—the Sixteenth, which allowed the income tax; the Seventeenth, which provided for the direct election of senators; the Eighteenth, which brought in the era of Prohibition; and the Nineteenth, which provided women the right to vote. The era ended around the beginning of the 1920s.

immoral purposes by actually repealing the act. In 1978 the statute was amended to replace the vague "immoral purpose" with "prohibited sexual conduct." Congress also amended the juvenile portion of the law, which had enhanced the possible punishment when the woman was under eighteen. It made the juvenile portion "gender neutral" in response to a large increase in juvenile homosexual prostitution.

MAJOR AMENDMENT

Finally, in 1986 the Mann Act was significantly amended, making the entire statute gender neutral. In other words, under the act the transportation of "any person" was prohibited, as was any purpose "to engage in prostitution, or in any sexual activity for which any person can be charged with a criminal offense." The federal government, aside from Native American reservations and military bases, has few laws making sexual activities as such a crime. The 1986 amendment essentially left it to the law of the state into which "any person" is transported to determine if a federal violation has occurred. Most states have decriminalized fornication and cohabitation; many have decriminalized adultery; and some have decriminalized sodomy. Therefore, the Mann Act is now effectively limited to interstate transportation for prostitution, forced sex (because it would be rape), homosexual couples (for travel into those states where sodomy is illegal), and adulterous couples (for travel into those states where adultery is illegal).

The act's unintended consequences included blackmail, selective prosecution by federal officials, and the repression of female sexuality.

The Mann Act failed to put a halt to interstate immorality; such repressive legislation seldom works. The act's unintended consequences included blackmail, selective prosecution by federal officials, and the repression of female sexuality. Worst of all, under the Mann Act people's sexuality became subject to the moral opinions of the majority. Some landed in prison for harmless conduct that did not conform to the majority's values.

BIBLIOGRAPHY

Connelly, Mark Thomas. *The Response to Prostitution in the Progressive Era.* Chapel Hill: University of North Carolina Press, 1980.

Kneeland, George J. *Commercialized Prostitution in New York City.* 1913. Reprint, Montclair, NJ: Patterson Smith, 1969.

Langum, David J. *Crossing over the Line: Legislating Morality and the Mann Act.* Chicago: University of Chicago Press, 1994.

Mackey, Thomas C. *Red Lights Out: A Legal History of Prostitution, Disorderly Houses, and Vice Districts, 1870–1917.* New York: Garland, 1987.

Vice Commission of Chicago. *The Social Evil in Chicago: A Study of Existing Conditions.* Chicago: American Vigilance Association, 1911.

MARINE MAMMAL PROTECTION ACT (1972)

Wendy Wagner

The Marine Mammal Protection Act of 1972 (P.L. 92–522, 86 Stat. 1027) is one of the first federal laws to protect animals for their own sake, rather

At the time the law was passed, there was a consensus in Congress that the act was needed to rectify the consequences of "man's impact upon marine mammals, which has ranged from what might be termed malign neglect to senseless slaughter."

than simply preventing extinction or keeping populations sustainable for harvesting. At the time the law was passed, there was a consensus in Congress that the act was needed to rectify the consequences of "man's impact upon marine mammals, which has ranged from what might be termed malign neglect to senseless slaughter." Because of competing visions of how vigorously marine mammals should be protected, however, Congress did not impose an absolute moratorium on the "taking" of marine mammals. Although the law prohibited the "harassing, catching and killing" of all "mammals which are physiologically adapted to the oceans," including whales, dolphins, seals, walruses, and manatees, it allowed for some exceptions. The most notable was allowing unintentional (or "incidental") takes of mammals from "nondepleted stocks" by commercial fishing operations, usually on the condition of obtaining a permit from the National Marine Fisheries Service (NMFS).

What Is Dolphin-Safe Tuna?

In the Eastern Tropical Pacific, tuna swim beneath schools of dolphin. During the 1950s, fishers began to encircle dolphin with nets to trap the tuna swimming below, killing thousands of dolphins in the process. Since 1991 the United States has allowed tuna to be sold with a label designating it "dolphin-safe" if nets were not intentionally set for dolphins as a means of catching the tuna. According to the National Marine Fisheries Service, this arrangement reduced dolphin deaths from hundreds of thousands to approximately 2,000 per year. In 2002, however, the regulations were relaxed so that tuna could be labeled dolphin-safe even if dolphins were encircled by the tuna nets, as long as an on-board observer certified that no dolphins were harmed or killed by the procedure. Environmental groups protested the change, arguing that the successes of the previous policy would be reversed. According to the Earth Island Institute, "The Bush administration's claim that chasing and netting of dolphins is 'safe' for dolphins is fraudulent and must be overturned by the courts."

JUDICIAL REVIEW

The MMPA is solidly grounded in Congress's power to regulate interstate commerce, as stated in the Constitution. In 1984 in *Balelo v. Baldrige*, the commercial fishery industry challenged the constitutionality of the act under the Fourth Amendment, alleging it was an unconstitutional search and seizure because it required federal observers to be stationed aboard large fishing fleets to ensure compliance. The United States Court of Appeals for the Ninth Circuit rejected this constitutional challenge, holding that commercial fishing fleets were closely regulated and did not enjoy a protected privacy right.

Beyond their role in resolving constitutional challenges to the MMPA, the courts have played a major role in the evolution of the statute, which has been amended regularly (at least once every seven years). In 1988, for example, the U.S. Court of Appeals for the District of Columbia invalidated the NFMS program for permitting the "incidental takes" of marine mammals by commercial fisheries in *Kokechik Fishermen's Association v. Secretary of Commerce*. The court held that NMFS's program did not provide adequate assurance that marine mammal populations would be maintained at optimal levels. In response, Congress amended the MMPA to provide a more comprehensive system for identifying marine mammal populations that could tolerate "incidental takes" and those populations below optimal levels which could not tolerate losses. The courts have also played an important role in enforcing the act, which authorizes both the Commerce and Interior Departments to seek civil and criminal sanctions against persons taking a marine mammal in violation of the act.

In 1991 a dispute resolution panel of the General Agreement on Tariffs and Trade (GATT) determined that the MMPA violated an international trade agreement. The panel found that the U.S. ban on the importation of tuna from Mexico, imposed because Mexican fleets caught tuna in a way that harmed dolphins, was not a justified basis for restricting trade. Although the United States lost the dispute, it resolved its differences with Mexico diplomatically. Congress passed a second statute, modified later, which banned imports from countries that did not catch tuna in a dolphin-safe manner.

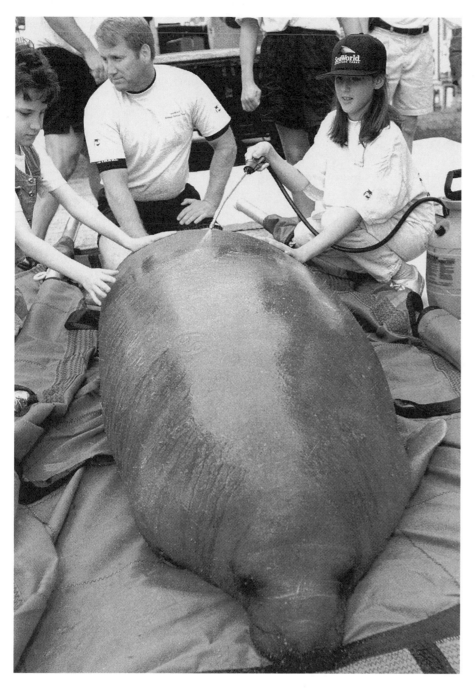

A manatee, rescued from underground drainage pipe in Cocoa Beach, Florida, is prepared for release into the Banana River. Once released, this manatee will be protected from humans by the Marine Mammal Protection Act. (© AP/WIDE WORLD PHOTOS)

EFFECTIVENESS

The MMPA appears to have made a significant difference in protecting marine mammals. For example, after the United States banned the import of tuna caught in ways that harm dolphins, the incidental deaths of dolphins dropped nearly 80 percent worldwide. The MMPA is complemented by the Marine Protection, Research, and Sanctuaries Act, which preserves marine mammal habitat more directly. The Endangered Species Act also provides more aggressive protections for marine mammals that are endangered or threatened with extinction.

See also: ENDANGERED SPECIES ACT; FISH AND WILDLIFE CONSERVATION ACT OF 1980.

BIBLIOGRAPHY

Bean, Michael J., and Melanie J. Rowland. *The Evolution of National Wildlife Law,* 3d ed. Westport, CN: Praeger, 1997.

INTERNET RESOURCES

The Marine Mammal Center. <http://www.tmmc.org/>.

National Oceanic And Atmospheric Administration. <http://www.nmfs.noaa.gov/prot_res/overview/mm.html>.

MARSHALL PLAN

See ECONOMIC COOPERATION ACT OF 1948

McKINNEY-VENTO ACT (1988)

Melanie B. Abbott

In the late 1970s the problem of homelessness became apparent to many Americans who had never before realized its scope. Throughout the United States, men, women and occasionally children were forced to live in cars, in private shelters, in overcrowded apartments, or even on the streets because they had no housing. Advocates for the homeless filed lawsuits, seeking to have courts order federal and state governments to provide shelter for those who could not provide it for themselves.

EVENTS LEADING TO THE ACT

The New York Coalition for the Homeless sued the city of New York in 1979, arguing that under the New York Constitution, in Article XVII, section 1, the state had a duty to care for the poor and must provide housing. In *Callahan v. Carey* (1981), the trial court agreed with the Coalition's argument, prompting the city to settle the case by agreeing to provide shelter for homeless New York City residents. *Callahan* represented one of relatively few court successes for advocates of the homeless. In general, litigation was not an effective approach to such a widespread and intractable problem.

In the 1980s the federal government reacted to the ever-increasing attention that states were paying to the homelessness problem. President Ronald Reagan declared in 1983, "the provision of a home and a suitable living environment for every American family continues to be a national housing goal" (Proclamation No. 5096, 48 Fed. Reg. 41,751). Despite this broad statement, however, the approach of the federal government throughout the 1980s was to focus efforts to address homelessness in the states rather than at the federal level. Many officials believed that social problems like housing were more effectively addressed by local governments.

Yet some federal officials did continue to press Congress to provide assistance for those in need of housing. One person who did so was Republican Congressman Stewart B. McKinney of Connecticut. McKinney, who represented Fairfield County, one of the wealthiest districts in the country, devoted much of his attention to the problem of homelessness. Shortly after his death in 1987, Congress passed legislation in which it acknowledged the "clear responsibility" of the federal government to deal with homelessness. In tribute to McKinney, the act was named the Stewart B. McKinney Homeless Assistance Act (P.L. 100-77, 101 Stat. 482 [1988]). In 2000 the act was renamed the McKinney-Vento Homeless Assistance Act, in memory of Democratic Congressman Bruce Vento of Minnesota, another official who was an advocate for the poor. The act was reauthorized in January 2002.

THE ORIGINAL ACT

In its original (1988) form, the McKinney-Vento Act sought to require state and local governments to implement aid programs for the homeless. In most cases, the act conditioned the awarding of federal funds on the receipt of matching funds from other sources. The act defined homelessness and created the Interagency Council on the Homeless, an independent agency within the executive branch of the government whose purpose was to coordinate and monitor federal programs for the homeless. Among the provisions authorized by the act were an emergency food and shelter program, a program for grants to **nonprofit** agencies seeking to create and operate emergency shelters, programs for the development of low-cost housing assistance and supportive services for those with mental illness or other disabilities, and programs requiring federal agencies to identify and make available surplus properties for the use of entities seeking to serve homeless people. Although the act mandates that states take the actions described, the awarding of funding in amounts sufficient to carry out the act's requirements has been uncertain. This uncertainty has become more pronounced as the federal budget has tightened.

In its original (1988) form, the McKinney-Vento Act sought to require state and local governments to implement aid programs for the homeless.

nonprofit: an organization whose business is not conducted or maintained for the purpose of making a profit, but is usually aimed at providing services for the public good

AMENDMENTS TO THE ACT

Some of the act's provisions have been strengthened in the years since its passage, in particular those concerning the education of homeless children. Under the act's original provisions, states were eligible for grants to aid local school districts in making sure homeless children received the same educational opportunities as other children. The McKinney Act was reauthorized in 2002 as part of President George W. Bush's education bill (No Child Left Behind Act of 2001).

The amended act mandated that states provide "equal access to the same free, appropriate public education" to "each child of a homeless individual and each homeless youth" (Subtitle B, Sec. 721). The act also required that homeless children be integrated into the mainstream school population and that states ensure that any residency requirements or other laws that would act as a barrier to enrollment or success of homeless children in schools be revised to remove those barriers. The revised McKinney-Vento Act also required that each state make plans to ensure that homeless children be given the opportunity to achieve the same newly created academic standards as other children in the state. Though the act required the federal government to provide funding to the states to carry out those mandates, the availability of sufficient funds has depended on the budget passed by Congress and signed by the president.

ISSUES UNDER THE ACT

The McKinney Act's provisions have an uncertain future regarding the question of whether it is appropriate for the act to be used to fund special schools

The two homeless people pictured, along with an estimated 200 other homeless persons, watched a 2000 presidential debate on a screen set up in Union Square, New York City, October 2000. The gathering was organized by the Coalition for the Homeless, a group that advocates for the homeless and affordable housing. The McKinney-Vento Act was reauthorized in January 2002, as part of the No Child Left Behind Act. (© AP/WIDE WORLD PHOTOS)

exclusively for homeless children. Such schools existed in a few places in the United States; however, successful court challenges have resulted in the limitation of plans for further development of exclusive schools. Other issues presented by the revised act's provisions included the need for transportation services for homeless children so they will be able both to attend school and to remain in the same school regardless of moves made necessary by their homeless condition, both of which are required by the act. The act also required schools to enroll homeless children immediately, even if they are unable to present the documents generally required prior to enrollment, such as school and medical records. It is likely, however, that these provisions will be challenged in court.

The McKinney-Vento Act is the basis for the federal government's attempts to address the persistent problem of homelessness. Although the act's provisions present some problems, it remains the best source for assistance available to the homeless at the federal level.

See also: HOUSING AND URBAN DEVELOPMENT ACT OF 1965.

BIBLIOGRAPHY

Kozol, Jonathan. *Rachel and Her Children: Homeless Families in America*. New York: Fawcett, 1989.

INTERNET RESOURCES

Department of Housing and Urban Development. <http://www.hud.gov/>.

National Coalition for the Homeless. <http://www.nationalhomeless.org/>.

MEDICAID ACT (1965)

Sara Rosenbaum

Enacted in 1965 as a legislative "afterthought" to Medicare, the Medicaid program (P.L. 89-97) has grown into a central part of the American health care system. Medicaid finances health needs throughout the entire life cycle: In 1999 the program funded nearly one-third of all U.S. births and approximately one-half of all nursing home care. It is the largest single funder in the treatment of HIV/AIDS and for serious mental illness, and provides more than a third of the revenues used to support the health care "safety net" for low-income, uninsured, and medically underserved persons. Medicaid insures nearly 14 percent of the nonelderly population and 20 percent of all children. In **fiscal year** 2002, combined federal and state Medicaid expenditures totaled nearly $250 billion, virtually equaling Medicare spending levels. Total program enrollment that year stood at forty-four million persons, making Medicaid the nation's largest single public insurance program.

Medicaid's structural elasticity and its resulting ability to respond to national health priorities involving individuals and conditions considered uninsurable in the commercial market explain its importance to the health

Statistics on Homelessness
Melanie B. Abbott

Homelessness tripled during the 1980s.

About 3.5 million people, 1.35 million of them children, are likely to experience homelessness in a given year.

As many as 20 percent of people seeking emergency shelter are turned away due to lack of resources.

In 1993, there were two million fewer low-rent homes on the market than there had been in 1973—because they were demolished or abandoned or because their prices increased.

In Miami, there is a seven-year wait for public housing.

In 1995, 36 million Americans lived in poverty.

Fourteen million families have critical housing needs. In 2002, families with children made up 41 percent of the urban homeless population.

Fifty percent of homeless women and children are fleeing abuse.

fiscal year: the term used for a business's accounting year; the period is usually twelve months which can begin during any month of the calendar year

Medicaid finances health needs throughout the entire life cycle: In 1999 the program funded nearly one-third of all U.S. births and approximately one-half of all nursing home care.

system. Legislators have amended Medicaid dozens of times since its original enactment to add numerous classes of eligible persons and covered services to address the range of priorities that have arisen over the nearly four decades since the law's original enactment. Examples include coverage for low-income pregnant women, uninsured women with breast and cervical cancer, community-based health care for children and adults with severe disabilities and at risk for institutionalization, workers with disabilities, and transitional insurance for families moving from welfare to work. Medicaid also has come to play a critical role in compensating for Medicare's limitations by offering premium and cost-sharing assistance to lower-income Medicare beneficiaries, as well as supplemental coverage for low income and medically needy beneficiaries for the many benefits and services that Medicare does not cover. This is particularly the case for prescription outpatient drugs and long-term care.

MEDICAID'S COMPLEXITY

The federal Medicaid statute is extremely complex, made so by two factors. The first is the program's historic ties to cash welfare payment principles. Originally Congress limited mandatory eligibility classifications to families with children and elderly and disabled persons receiving cash welfare. It significantly modified these rules over the years to either mandate or permit coverage for certain groups of low-income persons other than those who receive cash welfare assistance, but it never entirely replaced the original rules. The result is a complicated eligibility scheme that offers more than five dozen separate eligibility categories, some mandatory, others optional, encompassing pregnant women, children, families with children, and elderly and disabled adults. Poverty and low income (either outright or as the result of having incurred catastrophic medical expenses) are hallmarks of virtually all eligibility categories.

The federal Medicaid statute is extremely complex.

Ironically, no federal eligibility category exists for nondisabled, nonelderly, nonpregnant adults without children, even though these persons comprise a significant proportion of the nation's forty-two million uninsured persons. A number of states do extend coverage to such individuals by operating their Medicaid programs as "demonstrations" under the legal authority of Section 1115 of the Social Security Act. This provision of law, which dates back to 1963 (pre-Medicaid), permits the Secretary of the U.S. Department of Health and Human Services to waive otherwise applicable provisions of certain Social Security Act grant-in-aid programs in order to conduct welfare demonstrations that further federal objectives. Only a minority of states have expanded Medicaid eligibility standards in this fashion.

The second factor contributing to Medicaid's complexity is the program's special coverage structure. Several classes of benefits are federally required as a condition of state participation, and states must cover reasonable levels of benefits and services for their enrolled populations. Coverage is particularly comprehensive for children under twenty-one. The program either bars outright or severely curtails the use of patient cost-sharing and premiums. Unlike commercial health insurance or Medicare, Medicaid contains no pre-existing condition exclusion clauses or waiting periods. In addition, the statute bars discrimination in the provision of required services on the basis of a condition. For example, the types of hospital and medical care coverage limitations found in commercial plans for persons with HIV or mental illness would be impermissible in Medicaid.

Medicaid's legal structure accounts for its growth over the years. It is also this structure and its attendant costs that account for the deep controversy surrounding the program. Medicaid is a grant-in-aid program that provides federal assistance to states with approved plans to help defray the cost of extending covered benefits to eligible individuals when furnished by participating providers. The federal financial participation rate ranges from 50 to 77 percent of each dollar spent by a state on medical assistance under an approved state plan. Unlike other grant-in-aid programs, however, there is no aggregate upper limit on this federal contribution level: federal financing is open-ended and limited only by a state's own desires to contain the size and scope of their plans.

From a legal point of view, Medicaid is unique because unlike other grant-in-aid programs, it is an individually enforceable legal entitlement in the case of persons eligible for and receiving services under a state plan. Furthermore, enforceability is not simply an issue for beneficiaries. States have an enforceable right to payment, and participating health care providers that furnish covered services to eligible persons have a legally enforceable federal right to payment, although in recent years Congress has reduced provider protections by repealing key provider payment standards.

Medicaid is a grant-in-aid program that provides federal assistance to states with approved plans to help defray the cost of extending covered benefits to eligible individuals when furnished by participating providers.

FUNDING CONTROVERSIES

Medicaid's controversy also relates to its sheer size and its legal entitlements; the law mandates continued funding increases, even as the number of persons and the cost and intensity of health care increase. State officials facing the worst financial crisis since the **Great Depression** have responded in 2003 with efforts to reduce Medicaid spending through reductions in "optional" eligibility, benefits, and provider payments. Although two-thirds of all Medicaid expenditures are attributable to "optional" benefits and services, the reality is such that these "options" are politically sensitive. For example, most nursing home expenditures are optional, as is coverage of women with breast cancer, prescription drug coverage, and residential facilities for persons with mental retardation.

Great Depression: the longest and most severe economic depression in American history (1929–1939); its effects were felt throughout the world

Repeated calls for program reforms range from expanding existing eligibility and benefit rules in order to reduce the number of uninsured Americans or to respond to specific health problems (such as breast and cervical cancer) to eliminating much of the program and replacing it with aggregate **block grants** to states, as called for by the Bush administration in 2003. Most reform efforts are viewed as so politically and economically difficult that in many respects, Medicaid has remained essentially untouched since its original enactment, merely expanding in both scope and complexity over the years as needs arose. Whether this cycle of public outcry over program costs produces different results remains to be seen.

block grant: an unrestricted grant of federal money to state and local governments to support social welfare programs

See also: MEDICARE ACT; SOCIAL SECURITY ACT OF 1935.

BIBLIOGRAPHY

Schneider, Andy, et al. *The Medicaid Resource Book*. Washington, DC: Kaiser Family Foundation, 2003.

INTERNET RESOURCES

National Health Law Program. <http://www.healthlaw.org>.

Center for Medicare and Medicaid Services. <http://www.cms.gov>.

MEDICARE ACT (1965)

Kevin Outterson

Unlike most industrialized nations, the United States does not guarantee access to health care or health insurance for all of its population. Employers are the major providers of health insurance for working people and their dependents. But two major government programs also exist to ensure that Americans have access to health insurance: Medicaid provides health insurance for the poor, and Medicare provides health insurance for individuals sixty-five and over and the disabled. Gaps in coverage are evident, and approximately forty million Americans are uninsured at some point in a year.

Medicare is a federal program, funded from a mix of payroll taxes, premiums, and general tax revenues. On the benefits side, the government spent roughly $271 billion in 2003, 13 percent of the federal budget. Medicaid, by contrast, is a cooperative program between the states and the federal government. States administer the health insurance, and the federal government provides oversight and funding assistance. Approximately half of the Medicaid costs are borne by the states, with the federal government contributing the balance out of general tax revenues. Total Medicaid expenditures in 2002 were $210 billion.

THE CONSTITUTIONAL BASIS FOR MEDICARE

Congress designed Medicare to promote the general welfare of the United States. The program's financing mechanisms proceed under the taxing and spending powers, together with the **commerce clause**. Although some groups have challenged various features of the law, no litigant has challenged the Constitutional basis of the act as a whole.

CIRCUMSTANCES LEADING TO THE ADOPTION OF MEDICARE

Prior to the adoption of Medicare and Medicaid, health insurance in the United States was primarily an employee benefit. In the late 1950s, however, Congress observed that two groups were left out of the employment-focused model: the retired elderly and the unemployed poor. President Lyndon Johnson's landslide election in 1964 paved the way for the adoption of Medicare and Medicaid in 1965.

While the programs garnered much support in Congress, they were also subject to debate and negotiation. The American Medical Association, for example, opposed the federal intervention into healthcare as "socialized

Commerce Clause: the provision of the U.S. Constitution (Article I, section 8, clause 3) that gives Congress exclusive powers over interstate commerce—the buying, selling, or exchanging of goods between states

medicine." This opposition originally led Congress to make Medicare a voluntary program and led to provisions that awarded physicians with generous pay for their work. The language of the Medicare statute reflects the imprint of the American Medical Association:

> Nothing in this title shall be construed to authorize any Federal officer or employee to exercise any supervision or control over the practice of medicine or the manner in which medical services are provided ... or to exercise any supervision or control over the administration or operation of any such [health-care] institution, agency, or person.

More recently, however, Medicare has become less voluntary for the vast majority of providers, the payment rates are significantly less generous, and the federal government exercises great influence over the delivery of health care services.

ADMINISTRATION AND STRUCTURE OF THE MEDICARE PROGRAM

The Centers for Medicare and Medicaid Services (CMS), a federal agency within the Department of Health and Human Services (DHHS) administers Medicare and Medicaid. DHHS also includes the Food and Drug Administration, the Centers for Disease Control and Prevention (CDC) and the National Institutes of Health (NIH).

Medicare does not provide health care directly to seniors. The vast majority of physicians, hospitals, and related providers participate in the Medicare program. If a Medicare enrollee receives a "covered service" or product (such as a physician's visit or surgical procedure), Medicare will pay. Medicare only pays for covered services, which in 2003 still did not include important items such as outpatient prescription drugs or long-term nursing home care. A small minority of Medicare enrollees are able to purchase supplemental health insurance (known as "Medigap" policies) to provide coverage in these areas.

Congress divided Medicare into three parts, each of which covers unique services:

Medicare Part A covers inpatient hospital stays for ninety days per illness, plus sixty lifetime reserve days. Part A also covers up to 100 days per illness for post-hospital skilled nursing facility (SNF) care, hospice, and some home health care. Every person eligible for Social Security and over the age of sixty-five is eligible for Medicare Part A. Medicare enrollees are not charged premiums for Part A, but are subject to deductibles and co-insurance similar to commercial insurance programs. Part A is also a primary funding source for graduate medical education in the United States.

Part B covers physician services and many outpatient hospital, diagnostic, therapy, and many other medical services. Medicare Part B is optional, although most Part A enrollees also sign up for Part B. Part B enrollees must pay a monthly insurance premium to CMS, and are also subject to deductibles and co-insurance.

Part C is the Medicare HMO program, called Medicare Plus Choices. Medicare Part C is an optional Medicare HMO, which enrollees may choose instead of Parts A and B. The HMO sets the additional premiums for Part C, and any deductibles, coinsurance and additional benefits, within the limits set by CMS. For example, about 10 to 15 percent of Medicare enrollees receive some limited prescription drug benefit by enrolling in a Medicare HMO under Part C.

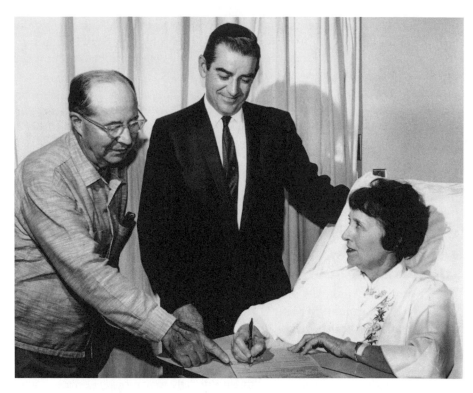

The nation's first Medicare beneficiary, Lillian Grace Avery, signs Medicare forms at Edward Hospital in Naperville, Illinois, July 1, 1966. (© AP/WIDE WORLD PHOTOS)

THE GROWTH AND EXPENSE OF THE MEDICARE PROGRAM

Many of the services now covered by Medicare were not part of the original benefit package. Over time, Congress has added coverage for home health, hospice, end-stage renal disease, and many other services in response to political demands and medical needs. Congress also added coverage for the disabled in 1972. The legislature is currently debating whether to add an outpatient prescription drug benefit to Medicare, one recommendation from the **Bipartisan** Commission on Medicare established under former President Bill Clinton.

The process of gradually adding benefits to Medicare is called *incrementalism*. In Medicaid, incrementalism has focused more on expanding eligibility to the near-poor and children. In July, 2003, Congress debated a new prescription drug benefit for Medicare. Expanded coverage predictably results in higher costs. National health care expenditures are more than 14 percent of the **gross domestic product** in 2003, up from seven percent in 1970. The **median** cost for health care in industrialized nations in 2000 was about eight percent. The growth in U.S. health care expenses continues to outpace the growth in the domestic economy, and to account for a large and growing share of government budgets at all levels. Medicare cost $7.7 billion in 1970; thirty years later the cost exceeded $224 billion per year. Medicaid and private health insurance have experienced **inflation**. Medicare has increasingly adopted price controls and managed care techniques in an attempt to control costs.

Cost-cutting measures in Medicare have either been patient-directed incentives to reduce medical utilization (deductibles, co-insurance, time limitations, and exclusions) and price controls to reduce payments to

bipartisan: involving members of two parties, especially the two political parties

gross domestic product: the total market value of goods and services produced within a nation in a given time period (usually one year)

median: the middle value in a distribution above and below which lie an equal number of values

inflation: a general rise in the prices of goods and services

providers. Medicare now sets specific prices for most health care services to enrollees. While the price is technically the only amount Medicare will reimburse, in practice the provider is not allowed to charge the patient any additional amount, other than the deductible and co-insurance. Medicare also punishes a provider for any discounts or rebates to patients, as a form of "fraud." As a result, the Medicare price list controls a large slice of the U.S. health care market.

MEDICARE LITIGATION

Medicare spawns much litigation nationwide. Some court controversies involve administrative issues, such as whether or not a particular service or product is covered by Medicare. Many providers run afoul of the complex Medicare rules and regulations regarding the provision of care and reimbursement under Medicare. Some of these cases are prosecuted as Medicare "fraud," although many providers claim the rules are so complex that innocent mistakes are common. The most significant litigation for patients has concerned the process that the government must follow when denying or limiting benefits, including the right to a hearing before benefits are restricted.

See also: MEDICAID ACT.

BIBLIOGRAPHY

Jost, Timothy S. *The Threats Facing our Public Health-care Programs and a Rights-based Response.* Oxford, NY: Oxford University Press, 2003.

Marmor, Theodore R. *The Politics of Medicare.* New York: A. de Gruyter, 2000.

Vladeck, Bruce C. "Medicare and the Politics of Incrementalism." 26 J *Health Politics, Policy and Law* 153 (Feb. 2001).

MERCHANT MARINE ACT OF 1920

Michael McClintock

The President of the United States has just been briefed by the national security advisor on a critical situation developing overseas. A close ally of the United States has come under attack from a hostile nation, and the president has decided to immediately deploy U.S. military forces to assist the defense of our ally. To whom will the president turn to in order to get the majority of U.S. military personnel, equipment, and weapons overseas? The answer is not the Army, Navy, Air Force, or Marines. Rather, the job of transporting our military forces and equipment in such a scenario is the job of the U.S. Merchant Marine.

The U.S. Merchant Marine is the fleet of civilian owned and crewed ships carrying imports and exports during peacetime, which becomes a naval auxiliary during wartime to deliver troops and war material. The Merchant Marine, as a

> *The U.S. Merchant Marine is the fleet of civilian owned and crewed ships carrying imports and exports during peacetime, which becomes a naval auxiliary during wartime to deliver troops and war material.*

cohesive and distinct arm of U.S. commerce and defense, began during the Revolutionary War and was then known as the Colonial Merchant Marine. The best known captain in the Colonial Merchant Marine was John Paul Jones, who committed his private merchant fleet to the development of the United States Navy. The Merchant Marine Act of 1920 is commonly referred to as the "Jones Act," named after the legislation's sponsor, Senator Wesly L. Jones of Washington, though it is a common misconception the act is named after Captain John Paul Jones.

At the turn of the nineteenth century the United States had completed a period of continental development and overcome the turmoil of the Civil War. By the dawn of the next century, the need for a strong and viable modern merchant fleet had become a political priority, driven by several factors. One consideration was the ascension of Britain as a world power, based in great part on its merchant fleet, control of the world's shipping lanes, and its steadfast adherence to a national maritime philosophy embodied in the quote by Sir Walter Raleigh, as "Whosoever commands the sea commands trade; whosoever commands the trade of the world commands the riches of the world, and consequently the world itself." Another important factor was America's need for a large sea lift capability in time of defense, realized during World War I. Lastly, the most important maritime development in this period was the converson of ships from coal to oil-burning, made possible through the development of a process to refine petroleum. Before World War I approximately only one percent of the world's merchant and naval vessels burned oil for fuel. By the end of 1918 the number of oil burning ships had risen to nearly 15 percent and continued to climb until coal-burning ships had become totally obsolete by the commencement of World War II.

At this same time, however, the volume of cargo and international trade for the U.S. merchant fleet had drastically decreased due to the economic decline and global turmoil caused by World War I. Further complicating the ability of the U.S. merchant fleet to compete in international commerce were higher construction and operation costs. For example, in 1926 the comparative monthly crew costs for ships of equal size were: $3,270 for the United States; $1,308 for Great Britain; and $777 for Japan. Historically, the United States curbed the impact of such issues through "cabotage laws," which are government measures used to protect or foster a domestic shipping industry by reserving all or a portion of international sea commerce to ships which fly the national flag.

Cabotage laws were first introduced with the Shipping Act of 1916. The Shipping Act provided, among other things, that only citizens of the United States, or companies in which a controlling interest was held by a citizen of the United States, could own a U.S. vessel. Additionally, the secretary of transportation had strict control over the transfer and chartering of U.S. vessels to foreign companies, and the Shipping Act provided for the regulation of rate agreements to avoid rate wars.

While most considered the Merchant Marine Act of 1920 the most important cabotage law, this act represented both the commitment of the United States to maintaining a strong and viable merchant fleet for commerce and defense, and its awareness that the fleet could not profitably operate in unregulated competition.

Subsequently, Congress passed the Merchant Marine Act of 1920, which was arguably the nation's most important cabotage law. At the time the Merchant Marine Act was passed into law, the act represented both the commitment of the United States to maintaining a strong and viable merchant fleet for commerce

World War II poster, advertising the Merchant Marine. The Merchant Marine played an important role in World War II, providing logistical support for the armed forces stationed across both the Atlantic and Pacific Oceans. (US NATIONAL ARCHIVES AND RECORDS ADMINISTRATION)

and defense, and its awareness that its merchant fleet could not profitably operate in unregulated competition. The opening paragraph of the act, entitled "Purpose and Policy of the United States," summarized this commitment:

> It is necessary for the national defense and for the proper growth of its foreign and domestic commerce that the United States shall have a merchant marine of the best equipped and most suitable types of vessels sufficient to

It is also important to note that many of the merchant fleets of other countries are highly subsidized by their governments, making it more difficult for the U.S. merchant fleet to compete in international commerce.

carry the greater portion of its commerce and serve as a naval auxiliary in time of war or national emergency, ultimately to be owned and operated privately by citizens of the United States; and it is the declared policy of the United States to do whatever may be necessary to develop and encourage the maintenance of such a merchant marine.

The Merchant Marine Act provided many measures to protect and foster the U.S. Merchant Marine. Most important, the act restricted the transport of goods from points within the United States to vessels constructed and registered in the United States and owned by U.S. citizens or companies. In this regard, the act further provided that any vessel lawfully engaging in the coastwise "Jones Act" trade must never have been foreign-owned at any time and never registered under a foreign flag or rebuilt abroad. Any cargo shipped in violation of the Jones Act is subject to seizure and forfeiture to the U.S. government.

The U.S. merchant fleet, however, continued to be plagued by its inability to compete in unregulated international commerce despite the passage of the Merchant Marine Act of 1920. The U.S. merchant fleet has declined steadily since the end of World War II and, from 1947 to 1999, the U.S. merchant fleet fell from approximately 4,400 vessels to less than 500 vessels. Numerous reasons are thought to have contributed to the decline, including lower standards of health, welfare, and safety for foreign merchant mariners leading to lower operating costs; discrimination by foreign countries against U.S. merchant vessels engaged in international trade; tax advantages of operating foreign-registered vessels; aggressive labor unions in the United States; and the decline of the nation's steel production industry. It is also important to note that many of the merchant fleets of other countries are highly subsidized by their governments, making it more difficult for the U.S. merchant fleet to compete in international commerce.

In response to the continual decline of the U.S. merchant fleet, Congress passed new legislation to assist the maritime industry, including the Maritime Security Act of 1996. Pursuant to this act, the government acquired and has been maintaining a fleet of merchant ships, known as the "Ready Reserve Fleet" (RRF) to ensure that there are sufficient U.S. merchant vessels to support military operations worldwide. Further, the United States continues to fund and operate the U.S. Merchant Marine Academy in Kings Point, New York, a four-year military academy vital to providing properly trained officers and executives for the transportation industry.

See also: SHIPPING ACTS.

MIGRATORY BIRD CONSERVATION ACT OF 1929

Marc A. Le Forestier

Excerpt from the Migratory Bird Conservation Act

For the acquisition, including the location, examination, and survey, of suitable areas of land, water, or land and water, for use as migratory bird reservations, and necessary expenses incident thereto, and for the administration, maintenance, and development of such areas and other preserves, reservations, or breeding grounds frequented by migratory birds and under the administration of the Secretary of the Interior, including the construction of dams, dikes, ditches, flumes, spillways, buildings, and other necessary improvements, and for the elimination of the loss of migratory birds from alkali poisoning, oil pollution of waters, or other causes, for cooperation with local authorities in wildlife conservation, for investigations and publications relating to North American birds, for personal services, printing, engraving, and issuance of circulars, posters, and other necessary matter and for the enforcement of the provisions of this subchapter, there are hereby authorized to be appropriated, in addition to all other amounts authorized by law to be appropriated, $200,000 for the fiscal year ending June 30, 1940, and for each fiscal year thereafter.

By the end of the nineteenth century, the wildlife conservation movement was beginning to develop support within American government. In 1900 Congress passed the first federal wildlife protection law, the Lacey Act, which made it a federal crime to transport wildlife across a state border if it had been taken in violation of state law. During the next thirty years such organizations as the National Audubon Society and the Wildlife Management Institute were formed to advance the objectives of the conservation movement. It is no coincidence that as the last of the passenger pigeons (*Ectopistes migratorius*) died in the Cincinnati Zoological Gardens in 1914, migratory birds became an early focus of the federal government's special attention. The extinction of game bird species also mobilized hunters and the sporting arms and ammunition industries, who convinced Congress to pass conservation laws that would assist states in protecting wildlife populations for sport.

The Migratory Bird Conservation Act of 1929 (45 Stat. 1222) exemplifies this cooperative federal-state approach. Migratory birds had already been placed under federal protection in 1913, and in 1916 they were the subject of a treaty between the United States and Great Britain (for Canada). This treaty, together with state and federal laws directed at the practice of plume hunting, would help reverse the decline in migratory bird populations. The Migratory Bird Conservation Act was designed to provide sanctuaries in which these birds could live.

The principal sponsor of the Migratory Bird Conservation Act was Senator Peter Norbeck, Republican from South Dakota. The act first emerged, in concept, in Senator Norbeck's 1923 proposal known as the "game refuge bill," which would have established a joint federal-state system of shorebird sanctuaries financed by federal hunting license fees. Conservationists, however, were alarmed that the bill would establish these game refuges as "public shooting grounds." Norbeck rewrote the proposal, eliminating the hunting provisions and providing that refuge funds would be appropriated directly from the federal treasury.

The act also established the Migratory Bird Conservation Commission to approve the purchase or rental of areas of land or water as sanctuaries for migratory birds and water fowl, upon the recommendation of the secretary of the Department of the Interior. Such acquisitions may be completed only after consultation with affected local and state governments, and are financed by the Migratory Bird Conservation Fund, also established by the act. The

The Migratory Bird Conservation Act was designed to provide sanctuaries in which these birds could live.

The wild ducks in this photo (c. 1930s) were seized from a market hunting operation—the mass hunting of game birds in order to sell them as food. (© US Fish and Wildlife Service)

fund also provides resources for maintenance of the acquired lands, the preservation of habitat, and for any other related expenses.

When it became clear that the $7.8 million dollars originally appropriated under the Migratory Bird Conservation Act would be insufficient to accomplish its purposes, Congress enacted the Migratory Bird Hunting Stamp Act of 1934, which required all hunters to attach stamps to their state hunting licenses, providing additional funds for the creation of sanctuaries. In 1937 the Pittman-Robertson Bill imposed an **excise tax** on guns and shells to extract more funds from hunters for the benefit of wildlife. Together, these acts have constituted the most effective wildlife conservation scheme on record.

excise tax: a tax levied on the manufacture or sale of specific—usually non-essential—commodities such as tobacco or liquor

BIBLIOGRAPHY

Gibbons, Felton. *Neighbors to the Birds: A History of Birdwatching in America.* New York: W.W. Norton & Company, 1988.

Lund, Thomas A. *American Wildlife Law.* Berkeley: University of California Press, 1980.

MILITIA ACT (1862)

Daniel W. Hamilton

On July 17, 1862, Congress passed the Militia Act, calling on the president to employ "persons of African descent" in military or naval service. This was, importantly, a change in policy. At the start of the Civil War, the War Department refused to accept blacks who volunteered for the Union army. In its relative openness the Militia Act was, however, far from egalitarian in design or practice. The act expressly provided that black soldiers would be paid significantly less than white soldiers. Similarly, while the act did not preclude blacks from serving as Union army soldiers, Lincoln instead initially used blacks in noncombatant roles as scouts, laborers, and nurses. In this clumsy, discriminatory fashion the Union took its first halting steps towards what became one of the most important social, military, and political developments of the Civil War—the widespread participation of black soldiers in the war.

Black abolitionists, most importantly Frederick Douglass, from the start of the war lobbied furiously for the enlistment of black soldiers. Fighting a popular perception that blacks would run from battle, Douglass pressed for black regiments not only to aid the war effort, but as an invaluable political tool in the fight against slavery and for greater racial equality. In Douglass' *Monthly,* he declared: "Once let the black man get upon his person the brass letters, U.S.; let him get an eagle on his button, and a musket on his shoulder and bullets in his pocket, and there is no power on earth which can deny that he has earned the right to citizenship."

On the same day as passage of the Militia Act Congress, the Second Confiscation Act similarly authorized the president to employ blacks in the suppression of the rebellion in any manner he deemed best. The president soon thereafter, in the Emancipation Proclamation issued on January 1, 1863,

The act also stipulated that any slave of a disloyal master who served in the military was to be freed, as were his family members.

announced his intention to enlist black soldiers and sailors. Union generals in the field in Kansas, in Louisiana, and the South Carolina Sea Islands had already, by the summer of 1862 organized black regiments. On August 25, 1862 the War Department officially authorized the recruitment of black regiments in the Sea Islands of South Carolina. A few months later, in October 1862, a Kansas regiment of black soldiers took part in a small battle in Missouri. Ten blacks were killed, and so became the first black combat casualties of the Civil War. A few months afterwards, Governor John Andrew of Massachusetts obtained permission from the War Department to form a black regiment. Andrew, however, received enough volunteers to form two regiments, and organized the 54th and 55th Massachusetts Regiments. In May of 1862 the War Department created a Bureau of Colored Troops. Ultimately, nearly 180,000 black troops fought for the Union army, comprising 10 percent of all Union soldiers.

The use of black soldiers sparked intense controversy in the North and South. In the Union, resistance to the use of black troops in battle remained steadfast. Black soldiers were consistently discriminated against in pay, in bounties, and even in receiving medicine. Only in June 1864, after a number of black soldiers complained to Lincoln himself, did the federal government end discriminatory pay practices. In the Confederacy the use of black troops provoked outrage. Some generals in the field declared that any black soldier captured would be summarily executed, and any white officer leading black troops be put on trial for promoting insurrection. This threat became real in April 1864, when Confederate troops under Nathan B. Forrest massacred hundreds of surrendering black soldiers at Fort Pillow, Tennessee. During the war, the extraordinary sacrifice of black troops in the field slowly changed Northern public opinion on the role of black troops. Most notably, the 54th Massachusetts Regiment lost nearly half its men in a heroic assault on Fort Wagner in Charleston Harbor on July 18, 1863, resulting in widespread commentary and admiration in the army and in the Northern press.

> *During the war, the extraordinary sacrifice of black troops in the field slowly changed northern public opinion on the role of black troops.*

The increasing numbers of black soldiers and their heroic sacrifices, made nearly impossible any negotiated peace with the Confederacy that preserved slavery. Some black soldiers were free men before the war, but the majority of black soldiers were slaves at the beginning of the war. Lincoln, who credited black soldiers with providing "the heaviest blow yet dealt to the rebellion," made it clear he would not permit the enslaving of any soldier. Otherwise, he feared: "I should be damned in eternity for so doing." Black soldiers, it was recognized, were fighting to end slavery and their devotion to this struggle was perhaps the most powerful testimony against the continuing existence of the institution. Frederick Douglass was, in short, right. Once blacks in sufficient numbers put on a Union uniform and carried a gun into battle on behalf of the Union, a peace settlement preserving slavery was an increasingly distant possibility.

See also: ENROLLMENT ACT; FIRST AND SECOND CONFISCATION ACTS.

BIBLIOGRAPHY

Andrews, William L., and William S. McFeely, eds. *Narrative of the Life of Frederick Douglass, An American Slave, Written by Himself.* New York: Norton 1997.

Donald, David H., et al. *The Civil War and Reconstruction.* New York: Norton, 2001.

Gienapp, William E. *Abraham Lincoln and Civil War America* New York: Oxford University Press, 2002.

McPherson, James M. *Battle Cry of Freedom*. New York: Ballentine Books, 1989.

MINERAL LEASING ACT (1920)

Brian E. Gray

The Mineral Leasing Act (41 Stat. 437) is one of the cornerstones of the reservation era in federal public lands policy. During this era, Congress recognized that certain public lands should be withdrawn from entry under the Homestead Act, the General Mining Law, and other statues authorizing the transfer of the federal public domain to private ownership. Instead, federal reserved lands would be retained by the United States for managed economic uses and preservation of certain natural resources in service of the national interest. The Mineral Leasing Act followed the Organic Act of 1897, which created the National Forest System, and the National Park Service Act of 1916.

BACKGROUND

At the beginning of the twentieth century, the vast oil reserves of the American West rested largely unknown and undeveloped. Although California was the fifth-largest petroleum producing state, the region as a whole contributed only about 9 percent of the nation's oil supplies. From 1900 to 1910, however, the petroleum industry, dominated by giants such as Standard Oil, Union Oil, Prairie Oil & Gas, Phillips Petroleum, and the Southern Pacific and Santa Fe Railroads, shifted its new exploration and drilling to the western lands. By 1911, the year the Supreme Court upheld the breakup of the Standard Oil Trust, the West's share of United States oil production had grown to 72 percent.

Most of the western drilling was on private or state lands in Texas, Oklahoma, Kansas, and California. As the demand for fuel oil rose, the petroleum companies turned to the federal public lands, particularly those in the northern Great Plains and California, for suitable crude oil. Deposits in the Los Angeles basin and San Joaquin Valley were highly valued, because the crude oil there was rich in high-octane hydrocarbons, which made it well suited for refinement into gasoline.

The petroleum deposits of the federal public lands were especially attractive to America's corporate oil barons for two reasons. First, the cost of exploration and extraction generally would be less than for the deposits located in the Gulf of Mexico or off the California coast. Second, Congress had confirmed in the Oil Placer Act of 1897 that all public lands "containing petroleum or other mineral oils and chiefly valuable therefore" were "free and open to occupation, exploration, and purchase" under the General Mining Law of 1872. The Mining Act authorized all citizens to enter onto the

> The Mining Act authorized all citizens to enter onto the public lands to prospect for minerals (such as gold, silver, copper, and lead, as well as oil and other fossil fuels), and it allowed the discoverer to stake multiple claims both to the minerals and to their surrounding lands.

public lands to prospect for minerals (such as gold, silver, copper, and lead, as well as oil and other fossil fuels), and it allowed the discoverer to stake multiple claims both to the minerals and to their surrounding lands. The only legal requirements for the establishment of a claim were that the mine be capable of producing minerals in "valuable quantities" and that the miner spend at least $100 each year on labor or capital improvements at the site. Upon satisfaction of these minimal conditions, the locator of the minerals could extract and market the minerals without royalty or other recompense to the United States. After expenditure of $500 of labor or capital investment, the miner also could purchase the land adjacent to the minerals for five dollars per acre.

OPEN-ACCESS POLICY

The advantages of the open-access policy were offset by two other realities. From the miner's perspective, free access encouraged competition for the mineral deposits and rewarded those who first located the minerals. The miner's custom of "first-in-time, first-in-right" meant that interests other than the big American oil companies could stake claims to the petroleum deposits of the western public lands. Indeed, in 1913 a subsidiary of Royal Dutch Shell claimed thousands of acres of rich oil fields in California's San Joaquin Valley and began pumping crude oil 200 miles north to the Shell refinery on San Francisco Bay.

An even greater flaw in the open-access policy had broader social implications.

CHANGING THE POLICY: THE PICKETT ACT

On September 17, 1909, the director of the U.S. Geological Survey reported to the secretary of the interior that companies acting under the General Mining Law were claiming the petroleum deposits of the public lands in California at such a rate that it would "be impossible for the people of the United States to continue ownership of oil lands for more than a few months. After that, the Government will be obliged to repurchase the very oil that it has practically

Oil Drilling in the Arctic National Wildlife Refuge

In August 2003, as the United States recovered from the biggest blackout in the nation's history, a major Congressional energy bill was stalled due to differences over increased oil drilling in Alaska's Arctic National Wildlife Refuge (ANWR). Republicans insisted that a provision for new drilling be included, arguing that domestic oil production should be stepped up to reduce dependence on international sources; Democrats refused to allow it, arguing that the environmentally sensitive refuge should be protected and that more effort should be directed toward developing alternative sources of fuel. A report by an independent advisory board, the National Research Council, maintained that the environmental damage from previous Alaskan drilling would probably never be corrected. The report stated: "Natural recovery in the Arctic is very slow, because of the cold; so the effects of abandoned structures and unrestored landscapes could persist for centuries and accumulate." The Council cited a broad range of problems including a drop in reproduction of nesting birds and an increase in diabetes in native communities. The report was developed at the request of Republican legislators who supported oil drilling in the ANWR.

given away." In view of the Navy's rapidly increasing demand for fuel oil, he continued, "there would appear to be an immediate necessity for assuring the conservation of a proper supply of petroleum for the Government's own use." The director concluded that "pending the enactment of adequate legislation on this subject, the filing of claims to oil lands in the State of California should be suspended."

Secretary of the Interior Richard A. Ballinger forwarded the report to President William Howard Taft, who agreed that the open-access policy of the General Mining Law threatened the national interest in maintaining strategic petroleum reserves. On September 27, 1909, the president issued a proclamation that temporarily withdrew from entry, location, and disposal 3,041,000 acres of oil-bearing lands in California and Wyoming. Uncertain of his constitutional authority to reserve federal lands from public use, Taft asked Congress to ratify his decision. Congress responded the following year by enacting the Pickett Act, which declared that the "President may, at any time in his discretion, temporarily withdraw from settlement, location, sale or entry any of the public lands of the United States ... and reserve the same for ... purposes to be

> *The oil reserves of the federal public lands were simply there for the taking, without consideration of the public interest in protecting the nation's oil supplies or compensating the citizens of the United States for the value of the petroleum extracted from their public lands.*

Oil and gas leasing, as authorized by the Mineral Leasing Act of 1920, in the Delta National Wildlife Refuge in Louisiana. Here, an employee of the U.S. Fish and Wildlife Service checks an oil well on the refuge. (© US Fish and Wildlife Service/Photo by John and Karen Hollingsworth)

specified in the orders of withdrawals, and such withdrawals or reservations shall remain in force until revoked by him or Congress." The Pickett Act did not retroactively approve Presidential land reservations that were made before the effective date of the statute, however.

CONSTITUTIONAL ISSUES

Prospectors in Wyoming entered an area of the public lands in Wyoming that were withdrawn by President Taft's proclamation, bored a well, and discovered oil. They assigned their interest in the oil and land to Midwest Oil Company, which extracted about 50,000 barrels. Upon learning of the illegal drilling, the United States sued to recover the land and for an accounting of the oil that had already been pumped out. Midwest defended itself on the grounds that the president's withdrawal of the land from entry and location under the General Mining Law was unconstitutional.

In *United States v. Midwest Oil Co.* (1915), the U.S. Supreme Court affirmed the president's constitutional power unilaterally to withdraw public land from entry, use, or settlement. Writing for a seven-member majority, Justice Joseph Rucker Lamar asserted that the Court "need not consider whether, as an original question, the President could have withdrawn from private acquisition what Congress had made free and open to occupation and purchase." Rather, he observed that a succession of presidents over the past eighty years had withdrawn land from the public domain and had done so without express statutory authority.

Justice Lamar cited ninety-nine executive orders that created or enlarged Native American reservations, 109 that established or enlarged military reservations, and forty-four that created bird reserves:

> When it appeared that the public interest would be served by withdrawing or reserving parts of the public domain, nothing was more natural than to retain what the Government already owned. And in making such orders, which were thus useful to the public, no private interest was injured. For prior to the initiation of some right given by law the citizen had no ... private right in land which was the property of the people.

Justice Lamar acknowledged the argument that "while these facts and rulings prove a usage they do not establish its validity." The Court concluded, however, that "government is a practical affair intended for practical men" and that "lawmakers and citizens naturally adjust themselves to any long-continued action of the Executive Department."

President Taft's withdrawal of the petroleum reserves in California and Wyoming focused public attention on the importance of safeguarding the nation's oil supplies. At the same time, the Supreme Court's confirmation of the government's power to reserve minerals from free entry and exploitation under the General Mining Law laid the constitutional foundation for a permanent reservation of petroleum-bearing lands.

MAJOR FEATURES OF THE ACT

Following more than ten years of debate, Congress enacted the Mineral Leasing Act, which President Woodrow Wilson signed into law on February 25, 1920. The Mineral Leasing Act applies to all deposits of oil, natural gas, oil shale, coal, bituminous rock, and other fossil fuels, as well as to fertilizers such as phosphate, sodium, and potassium. (The act also reserves all helium extracted from natural gas to the United States.) For these minerals, the act changed the open-access and free-extraction policies applicable to hardrock minerals.

Although the specific terms of the law vary depending on the type of mineral, the principal features of the Mineral Leasing Act are:

President Taft's withdrawal of the petroleum reserves in California and Wyoming focused public attention on the importance of safeguarding the nation's oil supplies.

- Permission to enter the public lands to explore for minerals must be obtained from the government. There is no right to prospect.
- The United States grants the authority to drill and extract minerals by lease. Coal and oil shale leases usually are for twenty years, while oil and natural gas leases generally are limited to ten-year terms.
- The government has the power to manage the exploitation of leasable minerals and may place conditions on leases to ensure that exploration, drilling, and reclamation of the lands on which the mineral development occurs are consistent with land- and resource-management plans and to protect the environment.
- The United States receives compensation from the lessee (the party that obtains a lease) for the privilege of extracting minerals from the federal public lands. In recent years, the royalty on coal is 12.5 percent of gross revenues. Royalties for oil and natural gas extraction range from 12.5 percent to 25 percent of gross receipts.

The Bureau of Land Management, an agency of the U.S. Department of the Interior, is the principal administrator of the Mineral Leasing Act. The act applies to approximately 564 million acres of federal lands (or about 28 percent of the land mass of the United States). Approximately 37 percent of the nation's coal, about 11 percent of its natural gas, and 5 percent of domestic oil production comes from the public lands. The states in which the minerals are extracted share approximately half of the royalties paid by lessees.

The Mineral Leasing Act significantly influenced the mineral exploration and leasing provisions of the Outer Continental Shelf Lands Act of 1953 (and its 1978 amendment), as well as the Geothermal Steam Act of 1970. The Mineral Leasing Act remains one of the most important statutes governing the federal public lands.

See also: NATIONAL PARK SERVICE ACT; OUTER CONTINENTAL SHELF LANDS ACT; YELLOWSTONE NATIONAL PARK ACT.

BIBLIOGRAPHY

Coggins, George Cameron, Charles F. Wilkinson, and John D. Leshy. *Federal Public Land and Resources Law,* 4th ed. New York: Foundation Press, 2001.

Gates, Paul W., and Robert W. Swenson. *History of Public Land Law.* Washington, DC: U.S. Government Printing Office, 1968.

Lamar, Howard R., ed. *The New Encyclopedia of the American West.* New Haven, CT: Yale University Press, 1998.

Leshy, John D. *The Mining Law: A Study in Perpetual Motion.* Washington, DC: Resources for the Future, 1987.

Wilkinson, Charles F. *Crossing the Next Meridian: Land, Water and the Future of the West.* Washington, DC: Island Press, 1992.

MISSOURI COMPROMISE (1820)

James L. Huston

Excerpt from the Missouri Compromise

And be it further enacted, That in all that territory ceded by France to the United States, under the name of Louisiana, which lies north of thirty-six degrees and thirty minutes north latitude, not included within the limits of the state, contemplated by this act, slavery and involuntary servitude, otherwise than in the punishment of crimes, where of the parties shall have been duly convicted, shall be, and is hereby, forever prohibited...

The compromise set a precedent for states to enter the Union in pairs (one free, one slave).

Louisiana Purchase

Sold to the United States by France in 1803, the Louisiana Purchase was a huge territory stretching from the Mississippi River to the Rocky Mountains and from the Gulf of Mexico to Canada. The property had gone from French rule to Spanish rule and then back again to the French under Napoleon. President Thomas Jefferson believed that control of the West hinged upon possession of New Orleans, at the mouth of the Mississippi. He wrote, "There is on the globe one single spot, the possessor of which is our natural and habitual enemy. It is New Orleans." He secured its control by purchasing the entire territory for $15 million, doubling the size of the United States, in what is now considered one of his greatest achievements.

embargo: a prohibition on commerce with a particular country for political or economic reasons

In 1819 Congress first confronted the frictions produced by a division of the country into free and slave states. In that year the territory of Missouri sought statehood, and Northern (free) states resisted its admission as a slave state. Northerners, believing the South had too much power already, opposed any expansion of slavery that might strengthen that power. In response to this Northern opposition, legislators came up with the Missouri Compromise of 1820 (10 Stat. 548), as a means to avoid the conflicts raised by territorial expansion.

The compromise set a precedent for states to enter the Union in pairs (one free, one slave). This was not a written part of the law but rather a general understanding among senators to ensure that the number of slave-state senators would equal the number of free-state senators. The compromise also divided the land acquired from France in the Louisiana Purchase into two areas: in the land above 36 degrees 30 minutes north latitude, slavery would be prohibited; in the land below the line, slavery would be permitted. The Missouri Compromise turned out to be a successful one, and after a few years many even viewed it as a part of the Constitution (though it never was). Until the Civil War broke out in April 1861, all attempted solutions to the question of slavery's expansion rested on the Missouri Compromise line of 36 degrees 30 minutes.

HISTORICAL BACKGROUND

By 1819 several Northern congressmen felt aggrieved by the power of the South in national affairs. Southerners dominated national politics through the operation of the Three-Fifths Compromise. Slaves, legally considered a form of property, were allowed to count as three-fifths of a person for the calculation of population to determine the number of congressional representatives a state would have. The Three-Fifths Compromise gave Southerners an edge in electing presidents and constructing majorities in Congress, and through it they managed to dominate the Democratic-Republican party, the party of Thomas Jefferson.

Northerners were also angry at the policies of the two presidents from Virginia, Jefferson (1801–1809) and James Madison (1809–1817). Restrictions on trade with Great Britain and France, including an **embargo** on American shipping in 1808, and the War of 1812 had all hurt the economy of Northern states. To make matters worse, the Federalist Party, which often pushed for policies that benefited the North, bungled its opposition to the war and managed to commit suicide by appearing traitorous.

Meanwhile, Southern slavery was spreading to the Great Lakes area (the present states of Ohio, Michigan, Indiana, Illinois, and Wisconsin), where it had been prohibited by the Northwest Ordinance of 1787. By 1818 it looked as if Southern migrants to Illinois and Indiana were trying to smuggle the "peculiar institution" into those states by calling the practice "indentured servitude" This too provoked the outrage of Northerners.

LEGISLATIVE DEBATE

On February 13, 1819 Representative James Tallmadge, Jr., a Democratic-Republican from New York, offered two amendments to the legislation admitting Missouri to the Union. One called for the prohibition of further importations of slaves into Missouri, and the other demanded gradual emancipation of slaves already there. The House of Representatives passed his two amendments by a sectional vote. In the Senate, where the numbers of slave states and free states were evenly balanced, the amendments were defeated. For the entire year, debate over slavery raged in Congress. This debate amazed the American people, because there was no agitation over the question in any other quarter.

A breakthrough came when the District of Maine, formerly an area controlled by the state of Massachusetts, sought statehood. Speaker of the House Henry Clay (from Kentucky) insisted that if Maine was to be admitted, then Missouri should be admitted as well. Thus the idea of letting states enter the Union in pairs, one free, the other slave, was formally presented. Then Illinois senator Jesse B. Thomas offered an amendment that would establish the line of 36 degrees 30 minutes in the Louisiana Purchase territory, below which slavery was allowed and above which it was not. (The line would approximately form the southern border of the new state of Missouri.) After much dispute between the Senate and the House on final versions of the bill, Congress passed the Missouri Compromise on March 2, 1820.

For the entire year, debate over slavery raged in Congress. This debate amazed the American people, because there was no agitation over the question in any other quarter.

The Dred Scott Case

Dred Scott was a slave who sued for his freedom in Missouri courts on the basis of having spent nine years in the free state of Illinois and the free territory of Wisconsin. Missouri courts had traditionally upheld the doctrine of "once free, always free," and the case was initially settled in Scott's favor. However, the Missouri Supreme Court stepped in to overturn the decision. The case eventually made its way to the Supreme Court, where each judge rendered a separate opinion. The only aspect of the case the justices agreed upon was that a slave was not a citizen, and therefore was not allowed to sue in federal court. The Court also ruled the Missouri Compromise unconstitutional, finding that the federal government did not have the right to outlaw slavery in the new western territories. Northerners were outraged at the decision, which intensified antagonism between the North and the South, contributed to the election of President Abraham Lincoln, and pushed the country toward civil war. The sons of Scott's first owner, Peter Blow, had helped pay Scott's legal fees during his decade-long legal battle. After the Supreme Court ruled against him, they purchased Scott and his wife and set them free. Scott died nine months later.

Antebellum Period
Alfred L. Brophy

During the antebellum period—the years before the Civil War—Congress's legislation aimed at continuing to promote economic development, expansion of the Union, and dealing with the conflict over slavery.

In the aftermath of the War of 1812, Congress passed extensive tariff legislation. When South Carolina opposed the tariff act of 1832, Congress passed the Force Bill that authorized Andrew Jackson to use federal troops to enforce the tariff; the nation was on the brink of civil war. War was avoided by a compromise tariff in 1833, yet the nation was well on the road to war. At the same time, Congress was spending money on internal improvements, known as the American System, which provided funding for roads, canals, and railroads. It also passed a bankruptcy act.

Slavery and settlement of the West were central issues of antebellum politics. In 1820 the Missouri Compromise attempted to settle the conflict by prohibiting slavery in the territories north of Missouri's southern border. Later, the Compromise of 1850, which included the Fugitive Slave Act, again tried to calm the conflict, as did the Kansas Nebraska Act.

It was not long after the Missouri debates that the proslavery argument began in earnest.

But the drama was not quite finished. Missourians, angry over Congress's intervention in the question of slavery, rewrote parts of their state constitution denying any free black person the ability to settle in the state. This provision clashed with the guarantee of the U.S. Constitution that citizens in one state would not be discriminated against in another state. So another major collision between Northerners and Southerners followed. The matter was solved by asking Missouri legislators to rewrite the offending section. (Although this was not done, few pursued the matter afterward.) On February 26, 1821, the House of Representatives passed the resolution to admit Missouri to the Union.

ILL WILL BETWEEN NORTH AND SOUTH

Much ill will was generated by the Missouri debates. Southerners did not believe that Northerners harbored any humanitarian concern for slaves. Rather, they believed Northerners merely used the slaves' existence as a way to resurrect the Federalist Party and to create a stronger central government. For Northerners, the debates showed that Southerners did not foresee a future end of slavery—to the contrary, the institution was becoming stronger. And Northerners realized that along with the growth of slavery came Southerners' desires to use national legislation to protect and extend the institution. It was not long after the Missouri debates that the proslavery argument began in earnest. Those in favor of slavery argued that Africans were meant by nature and by God to be slaves and never independent citizens.

EFFECTIVENESS OF THE COMPROMISE

Despite the ongoing tension between North and South, the Missouri Compromise handled the national issue of slavery smoothly for several decades. The first part of the compromise was roughly observed until 1850—the admission of states in pairs, one free and one slave, balancing the number of senators from each type of state. The admission of slave states ended with the Compromise of 1850, when California was admitted to the Union without an offsetting slave state.

But in many ways, the core of the Missouri Compromise was the line of 36 degrees 30 minutes. Before long, Northerners looked upon this section of the compromise, which "forever prohibited" slavery above it, as holy writ, not to be disturbed. However, it only operated in the Louisiana Purchase area. When the United States gained the territories of California and New Mexico in a war with Mexico, the compromise line again became a source of North-South wrangling. Southerners wanted to extend the line to the Pacific Ocean, but Northerners adamantly refused. When the Compromise of 1850 was written, there was no mention of the 36 degree 30 minute line. Then in 1854 the Kansas Nebraska Act repealed the 36 degree 30 minute line of the Missouri Compromise. This action led to a political explosion in the North, killing the Whig Party and giving birth to the Republican Party. The Republicans insisted that Congress could prohibit slavery in the territories, whereas Southern radicals (called "fireaters") insisted slavery had to be permitted and even protected in all U.S. territorial possessions.

In *Dred Scott v. Sanford* (1857), the chief justice of the Supreme Court, Roger B. Taney, declared the compromise line unconstitutional and in substance approved the radical Southern position. That case only infuriated the North, and by 1860 the Republicans successfully captured the presidency. In 1860–1861, in an effort to avoid the division of the nation, Kentucky senator John J. Crittenden used the Compromise Line as part of a general proposal, called the Crittenden resolutions, to reconcile North and South and reunify the country. It was the last public appearance of the compromise line.

The Civil War erupted following the attack on Fort Sumter on April 15, 1861. Congress passed a prohibition of slavery in the territories in June 1862, and with Union victory in 1865, slavery ceased in the United States.

See also: COMPROMISE OF 1850; FUGITIVE SLAVE ACTS; KANSAS NEBRASKA ACT OF 1854.

BIBLIOGRAPHY

Dangerfield, George. *The Awakening of American Nationalism, 1815–1828.* New York: Harper and Row, 1965.

Fehrenbacher, Don E. *Sectional Crisis and Southern Constitutionalism.* Baton Rouge: Louisiana State University Press, 1995.

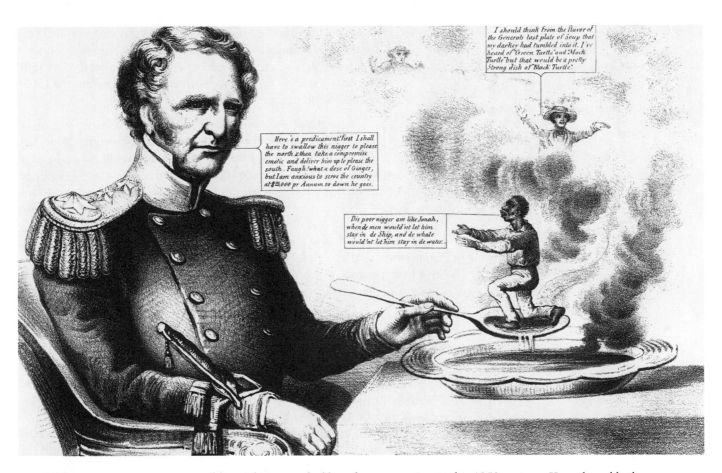

Winfield Scott, a prominent career soldier, is being mocked here for opportunism in this 1852 cartoon. He endorsed both abolitionism and the Missouri Compromise. He says here that he will have to swallow the black man in his soup to please the North, then take a "compromise emetic" so as to deliver him to please the South. "Faugh! What a dose of Ginger, but I am anxious to serve the country at $25,000 pr Annum so down he goes," he concludes. (LIBRARY OF CONGRESS, PRINTS AND PHOTOGRAPHS DIVISION)

Knupfer, Peter B. *The Union as It Is: Constitutional Unionism and Sectional Compromise, 1787–1861*. Chapel Hill: University of North Carolina Press, 1991.

Miller, John Chester. *The Wolf by the Ears: Thomas Jefferson and Slavery*. New York: Free Press, 1977.

Moore, Glover. *The Missouri Controversy, 1819–1821*. Lexington: University of Kentucky Press, 1966.

Wiecek, William M. *The Sources of Antislavery Constitutionalism in America, 1760–1848*. Ithaca, NY: Cornell University Press, 1977.

MORRILL LAND GRANT ACT OF 1862

Daniel W. Hamilton

During the Civil War, the Thirty-Seventh Congress was responsible for a striking amount of landmark legislation. The Homestead Act, the Enrollment Act, and the Internal Revenue Act were passed in a matter of months. Equally important, this energetic Congress also passed the Morrill Land Grant Act (MLGA). The MLGA transformed higher education and was responsible for the establishment of numerous colleges across the country. In this legislation, championed in the Congress by Justin Smith Morrill, the federal government took, for the first time, a leadership role in higher education in the United States.

The Morrill Land Grant Act transformed higher education and was responsible for the establishment of numerous colleges across the country.

Morrill, a representative from Vermont, was the most important proponent providing federal assistance for state colleges in Congress before the Civil War. Morrill, the son of a blacksmith, was unable to attend college because his father could not afford the tuition for all of his sons. Leaving school at fifteen, Morrill became a prosperous owner of a general store. He became active in public life and was elected in 1855 as a Whig to the House of Representatives before becoming a leader of the new Republican Party in Vermont. In Congress he rose to a position on the powerful Ways and Means Committee and became one of the most outspoken advocates for the democratic ideal that a college education should be available, at low cost, to all who desired one.

Morrill's thinking was heavily influenced by Jonathan Turner of Illinois College, who had long argued for the establishment of state agricultural colleges through the use of federal land grants. Morrill proposed plans for land grant colleges as early as 1857, and a plan of his passed the House in 1858. The bill faced opposition in the Senate from Southerners objecting to the increased federal role in dictating the course of higher education within the states. Morrill's bill eventually passed the Senate in 1859 in the midst of an economic downturn. President James Buchanan, however, vetoed the bill for both constitutional and economic reasons.

With a new president and the departure of the Southern congressional delegations, Morrill was able in the first Civil War Congress to finally steer his bill to passage. Under the terms of MLGA, the federal government distributed land proportionately to the states, which then sold it. The proceeds of the land sales supported colleges in the instruction of "agriculture and the mechanical arts." Some states used the money from the sale of land to aid existing schools, and other states used the money to establish new colleges and universities. Each state was given 30,000 acres of land for each senator and representative it had in the Congress. Most of the land given to the states was in the West, where the vast bulk of unsold federal land remained. Additionally, the most populous eastern states, such as New York and Pennsylvania, received a larger share of western land than the western states themselves. This provoked some opposition from western delegations in the Congress, but the simultaneous passage of the Homestead Act secured the support of enough western Republicans to pass the act on July 2, 1862. Although first applied in the Union states, after the Civil War, the MLGA was extended to the former Confederate states.

The passage of this legislation in the midst of war is emblematic of the dynamism and creativity of this Congress, even on nonmilitary matters. President Lincoln, consumed with the day-to-day fighting of the war, gave Congress a remarkably free hand in social and economic legislation. The Morrill

> *Under the terms of MLGA, the federal government distributed land proportionately to the states, which then sold it. The proceeds of the land sales supported colleges in the instruction of "agriculture and the mechanical arts."*

A student at Ohio State University, one of about 70 land grant universities created under the Morrill Act, walks in front of University Hall—the site where 24 students gathered for the first class of the Ohio Agricultural and Mechanical College on September 17, 1873. (© AP/WIDE WORLD PHOTOS)

Land Grant Act remains one of the great legislative achievements of the Civil War Congress, and countless Americans went to college as a direct result of this law. Through this legislation the state universities of Wisconsin, Illinois, California, Minnesota, and Ohio, as well as dozens of other state institutions were created or expanded. State universities from Maryland to Nebraska to Washington have a Morrill Hall on campus. Morrill was elected to the Senate in 1866, where he remained until he died in office in 1898.

BIBLIOGRAPHY

Donald, David H., et al. *The Civil War and Reconstruction*. New York: Norton, 2001.

McPherson, James M. *Battle Cry of Freedom*. New York: Ballentine Books, reissue ed., 1989.

Nevins, Allan. *The State Universities and Democracy* Urbana: University of Illinois Press, 1962.

MOTOR CARRIER ACT (1935)

Gary J. Edles

Excerpt from the Motor Carrier Act of 1935

to regulate transportation by motor carriers in such manner as to recognize and preserve the inherent advantages of, and foster sound economic conditions in, such transportation and among such carriers in the public interest; promote adequate, economic, and efficient service ... and reasonable charges ... without unjust discriminations ... and unfair or destructive competitive practices....

The Motor Carrier Act of 1935 (P.L. 74-255, 49 Stat. 543) gave the Interstate Commerce Commission (ICC), a federal government agency, the authority to regulate interstate truck and bus companies, known collectively as "motor carriers." The ICC's new powers with respect to motor carriers were similar to those it had over railroads, which it had regulated since 1887. The ICC could decide which companies could become motor carriers, what services they could offer, and what rates they could charge. The constitutionality of the act rests on Congress's authority to regulate interstate commerce under Article I, section 8 of the U.S. Constitution.

The ICC could decide which companies could become motor carriers, what services they could offer, and what rates they could charge.

FEATURES OF THE ACT

The act divided motor carriers into two categories: common carriers, which held out their service to the public generally, and contract carriers, which had agreements with one or only a limited number of customers. Applications by new truck or bus companies or applications by existing companies to expand their operations could be granted only if, in the words of the statute, the proposed service was "required by the present or future public convenience and necessity." The ICC had to decide precisely what this very general requirement meant. In an early case, it defined the public convenience and necessity by reference to three factors: whether a proposed operation would "serve a useful public purpose, responsive to a public demand or need," whether such purpose "could be served as well by existing firms or carriers," and whether the applicant could operate the service "without endangering or impairing the operations of existing [companies]." These requirements restricted the ability of new companies to enter the motor carrier business and existing companies to expand to new areas. It also inhibited competition between motor carriers and railroads and between common and contract carriers.

The act also stated that rates charged by motor carriers had to be "just and reasonable" and could not discriminate between customers of similar circumstances. The act required motor carriers to file rates thirty days before they were to become effective and allowed existing companies to protest. In 1948 Congress passed the Reed-Bulwinkle Act, which permitted rates to be set by "rate bureaus" representing groups of motor carriers. These bureaus could agree on uniform rates applicable to all its members. Such rates, when approved by the ICC, were immune from **antitrust** laws. In 1985 the U.S. Court of Appeals for the Eleventh Circuit noted that ICC regulation of motor carriers under this regime "discouraged rate competition." The Court called the rate-making regulation "rigid" and noted that collective rate making tended to prop up even the least efficient motor carrier companies (*Southern Motor Carriers Rate Conference v. United States*).

antitrust: laws protecting commerce and trade from monopolistic restraints on competition

The Motor Carrier Act specifically exempted certain individuals, companies, and products from regulation—for example, individuals using their own trucks as part of their own business, motor vehicles operated by farmers, and agricultural products.

INCREASED GOVERNMENT REGULATION

The Motor Carrier Act was one of several statutes enacted during the 1930s that brought key elements of American business under government regulation. Many believed that an unregulated marketplace had led to the **Great Depression** or otherwise harmed the public. Supporters of regulatory statutes argued that these acts could prevent a repetition of disastrous events. The ICC believed that tight control over motor carrier operations and rates was necessary to maintain the stable transportation industry Congress envisioned when it enacted the Motor Carrier Act.

Great Depression: the longest and most severe economic depression in American history (1929–1939); its effects were felt throughout the world

In the 1953 case *American Trucking Associations v. United States*, the U.S. Supreme Court noted that, before the Motor Carrier Act, the trucking industry "was unstable economically ... with small [companies] unable to satisfy even the most minimal standards of safety or financial responsibility." In another key decision in 1962, *United States v. Drum*, the Court noted that the licensing requirement is evidence of "congressional concern over diversions of traffic which may harm existing carriers upon whom the bulk of shippers must depend for access to market."

The Motor Carrier Act was one of several statutes enacted during the 1930s that brought key elements of American business under government regulation.

The regulatory system operated with little public notice or debate from 1935 to the 1970s. Nevertheless, regulation was the subject of some academic criticism and political interest. As former federal judge Abner Mikva observed in a 1990 law journal article, President John F. Kennedy as early as 1962 urged "greater reliance on the forces of competition and less reliance on the restraints of regulation." In 1971 President Richard Nixon's Council of Economic Advisers called for deregulation of the transportation industries. Both Gerald Ford and Jimmy Carter during their presidential terms supported a relaxation of regulation. They appointed to the ICC individuals who sought to increase competition under the existing regulatory regime. Over time, Congress also became convinced that regulation had a detrimental effect on the prices and services available to consumers.

FURTHER LEGISLATION: REDUCING REGULATION

In the 1980s Congress decided that less regulation would "promote competitive and efficient transportation services" and "allow a variety of quality and price options to meet changing market demands." The Motor Carrier Act of 1980 significantly reduced the level of ICC regulation of the trucking industry, though it did not eliminate regulation entirely. Congress modified the public convenience and necessity standard so the ICC could no longer consider new entries undesirable simply because they might divert traffic or revenues away from existing companies. The 1980 act modified the distinction between common and contract carriers to foster competition between the two groups. Congress also gave individual motor carriers greater freedom to set rates in response to customer demand with less ICC involvement and banned rate bureaus from discussing rates applicable solely to individual companies. As a result, between 1980 and 1990, the number of trucking companies doubled.

Congress finally ended sixty years of motor carrier regulation with the ICC Termination Act of 1995.

In 1982 Congress substantially reduced regulatory control of bus companies in the Bus Regulatory Reform Act. Despite this change in direction, financial hardships in the bus industry forced the ICC in 1988 to approve the absorption of the Trailways Bus Company by Greyhound, which became the only nationwide bus company. Nevertheless, most major cities and towns receive bus service from regional operators, mostly offering charter or tour service.

Congress finally ended sixty years of motor carrier regulation with the ICC Termination Act of 1995. This act eliminated virtually all economic control of motor carriers and abolished the ICC. Most motor carriers need only register with the Department of Transportation and meet minimum financial, insurance, and safety requirements to exist today.

See also: INTERSTATE COMMERCE ACT OF 1887.

BIBLIOGRAPHY

Dempsey, Paul Stephen. *The Social and Economic Consequences of Deregulation.* New York: Quorum Books, 1989.

Derthick, Martha, and Paul J. Quirk. *The Politics of Deregulation.* Washington, DC: Brookings Institution, 1985.

Landis, James M. *The Administrative Process.* Westport, CN: Greenwood, 1974 [1938].

Meyer, John R., Merton J. Peck, John Stenason, and Charles Zwick. *The Economics of Competition in the Transportation Industries.* Cambridge, MA: Harvard University Press, 1959.

Mikva, Abner. "Deregulating Through the Back Door: The Hard Way to Fight a Revolution." 57 *University of Chicago Law Review* 521 (1990).

Moore, Thomas Gale. "Trucking Deregulation." *The Concise Encyclopedia of Economics*. <http://www.econlib.org/library/Enc/TruckingDeregulation.html>.

MOTOR VEHICLE SAFETY ACT

See NATIONAL TRAFFIC AND MOTOR VEHICLE SAFETY ACT OF 1966

MUTUAL SECURITY ACT (1951)

Lynne K. Zusman and Neil S. Helfand

In the aftermath of World War II, a redistribution of military and economic power left two supreme powers, the United States and the Soviet Union. The remaining world order consisted of the war torn nations of the European continent and the less-developed nations of Asia, Africa, and South America, many of which would gain their independence in the post–World War II era. Ideologically divided and with competing aims, the Soviet Union and the United States each vied for control over the reshaping and development of this remaining world order.

From the standpoint of U.S. foreign policy makers, the vulnerability of these nations to the threat of communist influence and aggression posed a direct threat to the national security of the United States and the rest of the free world. In response to this security threat, the United States enacted the Mutual Security Act of 1951, an ambitious piece of legislation with its stated aim "to maintain the security and promote the foreign policy and provide for the general welfare of the United States by furnishing assistance to friendly nations in the interest of international peace and security."

The ideological purpose of this act was the defense of democracy in the continual struggle against communism. The chosen means by which to mount this defense was the strengthening and development of the military and economic structure of friendly nations, in other words those nations opposed to communism. The goal of the act was to make these nations viable partners in the building of an effective "collective security" against communist domination. Such self-sustaining countries could contribute to the common defense of the free world, including the defense of the United States.

> *The ideological purpose of this act was the defense of democracy in the continual struggle against communism.*

FEATURES OF THE ACT

The act authorized military, economic, and technical assistance to countries with the aim of developing their resources in the interest of their security and independence on the condition that such assistance be in the national interest of the United States. However, the act also reflected the idealism of the post-

Under the Mutual Security Act the United States provided not only military funding and training but also assistance to bolster the economies and the standards of living and health of recipient countries.

war era, as embodied in the Charter of the United Nations, in its ambition to promote world peace, international understanding, and good will and to bring about the participation of recipient countries in the United Nations system for collective security. The act provided for the distribution of funds based on geographical regions, namely Europe, the Near East and Africa, Asia, and the American republics, taking into account the unique circumstances and needs of each region.

HISTORICAL IMPACT

As Western Europe quickly rebounded from the ravages of war, United States assistance became increasingly focused on the less-developed nations of the Southern Hemisphere. It was widely believed that the southern half of the globe was the battleground between the free world and the communist world. Under this act the United States provided not only military funding and training but also assistance to bolster the economies and the standards of living and health of recipient countries.

See also: MUTUAL DEFENSE ASSISTANCE ACT.

APPENDICES

CONSTITUTION OF THE UNITES STATES OF AMERICA

We the People of the United States, in Order to form a more perfect Union, establish Justice, insure domestic Tranquility, provide for the common defense, promote the general Welfare, and secure the Blessings of Liberty to ourselves and our Posterity, do ordain and establish this Constitution for the United States of America.

ARTICLE I

Items in italic have since been amended or superseded. A portion of Article I, Section 2, was modified by Section 2 of the Fourteenth Amendment; Article I, Section 3, was modified by the Seventeenth Amendment; Article I, Section 4, was modified by Section 2 of the Twentieth Amendment; and Article I, Section 9, was modified by the Sixteenth Amendment.

Section 1: All legislative Powers herein granted shall be vested in a Congress of the United States, which shall consist of a Senate and House of Representatives.

Section 2: The House of Representatives shall be composed of Members chosen every second Year by the People of the several States, and the Electors in each State shall have the Qualifications requisite for Electors of the most numerous Branch of the State Legislature.

No Person shall be a Representative who shall not have attained to the Age of twenty five Years, and been seven Years a Citizen of the United States, and who shall not, when elected, be an Inhabitant of that State in which he shall be chosen.

Representatives and direct Taxes shall be apportioned among the several States which may be included within this Union, according to their respective Numbers, which shall be determined by adding to the whole Number of free Persons, including those bound to Service for a Term of Years, and excluding Indians not taxed, three fifths of all other Persons. The actual Enumeration shall be made within three Years after the first Meeting of the Congress of the United States, and within every subsequent Term of ten Years, in such Manner as they shall by Law direct. The Number of Representatives shall not exceed one for every thirty Thousand, but each State shall have at Least one Representative; and until such enumeration shall be made, the State of New Hampshire shall be entitled to chuse three, Massachusetts eight, Rhode-Island

and Providence Plantations one, Connecticut five, New-York six, New Jersey four, Pennsylvania eight, Delaware one, Maryland six, Virginia ten, North Carolina five, South Carolina five, and Georgia three.

When vacancies happen in the Representation from any State, the Executive Authority thereof shall issue Writs of Election to fill such Vacancies.

The House of Representatives shall chuse their Speaker and other Officers; and shall have the sole Power of Impeachment.

Section 3: The Senate of the United States shall be composed of two Senators from each State, *chosen by the Legislature thereof* for six Years; and each Senator shall have one Vote.

Immediately after they shall be assembled in Consequence of the first Election, they shall be divided as equally as may be into three Classes. The Seats of the Senators of the first Class shall be vacated at the Expiration of the second Year, of the second Class at the Expiration of the fourth Year, and of the third Class at the Expiration of the sixth Year, so that one third may be chosen every second Year; *and if Vacancies happen by Resignation, or otherwise, during the Recess of the Legislature of any State, the Executive thereof may make temporary Appointments until the next Meeting of the Legislature, which shall then fill such Vacancies.*

No Person shall be a Senator who shall not have attained to the Age of thirty Years, and been nine Years a Citizen of the United States, and who shall not, when elected, be an Inhabitant of that State for which he shall be chosen.

The Vice President of the United States shall be President of the Senate, but shall have no Vote, unless they be equally divided.

The Senate shall chuse their other Officers, and also a President pro tempore, in the Absence of the Vice President, or when he shall exercise the Office of President of the United States.

The Senate shall have the sole Power to try all Impeachments. When sitting for that Purpose, they shall be on Oath or Affirmation. When the President of the United States is tried, the Chief Justice shall preside: And no Person shall be convicted without the Concurrence of two thirds of the Members present.

Judgment in Cases of Impeachment shall not extend further than to removal from Office, and disqualification to hold and enjoy any Office of honor, Trust or Profit under the United States: but the Party convicted shall nevertheless be liable and subject to Indictment, Trial, Judgment and Punishment, according to Law.

Section 4: The Times, Places and Manner of holding Elections for Senators and Representatives, shall be prescribed in each State by the Legislature thereof; but the Congress may at any time by Law make or alter such Regulations, except as to the Places of chusing Senators.

The Congress shall assemble at least once in every Year, and such Meeting shall *be on the first Monday in December,* unless they shall by Law appoint a different Day.

Section 5: Each House shall be the Judge of the Elections, Returns and Qualifications of its own Members, and a Majority of each shall constitute a Quorum to do Business; but a smaller Number may adjourn from day to day, and may be authorized to compel the Attendance of absent Members, in such Manner, and under such Penalties as each House may provide.

Each House may determine the Rules of its Proceedings, punish its Members for disorderly Behaviour, and, with the Concurrence of two thirds, expel a Member.

Each House shall keep a Journal of its Proceedings, and from time to time publish the same, excepting such Parts as may in their Judgment require Secrecy; and the Yeas and Nays of the Members of either House on any question shall, at the Desire of one fifth of those Present, be entered on the Journal.

Neither House, during the Session of Congress, shall, without the Consent of the other, adjourn for more than three days, nor to any other Place than that in which the two Houses shall be sitting.

Section 6: The Senators and Representatives shall receive a Compensation for their Services, to be ascertained by Law, and paid out of the Treasury of the United States. They shall in all Cases, except Treason, Felony and Breach of the Peace, be privileged from Arrest during their Attendance at the Session of their respective Houses, and in going to and returning from the same; and for any Speech or Debate in either House, they shall not be questioned in any other Place.

No Senator or Representative shall, during the Time for which he was elected, be appointed to any civil Office under the Authority of the United States, which shall have been created, or the Emoluments whereof shall have been encreased during such time; and no Person holding any Office under the United States, shall be a Member of either House during his Continuance in Office.

Section 7: All Bills for raising Revenue shall originate in the House of Representatives; but the Senate may propose or concur with Amendments as on other Bills.

Every Bill which shall have passed the House of Representatives and the Senate, shall, before it become a Law, be presented to the President of the United States: If he approve he shall sign it, but if not he shall return it, with his Objections to that House in which it shall have originated, who shall enter the Objections at large on their Journal, and proceed to reconsider it. If after such Reconsideration two thirds of that House shall agree to pass the Bill, it shall be sent, together with the Objections, to the other House, by which it shall likewise be reconsidered, and if approved by two thirds of that House, it shall become a Law. But in all such Cases the Votes of both Houses shall be determined by yeas and Nays, and the Names of the Persons voting for and against the Bill shall be entered on the Journal of each House respectively. If any Bill shall not be returned by the President within ten Days (Sundays excepted) after it shall have been presented to him, the Same shall be a Law, in like Manner as if he had signed it, unless the Congress by their Adjournment prevent its Return, in which Case it shall not be a Law.

Every Order, Resolution, or Vote to which the Concurrence of the Senate and House of Representatives may be necessary (except on a question of

Adjournment) shall be presented to the President of the United States; and before the Same shall take Effect, shall be approved by him, or being disapproved by him, shall be repassed by two thirds of the Senate and House of Representatives, according to the Rules and Limitations prescribed in the Case of a Bill.

Section 8: The Congress shall have Power To lay and collect Taxes, Duties, Imposts and Excises, to pay the Debts and provide for the common Defence and general Welfare of the United States; but all Duties, Imposts and Excises shall be uniform throughout the United States;

To borrow Money on the credit of the United States;

To regulate Commerce with foreign Nations, and among the several States, and with the Indian Tribes;

To establish an uniform Rule of Naturalization, and uniform Laws on the subject of Bankruptcies throughout the United States;

To coin Money, regulate the Value thereof, and of foreign Coin, and fix the Standard of Weights and Measures;

To provide for the Punishment of counterfeiting the Securities and current Coin of the United States;

To establish Post Offices and post Roads;

To promote the Progress of Science and useful Arts, by securing for limited Times to Authors and Inventors the exclusive Right to their respective Writings and Discoveries;

To constitute Tribunals inferior to the supreme Court;

To define and punish Piracies and Felonies committed on the high Seas, and Offences against the Law of Nations;

To declare War, grant Letters of Marque and Reprisal, and make Rules concerning Captures on Land and Water;

To raise and support Armies, but no Appropriation of Money to that Use shall be for a longer Term than two Years;

To provide and maintain a Navy;

To make Rules for the Government and Regulation of the land and naval Forces;

To provide for calling forth the Militia to execute the Laws of the Union, suppress Insurrections and repel Invasions;

To provide for organizing, arming, and disciplining, the Militia, and for governing such Part of them as may be employed in the Service of the United States, reserving to the States respectively, the Appointment of the Officers, and the Authority of training the Militia according to the discipline prescribed by Congress;

To exercise exclusive Legislation in all Cases whatsoever, over such District (not exceeding ten Miles square) as may, by Cession of particular States, and the Acceptance of Congress, become the Seat of the Government of the United States, and to exercise like Authority over all Places purchased by the

Consent of the Legislature of the State in which the Same shall be, for the Erection of Forts, Magazines, Arsenals, dock-Yards, and other needful Buildings;—And

To make all Laws which shall be necessary and proper for carrying into Execution the foregoing Powers, and all other Powers vested by this Constitution in the Government of the United States, or in any Department or Officer thereof.

Section 9: The Migration or Importation of such Persons as any of the States now existing shall think proper to admit, shall not be prohibited by the Congress prior to the Year one thousand eight hundred and eight, but a Tax or duty may be imposed on such Importation, not exceeding ten dollars for each Person.

The Privilege of the Writ of Habeas Corpus shall not be suspended, unless when in Cases of Rebellion or Invasion the public Safety may require it.

No Bill of Attainder or ex post facto Law shall be passed.

No Capitation, or other direct, Tax shall be laid, *unless in Proportion to the Census or enumeration herein before directed to be taken.*

No Tax or Duty shall be laid on Articles exported from any State.

No Preference shall be given by any Regulation of Commerce or Revenue to the Ports of one State over those of another; nor shall Vessels bound to, or from, one State, be obliged to enter, clear, or pay Duties in another.

No Money shall be drawn from the Treasury, but in Consequence of Appropriations made by Law; and a regular Statement and Account of the Receipts and Expenditures of all public Money shall be published from time to time.

No Title of Nobility shall be granted by the United States: And no Person holding any Office of Profit or Trust under them, shall, without the Consent of the Congress, accept of any present, Emolument, Office, or Title, of any kind whatever, from any King, Prince, or foreign State.

Section 10: No State shall enter into any Treaty, Alliance, or Confederation; grant Letters of Marque and Reprisal; coin Money; emit Bills of Credit; make any Thing but gold and silver Coin a Tender in Payment of Debts; pass any Bill of Attainder, ex post facto Law, or Law impairing the Obligation of Contracts, or grant any Title of Nobility.

No State shall, without the Consent of the Congress, lay any Imposts or Duties on Imports or Exports, except what may be absolutely necessary for executing it's inspection Laws: and the net Produce of all Duties and Imposts, laid by any State on Imports or Exports, shall be for the Use of the Treasury of the United States; and all such Laws shall be subject to the Revision and Controul of the Congress.

No State shall, without the Consent of Congress, lay any Duty of Tonnage, keep Troops, or Ships of War in time of Peace, enter into any Agreement or Compact with another State, or with a foreign Power, or engage in War, unless actually invaded, or in such imminent Danger as will not admit of delay.

ARTICLE II

Article II, Section 1, was superseded by the Twelfth Amendment; Article II, Section 1, was modified by the Twenty-fifth Amendment.

Section 1: The executive Power shall be vested in a President of the United States of America. He shall hold his Office during the Term of four Years, and, together with the Vice President, chosen for the same Term, be elected, as follows:

Each State shall appoint, in such Manner as the Legislature thereof may direct, a Number of Electors, equal to the whole Number of Senators and Representatives to which the State may be entitled in the Congress: but no Senator or Representative, or Person holding an Office of Trust or Profit under the United States, shall be appointed an Elector.

The Electors shall meet in their respective States, and vote by Ballot for two Persons, of whom one at least shall not be an Inhabitant of the same State with themselves. And they shall make a List of all the Persons voted for, and of the Number of Votes for each; which List they shall sign and certify, and transmit sealed to the Seat of the Government of the United States, directed to the President of the Senate. The President of the Senate shall, in the Presence of the Senate and House of Representatives, open all the Certificates, and the Votes shall then be counted. The Person having the greatest Number of Votes shall be the President, if such Number be a Majority of the whole Number of Electors appointed; and if there be more than one who have such Majority, and have an equal Number of Votes, then the House of Representatives shall immediately chuse by Ballot one of them for President; and if no Person have a Majority, then from the five highest on the List the said House shall in like Manner chuse the President. But in chusing the President, the Votes shall be taken by States, the Representation from each State having one Vote; A quorum for this purpose shall consist of a Member or Members from two thirds of the States, and a Majority of all the States shall be necessary to a Choice. In every Case, after the Choice of the President, the Person having the greatest Number of Votes of the Electors shall be the Vice President. But if there should remain two or more who have equal Votes, the Senate shall chuse from them by Ballot the Vice President.

The Congress may determine the Time of chusing the Electors, and the Day on which they shall give their Votes; which Day shall be the same throughout the United States.

No Person except a natural born Citizen, or a Citizen of the United States, at the time of the Adoption of this Constitution, shall be eligible to the Office of President; neither shall any Person be eligible to that Office who shall not have attained to the Age of thirty five Years, and been fourteen Years a Resident within the United States.

In Case of the Removal of the President from Office, or of his Death, Resignation, or Inability to discharge the Powers and Duties of the said Office, the Same shall devolve on the Vice President, and the Congress may by Law provide for the Case of Removal, Death, Resignation or Inability, both of the President and Vice President, declaring what Officer shall then act as President, and such Officer shall act accordingly, until the Disability be removed, or a President shall be elected.

The President shall, at stated Times, receive for his Services, a Compensation, which shall neither be increased nor diminished during the Period for which he shall have been elected, and he shall not receive within that Period any other Emolument from the United States, or any of them.

Before he enter on the Execution of his Office, he shall take the following Oath or Affirmation:—"I do solemnly swear (or affirm) that I will faithfully execute the Office of President of the United States, and will to the best of my Ability, preserve, protect and defend the Constitution of the United States."

Section 2: The President shall be Commander in Chief of the Army and Navy of the United States, and of the Militia of the several States, when called into the actual Service of the United States; he may require the Opinion, in writing, of the principal Officer in each of the executive Departments, upon any Subject relating to the Duties of their respective Offices, and he shall have Power to grant Reprieves and Pardons for Offences against the United States, except in Cases of Impeachment. He shall have Power, by and with the Advice and Consent of the Senate, to make Treaties, provided two thirds of the Senators present concur; and he shall nominate, and by and with the Advice and Consent of the Senate, shall appoint Ambassadors, other public Ministers and Consuls, Judges of the supreme Court, and all other Officers of the United States, whose Appointments are not herein otherwise provided for, and which shall be established by Law: but the Congress may by Law vest the Appointment of such inferior Officers, as they think proper, in the President alone, in the Courts of Law, or in the Heads of Departments.

The President shall have Power to fill up all Vacancies that may happen during the Recess of the Senate, by granting Commissions which shall expire at the End of their next Session.

Section 3: He shall from time to time give to the Congress Information of the State of the Union, and recommend to their Consideration such Measures as he shall judge necessary and expedient; he may, on extraordinary Occasions, convene both Houses, or either of them, and in Case of Disagreement between them, with Respect to the Time of Adjournment, he may adjourn them to such Time as he shall think proper; he shall receive Ambassadors and other public Ministers; he shall take Care that the Laws be faithfully executed, and shall Commission all the Officers of the United States.

Section 4. The President, Vice President and all civil Officers of the United States, shall be removed from Office on Impeachment for, and Conviction of, Treason, Bribery, or other high Crimes and Misdemeanors.

ARTICLE III

A portion of Section 2 was modified by the Eleventh Amendment

Section 1: The judicial Power of the United States shall be vested in one supreme Court, and in such inferior Courts as the Congress may from time to time ordain and establish. The Judges, both of the supreme and inferior Courts, shall hold their Offices during good Behaviour, and shall, at stated Times, receive for their Services a Compensation, which shall not be diminished during their Continuance in Office.

Section 2: The judicial Power shall extend to all Cases, in Law and Equity, arising under this Constitution, the Laws of the United States, and Treaties made, or which shall be made, under their Authority;—to all Cases affecting Ambassadors, other public Ministers and Consuls;—to all Cases of admiralty and maritime Jurisdiction;—to Controversies to which the United States shall be a Party; to Controversies between two or more States;—*between a State and Citizens of another State;*—between Citizens of different States; between Citizens of the same State claiming Lands under Grants of different States, and between a State, or the Citizens thereof, and foreign States, Citizens or Subjects.

In all Cases affecting Ambassadors, other public Ministers and Consuls, and those in which a State shall be Party, the supreme Court shall have original Jurisdiction. In all the other Cases before mentioned, the supreme Court shall have appellate Jurisdiction, both as to Law and Fact, with such Exceptions, and under such Regulations as the Congress shall make.

The Trial of all Crimes, except in Cases of Impeachment, shall be by Jury; and such Trial shall be held in the State where the said Crimes shall have been committed; but when not committed within any State, the Trial shall be at such Place or Places as the Congress may by Law have directed.

Section 3: Treason against the United States, shall consist only in levying War against them, or in adhering to their Enemies, giving them Aid and Comfort. No Person shall be convicted of Treason unless on the Testimony of two Witnesses to the same overt Act, or on Confession in open Court.

The Congress shall have Power to declare the Punishment of Treason, but no Attainder of Treason shall work Corruption of Blood, or Forfeiture except during the Life of the Person attainted.

ARTICLE IV
A portion of Section 2 was superseded by the Thirteenth Amendment.

Section 1: Full Faith and Credit shall be given in each State to the public Acts, Records, and judicial Proceedings of every other State. And the Congress may by general Laws prescribe the Manner in which such Acts, Records and Proceedings shall be proved, and the Effect thereof.

Section 2: The Citizens of each State shall be entitled to all Privileges and Immunities of Citizens in the several States.

A Person charged in any State with Treason, Felony, or other Crime, who shall flee from Justice, and be found in another State, shall on Demand of the executive Authority of the State from which he fled, be delivered up, to be removed to the State having Jurisdiction of the Crime.

No Person held to Service or Labour in one State, under the Laws thereof, escaping into another, shall, in Consequence of any Law or Regulation therein, be discharged from such Service or Labour, but shall be delivered up on Claim of the Party to whom such Service or Labour may be due.

Section 3: New States may be admitted by the Congress into this Union; but no new State shall be formed or erected within the Jurisdiction of any other State; nor any State be formed by the Junction of two or more States, or Parts of States, without the Consent of the Legislatures of the States concerned as well as of the Congress.

The Congress shall have Power to dispose of and make all needful Rules and Regulations respecting the Territory or other Property belonging to the United States; and nothing in this Constitution shall be so construed as to Prejudice any Claims of the United States, or of any particular State.

Section 4: The United States shall guarantee to every State in this Union a Republican Form of Government, and shall protect each of them against Invasion; and on Application of the Legislature, or of the Executive (when the Legislature cannot be convened), against domestic Violence.

ARTICLE V

The Congress, whenever two thirds of both Houses shall deem it necessary, shall propose Amendments to this Constitution, or, on the Application of the Legislatures of two thirds of the several States, shall call a Convention for proposing Amendments, which, in either Case, shall be valid to all Intents and Purposes, as Part of this Constitution, when ratified by the Legislatures of three fourths of the several States, or by Conventions in three fourths thereof, as the one or the other Mode of Ratification may be proposed by the Congress; Provided that no Amendment which may be made prior to the Year One thousand eight hundred and eight shall in any Manner affect the first and fourth Clauses in the Ninth Section of the first Article; and that no State, without its Consent, shall be deprived of its equal Suffrage in the Senate.

ARTICLE VI

All Debts contracted and Engagements entered into, before the Adoption of this Constitution, shall be as valid against the United States under this Constitution, as under the Confederation.

This Constitution, and the Laws of the United States which shall be made in Pursuance thereof; and all Treaties made, or which shall be made, under the Authority of the United States, shall be the supreme Law of the Land; and the Judges in every State shall be bound thereby, any Thing in the Constitution or Laws of any State to the Contrary notwithstanding.

The Senators and Representatives before mentioned, and the Members of the several State Legislatures, and all executive and judicial Officers, both of the United States and of the several States, shall be bound by Oath or Affirmation, to support this Constitution; but no religious Test shall ever be required as a Qualification to any Office or public Trust under the United States.

ARTICLE VII

The Ratification of the Conventions of nine States, shall be sufficient for the Establishment of this Constitution between the States so ratifying the Same.

Attest William Jackson Secretary

Done in Convention by the Unanimous Consent of the States present the Seventeenth Day of September in the Year of our Lord one thousand seven hundred and Eighty seven and of the Independence of the United States of America the Twelfth In witness whereof We have hereunto subscribed our Names,

Go. Washington Presidt and deputy from Virginia

Delaware: Geo: Read, Gunning Bedford jun, John Dickinson, Richard Bassett, Jaco: Broom

Maryland: James McHenry, Dan of St Thos. Jenifer, Danl. Carroll

Virginia: John Blair—, James Madison Jr.

North Carolina: Wm. Blount, Richd. Dobbs Spaight, Hu Williamson

South Carolina: J. Rutledge, Charles Cotesworth Pinckney, Charles Pinckney, Pierce Butler

Georgia: William Few, Abr Baldwin

New Hampshire: John Langdon, Nicholas Gilman

Massachusetts: Nathaniel Gorham, Rufus King

Connecticut: Wm. Saml. Johnson Roger Sherman

New York: Alexander Hamilton

New Jersey: Wil: Livingston, David Brearley, Wm. Paterson, Jona: Dayton

Pennsylvania: B Franklin, Thomas Mifflin, Robt. Morris, Geo. Clymer, Thos. FitzSimons, Jared Ingersoll, James Wilson, Gouv Morris

AMENDMENTS TO THE CONSTITUTION

The first 10 amendments to the Constitution were ratified December 15, 1791, and form what is known as the "Bill of Rights."

AMENDMENT I

Congress shall make no law respecting an establishment of religion, or prohibiting the free exercise thereof; or abridging the freedom of speech, or of the press; or the right of the people peaceably to assemble, and to petition the Government for a redress of grievances.

AMENDMENT II

A well regulated Militia, being necessary to the security of a free State, the right of the people to keep and bear Arms, shall not be infringed.

AMENDMENT III

No Soldier shall, in time of peace be quartered in any house, without the consent of the Owner, nor in time of war, but in a manner to be prescribed by law.

AMENDMENT IV

The right of the people to be secure in their persons, houses, papers, and effects, against unreasonable searches and seizures, shall not be violated, and no Warrants shall issue, but upon probable cause, supported by Oath or affirmation, and particularly describing the place to be searched, and the persons or things to be seized.

AMENDMENT V

No person shall be held to answer for a capital, or otherwise infamous crime, unless on a presentment or indictment of a Grand Jury, except in cases arising in the land or naval forces, or in the Militia, when in actual service in time of War or public danger; nor shall any person be subject for the same offence to be twice put in jeopardy of life or limb; nor shall be compelled in any criminal case to be a witness against himself, nor be deprived of life, liberty, or property, without due process of law; nor shall private property be taken for public use, without just compensation.

AMENDMENT VI

In all criminal prosecutions, the accused shall enjoy the right to a speedy and public trial, by an impartial jury of the State and district wherein the crime shall have been committed, which district shall have been previously ascertained by law, and to be informed of the nature and cause of the accusation; to be confronted with the witnesses against him; to have compulsory process for obtaining witnesses in his favor, and to have the Assistance of Counsel for his defence.

AMENDMENT VII

In suits at common law, where the value in controversy shall exceed twenty dollars, the right of trial by jury shall be preserved, and no fact tried by a jury, shall be otherwise reexamined in any Court of the United States, than according to the rules of the common law.

AMENDMENT VIII

Excessive bail shall not be required, nor excessive fines imposed, nor cruel and unusual punishments inflicted.

AMENDMENT IX

The enumeration in the Constitution, of certain rights, shall not be construed to deny or disparage others retained by the people.

AMENDMENT X

The powers not delegated to the United States by the Constitution, nor prohibited by it to the States, are reserved to the States respectively, or to the people.

AMENDMENT XI

Passed by Congress March 4, 1794. Ratified February 7, 1795. A portion of Article III, Section 2, was modified by the Eleventh Amendment.

The Judicial power of the United States shall not be construed to extend to any suit in law or equity, commenced or prosecuted against one of the United States by Citizens of another State, or by Citizens or Subjects of any Foreign State.

AMENDMENT XII

Passed by Congress December 9, 1803. Ratified June 15, 1804. A portion of Article II, Section 1, was superseded by the Twelfth Amendment. A portion of the Twelfth Amendment was superseded by Section 3 of the Twentieth Amendment.

The Electors shall meet in their respective states and vote by ballot for President and Vice-President, one of whom, at least, shall not be an inhabitant of the same state with themselves; they shall name in their ballots the person voted for as President, and in distinct ballots the person voted for as Vice-President, and they shall make distinct lists of all persons voted for as President, and of all persons voted for as Vice-President, and of the number of votes for each, which lists they shall sign and certify, and transmit sealed to the seat of the government of the United States, directed to the President of the Senate;—the President of the Senate shall, in the presence of the Senate and House of Representatives, open all the certificates and the votes shall then be counted;—The person having the greatest number of votes for President, shall be the President, if such number be a majority of the whole number of Electors appointed; and if no person have such majority, then from the persons having the highest numbers not exceeding three on the list of those voted for as President, the House of Representatives shall choose immediately, by ballot, the President. But in choosing the President, the votes shall be taken by states, the representation from each state having one vote; a quorum for this purpose shall consist of a member or members from two-thirds of the states, and a majority of all the states shall be necessary to a choice. *And if the House of Representatives shall not choose a President whenever the right of choice shall devolve upon them, before the fourth day of March next following, then the Vice-President shall act as President, as in case of the death or other constitutional disability of the President.*—The person having the greatest number of votes as Vice-President, shall be the Vice-President, if such number be a majority of the whole number of Electors appointed, and if no person have a majority, then from the two highest numbers on the list, the Senate shall choose the Vice-President; a quorum for the purpose shall consist of two-thirds of the whole number of Senators, and a majority of the whole number shall be necessary to a choice. But no person constitutionally ineligible to the office of President shall be eligible to that of Vice-President of the United States.

AMENDMENT XIII

Passed by Congress January 31, 1865. Ratified December 6, 1865. A portion of Article IV, Section 2, was superseded by the Thirteenth Amendment.

Section 1: Neither slavery nor involuntary servitude, except as a punishment for crime whereof the party shall have been duly convicted, shall exist within the United States, or any place subject to their jurisdiction.

Section 2: Congress shall have power to enforce this article by appropriate legislation.

AMENDMENT XIV

Passed by Congress June 13, 1866. Ratified July 9, 1868. A portion of Article I, Section 2, was modified by Section 2 of the Fourteenth Amendment. A portion of the Fourteenth Amendment was modified by Section 1 of the Twenty-sixth Amendment.

Section 1: All persons born or naturalized in the United States, and subject to the jurisdiction thereof, are citizens of the United States and of the State wherein they reside. No State shall make or enforce any law which shall abridge the privileges or immunities of citizens of the United States; nor shall any State deprive any person of life, liberty, or property, without due process of law; nor deny to any person within its jurisdiction the equal protection of the laws.

Section 2: Representatives shall be apportioned among the several States according to their respective numbers, counting the whole number of persons in each State, excluding Indians not taxed. But when the right to vote at any election for the choice of electors for President and Vice-President of the United States, Representatives in Congress, the Executive and Judicial officers of a State, or the members of the Legislature thereof, is denied to any of the male inhabitants of such State, *being twenty-one years of age,* and citizens of the United States, or in any way abridged, except for participation in rebellion, or other crime, the basis of representation therein shall be reduced in the proportion which the number of such male citizens shall bear to the whole number of male citizens twenty-one years of age in such State.

Section 3: No person shall be a Senator or Representative in Congress, or elector of President and Vice-President, or hold any office, civil or military, under the United States, or under any State, who, having previously taken an oath, as a member of Congress, or as an officer of the United States, or as a member of any State legislature, or as an executive or judicial officer of any State, to support the Constitution of the United States, shall have engaged in insurrection or rebellion against the same, or given aid or comfort to the enemies thereof. But Congress may by a vote of two-thirds of each House, remove such disability.

Section 4: The validity of the public debt of the United States, authorized by law, including debts incurred for payment of pensions and bounties for services in suppressing insurrection or rebellion, shall not be questioned. But neither the United States nor any State shall assume or pay any debt or obligation incurred in aid of insurrection or rebellion against the United States, or any claim for the loss or emancipation of any slave; but all such debts, obligations and claims shall be held illegal and void.

Section 5: The Congress shall have the power to enforce, by appropriate legislation, the provisions of this article.

AMENDMENT XV
Passed by Congress February 26, 1869. Ratified February 3, 1870.

Section 1: The right of citizens of the United States to vote shall not be denied or abridged by the United States or by any State on account of race, color, or previous condition of servitude—

Section 2: The Congress shall have the power to enforce this article by appropriate legislation.

AMENDMENT XVI

Passed by Congress July 12, 1909. Ratified February 3, 1913. A portion of Article I, Section 9, was modified by the Sixteenth Amendment.

The Congress shall have power to lay and collect taxes on incomes, from whatever source derived, without apportionment among the several States, and without regard to any census or enumeration.

AMENDMENT XVII

Passed by Congress May 13, 1912. Ratified April 8, 1913. Portions of Article I, Section 3, were modified by the Seventeenth Amendment.

The Senate of the United States shall be composed of two Senators from each State, elected by the people thereof, for six years; and each Senator shall have one vote. The electors in each State shall have the qualifications requisite for electors of the most numerous branch of the State legislatures.

When vacancies happen in the representation of any State in the Senate, the executive authority of such State shall issue writs of election to fill such vacancies: Provided, That the legislature of any State may empower the executive thereof to make temporary appointments until the people fill the vacancies by election as the legislature may direct.

This amendment shall not be so construed as to affect the election or term of any Senator chosen before it becomes valid as part of the Constitution.

AMENDMENT XVIII

Passed by Congress December 18, 1917. Ratified January 16, 1919. Repealed by the Twenty-first Amendment.

Section 1: After one year from the ratification of this article the manufacture, sale, or transportation of intoxicating liquors within, the importation thereof into, or the exportation thereof from the United States and all territory subject to the jurisdiction thereof for beverage purposes is hereby prohibited.

Section 2: The Congress and the several States shall have concurrent power to enforce this article by appropriate legislation.

Section 3: This article shall be inoperative unless it shall have been ratified as an amendment to the Constitution by the legislatures of the several States, as provided in the Constitution, within seven years from the date of the submission hereof to the States by the Congress.

AMENDMENT XIX

Passed by Congress June 4, 1919. Ratified August 18, 1920.

The right of citizens of the United States to vote shall not be denied or abridged by the United States or by any State on account of sex.

Congress shall have power to enforce this article by appropriate legislation.

AMENDMENT XX

Passed by Congress March 2, 1932. Ratified January 23, 1933. A portion of Article 1, Section 4, was modified by Section 2 of the Twentieth Amendment. In addition, a portion of the Twelfth Amendment was superseded by Section 3 of the Twentieth Amendment.

Section 1: The terms of the President and the Vice President shall end at noon on the 20th day of January, and the terms of Senators and Representatives at noon on the 3d day of January, of the years in which such terms would have ended if this article had not been ratified; and the terms of their successors shall then begin.

Section 2: The Congress shall assemble at least once in every year, and such meeting shall begin at noon on the 3d day of January, unless they shall by law appoint a different day.

Section 3: If, at the time fixed for the beginning of the term of the President, the President elect shall have died, the Vice President elect shall become President. If a President shall not have been chosen before the time fixed for the beginning of his term, or if the President elect shall have failed to qualify, then the Vice President elect shall act as President until a President shall have qualified; and the Congress may by law provide for the case wherein neither a President elect nor a Vice President shall have qualified, declaring who shall then act as President, or the manner in which one who is to act shall be selected, and such person shall act accordingly until a President or Vice President shall have qualified.

Section 4: The Congress may by law provide for the case of the death of any of the persons from whom the House of Representatives may choose a President whenever the right of choice shall have devolved upon them, and for the case of the death of any of the persons from whom the Senate may choose a Vice President whenever the right of choice shall have devolved upon them.

Section 5: Sections 1 and 2 shall take effect on the 15th day of October following the ratification of this article.

Section 6: This article shall be inoperative unless it shall have been ratified as an amendment to the Constitution by the legislatures of three-fourths of the several States within seven years from the date of its submission.

AMENDMENT XXI

Passed by Congress February 20, 1933. Ratified December 5, 1933.
Repealed the Eighteenth Amendment.

Section 1: The eighteenth article of amendment to the Constitution of the United States is hereby repealed.

Section 2: The transportation or importation into any State, Territory, or Possession of the United States for delivery or use therein of intoxicating liquors, in violation of the laws thereof, is hereby prohibited.

Section 3: This article shall be inoperative unless it shall have

been ratified as an amendment to the Constitution by conventions in the several States, as provided in the Constitution, within seven years from the date of the submission hereof to the States by the Congress.

AMENDMENT XXII
Passed by Congress March 21, 1947. Ratified February 27, 1951.

Section 1: No person shall be elected to the office of the President more than twice, and no person who has held the office of President, or acted as President, for more than two years of a term to which some other person was elected President shall be elected to the office of President more than once. But this Article shall not apply to any person holding the office of President when this Article was proposed by Congress, and shall not prevent any person who may be holding the office of President, or acting as President, during the term within which this Article becomes operative from holding the office of President or acting as President during the remainder of such term.

Section 2: This article shall be inoperative unless it shall have been ratified as an amendment to the Constitution by the legislatures of three-fourths of the several States within seven years from the date of its submission to the States by the Congress.

AMENDMENT XXIII
Passed by Congress June 16, 1960. Ratified March 29, 1961.

Section 1: The District constituting the seat of Government of the United States shall appoint in such manner as Congress may direct:

A number of electors of President and Vice President equal to the whole number of Senators and Representatives in Congress to which the District would be entitled if it were a State, but in no event more than the least populous State; they shall be in addition to those appointed by the States, but they shall be considered, for the purposes of the election of President and Vice President, to be electors appointed by a State; and they shall meet in the District and perform such duties as provided by the twelfth article of amendment.

Section 2: The Congress shall have power to enforce this article by appropriate legislation.

AMENDMENT XXIV
Passed by Congress August 27, 1962. Ratified January 23, 1964.

Section 1: The right of citizens of the United States to vote in any primary or other election for President or Vice President, for electors for President or Vice President, or for Senator or Representative in Congress, shall not be denied or abridged by the United States or any State by reason of failure to pay poll tax or other tax.

Section 2: The Congress shall have power to enforce this article by appropriate legislation.

AMENDMENT XXV

Passed by Congress July 6, 1965. Ratified February 10, 1967. A portion of Article II, Section 1, was modified by the Twenty-fifth Amendment.

Section 1: In case of the removal of the President from office or of his death or resignation, the Vice President shall become President.

Section 2: Whenever there is a vacancy in the office of the Vice President, the President shall nominate a Vice President who shall take office upon confirmation by a majority vote of both Houses of Congress.

Section 3: Whenever the President transmits to the President pro tempore of the Senate and the Speaker of the House of Representatives his written declaration that he is unable to discharge the powers and duties of his office, and until he transmits to them a written declaration to the contrary, such powers and duties shall be discharged by the Vice President as Acting President.

Section 4: Whenever the Vice President and a majority of either the principal officers of the executive departments or of such other body as Congress may by law provide, transmit to the President pro tempore of the Senate and the Speaker of the House of Representatives their written declaration that the President is unable to discharge the powers and duties of his office, the Vice President shall immediately assume the powers and duties of the office as Acting President.

Thereafter, when the President transmits to the President pro tempore of the Senate and the Speaker of the House of Representatives his written declaration that no inability exists, he shall resume the powers and duties of his office unless the Vice President and a majority of either the principal officers of the executive department or of such other body as Congress may by law provide, transmit within four days to the President pro tempore of the Senate and the Speaker of the House of Representatives their written declaration that the President is unable to discharge the powers and duties of his office. Thereupon Congress shall decide the issue, assembling within forty-eight hours for that purpose if not in session. If the Congress, within twenty-one days after receipt of the latter written declaration, or, if Congress is not in session, within twenty-one days after Congress is required to assemble, determines by two-thirds vote of both Houses that the President is unable to discharge the powers and duties of his office, the Vice President shall continue to discharge the same as Acting President; otherwise, the President shall resume the powers and duties of his office.

AMENDMENT XXVI

Passed by Congress March 23, 1971. Ratified July 1, 1971. A portion of the Fourteenth Amendment, Section 2, was modified by Section 1 of the Twenty-sixth Amendment.

Section 1: The right of citizens of the United States, who are eighteen years of age or older, to vote shall not be denied or abridged by the United States or by any State on account of age.

Section 2: The Congress shall have power to enforce this article by appropriate legislation.

AMENDMENT XXVII

Originally proposed Sept. 25, 1789. Ratified May 7, 1992.

No law, varying the compensation for the services of the Senators and Representatives, shall take effect, until an election of representatives shall have intervened.

TIMELINE

YEAR	PRESIDENT	CONGRESS	US HISTORY	LEGISLATION
1787			Constitutional Convention, Independence Hall, Philadelphia	Northwest Ordinance
1788			Congress picks New York City as site of government	
1789	George Washington: 1789–1797 (Nonpartisan)	1st 1789–1791 Senate: 17 F; 9 Opp. House: 38 F; 26 Opp.	House of Representatives, Senate, executive branch organized, Supreme Court is established George Washington inaugurated in New York City Pres. Washington signs first act of Congress	Judiciary Act Tariff Act of 1789
1790			1st census: U.S. population 3,929,214 Congress meets in Philadelphia, new temporary capital Congress submits Bill of Rights to states for ratification Supreme Court meets for the first time	Copyright Act of 1790 Naturalization Act Patent Act Southwest Ordinance
1791		2d 1791–1793 Senate: 16 F; 13 DR House: 37 F; 33 DR	Bill of Rights ratified	Bank of the United States
1792			U.S. Mint established through Coinage Act New York Stock Exchange organized Cornerstone to White House laid	Coinage Act of 1792
1793		3d 1793–1795 Senate: 17 F; 13 DR House: 57 DR; 48 F	Cotton gin invented by Eli Whitney	Anti-Injunction Act Fugitive Slave Act of 1793

YEAR	PRESIDENT	CONGRESS	US HISTORY	LEGISLATION
1794			Excise tax on distilled liquor causes Whiskey Rebellion Creation of U.S. Navy authorized by Congress	
1795		4th 1795–1797 Senate: 19 F; 13 DR House: 54 F; 52 DR	Eleventh Amendment goes into effect (limits judicial powers) First state university, University of North Carolina, opens	
1796			*Hylton v. United States* is first Supreme Court case that upholds an act of Congress George Washington's farewell address is published, but never delivered as speech	
1797	John Adams: 1797–1801 (Federalist)	5th 1797–1799 Senate: 20 F; 12 DR House: 58 F; 48 DR	Congress creates 80,000 member militia	
1798			Undeclared war with France begins (conflict ends 1800) Rebellion in Haiti ends slavery there; many white Haitians flee to U.S., increasing fears among whites of slave rebellion and French revolution	Alien and Sedition Acts
1799		6th 1799–1801 Senate: 19 F; 13 DR House: 64 F; 42 DR		
1800			2d census: U.S. population 5,308,483 Library of Congress established Site of government moves to Washington, DC	
1801	Thomas Jefferson: 1801–1809 (Democratic-Republican)	7th 1801–1803 Senate: 18 DR; 13 F House: 69 DR; 36 F		Judiciary Act of 1801
1802				
1803		8th 1803–1805 Senate: 25 DR; 9 F House: 102 DR; 39 F	*Marbury v. Madison* is first Supreme Court case that declares an act of Congress unconstitutional Lewis and Clark expedition begins Louisiana Purchase (U.S. purchased about 828,000 square miles between the Mississippi River and Rocky Mountains from France, for $15 million)	
1804			Twelfth amendment ratified (separate ballots for president and vice president)	

YEAR	PRESIDENT	CONGRESS	US HISTORY	LEGISLATION
1805		9th 1805–1807 Senate: 27 DR; 7F House: 116 DR; 25 F		
1806				
1807		10th 1807–1809 Senate: 28 DR; 6 F House: 118 DR; 24 F	Steamboat (Robert Fulton's *Clermont*) completes round trip from New York to Albany in 62 hours, first practical steamboat trip Importation of slaves into the U.S. prohibited	Prohibition of the Slave Trade
1808			Anthracite coal first used as stove fuel in Pennsylvania	
1809	James Madison: 1809–1817 (Democratic-Republican)	11th 1809–1811 Senate: 28 DR; 6 F House: 94 DR; 48 F	Supreme Court case *United States v. Peters* affirms federal government power over states	Nonintercourse Act
1810			3d census: U.S. population 7,239,881 Revolt against Spanish by southern expansionists results in the U.S. gaining territory in the south	
1811		12th 1811–1813 Senate: 30 DR; 6 F House: 108 DR; 36 F	Non-intercourse policy against Great Britain renewed Senate declines to renew charter of Bank of the United States Construction of Cumberland Road begins (completed 1818; Cumberland, MD, to Wheeling, WV)	
1812			First war-bond issue; first interest-bearing U.S. Treasury notes are authorized War is declared on Great Britain (War of 1812, 1812–1814)	
1813		13th 1813–1815 Senate: 27 DR; 9 F House: 112 DR; 68 F	Creek War with Indian nations in southern United States	
1814			Peace treaty signed ending Creek War; Americans led to victory over Native Americans by Gen. Andrew Jackson Treaty of Ghent (Belgium) signed ending war with Britain	
1815		14th 1815–1817 Senate: 25 DR; 11 F House: 117 DR; 65 F	Treaties signed with Algiers, Tunis, and Tripoli ending piracy on U.S. ships	

YEAR	PRESIDENT	CONGRESS	US HISTORY	LEGISLATION
1816			Second Bank of United States is created	
1817	James Monroe: 1817–1825 (Democratic-Republican)	15th 1817–1819 Senate: 34 DR; 10 F House: 141 DR; 42 F	First Seminole War begins; Andrew Jackson named as commander of U.S. forces	
1818			Seminole War ends after American capture of St. Marks and Pensacola, FL	
1819		16th 1819–1821 Senate: 35 DR; 7 F House: 156 DR; 27 F	Adams-Onis treaty signed with Spain; Spain cedes East Florida to U.S., ends claim on West Florida Financial panic of 1819, economic recession begins First American savings banks open and begin paying interest on deposits	
1820			4th census: U.S. population 9,638,453	Missouri Compromise
1821		17th 1821–1823 Senate: 44 DR; 4 F House: 158 DR; 25 F	Republic of Liberia founded by American Colonization Society as haven for freed African-American slaves Sante Fe trail opened (Independence, MO, to Sante Fe, NM)	
1822			Planned slave revolt in Charleston, SC, blocked	
1823		18th 1823–1825 Senate: 44 DR; 4 F House: 187 DR; 26 F	In annual message to Congress, Pres. Monroe lays out what will become known as the Monroe Doctrine Treaties signed with Osage and Kansa Indian nations that cede lands in present-day Kansas, Oklahoma, and Missouri to the U.S. Great Britain abolishes slavery in its territories	
1824			Supreme Court case *Gibbons v. Ogden* upholds Congress's power to regulate interstate commerce	
1825	John Quincy Adams: 1825–1829 (Democratic-Republican)	19th 1825–1827 Senate: 26 A; 20 J House: 105 A; 97 J	Erie canal opens between Buffalo, NY, and New York City	
1826			John Stevens demonstrates use of first steam locomotive in Hoboken, NJ	

YEAR	PRESIDENT	CONGRESS	US HISTORY	LEGISLATION
1827		20th 1827–1829 Senate: 28 J; 20 A House: 119 J; 94 A	Mechanics Union of Trades Association, first central labor union, is created in Philadelphia	
1828			Treaty signed by United States and Mexico establishes Sabine River as common boundary	
1829	Andrew Jackson: 1829–1837 (Democratic)	21st 1829–1831 Senate: 26 D; 22 NR House: 139 D; 74 NR		
1830			5th census: U.S. population 12,860,702 Various Native American tribes sign treaties ceding western lands of present-day Iowa, Missouri, and Minnesota Mexico prohibits further settlement of Texas by Americans Baltimore & Ohio Railroad begins operation (first U.S. passenger railroad)	Indian Removal Act
1831		22d 1831–1833 Senate: 25 D; 21 NR; 2 O House: 141 D; 58 NR; 14 O	Nat Turner leads a slave rebellion in Virginia, is captured and executed along with 19 other blacks First U.S. built locomotive goes into service	
1832			Black Hawk War with Sac and Fox Indians; Creek nation cedes all its lands east of the Mississippi River to the United States; Seminoles cede lands in Florida Virginia legislature considers, but rejects, gradual termination of slavery	
1833		23d 1833–1835 Senate: 20 D; 20 NR; 8 O House: 147 D; 53 AM; 60 O	Oberlin College (Ohio) is first college in U.S. to adopt coeducation	
1834				
1835		24th 1835–1837 Senate: 27 D; 25 W House: 145 D; 98 W	Texas declares independence from Mexico; Mexico establishes military state in Texas Second Seminole War begins in response to attempts to remove Seminoles by force Cherokee nation cedes lands east of the Mississippi River	

YEAR	PRESIDENT	CONGRESS	US HISTORY	LEGISLATION
1836			Siege of the Alamo in San Antonio, TX, by Mexicans; entire garrison killed Mexican general Santa Anna captured at Battle of San Jacinto; Sam Houston installed as president of Republic of Texas	
1837	Martin Van Buren: 1837–1841 (Democratic)	25th 1837–1839 Senate: 30 D; 18 W; 4 O House: 108 D; 107 W; 24 O	Financial panic of 1837 leads to economic depression that lasts until 1842	
1838			Underground railroad becomes force in assisting slaves to reach the North and Canada Forced removal of Cherokee Indians from their native land in Georgia to Oklahoma begins (Trail of Tears)	
1839		26th 1839–1841 Senate: 28 D; 22 W House: 124 D; 118 W		
1840			6th census: U.S. population 17,063,353 Great National Pike completed (Cumberland, MD, to Vandalia, IL; formerly known as the Cumberland Road)	
1841	William Henry Harrison: 1841 (Whig) John Tyler: 1841–1845 (Whig)	27th 1841–1843 Senate: 28 W; 22 D; 2 O House: 133 W; 102 D; 6 O	First wagon train leaves for California from Independence, MO (47 people)	Bankruptcy Act of 1841
1842			Dorr's Rebellion in Rhode Island (demanded new state constitution guaranteeing equal voting rights) Settlement of Oregon begins via Oregon Trail Webster-Ashburton Treaty fixes northern border of U.S. in Maine and Minnesota	
1843		28th 1843–1845 Senate: 28 W; 25 D; 1 O House: 142 D; 79 W; 1 O		
1844			Treaty of Wanghia signed with China; opens five Chinese ports to American commerce Commercial telegraph service begins	
1845	James K. Polk: 1845–1849 (Democratic)	29th 1845–1847 Senate: 31 D; 25 W House: 143 D; 77 W; 6 O	Texas annexed by U.S.; Mexico breaks off relations with U.S.	

YEAR	PRESIDENT	CONGRESS	US HISTORY	LEGISLATION
1846			Mexican-American War begins (1846–1848) Treaty with Great Britain setting northern boundary of Oregon Territory at 49th parallel	
1847		30th 1847–1849 Senate: 36 D; 21 W; 1 O House: 115 W; 108 D; 4 O	Establishment of new government in California begins after treaty ends Mexican-American War hostilities there	
1848			Treaty of Guadelupe Hidalgo ends Mexican-American War California gold rush begins First women's rights convention in Seneca Falls, NY	
1849	Zachary Taylor: 1849–1850 (Whig)	31st 1849–1851 Senate: 35 D; 25 W; 2 O House: 112 D; 109 W; 9 O	Mormons establish state of Deseret after migration to Utah from Illinois (1846); Deseret becomes Territory of Utah in 1850	
1850	Millard Fillmore: 1850–1853 (Whig)		7th census: U.S. population 23,191,876	Compromise of 1850 Fugitive Slave Act of 1850
1851		32d 1851–1853 Senate: 35 D; 24 W; 3 O House: 140 D; 88 W; 5 O		
1852			Harriet Beecher Stowe publishes *Uncle Tom's Cabin*	
1853	Franklin Pierce: 1853–1857 (Democratic)	33d 1853–1855 Senate: 38 D; 22 W; 2 O House: 159 D; 71 W; 4 O	Commodore Matthew Perry arrives in Japan to deliver letter from the president, who wants to open trade Gadsden Purchase (southern areas of present-day Arizona and New Mexico)	
1854			Treaty of Kanagawa opens Japanese ports to the U.S. Large-scale immigration of Chinese begins First American oil company incorporated (Pennsylvania Rock Oil Co.)	Kansas Nebraska Act
1855		34th 1855–1857 Senate: 40 D; 15 R; 5 O House: 108 R; 83 D; 43 O	U.S. Court of Claims established Congress authorizes construction of telegraph line from Mississippi River to Pacific Ocean	

YEAR	PRESIDENT	CONGRESS	US HISTORY	LEGISLATION
1856			Violence in Kansas breaks out between pro- and anti-slavery factions over question of slavery; federal troops keep temporary peace	
1857	James Buchanan: 1857–1861 (Democratic)	35th 1857–1859 Senate: 36 D; 20 R; 8 O House: 118 D; 92 R; 26 O	Dred Scott case decided by Supreme Court (decision says Scott is not a citizen, therefore cannot sue in federal court; his residence in a free state does not make him free; Missouri Compromise is unconstitutional) Financial panic results from speculation in railroad securities and real estate	
1858				
1859		36th 1859–1861 Senate: 36 D; 26 R; 4 O House: 114 R; 92 D; 31 O	Kansas approves constitution making it a free state Harper's Ferry incident (abolitionist John Brown and 21 other men seize a U.S. Armory, are captured, Brown is hanged) First trip of a Pullman sleeping car on a railroad is completed	
1860			8th census: U.S. population 31,443,321 South Carolina is first state to secede from Union	
1861	Abraham Lincoln: 1861–1865 (Republican)	37th 1861–1863 Senate: 31 R; 10 D; 8 O House: 105 R; 43 D; 30 O	Confederate government created; Jefferson Davis elected president of the Confederacy Civil War begins (1861–1865) First transcontinental telegraph line is completed	Civil War Pensions First Confiscation Act
1862				Homestead Act Militia Act Morrill Land Grant Act Second Confiscation Act
1863		38th 1863–1865 Senate: 36 R; 9 D; 5 O House: 102 R; 75 D; 9 O	Pres. Lincoln issues Emancipation Proclamation Draft riots in New York City, about 1000 killed, some blacks lynched	Enrollment Act (Conscription Act)
1864			J. P. Morgan & Co. established	National Bank Act

YEAR	PRESIDENT	CONGRESS	US HISTORY	LEGISLATION
1865	Andrew Johnson: 1865–1869 (Democratic)	39th 1865–1867 Senate: 42 U; 10 D House: 149 U; 42 D	Gen. Robert E. Lee surrenders to Gen. U. S. Grant at Appomattox Court House Pres. Abraham Lincoln assassinated in Ford's Theater, Washington, DC Thirteenth Amendment is ratified (abolished slavery)	Freedmen's Bureau Act
1866			Reconstruction of the South begins Ku Klux Klan founded Fourteenth Amendment enacted by Congress (guarantees that no person is to be denied life, liberty, or pursuit of happiness by a state without due process of law) First refrigerated rail car built	Civil Rights Act of 1866
1867		40th 1867–1869 Senate: 42 R; 11 D House: 143 R; 49 D	U.S. purchases Alaska from Russia for $7.2 million National Grange is formed to protect farmer's interests	Reconstruction Acts (1867–1868)
1868			House of Representatives votes to impeach Andrew Johnson for violating the Tenure of Office Act after he tries to remove the secretary of war from office; Senate one vote short of two-thirds required for conviction	
1869	Ulysses S. Grant: 1869–1877 (Republican)	41st 1869–1871 Senate: 56 R; 11 D House: 149 R; 63 D	Congress enacts Fifteenth Amendment (makes it illegal to deprive a citizen of the right to vote based on race, color, or previous condition of servitude) National Woman Suffrage Association organized Freedmen's Bureau goes out of operation First transcontinental railroad completed with the joining of Union Pacific and Central Pacific railroads at Promontory, UT Knights of Labor (national labor union) formed	
1870			9th census: U.S. population 38,558,371 Justice Department is created Standard Oil Co. is incorporated	

YEAR	PRESIDENT	CONGRESS	US HISTORY	LEGISLATION
1871		42d 1871–1873 Senate: 52 R; 17 D 5 O House: 134 R; 104 D; 5 O	The Tweed Ring in New York City (led by Boss William Tweed of Tammany Hall) is broken up Race riots against Chinese in Los Angeles; 15 lynched Disastrous fire in Chicago destroys over 17,000 buildings, leaves 100,000 homeless	Ku Klux Klan Act Force Act
1872				Mail Fraud Statute Yellowstone National Park Act
1873		43d 1873–1875 Senate: 49 R; 19 D; 5 O House: 194 R; 92 D; 14 O	U.S. monetary policy shifts from bimetallic standard to gold standard Financial panic of 1873 results in New York Stock Exchange closing for ten days, substantial unemployment, and drastic fall in security prices Bethlehem Steel Co. begins operating	Coinage Act Comstock Act
1874				
1875		44th 1875–1877 Senate: 45 R; 29 D; 2 O House: 169 D; 109 R; 14 O		Civil Rights Act of 1875
1876			Battle of Little Bighorn in Montana; Col. George Custer and 266 are surrounded and killed in "Custer's last stand" Alexander Graham Bell receives patent for telephone, makes first telephone call	
1877	Rutherford B. Hayes: 1877–1881 (Republican)	45th 1877–1879 Senate: 39 R; 36 D; 1 O House: 153 D; 140 R	Federal troops withdraw from South in return for allowing Rutherford B. Hayes to become president in disputed election (Compromise of 1877) Strike on Baltimore & Ohio Railroad in protest of wage cuts leads to strikes on other railroads; 100,000 workers eventually involved	

YEAR	PRESIDENT	CONGRESS	US HISTORY	LEGISLATION
1878			First commercial telephone exchange opened, New Haven, CT	Bland-Allison Act Posse Comitatus Act
1879		46th 1879–1881 Senate: 42 D; 33 R; 1 O House: 149 D; 130 R; 14 O	First Woolworth five-and-dime store opens Incandescent electric lamp invented by Thomas Edison	
1880			10th census: U.S. population 50,155,783	
1881	James A. Garfield: 1881 (Republican) Chester A. Arthur: 1881–1885 (Republican)	47th 1881–1883 Senate: 37 R; 37 D; 1 O House: 147 R; 135 D; 11 O	Pres. Garfield shot and killed in Washington, DC, by disappointed office seeker Sitting Bull and Sioux surrender to U.S. Army Southern Pacific Railroad completed (New Orleans to Pacific) Tuskegee Institute founded by Booker T. Washington Western Union Telegraph Co. formed	
1882			First trust formed by Standard Oil Co. Severe strikes in iron and steel industry	Chinese Exclusion Act
1883		48th 1883–1885 Senate: 38 R; 36 D; 2 O House: 197 D; 118 R; 10 O	Brooklyn Bridge in New York City completed Northern Pacific Railroad completed	Civil Services Act (Pendleton Act)
1884			Statue of Liberty presented to U.S. by France (arrives in U.S. 1885, dedicated 1886) First tall building to use steel beams is erected (Home Insurance Building, Chicago) First large-scale electric street car system established in Richmond, VA First long-distance telephone service established between New York and Boston	
1885	Grover Cleveland: 1885–1889 (Democratic)	49th 1885–1887 Senate: 43 R; 34 D House: 183 D; 140 R; 2 O		
1886			Apache Indians (Southwest) surrender to U.S. Haymarket Massacre in Chicago American Federation of Labor (AFL) organized by 25 labor groups	

YEAR	PRESIDENT	CONGRESS	US HISTORY	LEGISLATION
1887		50th 1887–1889 Senate: 39 R; 37 D House: 169 D; 152 R; 4 O	Free mail delivery begins in cities of 10,000 or more The Interstate Commerce Commission, first U.S. regulatory commission, is created to regulate railroads	Indian General Allotment Act (Dawes Act) Interstate Commerce Act
1888			Department of Labor established	
1889	Benjamin Harrison: 1889–1893 (Republican)	51st 1889–1891 Senate: 39 R; 37 D House: 166 R; 159 D	Carnegie Steel Co. organized by Andrew Carnegie	
1890			11th census: U.S. population 62,979,766 Sioux Indians are defeated at Wounded Knee; last major battle of Indian wars	Sherman Antitrust Act
1891		52d 1891–1893 Senate: 47 R; 39 D; 2 O House: 235 D; 88 R; 9 O	Immigration and Naturalization Service is established	
1892			Ellis Island opens as an immigration receiving station	
1893	Grover Cleveland: 1893–1897 (Democratic)	53d 1893–1895 Senate: 44 D; 38 R; 3 O House: 218 D; 127 R; 11 O	Free mail delivery extended to rural communities Stock market crash, financial panic of 1893 begins, 491 banks and 15,000 commercial institutions fail; economy in severe depression until 1897	
1894			American Railway Union strikes at Pullman plant in Chicago; federal injunction breaks strike	1894 Income Tax and the Wilson-Gorman Tariff Act
1895		54th 1895–1897 Senate: 43 R; 39 D; 6 O House: 244 R; 105 D; 7 O	Internal combustion engine patented; first automobile company started	
1896			Supreme Court upholds Louisiana law calling for "separate but equal" accommodations on public transportation in *Plessy v. Ferguson*	
1897	William McKinley: 1897–1901 (Republican)	55th 1897–1899 Senate: 47 R; 34 D; 7 O House: 204 R; 113 D; 40 O	Thomas Edison patents a movie camera First section of a U.S. subway opens, in Boston	

YEAR	PRESIDENT	CONGRESS	US HISTORY	LEGISLATION
1898			Spanish-American War begins and ends; Spain cedes Puerto Rico, Philippines, and Guam to U.S. and relinquishes all claims to Cuba	
1899		56th 1899–1901 Senate: 53 R; 26 D; 8 O House: 197 R; 151 D; 9 O	Filipino nationalists revolt against U.S. First Hague Conference held; 26 nations participate	
1900			12th census: U.S. population 76,212,168 U.S. announces Open Door Policy in China (opens Chinese markets to all nations)	Gold Standard Act
1901	Theodore Roosevelt: 1901–1909 (Republican)	57th 1901–1903 Senate: 55 R; 31 D; 4 O House: 197 R; 151 D; 9 O	Pres. McKinley assassinated in Buffalo, NY, by an anarchist	
1902			Pres. Roosevelt asks attorney general to bring first antitrust suit to dissolve a railroad holding company	National Reclamation Act Panama Canal Purchase Act
1903		58th 1903–1905 Senate: 57 R; 33 D House: 208 R; 178 D	Hay-Herran Treaty with Colombia provides for 100-year lease of 10-mile-wide strip across isthmus of Panama for canal Wright brothers demonstrate first motor-driven airplane	
1904			Muckraker Ida Tarbell publishes *The History of the Standard Oil Company* First section of New York City subway opens	
1905		59th 1905–1907 Senate: 57 R; 33 D House: 250 R; 136 D		
1906			Upton Sinclair publishes *The Jungle*, muckraking account of the meat-packing industry Dow Jones Industrial Average closes over 100 for the first time	Antiquities Act Pure Food and Drug Act
1907		60th 1907–1909 Senate: 61 R; 31 D House: 222 R; 164 D	Food and Drug Administration begins operation Financial panic of 1907 Indiana passes world's first compulsory sterilization law for "all confirmed criminals, idiots, rapists, and imbeciles" held in state institutions; 32 states eventually adopt such laws	

YEAR	PRESIDENT	CONGRESS	US HISTORY	LEGISLATION
1908			Bureau of Investigation formed (later to become FBI) Model T automobile introduced by Henry Ford, sells for $850	Federal Employers' Liability Act
1909	William Howard Taft:1909–1913 (Republican)	61st 1909–1911 Senate: 61 R; 32 D House: 219 R; 172 D	Congress passes Sixteenth Amendment (allows federal income tax; ratified 1913) NAACP created	Corporate Income Tax Act
1910			13th Census: U.S. population 92,228,496	Mann Act
1911		62d 1911–1913 Senate: 51 R; 41 D House: 228 D; 161 R; 1 O	Supreme Court orders dissolution of Standard Oil Co. as a monopoly; same goes for the American Tobacco Co. and the DuPont Co.	
1912				
1913	Woodrow Wilson: 1913–1921 (Democratic)	63d 1913–1915 Senate: 51 D; 44 R; 1 O House: 291 D; 127 R; 17 O	Seventeenth Amendment ratified (calls for popular election of senators) First drive-in gasoline station opens in Pittsburgh, PA Ford Motor Co. introduces conveyor-belt assembly-line production of cars	Federal Income Tax Act of 1913 Federal Reserve Act
1914			War breaks out in Europe; Woodrow Wilson issues neutrality proclamation Federal Trade Commission established Commercial traffic begins on Panama Canal Margaret Sanger launches *The Woman Rebel*, feminist magazine dedicated to birth control; is indicted for "inciting violence and promoting obscenity" (goes on to found first family planning clinic, 1916; American Birth Control League, precursor to planned parenthood, 1921)	Clayton Act Federal Trade Commission Act Narcotics Act
1915		64th 1915–1917 Senate: 56 D; 40 R House: 230 D; 196 R; 9 O	First transcontinental telephone call Film *Birth of a Nation* debuts and increases support for the new Ku Klux Klan	

YEAR	PRESIDENT	CONGRESS	US HISTORY	LEGISLATION
1916			Congress votes to increase size of army; authorizes 450,000 person national guard U.S. buys Danish West Indies In first half of year, nearly 2,100 strikes and lockouts occur First woman elected to House of Representatives (Jeanette Rankin, R-MT)	Keating-Owen Act National Park Service Act
1917		65th 1917–1919 Senate: 53 D; 42 R House: 216 D; 210 R; 6 O	U.S. declares war on Germany and on Austria-Hungary; first U.S. troops arrive in Europe Puerto Rico becomes U.S. territory	Espionage Act Selective Service Act Trading With the Enemy Act Vocational Education Act
1918			Woodrow Wilson outlines "Fourteen Points" for a peace program Armistice signed with Germany and Austria-Hungary Regular airmail service established (between Washington, DC, and New York City) Influenza epidemic kills around 20 million people worldwide; 548,000 die in U.S.	Sedition Act
1919		66th 1919–1921 Senate: 49 R; 47 D House: 240 R; 190 D; 3 O	Treaty of Versailles signed by Germany and Allies (excluding Russia) In *Schenck v. United States*, Supreme Court finds that free speech can be restricted in wartime, upholding Espionage and Sedition Acts Riots in Chicago, Washington, and many other cities	National Prohibition Act
1920			14th Census: U.S. population 106,021,537 Eighteenth Amendment goes into effect (Prohibition) Nineteenth Amendment goes into effect (women's suffrage) American Civil Liberties Union founded First commercial radio broadcasts	Merchant Marine Act Mineral Leasing Act

YEAR	PRESIDENT	CONGRESS	US HISTORY	LEGISLATION
1921	Warren G. Harding: 1921–1923 (Republican)	67th 1921–1923 Senate: 59 R; 37 D House: 301 R; 131 D; 1 O	Congress limits the number of immigrants from each country to 3 percent of the number of that foreign-born nationality living in U.S. First state sales tax levied (West Virginia)	
1922				
1923	Calvin Coolidge: 1923–1929 (Republican)	68th 1923–1925 Senate: 51 R; 43 D; 2 O House: 225 R; 205 D; 5 O	Pres. Harding dies in San Francisco during return trip from Alaska First transcontinental nonstop plane flight First sound-on-film motion picture (*Phonofilm*) shown in New York City	
1924			Regular transcontinental air service begins Annual immigration quota reduced to 2 percent of number of that foreign-born nationality living in U.S. Congress passes law making all Indians U.S. citizens First woman elected state governor (Nellie Tayloe Ross, D-WY)	Bonus Bill (Adjusted Compensation Act)
1925		69th 1925–1927 Senate: 56 R; 39 D; 1 O House: 247 R; 183 D; 4 O	National Aircraft Board created to investigate government's role in aviation	
1926			First liquid-fuel rocket demonstrated by Robert H. Goddard, Auburn, MA	
1927		70th 1927–1929 Senate: 49 R; 46 D; 1 O House: 237 R; 195 D; 3 O	Charles Lindbergh makes first New York–Paris nonstop flight	
1928				
1929	Herbert Hoover: 1929–1933 (Republican)	71st 1929–1931 Senate: 56 R; 39 D; 1 O House: 267 R; 167 D;1 O	Teapot Dome scandal (former secretary of state is found guilty of leasing government land for bribes) Stock market crash sets off Great Depression (1929–1939)	Migratory Bird Conservation Act
1930			15th census: U.S. population 123,202,624 Bank of the United States in New York closes; over 2,100 banks close between late 1929 and end of 1930	Smoot-Hawley Tariff Act

YEAR	PRESIDENT	CONGRESS	US HISTORY	LEGISLATION
1931		72d 1931–1933 Senate: 48 R; 47 D; 1 O House: 220 R; 214 D; 1 O		
1932			Bonus March on Washington, DC (WWI veterans demand early payment of their bonus) First woman elected to U.S. Senate (Hattie W. Caraway, D-AR)	Federal Home Loan Bank Act Norris-LaGuardia Act
1933	Franklin D. Roosevelt: 1933–1945 (Democratic)	73d 1933–1935 Senate: 60 D; 35 R; 1 O House: 310 D; 117 R; 5 O	An estimated 25 percent of the workforce is unemployed First 100 days of Roosevelt administration marked by passage of much New Deal social and economic legislation U.S. officially goes off gold standard Congress passes legislation providing for independence of the Philippine Islands after 12 years U.S. recognizes U.S.S.R. Twentieth Amendment ratified (moves presidential inauguration and beginning of congressional term to January; were previously in March) Twenty-first Amendment goes into effect (repeals Eighteenth Amendment)	Agricultural Adjustment Act Farm Credit Act Federal Deposit Insurance Act Glass-Steagall Act National Industrial Recovery Act Securities Act of 1933 Tennessee Valley Authority Act
1934			Dust storms in Midwest blow thousands of tons of topsoil away (Dust Bowl) Longshoremen strike in San Francisco leads to first general strike in the U.S.	Communications Act Gold Reserve Act Indian Reorganization Act Securities Exchange Act
1935		74th 1935–1937 Senate: 69 D; 25 R; 2 O House: 319 D; 103 R; 10 O	George H. Gallup founds Institute of Public Opinion, which holds Gallup polls First U.S. Savings Bonds issued Committee of Industrial Organization, precursor to Congress of Industrial Organizations (CIO), created	Aid to Dependent Children Motor Carrier Act National Labor Relations Act Neutrality Acts (1935–1939) Public Utility Holding Company Act Social Security Act Soil Conservation and Domestic Allotment Act
1936				Commodity Exchange Act Rural Electrification Act Walsh-Healey Public Contracts Act

YEAR	PRESIDENT	CONGRESS	US HISTORY	LEGISLATION
1937		75th 1937–1939 Senate: 76 D; 16 R; 4 O House: 331 D; 89 R; 13 O	First African-American federal judge (William H. Hastie) Pres. Roosevelt's plan to increase number of Supreme Court justices from 9 to 16 is defeated	United States Housing Act
1938			House Committee on Un-American Activities created to investigate subversive activities Federal minimum wage established	Civil Aeronautics Act Fair Labor Standards Act Federal Food, Drug, and Cosmetic Act Natural Gas Act
1939		76th 1939–1941 Senate: 69 D; 23 R; 4 O House: 261 D; 164 R; 4 O	U.S. declares neutrality in World War II Scientists, including Albert Einstein, warn Pres. Roosevelt of possibility of atomic bomb	Federal Unemployment Tax Act Hatch Act
1940			16th census: U.S. population 132,164,569 Congress approves first peacetime draft	
1941		77th 1941–1943 Senate: 66 D; 28 R; 2 O House: 268 D; 162 R; 5 O	First commercial television license issued to NBC Japanese attack on Pearl Harbor U.S. enters World War II	Lend-Lease Act Public Debt Act
1942			Manhattan Project organized for production of atomic bomb 10,000 Japanese-Americans on West Coast are relocated to camps in the interior	
1943		78th 1943–1945 Senate: 58 D; 37 R; 1 O House: 218 D; 208 R; 4 O	Building of Pentagon (to house Department of Defense) completed	
1944			Conference at Dumbarton Oaks, Washington, DC, lays groundwork for United Nations First large scale digital computer completed by IBM, given to Harvard University	Veterans' Preference Act

YEAR	PRESIDENT	CONGRESS	US HISTORY	LEGISLATION
1945	Harry S. Truman: 1945–1953 (Democratic)	79th 1945–1947 Senate: 56 D; 38 R; 1 O House: 242 D; 190 R; 2 O	Pres. Roosevelt dies suddenly while on vacation First atomic bomb detonated successfully in New Mexico Germany agrees to unconditional surrender; German occupational zones established Pres. Truman orders dropping of two atomic bombs on Japanese cities of Hiroshima and Nagasaki; Japan quickly surrenders; U.S. begins occupation United Nations is formed as representatives of 50 nations meet in San Francisco Nuremberg War Crimes Trials begin Lend-Lease program ends	Export-Import Bank Act United Nations Participation Act
1946			U.S. gives Philippine Islands independence U.N. General Assembly holds first session World Bank organizes	Administrative Procedure Act Atomic Energy Act Employment Act of 1946 Farmers Home Administration Act Federal Tort Claims Act Foreign Service Act Hill-Burton Act Hobbs Anti-Racketeering Act Richard B. Russell National School Lunch Act
1947		80th 1947–1949 Senate: 51 R; 45 D House: 245 R; 188 D; 1 O	The president pledges aid to Greece and Turkey (to prevent the spread of communism), known as the "Truman Doctrine" U.S. Army, Navy, and Air Force combined into Defense Department; Joint Chiefs of Staff and National Security Council created (National Security Act)	National Security Act Taft-Hartley Act
1948			U.S.S.R. blockades Allied sectors of Berlin; U.S. and British airlift food and coal into city (blockade ends in 1949) Universal Declaration on Human Rights adopted by U.N. General Assembly Israel declared an independent state Executive order issued by Pres. Truman outlawing racial segregation in armed forces Organization of American States formed by 21 Western Hemisphere nations	Economic Cooperation Act (Marshall Plan) United States Information and Educational Exchange Act Federal Water Pollution Control Act

YEAR	PRESIDENT	CONGRESS	US HISTORY	LEGISLATION
1949		81st 1949–1951 Senate: 54 D; 42 R House: 263 D; 171 R; 1 O	North Atlantic Treaty signed; NATO created	Central Intelligence Agency Act
1950			17th census: U.S. population 151,325,798 Korean War begins when North Korea invades South Korea; U.S. leads U.N. troops Thirty-five military advisers, along with arms and supplies, sent to South Vietnam to aid anti-Communist government Army seizes railroads to prevent general strike (ordered by Pres. Truman)	Federal Civil Defense Act
1951		82d 1951–1953 Senate: 49 D; 47 R House: 234 D; 199 R; 1 O	Twenty-second Amendment ratified (sets a maximum of two terms for the presidency) Credit card is introduced by Franklin National Bank of New York	Mutual Security Act
1952			First hydrogen bomb tested Pres. Truman orders seizure of steel mills to prevent strike; Supreme Court rules seizure is unconstitutional Ralph Ellison's novel *Invisible Man* published	Immigration and Nationality Act
1953	Dwight D. Eisenhower: 1953–1961 (Republican)	83d 1953–1955 Senate: 48 R; 47 D; 1 O House: 221 R; 211 D; 1 O	Armistice signed in Korea	Outer Continental Shelf Lands Act Small Business Act
1954			Supreme Court rules that racial segregation in public schools violates the Fourteenth Amendment (*Brown v. Board of Education of Topeka, Kansas*) Senator Joseph McCarthy conducts televised hearings concerning Communists in the U.S. government and Democratic Party Southeast Treaty Organization created First atomic-powered submarine is launched	Communist Control Act Federal National Mortgage Association Charter Act Internal Revenue Act of 1954

YEAR	PRESIDENT	CONGRESS	US HISTORY	LEGISLATION
1955		84th 1955–1957 Senate: 48 D; 47 R; 1 O House: 232 D; 203 r	American occupation of Germany ends U.S. agrees to help train South Vietnamese Army Rosa Parks refuses to give up her seat to a white man on a bus in Montgomery, AL; this leads to a boycott of buses and to Supreme Court decision that outlaws segregation in public transportation AFL and CIO, two largest labor organizations in U.S., merge McDonald's fast-food chain founded	National Housing Act (Capehart Act)
1956			Commercial telephone service over transatlantic cable begins Minimum wage raised to $1 per hour Dow Jones Industrial Average closes over 500 for the first time	Highway Act of 1956
1957		85th 1957–1959 Senate: 49 D; 47 R House: 233 D; 200 R	Southern Christian Leadership Conference founded, Martin Luther King, Jr., president	Civil Rights Act of 1957
1958			National Aeronautics and Space Administration (NASA) created	Federal Aviation Act National Aeronautics and Space Act
1959		86th 1959–1961 Senate: 64 D; 34 R House: 283 D; 153 R	Nikita Khrushchev, Soviet premier, visits U.S.	
1960			18th Census: U.S. population 179,323,175 Russia announces it shot down an American U-2 spy plane; President Eisenhower says he authorized the flight Sit-ins begin when 4 black college students refuse to move from a Woolworth lunch counter in Greensboro, NC Student Non-Violent Coordinating Committee established	

YEAR	PRESIDENT	CONGRESS	US HISTORY	LEGISLATION
1961	John F. Kennedy: 1961–1963 (Democratic)	87th 1961–1963 Senate: 65 D; 35 R House: 263 D; 174 R	Bay of Pigs invasion by Cuban exiles is crushed Peace Corps created by executive order; legislation follows Twenty-third Amendment ratified (allows residents of District of Columbia to vote for president) Minimum wage raised to $1.25 per hour	Arms Control and Disarmament Act Foreign Assistance Act Peace Corps Act
1962			Cuban missile crisis (Soviet missile buildup in Cuba) Cesar Chavez organizes National Farm Workers Association John Glenn becomes first U.S. astronaut to orbit the Earth	Bribery Act
1963	Lyndon B. Johnson: 1963–1969 (Democratic)	88th 1963–1965 Senate: 67 D; 33 R House: 258 D; 177 R	Pres. Kennedy is assassinated in Dallas, TX Dr. Martin Luther King gives "I have a dream" speech during March on Washington for equal rights, Washington, DC Ninety-nine nations, including U.S., U.S.S.R., and Great Britain agree to limited Nuclear Test Ban Treaty	Clean Air Act Equal Pay Act
1964			Pres. Johnson announces air attacks on Vietnam; Gulf of Tonkin Resolution passed by Congress gives the president broad authority for military action in Vietnam Three civil rights workers murdered in Philadelphia, MS; 21 white men arrested, 7 convicted of conspiracy in killings Twenty-fourth Amendment ratified (bars poll tax in federal elections)	Civil Rights Act of 1964 Economic Opportunity Act Food Stamp Act Urban Mass Transportation Act

YEAR	PRESIDENT	CONGRESS	US HISTORY	LEGISLATION
1965		89th 1965–1967 Senate: 68 D; 32 R House: 295 D; 140 R	First combat troops land in South Vietnam (125,000 total troops in Vietnam by year's end) Malcolm X assassinated in New York City Civil rights activists march 54 miles from Selma to Montgomery, AL	Elementary and Secondary Education Act Federal Cigarette Labeling and Advertising Act Higher Education Act Highway Beautification Act Housing and Urban Development Act Medicaid Act Medicare Act National Emissions Standard Act Solid Waste Disposal Act Voting Rights Act
1966			More than 10,000 protest Vietnam War in front of White House National Organization for Women (NOW) established	Freedom of Information Act Highway Safety Act National Historic Preservation Act National Traffic and Motor Vehicle Safety Act National Wildlife Refuge System Administration Act
1967		90th 1967–1969 Senate: 64 D; 36 R House: 246 D; 187 R	First African-American Supreme Court justice (Thurgood Marshall) Blacks riot in Newark, NJ, and Detroit, MI Twenty-fifth Amendment ratified (sets up presidential succession scheme)	Age Discrimination in Employment Act Public Broadcasting Act
1968			Martin Luther King, Jr., and Robert Kennedy are assassinated Lyndon B. Johnson announces that he will not seek reelection	Alcoholic and Narcotic Rehabilitation Act Fair Housing Act Gun Control Act Indian Civil Rights Act Omnibus Crime Control and Safe Streets Act
1969	Richard M. Nixon: 1969–1974 (Republican)	91st 1969–1971 Senate: 57 D; 43 R House: 245 D; 189 R	Peace talks to end Vietnam War begin; 250,000 protest war in Washington, DC U.S. astronauts land on moon	Consumer Credit Protection Act National Environmental Policy Act Truth in Lending Act
1970			19th Census: U.S. population 203,302,031 Four students at Kent State College in Ohio are killed during an antiwar demonstration First draft lottery since WWII is held Intel introduces its first computer memory chip	Controlled Substances Act Occupational Safety and Health Act Organized Crime Control Act Plant Variety Protection Act Rail Passenger Service Act

YEAR	PRESIDENT	CONGRESS	US HISTORY	LEGISLATION
1971		92d 1971–1973 Senate: 54 D; 44 R; 2 O House: 254 D; 180 R	Pentagon Papers, classified documents on Vietnam War leaked to the press, published in newspapers Amtrak begins operation Twenty-sixth Amendment ratified (lowers voting age to 18)	Alaska Native Claims Settlement Act Federal Election Campaign Act
1972			Pres. Nixon makes historic visits to China and U.S.S.R. Peace talks on Vietnam War begin and then stall Strategic Arms Limitation Treaty I signed with U.S.S.R. Five men are arrested for breaking into Democratic National Headquarters at the Watergate building in Washington, DC, beginning a series of events that would lead to Richard Nixon's resignation Dow Jones Industrial Average closes over 1,000 for the first time	Federal Advisory Committee Act Marine Mammal Protection Act Title IX, Education Amendments
1973		93d 1973–1975 Senate: 56 D; 42 R; 2 O House: 239 D; 192 R; 1 O	Cease fire signed between U.S., South Vietnam, and North Vietnam OPEC oil embargo (Arab countries ban oil exports to U.S. because of U.S. support to Israel in Arab-Israeli War) In *Roe v. Wade* Supreme Court rules that a state cannot prevent a woman from having an abortion in the first six months of pregnancy	Domestic Volunteer Service Act (VISTA) Endangered Species Act War Powers Resolution
1974	Gerald R. Ford: 1974–1977 (Republican)		House of Representatives authorizes an impeachment investigation of Pres. Nixon, votes and approves three impeachment articles; Nixon resigns Work begins on Alaskan oil pipeline Minimum wage raised to $2.00 per hour	Congressional Budget and Impoundment Control Act Employee Retirement Income Security Act Juvenile Justice and Delinquency Prevention Act Legal Services Corporation Act Privacy Act Safe Drinking Water Act Trade Act of 1974

YEAR	PRESIDENT	CONGRESS	US HISTORY	LEGISLATION
1975		94th 1975–1977 Senate: 61 D; 37 R; 2 O House: 291 D; 144 R	Remaining U.S. military evacuated from Vietnam after the shelling of Saigon by Communist forces; South Vietnam surrenders unconditionally to the Viet Cong U.S. military academies open to women Minimum wage raised to $2.10 per hour	Individuals with Disabilities Education Act Hazardous Materials Transportation Act
1976			Homestead Act of 1862 repealed for all states except Alaska Apple I desktop computer introduced Minimum wage raised to $2.30 per hour	Copyright Act of 1976 Federal Land Policy and Management Act Government in the Sunshine Act National Forest Management Act Toxic Substances Control Act
1977	James E. Carter: 1977–1981 (Democratic)	95th 1977–1979 Senate: 61 D; 38 R; 1 O House: 292 D; 143 R	Agreement between U.S. and Canada for oil pipeline from Alaska to continental U.S. Pres. Carter pardons most Vietnam War draft evaders Microsoft corporation is formed	Community Reinvestment Act Department of Energy Organization Act Foreign Corrupt Practices Act International Emergency Economic Powers Act Surface Mining Control and Reclamation Act
1978			Deregulation of the airline industry Minimum wage raised to $2.65 per hour	Bankruptcy Act of 1978 Civil Service Reform Act Contract Disputes Act Ethics in Government Act Foreign Intelligence Surveillance Act National Energy Conservation Policy Act Nuclear Non-Proliferation Act Pregnancy Discrimination Act Whistleblower Protection Laws
1979		96th 1979–1981 Senate: 58 D; 41 R; 1 O House: 276 D; 157 R	Sixty-three U.S. citizens taken hostage when Iranian militants seize U.S. embassy in Tehran; black and women hostages released in just over two weeks Nuclear accident (partial meltdown) at Three Mile Island, Middletown, PA Minimum wage raised to $2.90 per hour	

YEAR	PRESIDENT	CONGRESS	US HISTORY	LEGISLATION
1980			20th Census: U.S. population 226,542,203 Military mission to rescue U.S. hostages in Iran fails Residents are evacuated from homes in Love Canal, Niagara Falls, NY, a former toxic waste dump Minimum wage raised to $3.10 per hour	Comprehensive Environmental Response, Compensation, and Liability Act Drug Abuse Prevention, Treatment, and Rehabilitation Act Fish and Wildlife Conservation Act Paperwork Reduction Act Regulatory Flexibility Act Staggers Rail Act
1981	Ronald W. Reagan: 1981–1989 (Republican)	97th 1981–1983 Senate: 53 R; 46 D; 1 O House: 242 D; 189 R	Iran releases remaining 52 U.S. hostages First manned space shuttle (*Columbia*) launched into space Nationwide strike by Professional Air Traffic Controllers Association; most controllers are fired Sandra Day O'Connor becomes first woman Supreme Court justice Minimum wage raised to $3.35 per hour	
1982			Equal Rights Amendment to Constitution defeated (would assure equal rights regardless of sex) Unemployment reaches 10.8 percent of the labor force, highest since 1940 U.S. and Soviet Union hold arms control talks in Geneva, Switzerland	Nuclear Waste Policy Act
1983		98th 1983–1985 Senate: 54 R; 46 D House: 268 D; 167 R	Soviet Union shoots down a Korean Airlines plane, killing all 269 passengers, including 52 Americans U.S. Embassy in Beirut is bombed, killing 17 U.S. citizens; a truck bomb kills 241 Americans at a U.S. Marine compound in Beirut	
1984			Truck filled with explosives strikes U.S. Embassy annex in Beirut; U.S. Marines are withdrawn from Beirut As a result of an antitrust settlement, AT&T gives up 22 local Bell System telephone companies	Counterfeit Access Device and Computer Fraud and Abuse Act Hazardous and Solid Waste Amendments Sentencing Reform Act

YEAR	PRESIDENT	CONGRESS	US HISTORY	LEGISLATION
1985		99th 1985–1987 Senate: 53 R; 47 D House: 253 D; 182 R	U.S. and Soviet Union hold arms control talks in Geneva	Balanced Budget and Emergency Deficit Control Act (Gramm-Rudman-Hollings Act)
1986			Pres. Reagan signs secret order authorizing sale of arms to Iran; Lt. Col. Oliver North is dismissed when it is learned that some proceeds from the arms sales helped finance Nicaraguan Contras Space shuttle *Challenger* explodes in air after liftoff, killing entire crew	Anti-Drug Abuse Act Electronic Communications Privacy Act Emergency Planning and Community Right-To-Know Act Immigration Reform and Control Act Tax Reform Act
1987		100th 1987–1989 Senate: 55 D; 45 R House: 258 D; 177 R	Iran-Contra hearings in Congress last about three months U.S. and U.S.S.R. sign treaty banning medium- and short-range missiles Dow Jones Industrial Average closes over 2,000 for the first time	Computer Security Act McKinney-Vento Act
1988			Senate approves free trade agreement made with Canada (1987), all tariffs between the two countries will be eliminated by 1999	Civil Liberties Act Indian Gaming Regulatory Act
1989	George H. W. Bush: 1989–1993 (Republican)	101st 1989–1991 Senate: 55 D; 45 R House: 260 D; 175 R	Oil tanker, *Exxon Valdez*, runs aground on a reef in Prince William Sound, off the coast of Alaska, creating largest oil spill in American history Failing savings and loan industry receives $159 million bailout legislated by Congress 20,000 U.S. troops invade Panama, overthrow regime of Manuel Noriega Minimum wage raised to $4.25 per hour	Flag Protection Act
1990			21st census: U.S. population 249,632,692 U.N. forces begin air attacks on Iraq, after Iraq invades Kuwait	Administrative Dispute Resolution Act Americans with Disabilities Act Negotiated Rulemaking Act Oil Pollution Act

YEAR	PRESIDENT	CONGRESS	US HISTORY	LEGISLATION
1991		102d 1991–1993 Senate: 56 D; 44 R House: 267 D; 167 R; 1 O	First Persian Gulf War begins and ends, freeing Kuwait from Iraqi occupation U.S.S.R. is formally dissolved, effectively ending the Cold War Dow Jones Industrial Average closes over 3,000 for the first time	
1992			Representatives from Canada, Mexico, and U.S. approve draft agreement establishing free trade among the three nations in 15 years Riots in south-central Los Angeles after a jury acquits four white police officers on charges of brutality against a black man, Rodney King Twenty-seventh Amendment is ratified (legislated pay raises for congress don't take effect until a new Congress is convened)	Weapons of Mass Destruction Control Act
1993	William J. Clinton: 1993–2001 (Democratic)	103d 1993–1995 Senate: 56 D; 44 R House: 258 D; 176 R; 1 O	Bomb explodes in parking garage beneath World Trade Center, killing 6 people Twenty U.S. soldiers are killed in Mogadishu, Somalia, in an effort to protect food shipment and distribution to the population Second Strategic Arms Reduction Treaty signed with Russia U.S. and 117 other countries agree to GATT (General Agreement on Tariffs and Trade), to be signed in 1995, will remove export barriers and tariffs on thousands of products	Brady Handgun Violence Protection Act Family and Medical Leave Act NAFTA Implementation Act Religious Freedom Restoration Act
1994			U.S. and North Korea sign agreement that allows for U.N. inspection of North Korea nuclear facilities Republicans win control of Congress for the first time since 1952; Newt Gingrich to become Speaker of the House (1995–1999)	Community Development Banking and Financial Institutions Act Federal Blackmail Statute Freedom of Access to Clinic Entrances Act Violence Against Women Act Violent Crime Control and Law Enforcement Act

YEAR	PRESIDENT	CONGRESS	US HISTORY	LEGISLATION
1995		104th 1995–1997 Senate: 52 R; 48 D House: 230 R; 204 D; 1 O	U.S. troops arrive in Balkans as part of U.N. force, mission is to halt years of fighting in Bosnia Bombing of Oklahoma City Federal Building, killing 160 people Dow Jones Industrial Average closes over 4,000 (Feb.) and 5,000 (Nov.) for the first time	Lobbying Disclosure Act
1996			Nineteen U.S. military personnel die, several hundred wounded, in bombing of military complex near Dhahran, Saudi Arabia Minimum wage raised to $4.75 per hour Dow Jones Industrial Average closes over 6,000 for the first time	Antiterrorism and Effective Death Penalty Act Communications Decency Act Defense of Marriage Act Food Quality Protection Act Personal Responsibility and Work Opportunity Reconciliation Act
1997		105th 1997–1999 Senate: 55 R; 45 D House: 226 R; 208 D; 1 O	Settlement for $368.5 billion reached between four major tobacco companies and several state attorneys general (a $200 billion settlement with 46 states would happen in 1998) Minimum wage raised to $5.15 Dow Jones Industrial Average closes over 7,000 (Feb.) and 8,000 (July) for the first time	
1998			House of Representatives approves two articles of impeachment against Pres. Clinton for perjury and obstruction of justice; he is accused of lying under oath about his relationship with a White House intern Newt Gingrich steps down as Speaker of the House and leaves Congress amid ethics charges and poor results in the midterm congressional elections Dow Jones Industrial Average closes over 9,000 for the first time	Children's Online Privacy Protection Act Taxpayer Bill of Rights III

YEAR	PRESIDENT	CONGRESS	US HISTORY	LEGISLATION
1999		106th 1999–2001 Senate: 54 R; 46 D House: 222 R; 208 D; 1 O	Two students of Columbine High School in Littleton, CO, open fire and kill 12 students and a teacher, then commit suicide; at least 4 other school shootings occur during the year Pres. Clinton impeached but not convicted; investigation led by independent council Kenneth Starr reveals much about Clinton's sexual indiscretions Dow Jones Industrial Average closes over 10,000 (Mar.) and 11,000 (May) for the first time	
2000			Disputed results in the presidential election, centering around election results and ballot irregularities in Florida, lead to a Supreme Court decision that does not allow a vote recount to proceed in that state; George W. Bush declared winner over Al Gore, who won the popular vote U.S.S. *Cole*, an American ship, is bombed by terrorists while refueling in Yemen; 17 sailors killed, 39 injured in the blast "Dot com" boom experienced throughout the late 1990s begins to go bust, starting with the bursting of the stock market "bubble" in March; 4 of the 10 greatest point losses on the Dow Jones Industrial Average occur this year (3 of the 10 greatest point increases occur as well)	Electronic Signatures in Global and National Commerce Act

YEAR	PRESIDENT	CONGRESS	US HISTORY	LEGISLATION
2001	George W. Bush: 2001– (Republican)	107th 2001–2003 Senate: 50 D; 49 R; 1 O House: 222 R; 211 D; 1 O	On September 11, the U.S. comes under terrorist attack when two hijacked planes fly into the towers of the World Trade Center in New York, another plane flies into the Pentagon, and a fourth crashes in Pennsylvania Letters containing Anthrax spores, sent to congressmen and journalists, contaminate the U.S. mail system U.S. begins bombing of Afghanistan to oust the Taliban (Islamic fundamentalist party in power) and capture Osama Bin Laden (leader of Al-Qaeda, the group thought responsible for the September 11 attacks); Taliban removed from power, Bin Laden not captured	No Child Left Behind Act USA Patriot Act
2002			The Enron Corporation collapses as a scandal regarding the company's accounting practices emerges, its share prices plummet and the company declares bankruptcy; other similar corporate scandals follow Bush administration begins to announce an aggressive policy toward Iraq, including the possibility of a "preemptive" strike with the aim of "regime change"; U.N. passes resolution sending weapons inspectors to Iraq; Congress passes resolution authorizing the president to use military force in Iraq	Born-Alive Infants Protection Act Department of Homeland Security Act

YEAR	PRESIDENT	CONGRESS	US HISTORY	LEGISLATION
2003		108th 2003-2005 Senate: 51 R; 48 D; 1 O House: 229 R; 205 D; 1 O	Although U.N. weapons inspectors are still at work, U.S., Britain, and allies declare that Iraq has not disarmed and is in violation of a U.N. resolution passed in November 2002; U.S. is unable to get U.N. approval for the use of force against Iraq because of international opposition; U.S. and a "coalition of the willing" attack Iraq without U.N. approval and win war easily; after Pres. Bush declares an end to major combat a guerilla war ensues; reconstruction of Iraq's infrastructure proves to be more costly than thought; as of five months after Bush's declaration of victory, banned weapons—the major rationale for the war—had not been found Space shuttle *Columbia* breaks apart during reentry killing all seven crew members; independent investigation of accident lasts nearly seven months and concludes that flaws in NASA's management and culture were underlying causes of the disaster In California, a petition gathers enough signatures to force a recall election for governor (incumbent is Gray Davis [D]); 135 candidates to appear on ballot, including actor Arnold Schwarzenegger (R) Massive, rolling blackout across northern Midwest, Canada, and northeastern U.S. results in 50 million people losing power	

GLOSSARY

abate:
to reduce in amount; put an end to; make void or annul

abet: to actively, knowingly, and intentionally assist another in the committing (or attempt) of a crime

abolitionist: one favoring principles or measures fostering the end of slavery

absolute: complete, pure, free from restriction or limitation

adherent: a follower of a leader or party, or a believer in a cause

adjournment: the closing, or end, of a session

adjudicate: to settle something judicially

adjudicated: a matter or controversy that has already been decided through judicial procedure

adjudication: the act of settling something judicially

adjudicatory: having to do with the process of settling something judicially

adverse: contrary to one's interests; harmful or unfavorable

aggrieved: suffering physical injury or a loss of one's property interest, monetary interest, or personal rights

agrarian: having to do with farming or farming communities and their interests

alien: a citizen of another country

alternative dispute resolution: any means of settling disputes outside of the courtroom, typically including arbitration, mediation, early neutral evaluation, and conciliation

amend: to alter or change

antitrust: laws protecting commerce and trade from monopolistic restraints on competition

appellate: a court having jurisdiction to review the findings of lower courts

appoint: to select someone to fill an office or position

apportion: to divide and assign according to a plan

appropriate: to set aside for or assign to a particular purpose or group

arbitrate: to resolve disagreements whereby parties choose a person or group of people familiar with the issues in question to hear and settle their dispute

arbitration the settling of a dispute by a neutral third party

Articles of Confederation: first constitution of the United States (in effect 1781–1789); it established a union between the thirteen states, but with a weak central government

bipartisan: involving members of two parties, especially the two major political parties

blacklist: a list of persons who are to be denied employment

block grant: an unrestricted grant of federal money to state and local governments to support social welfare programs

bondage: a state of being involuntarily bound or subjugated to someone or something

boycott: to refuse to purchase goods or services from a specific company

capitulate: to surrender under specific conditions; to give up resistance

carcinogenic: cancer-causing

cause of action: reason or ground for initiating a proceeding in court

censor: to restrict the expression of something considered objectionable

charter: document that creates a public or private corporation and outlines the principles, functions, and organization of the corporate body

checks and balances: the limiting powers that each branch of government has over the other two. (The government is divided into three branches: legislative, executive, and judicial, each with distinct powers.)

civil action: a lawsuit brought to protect an individual right or redress a wrong, as distinct from criminal proceedings

civil disobedience: nonviolent protest

civil libertarian: one who is actively concerned with the protection of the fundamental freedoms guaranteed to the individual in the Bill of Rights

civil penalties: fines or money damages imposed as punishment

Civil Rights movement: the movement to win political, economic, and social equality for African Americans

class action: a lawsuit brought by a representative member of a large group of people who have suffered the same injury or damages

Cold War: a conflict over ideological differences carried on by methods short of military action and usually without breaking off diplomatic relations; usually refers to the ideological conflict between the U.S. and former U.S.S.R.

collateral: property put up by a borrower to secure a loan that could be seized if the borrower fails to pay back the debt

collective bargaining: a method of negotiations, usually between employees and an employer, in which a representative negotiates on behalf of an organized group of people

commerce: the large-scale exchange of goods, involving transportation from one place to another

commerce clause: the provision of the U.S. Constitution (Article I, section 8, clause 3) that gives Congress exclusive powers over interstate commerce—the buying, selling, or exchanging of goods between states

commodity: an article of trade or commerce that can be transported; especially an agricultural or mining product

common law: a system of laws developed in England—and later applied in the U.S.—based on judicial precedent rather than statutory laws passed by a legislative body

communism: an economic and social system characterized by the absence of classes and by common ownership of the means of production and subsistence

comply: to act in accordance with a wish, request, demand, rule, order, or statute

constraint: a restriction

consumer credit information: credit experiences, such as your bill-paying history, the number and type of accounts you have, late payments, collection actions, outstanding debt, and the age of your accounts

consumption tax: tax imposed on outlay for goods and services

contempt: disobedience of a court's order; interference with the court's operation

Continental Congress: the first central governing body of the United States (1774–1789)

contract: a formal agreement, usually in writing, between two or more parties that can be legally enforced

conventional mortgage: a home mortgage loan that is not federally insured

de novo: (Latin) anew, a second time; the same as if it had not been heard before

debtor: one who owes payment or other performance on an obligation; anyone liable on a claim

decedent: one who has died; the deceased

deduction: an amount subtracted from the amount of income that is used to calculate income tax due

default: the failure by the borrower to comply with the terms of the loan, usually the failure to make payments

defaulter: one who fails to comply with the terms of a loan or contract, usually by failing to make payments on a debt

defendant: one against whom a legal action is brought

deflation: a general decline in the prices of goods and services

demagogue: a leader who obtains power by means of impassioned appeals to the emotions and prejudices of the populace

dependency: a territory under the jurisdiction of a sovereign nation

detain: to keep in custody or temporary confinement

directors: those who establish the policies of the corporation

discharge petition: a method for moving a bill from a committee to the floor of the House when a committee refuses to do so itself. The bill must have been held by a committee for at least thirty legislative days, and half of the House membership must sign the petition for release that is filed

disclosure: obligation of parties to reveal material facts deemed necessary for one to make an informed decision

discount window: a lending facility available to member banks of the Federal Reserve System

dividend: a payment made by a company, based on its earnings, to its shareholders

dogma: an established opinion expressed as an authoritative statement

draconian: severe, harsh

Dust Bowl: a semiarid region in the south-central United States where the topsoil was lost by wind erosion in the mid-1930s

egalitarian: marked by a belief in human equality

electorate: the body of people qualified to vote

emancipate: to free from another's control, restraint, or bondage

embargo: a prohibition on commerce with a particular country for political or economic reasons

encroach: to infringe upon or violate

equal protection: Constitutional guarantee that prevents states from denying a person or class of persons from the same protection under the law as those enjoyed by other persons or classes of persons

espionage: the act of spying on the government to obtain secret information

ex officio: (Latin) from office, by virtue of office; powers may be exercised by an officer which are not specifically conferred upon him, but are necessarily implied in his office

excise tax: a tax levied on the manufacture or sale of specific—usually non-essential—commodities such as tobacco or liquor

executive order: an order issued by the president that has the force of law

exorbitant: an amount that far exceeds what is fair or customary

extortion: the obtaining of money (or other concessions) by force or intimidation

faction: a party or group united by a common cause

Federal Register: a newspaper published daily by the National Archives and Records Administration to notify the public of federal agency regulations, proposed rules and notices, executive orders, and other executive branch documents

federal securities laws: federal securities laws include the Securities Act of 1933, the Securities Exchange Act of 1934, and various rules and regulations under these acts. These acts regulate the offer and sales of securities as well as secondary markets for securities. They require numerous disclosures and prohibit deceptive practices

federalism: a system of political organization; a union formed of separate states or groups that are ruled by a central authority on some matters but are otherwise permitted to govern themselves independently

felony: a crime punished with a lengthy prison sentence (more than one year) or the death penalty

filibuster: a tactic involving unlimited debate on the floor of the Senate designed to delay or prevent legislative action

fiscal year: the term used for a business's accounting year; the period is usually twelve months which can begin during any month of the calendar year

foreclosure: when a person defaults on (fails to pay) a mortgage debt, the owner's legal right to the property is terminated. The real estate may be sold at an auction by the creditor; the money raised is then put toward the mortgage debt

forfeiture: the loss of something (property, assets) as a result of breaking the law

free expression: the right to state opinions without interference or censorship

freedman: one freed from slavery

garnish: process whereby one's property or money that is in the possession of a third party is paid to another to satisfy one's debt

gold standard: a monetary standard under which the basic unit of currency is equal in value to and can be exchanged for a specified amount of gold

graduated rate schedule: tax structured so that the rate increases as the amount of taxpayer income increases

grassroots: originating or operating at the basic level of society

Great Depression: the longest and most severe economic depression in American history (1929–1939); its effects were felt throughout the world

Great Society: broad term for the domestic programs of President Lyndon B. Johnson, in which he called for "an end to poverty and racial injustice

gross domestic product: the total market value of goods and services produced within a nation in a given time period (usually one year)

habeas corpus: (Latin, "you should have the body") a written order to bring a prisoner in front of a judge, to determine whether his or her detention is lawful

high-rate mortgages: a mortgage with a high interest rate because it is perceived to be a higher risk based on the purchaser's credit history

illiquid: incapable of being readily converted to cash

immigrant: one who comes to a country to take up permanent residence

immunity: protection from legal action

impair: to lessen or reduce

impeach: to set up a formal hearing on charges of high crimes and misdemeanors which could result in removal from office

imperial presidency: a powerful president who is being belligerent internationally, being intrusive domestically, and running roughshod over another branch of government

import: to bring in merchandise from another country as part of a commercial business

individual retirement account (IRA): an account into which a person can deposit up to a certain amount of money annually without being taxed until either retirement or early withdrawal (withdrawal when the person is under a certain age)

inflation: a general rise in the prices of goods and services

infringe: to exceed the limits of; to violate

ingress: a means or place for entering

injunctive relief: a court order that requires a person to refrain from doing something; the order guards against future damages rather than remedies past damages

insurgent: one who revolts against authority; especially a member of a political party who rebels against its leadership

insurrection: a rebellion against a government or civil authority

interest expense: the money a corporation or individual pays out in interest on loans

interest rate: the fee for borrowing money, expressed as a percentage of the amount borrowed

interstate commerce: trade involving the transportation of goods from one state to another, or the transfer of property between a person in one state and a person in another

interventionism: a policy of getting involved in international affairs through membership in international organizations and multinational alliances

invidious: tending to arouse ill will or animosity; an offensive or discriminatory action

involuntary servitude: forced service to a master

isolationism: a policy of not getting involved in international affairs

Jim Crow: the systematic practice of segregating and suppressing African Americans; the name is from a character in a nineteenth-century minstrel show

judgment debtor: one who owes money as a result of a judgment in favor of a creditor

judicial: having to do with judgments in courts of law or with the administration of justice

judicial decree: the ruling of a court

jurisdiction: the territory or area within which authority may be exercised

labor union: an organization of workers whose main purpose is to collectively bargain with employers about the terms and conditions of employment

laissez-faire: a doctrine opposing governmental interference in economic affairs beyond the minimum necessary for the maintenance of peace and property rights

lame-duck: an elected officer holder who is to be succeeded by another; in the case of Congress, the time it is in session between the November elections and the convening of the new Congress the following year

legal tender: an offer of money in the form of coin, paper money, or another circulating medium that the law compels a creditor to accept in payment of a debt

liability: an obligation, responsibility, or duty that one is bound by law to perform

libel: the publication of statements that wrongfully damage another's reputation

libertarian: one who upholds the principles of absolute and unrestricted liberty and strongly opposes any government-imposed restrictions

licentious: lacking moral discipline or sexual restraint

lien: legal claim to property by a creditor (one who makes a loan) as a condition of a contract

life estate: an estate that lasts for the duration of the life of the person holding it

litigation: a lawsuit

lobby: to try to persuade the legislature to pass laws and regulations that are favorable to one's interests and to defeat laws that are unfavorable to those interests

lockout: the withholding of work from employees by management, to get them to agree to certain terms and conditions

long-term capital gains: profit made on the sale or exchange of a capital asset (usually stock or real estate) that has been owned for more than twelve months

loophole: a means of evading or escaping an obligation or enforcement of a law or contract

mandate: an order or requirement

marginal rates: the total percentage of tax one pays on one's income, taking into account all the separate taxes levied on one's wages or salary

Mason-Dixon line: the boundary line between Pennsylvania on the north and Maryland on the south which, before the end of slavery, was the line between the slave and the free states

median: the middle value in a distribution, above and below which lie an equal number of values

migrate: to move from one place to another

militia: a part-time army made up of ordinary citizens

mirabile dictu "wonderful to relate"

monopoly: exclusive control of a market by one company, often marked by the controlling of prices and exclusion of competition

moratorium: a legally required suspension of activity

mortgage loan: a loan to purchase real estate; the real estate purchased with the loan usually serves as collateral against default

muckraker: one who tries to find and expose real or alleged evidence of corruption

multilateral: undertaken by multiple persons, parties, or entities, in conjunction with one another

N

nadir: lowest point

naturalize: to grant the privileges and rights of citizenship

necessary and proper clause: provision in the U.S. Constitution (Article I, section 8, clause 18) that authorizes Congress to pass laws needed in order to exercise its constitutional powers

negotiate: to deal or bargain with another as in the preparation of a treaty or contract

New Deal: the legislative and administrative program of President Franklin D. Roosevelt designed to promote economic recovery and social reform (1933–1939)

nominate: to propose one for appointment to office

nonprofit: an organization whose business is not conducted or maintained for the purpose of making a profit but is usually aimed at providing services for the public good

nonpunitive: not having the character of punishment or penalty

notice and disclosure requirements: in contracts and other transactions, the law requires that key provisions and penalties be disclosed in plain English so a consumer can make an informed decision

null and void: having no legal force; invalid

O

obscene: morally offensive; designed to degrade or corrupt

offender: one who breaks a rule or law

omnibus: including many things at once

OPEC oil embargo: in October 1973, the Organization of Petroleum Exporting Countries (OPEC) banned oil exports to the United States because the United States sold arms to Israel during the Arab-Israeli War of 1973

open market operations: purchases and sales of government securities by the Federal Reserve Bank, designed to control the money supply and short-term interest rates

opining: to hold or state as an opinion

ordinance: a law

originate: a loan is originated when the loan is first made by the lender to a borrower. The origination function includes taking the borrower's loan application, checking the borrower's credit history and employment, obtaining an appraisal of valuation of the home, and funding the loan

override: if the President vetoes a bill passed by Congress, the bill can still become law if two-thirds of each house of Congress votes to override the veto

P

partisan: someone loyal to a particular party, cause, or person

paternalism: a policy or practice of treating or governing people in a fatherly manner especially by providing for their needs without giving them responsibility

penal: having to do with punishments or penalties

perjury: lying under oath or otherwise breaking an oath by not doing what was promised

personal consumption goods: goods purchased for personal use

photovoltaic: relating to the technology used to capture radiation (light) from the sun and turn it into electricity

plaintiff: one who brings legal action against another

populist: someone who identifies with and believes in the rights and virtues of the common people (often as the foundation of a political philosophy)

poverty line: level of personal or family income below which a person or family is classified as poor. The standard is set by the government

powers of appointment: the right to appoint or give away property

preemption when a conflict of authority arises between the federal and state governments, the federal government prevails

president-elect: one who has been elected president but has not yet begun his term of office

preventive relief: relief granted to prevent a foreseen harm

private litigation: a civil lawsuit (one brought to protect an individual right or redress a wrong), as distinct from criminal proceedings

private sector: the part of the economy that is not controlled by the government

Prohibition: period from 1919 to 1933, during which the making, transport, and sale of alcoholic beverages was illegal in the United States

promulgate: to make the terms of a law known by formal public announcement

proponent: an advocate

prosecute: to begin and carry on a lawsuit; to bring legal action against

protectionism: the use of tariffs to protect domestic industries from foreign competition

protectionist: advocating the use of tariffs to protect domestic industries from foreign competition

public held company: a corporation whose stock anyone can buy on a stock exchange

public offering: the making available of corporate stocks or bonds to the general public

pursuant: to execute or carry out in accordance with or by reason of something

quid pro quo: (Latin, "something for something") an equal exchange or substitution

quorum: the number of members required to be present for a vote to take place

ratify: to formally approve; three-fourths of all states in the Union must approve an amendment for it becomes part of the Constitution

real income: income of an individual, organization, or country, after taking into consideration the effects of inflation on purchasing power

recession: a period of reduced economic activity, but less severe than a depression

Reconstruction: the political and economic reorganization and reestablishment of the South after the Civil War

redress: to make right what is wrong

refinance: to pay off existing loans with funds secured from new loans

Regulation Q: a banking regulation that prohibits paying interest on short-term deposits; the scope of this regulation has narrowed over time, so that most non-commercial deposits are unaffected

remedy: the means to compensate a person whose rights have been violated, which usually takes the form of money damages

repatriate: to return to the country of one's birth or citizenship

repeal: to revoke or cancel

rescind: to declare a contract void in its inception and to put an end to it as though it never existed

rescission provisions: provisions in a contract that, if they occur or fail to occur, allow the contract to be rescinded

resolution: a formal statement of opinion, intent, or will voted by an official body

reverse mortgage: a type of home mortgage under which an elderly homeowner is allowed a long-term loan in the form of monthly payments against his or her paid-off equity as collateral, repayable when the home is eventually sold

sabotage: the destruction of property or obstruction of an action intended to hinder the normal operations of a company or government

secede: to depart or withdraw from an organization

secondary market: the market that exists for an issue of stock after large blocks of shares have been publicly distributed, or items not obtained directly from the manufacturer

sectarian characteristic of a group following a specific doctrine or leader

securities: stocks, bonds, and certain other instruments of investment

security interest: a form of interest in property which provides that the property may be sold on default in order to satisfy the obligation for which the security interest is given; a mortgage is used to grant a security interest in real property

seditious: urging resistance to or overthrow of the government

seed money: money needed or provided to start a new project

self-incrimination: the giving of testimony that will likely subject one to criminal prosecution

separation of powers: the division of the government into three branches: legislative, executive, and judicial, each with distinct powers. This separation supports a system of checks and balances

Sexual Revolution: the liberalization of social and moral attitudes toward sex and sexual relations

slander: to make a false statement that defames and damages another's reputation

socialism: any of various economic and political theories advocating collective or governmental ownership and administration of the means of production and distribution of goods

sovereign: self-governing and independent

sovereign immunity: the doctrine that prevents bringing a lawsuit against the government without the government's consent

special session: an extraordinary or special session of Congress is called to meet in the interval between regular sessions

specie: money in the form of coins, usually in a metal with intrinsic value, such as gold or silver

speculate: to engage in the buying or selling of a commodity with the expectation (or hope) of making a profit

statute: a law enacted by the legislative branch of government

stipend: a fixed or regular payment, such as a salary for services rendered or an allowance

stipulate: to specify as a condition of an agreement

strike: to stop work in protest, usually so as to make an employer comply with demands

subpoena: a writ issued under authority of a court to compel the appearance of a witness at a judicial hearing

superannuated: retired or discharged because of age; obsolete; out of date

surveillance: the close observation of a person, place, or process

T

tariff: a tax imposed on goods when imported into a country

tax credit: a reduction in the amount an individual or corporation owes in taxes

tax shelter: a strategy or method that allows one to legally reduce or avoid tax liabilities

temperance: moderation in or abstinence from the consumption of alcohol

tender offer: a public offer to purchase shares of a specific corporation, usually at a price above what the market offers, in an attempt to accumulate enough shares to take control of the company

terminology: the vocabulary of technical terms and usages appropriate to a particular trade, science, or art

tort: any wrongdoing other than a breach of contract for which a civil lawsuit can be brought. Examples include physical injury, damage to property, and damage to one's reputation

tortuous: unlawful conduct that subjects a person to tort liability

totalitarian: the political concept that the citizen should be totally subject to an absolute state authority

treason: the offense of attempting to overthrow the government of one's own state or country

treaty: a binding international agreement

treaty clause: provision of the U.S. Constitution (Article II, section 2, clause 2) that grants the power to make treaties with foreign nations to the president, which are subject to approval by the Senate

truancy: skipping out of school

U

underwrite: to assume financial responsibility and risk for something

unilateral: undertaken by one person, party, or entity

United States Trade Representative (USTR): a cabinet-level official appointed by the president who has primary responsibility for directing U.S. trade policy and trade negotiations

unprecedented: not resembling something already in existence

unsolicited: not wanted or requested

V

veto: when the president returns a bill to Congress with a statement of objections

vigilante: a member of a self-appointed group of citizens who undertake law enforcement within their community without legal authority

W

waive: to give up voluntarily

waivers of immunity: legal statement that gives up the government's right to sovereign immunity (the doctrine that the government cannot be sued without its consent)

warrant: a document issued by a judge granting authority to do something

Watergate: the scandal following the break-in at the Democratic National Committee headquarters located in the Watergate apartment and office complex in Washington, D.C., in 1972

COURT CASE INDEX

Each entry has (in order): the case name and the year the act became law (in parenthesis). The numbers after the date denote the volume and page number(s) where information can be found in Major Acts of Congress.

CUMULATIVE INDEX

Page numbers in boldface type indicate article titles; those in italic type indicate illustrations. The number preceding the colon indicates the volume number; the number after a colon indicates the page number.

E-SIGN. *See* Electronic Signatures in Global and National Commerce Act

Espionage, defined, **1:**251

Espionage Act and Sedition Act, **1:251–257, 1:***253*, **1:***255*
See also Alien and Sedition Acts; Communist Control Act

Espy, Mike, **1:**75

Estate and gift taxation, **1:257–260, 1:***259*

Ethics in Government Act, **1:260–264**

Ethyl Corp. v. Environmental Protection Agency, **1:**130

European Central Bank, **2:**66

European Common Market, **1:**218

European recovery plan, **1:**214–219

European Union, **2:**66

Evans, Alona E., **2:**114

Evans, George Henry, **2:**172

Exchange, under Commodity Exchange Act, **1:**140

Excise tax, defined, **1:**190, **2:**49

Exclusive dealing, under Clayton Act, **1:**125

Exclusivity principle, **3:**38

Executive order, defined, **1:**91, **2:**139, **3:**121

Exhaustion requirement, and habeas corpus, **1:**41, **1:**42

Ex officio, defined, **2:**68

Exon, James, **1:**147

Exorbitant, defined, **3:**144

Ex parte, defined, **1:**6

Ex parte Jackson, **2:**249–250

Ex parte Royall, **1:**41

Export Administration Act, **2:**210

Export-Import Bank Act, **1:264–267, 1:***265*

Export-Import Bank of the United States, **1:**265–266

Export-Import Bank of Washington, **1:**264–265

Export-Import Reauthorization Act, **1:**266

Extortion
defined, **1:**157, **2:**168
Hobbs Anti-Racketeering Act, **2:**24–25, **2:**168–169

Exxon Corp. v. Chick Kam Choo, **1:**36

Exxon Valdez (ship), **3:**99, **3:***100*

F

FAA. *See* Foreign Assistance Act; U.S. Federal Aviation Administration

(FAA); U.S. Federal Aviation Agency (FAA)

FAC. *See* U.S. Federal Aviation Commission (FAC)

FACA. *See* Federal Advisory Committee Act

FACE. *See* Freedom of Access to Clinic Entrances Act

Faction, defined, **1:**22

Fair Credit Reporting Reform Act, **1:**173

Fair Debt Collection Practices Act, **1:**174–175

Fair Housing Act, **2:1–5, 2:***3*, **3:**252, **3:**274
See also Housing and Urban Development Act

Fair Housing Act Amendments, **1:**28

Fair Labor Standards Act, **2:5–10, 2:***7*
child labor, **2:**233
Congress considers a broader bill, **2:**6–7
and Equal Pay Act, **1:**248, **1:**249–250
expanding coverage, **2:**9
in the House, **2:**8
Hugo Black's bill, **2:**5–6
importance, **2:**9–10
and National Industrial Recovery Act, **3:**36
passage, **2:**8
Supreme Court, **2:**6, **2:**8–9

Fairness doctrine, **1:**146

Fair Pay Act, **1:**250

Fair use, and copyright, **1:**182, **1:**183, **1:**188

Fall, Albert B., **1:**74

Fallon, George H., **2:**161

False Claims Act, **3:**292

Family and Medical Leave Act, **2:10–13, 2:***11,* **3:**135

Family Limitation (Sanger), **1:**168

Family Time Flexibility Act, **2:**10

Fannie Mae. *See* Federal National Mortgage Association Charter Act

FAPE (free appropriate public education), **2:**200–203

Farm Bankruptcy Act, **1:**11

Farm Bill, **2:**97

Farm Credit Act of 1933, **2:14–16**
See also Farmers Home Administration Act

Farm Credit Act of 1971, **2:**15

Farmers Home Administration Act, **2:16–17**

Farmers' & Mechanics' National Bank v. Dearing, **3:**8

Farm Tenancy Act, **2:**15

Farwell v. Boston & Worcester Railway, **2:**40

Fay v. Noia, **1:**41

FBI. *See* U.S. Federal Bureau of Investigation (FBI)

FBN. *See* U.S. Federal Bureau of Narcotics (FBN)

FCC. *See* U.S. Federal Communications Commission (FCC)

FCC v. ITT World Communications, **2:**145

FCDA. *See* U.S. Federal Civil Defense Administration (FCDA)

FCPA. *See* Foreign Corrupt Practices Act

FDA. *See* U.S. Food and Drug Administration (FDA)

FDA v. Brown and Williamson Tobacco Corp., **2:**46

FDCA. *See* Federal Food, Drug, and Cosmetic Act

FDIC. *See* U.S. Federal Deposit Insurance Corporation (FDIC)

FDIC v. Philadelphia Gear Corp., **2:**32

FEC. *See* U.S. Federal Election Commission (FEC)

FECA. *See* Federal Election Campaign Act

Federal Advisory Committee Act, **2:17–20**
See also Civil Aeronautics Act

Federal-Aid Highway Act, **3:**254

Federal Anti-Price Discrimination Act, **3:**189

Federal Arbitration Act, **1:**1

Federal Aviation Act, **1:**89, **2:20–24, 2:***23*

Federal Blackmail Statute, **2:24–26**
See also Hobbs Anti-Racketeering Act

"Federal Box," and Truth in Lending Act, **3:**243

Federal Cigarette Labeling and Advertising Act, **2:26–28, 2:***27*

Federal Civil Defense Act, **2:28–31, 2:***30*

Federal Corrupt Practices Act, **2:**35

Federal Debt Collection Procedures Act, **2:**160

Federal Deposit Insurance Acts, **2:31–34, 2:***33*
See also Glass-Steagall Act

Federal Deposit Insurance Corporation Improvement Act, **1:**156, **2:**34

Federal Election Campaign Act, **2:34–39, 2:***37,* **2:**248

Federal employees
Civil Service Acts, **1:**115–119, **1:***117*

NWPA. *See* Nuclear Waste Policy Act

NYSSV (New York Society for the Suppression of Vice), **1:**167

O

Oath clause, **2:**110

Obscene
 under Comstock Act, **1:**166, **1:**167, **1:**168
 defined, **1:**166

OCCA. *See* Organized Crime Control Act

Occidental Chemical Company, **1:**159

OCCSSA. *See* Omnibus Crime Control and Safe Streets Act

Occupational Safety and Health Act, **1:**234–235, **3:**94–98, **3:**95, *3:97*

OCD. *See* U.S. Civilian Defense Office (OCD)

O'Connor, Sandra Day, **1:**148, **3:**277

OCSLA. *See* Outer Continental Shelf Lands Act

OECD (Organisation of Economic Cooperation and Development), **2:**109

Offender, defined, **1:**21

Offender rehabilitation, **3:**182–183

Offers in Compromise, **3:**224

OFHEO. *See* U.S. Federal Housing Enterprise Oversight (OFHEO)

Ohio Agricultural and Mechanical College, **2:***285*

Ohio Company, **3:**84

Ohio State University, **2:***285*

Oil and gas
 Mineral Leasing Act, **2:**275–279, **2:***277*
 Natural Gas Act, **3:**62–63
 Outer Continental Shelf Lands Act, **3:**109–110

Oil Placer Act, **2:**275

Oil Pollution Act of 1924, **3:**99

Oil Pollution Act of 1961, **3:**99

Oil Pollution Act of 1990, **3:**99

Oil Pollution Acts, **3:**99–101, **3:***100*

Oil reserves, in Alaska, **1:***18*, **1:**19

Oil Spill Liability Trust Fund, **3:**99

OIRA. *See* U.S. Information and Regulatory Affairs Office (OIRA)

Oklahoma City bombing, **1:***40*, **1:**42

Old Order Amish, and religious freedom, **3:**161–162

Oligopoly pricing, **2:**76

OMB. *See* U.S. Management and Budget Office (OMB)

Omnibus, defined, **1:**161, **3:**183

Omnibus Adjustment Act, **3:**52

Omnibus Anti-Drug Abuse Act, **1:**180, **1:**213

Omnibus Crime Control and Safe Streets Act, **1:**229, **3:**101–104, **3:**267
 See also Violent Crime Control and Law Enforcement Act

Omnibus Trade and Competitiveness Act, **3:**238

Oncomouse, patents on, **3:**120

"One-Click Shopping Method" patent, **3:**118

Online services. *See* Internet

OPEC Oil Embargo, defined, **1:**200, **3:**15

"Open government" statutes. *See* Federal Advisory Committee Act; Freedom of Information Act; Government in the Sunshine Act; Privacy Act

Open market operations, defined, **2:**69

Operation Rescue, **2:**119–121, **2:**123, **2:**238–239

Operation Whiteout, **1:***179*

Opining, defined, **1:**15

Opium problem, **3:**1–2

OPS. *See* U.S. Pipeline Safety Office (OPS)

Options, under Commodity Exchange Act, **1:**140

ORA. *See* U.S. Redress Administration Office (ORA)

Ordinance, defined, **3:**84

Ordinance of 1784, **3:**84, **3:**209

Ordinance of 1787. *See* Northwest Ordinance

Organic Act of 1884, **1:**18

Organic Act of 1897, **3:**21

Organisation of Economic Cooperation and Development (OECD), **2:**109

Organization for Security and Cooperation in Europe, **2:**104

Organized Crime Control Act, **2:**169, **3:**104–109, **3:***107*, **3:***108*
 See also Hobbs Anti-Racketeering Act

Organized labor
 National Industrial Recovery Act, **3:**34, **3:***35*
 National Labor Relations Act, **3:**37–42
 Norris-LaGuardia Act, **3:**74–79
 Occupational Safety and Health Act, **3:**96
 Taft-Hartley Act, **2:**35, **3:**213–218

Originate, defined, **2:**62

Orth, Franklin L., **2:**148

Osborn v. Bank of the United States, **3:**8

OSHA. *See* Occupational Safety and Health Act; U.S. Occupational

Safety and Health Administration (OSHA)

OSS. *See* U.S. Strategic Services Office (OSS)

O'Sullivan, John L., **2:**172

The Other America: Poverty In the United States (Harrington), **1:**221

Outer Continental Shelf Lands Act, **2:**279, **3:**109–110
 See also Mineral Leasing Act

Outer Space Treaty, **1:**44, **1:**46

Override, defined, **1:**71, **2:**117, **3:**284

Over-the-counter derivative instruments, under Commodity Exchange Act, **1:**140

P

Pacific Northwest endangered species, **1:**245

Pacific Railroad Act, **2:**41

Pacific Railway Acts of 1862 and 1864, **2:**174

Packwood, Robert, **3:**223

Page, Carroll, **3:**270–271

Page Law, **1:**82

Panama Canal Purchase Act, **3:**111–113, **3:***112*

Pan-American Petroleum, **1:**74

Panic of 1837, **1:**58

Panic of 1893, **1:**65, **2:**50–51

Panic of 1907, **2:**51, **2:**67

Paperwork Reduction Act, **3:**114–116

Parity prices, **1:**9–10

Park policy, **3:**42–45

Parole, **3:**182, **3:**184

Parrino, Sandra, **1:***26*

Partisan, defined, **2:**39

Passive loss rules, **3:**221

Patent Act (1790), **3:**117

Patent Act (1836), **3:**117

Patent Act (1870), **3:**117

Patent Act (1952), **3:**117

Patent Acts, **3:**116–121, **3:***119*

"Patently offensive" materials, under Communications Decency Act, **1:**147

Patents
 of importation, **3:**118–120
 for plants, **3:**129
 Sherman Antitrust Act (1890), **3:**188

Paternalism, defined, **1:**241

Patrick, William, **3:***289*

Paycheck Fairness Act, **1:**250

Payne, Sereno, **2:**51

Payne-Aldrich Tariff, **1:**192, **3:**196–197

Payne-Aldrich Tariff Act, **2:**51